ATLA Bibliography Series
edited by Dr. Kenneth E. Rowe

1. *A Guide to the Study of The Holiness Movement,* by Charles Edwin Jones. 1974.
2. *Thomas Merton: A Bibliography,* by Marquita E. Breit. 1974.
3. *The Sermon on the Mount: A History of Interpretation and Bibliography,* by Warren S. Kissinger. 1975.

12.50

The Sermon on the Mount:

A History of Interpretation
And
Bibliography

by

Warren S. Kissinger

ATLA Bibliography Series, No. 3

The Scarecrow Press, Inc., Metuchen, N.J.
and
The American Theological Library Association
1975

The bibliography portion of this book was developed and greatly expanded from the bibliography and the extensive private collection of
books on the Sermon on the Mount of the late
W. Harold Row.

Library of Congress Cataloging in Publication Data
Kissinger, Warren S   1922-
    The Sermon on the Mount.

    (ATLA bibliography series ; no. 3)
    Part II was developed and greatly expanded from the
bibliography and books of the late W. Harold Row.
    Bibliography: p.
    Includes index.
    1. Sermon on the mount. 2. Sermon on the mount--
Bibliography. 3. Beatitudes--Bibliography. I. Title.
II. Series: American Theological Library Association.
ATLA bibliography series ; no. 3.
BT380.2.K5 1975   226'.9'06   75-29031
ISBN 0-8108-0843-9

to

W. HAROLD ROW

1912-1971

Blessed are the peacemakers
for they shall be called sons of God

EDITOR'S NOTE

The American Theological Library Association Bibliography
Series is designed to stimulate and encourage the preparation of re-
liable bibliographies and guides to the literature of religious studies
in all of its scope and variety. Each compiler is free to define his
field, make his own selections, and work out internal organization
as the unique demands of his subject indicate.

Warren S. Kissinger studied theology at Yale Divinity School
and at the Lutheran Theological Seminary in Gettysburg, Pa., and
library science at Drexel University in Philadelphia. An ordained
minister in the Church of the Brethren, he has served several pastorates in Pennsylvania, taught religion at Juniata College in Hunting-
ton, Pa., and currently serves as Subject Cataloger in Religion at
the Library of Congress.

We are pleased to publish this guide to the literature of the
Sermon on the Mount, the bibliography for which was developed
from the collection of the late W. Harold Row, as number three in
our series.

Kenneth E. Rowe, Editor
Drew University Library
Madison, New Jersey

IN APPRECIATION: W. HAROLD ROW

The Sermon on the Mount held an unrelenting fascination for Harold Row from his early student days to his death. In the first years of our marriage moments of leisure were spent in secondhand book stores seeking books on the Sermon which he hoped to include in our library when the budget would allow. Quite often he would find a copy which he wanted very much, but the price was too high. He would say, "That's too much now. Let's wait awhile." So a mental note was made that this book would be a birthday or Christmas gift.

The collection grew over the years, and with it a list of titles yet to be collected. As his work took him over the United States and to other countries, he carried this list of titles. When a free moment presented itself he would visit book stores, libraries at colleges, universities, and theological schools to locate other writings on the Sermon on the Mount. As a result, he added books in other languages (German, Russian, etc.) to his English collection. But more importantly, his bibliography kept growing. It was his plan to annotate these titles, and publish his findings for the use of persons interested in the Sermon.

During his illness (after moving to Washington, D.C. from Elgin, Illinois), he worked with the author, the Rev. Warren Kissinger, who is employed at the Library of Congress, adding new titles as they were discovered. Many long, painful days for Harold were brightened by a visit from Warren bringing still a new title.

A natural sequence followed in the discovery that Warren was interested in completing the project after Harold's death. Not only did he follow through with Harold's idea, but went further to write a History of Interpretation of the Sermon. This has been deeply satisfying to our family to see this dream of Harold's completed.

Our warm personal thanks go to Warren Kissinger for his many acts of kindness before Harold's death, and now, for his thorough and comprehensive work to complete and expand the idea started as a "hobby."

Dr. Andrew W. Cordier, in the Foreword for the Bibliography has enlarged this idea. We are appreciative of the Foreword, as well as the enriching friendship over the years.

In addition, our deep gratitude goes to librarians and religious leaders who aided in this quest. Many of these we visited together while Harold was on sabbatical leave. Others were contacted in leisure moments when he was alone. Countries and libraries listed are only those of which I am aware. They are: Austria (Vienna), Denmark (Copenhagen), England (London), France (Paris), Germany (Berlin, Göttingen, Leipzig, Hamburg, Tübingen, Munich, Stuttgart, Bonn, Freiburg, Düsseldorf), Greece (Athens), Holland (The Hague, Amsterdam), Italy (Naples), U.S.S.R. (Moscow, Leningrad, others), Sweden (Stockholm), Finland (Helsinki), and Switzerland (Basel, Bern, Zürich).

Leona Z. Row
Washington, D.C.

CONTENTS

INTRODUCTION

Like a mighty mountain, the Sermon on the Mount continues to attract persons of different backgrounds and traditions. There is general agreement that the Sermon offers a compendium of the teachings of Jesus, and that it is one of the most lofty and powerful expressions of the essence of the moral life. Gandhi was much impressed by it, and its impact upon him was second only to that of the Bhagavad Gita. Tolstoy came to a new Weltanschauung through his reading and study of it. Claude Montefiore, writing from a liberal Jewish perspective, spoke of the Sermon's great nobility, significance, and power. Nietzsche was one who did not share this almost universal admiration. For him the Sermon on the Mount represented a significant part of Jesus' ethics, which was a "slave morality."

When one turns to questions about the Sermon's meaning and relevance, there is far from unanimity of opinion. A cluster of problems has divided interpreters from the first centuries of the Christian era to the present. Among them are: Was the Sermon delivered as it stands? or Is it a composite of Jesus' sayings given at different times and places? To whom was it addressed? Is it original with Jesus? or Is it paralleled in rabbinic sources? What was its status and authority in primitive Christianity? Did Jesus institute a new law in the Sermon on the Mount that was as binding as the Torah had been in Judaism? What bearing did Jesus' eschatological outlook have upon the Sermon's content and relevance? How can one reconcile the Sermon's emphasis upon works and merit with the Pauline understanding of "grace alone?" In what sense is the Sermon on the Mount relevant for us today who live in different times and are perplexed by other problems than those prevailing in first-century Palestine? The essay and bibliography which follow

reflect some of the many attempts which have been made to wrestle
with these problems.

Part I traces in 35 sections the history of interpretation of the
Sermon on the Mount from the patristic period to the twentieth century. Most of the authors discussed have written significant monographs on the Sermon on the Mount. But I have also chosen others
who have interpreted the Sermon through works devoted to other subjects such as Christian ethics, New Testament criticism, teachings
of Jesus, etc. In addition I have examined movements such as Anabaptism, Protestant Liberalism, Consistent Eschatology, Dispensationalism, whose distinctive emphases have had important consequences for Sermon on the Mount interpretation.

Part II comprises a bibliography of the Sermon on the Mount.
This bibliography had its origin with the late W. Harold Row who
for many years was an avid collector of books on the Sermon on
the Mount. In his travels here and abroad he was always eager to
enlarge his collection, which was probably the largest anywhere. He
intended to prepare an annotated bibliography, but unfortunately his
long illness and untimely death prevented him. Following Harold's
death, Mrs. Row encouraged me to complete this work. Beginning
with the Harold Row collection and the bibliography he compiled,
which included about 540 unannotated entries, I made additions from
the Library of Congress and its extensive bibliographical resources,
and from the following libraries: Associated Mennonite Biblical
Seminaries, Catholic University of America, Drew University, Gettysburg Lutheran Seminary, Hartford Seminary Foundation, Harvard
Divinity School, Notre Dame University, Princeton Theological Seminary, Union Theological Seminary (New York), Union Theological
Seminary (Richmond, Va.), Wesley Theological Seminary, and the
Yale Divinity School.

The bibliography is generally limited to studies that have the
Sermon on the Mount and/or the Beatitudes as their major emphasis. Omitted are Bible commentaries and commentaries on Matthew and Luke, works on the life and teachings of Jesus, New Testament and Christian ethics, New Testament theology, and the Christian life, all of which usually contain some material on the Sermon

on the Mount. These are recommended as additional and supplemental resources to the bibliography. Also omitted are two other well-known parts of the Sermon on the Mount--the Lord's Prayer and the Golden Rule.

Part II contains three sections. First, there is a partial listing of texts of the Sermon on the Mount in many languages. Some of these were translated and printed by missionaries. Consequently, some people had their first introduction to the Bible via the Sermon on the Mount. Other editions were privately printed and have ornate illuminations and binding. The second and third parts are partially-annotated bibliographies of criticism, interpretation, sermons, meditations, etc., the first on the Sermon on the Mount, and the second on the Beatitudes.

My indebtedness is acknowledged to numerous persons who assisted in this project. First, to Leona Z. Row for her encouragement, support, and zealous interest; to various librarians of the above-named institutions who manifested the librarian's usual skill, courtesy, and helpfulness; to a number of colleagues at the Library of Congress, especially Dr. Edwin Bonsack, for their generous assistance with certain language problems and constructions; to Dr. David J. Wieand of Bethany Theological Seminary and Dr. Clarence Bauman of Mennonite Biblical Seminary for reading Part I of the manuscript and offering helpful criticism and suggestions; and to Darlene Rose for her assistance in typing Part II of the manuscript.

Warren S. Kissinger

University Park, Md.
November 1974

Part I

HISTORY OF INTERPRETATION

1 THE LITERATURE

In his Introduction to The Preaching of Chrysostom; Homilies
on the Sermon on the Mount, Jeroslav Pelikan states that the history
of the exposition of the Sermon on the Mount has not yet been written and that if one were to include in that history all the references
to the Sermon on the Mount in the history of exegesis, and especially
the expositions of the Lord's Prayer, it would be a massive historical enterprise. Clarence Tucker Craig in a review of Martin Dibelius' The Sermon on the Mount, speaks of three main types of
books that are written on the Sermon on the Mount. The majority
are homiletical applications to contemporary life with little endeavor
to discover the circumstances under which the words were originally
spoken. The second type is apologetic, discussing the Jewish parallels in order to estimate the degree of originality of Jesus in relation to the rabbis. Craig says that there have been all too few gen-
uinely historical works of which Dibelius' book is a significant type
[Journal of Religion 21 (Jan 1941), 70]. The bibliography which follows this essay confirms the above observations by Pelikan and Craig.
While there are no systematic histories of the exposition of the Sermon on the Mount, there are a number of works which do deal with
this area. In addition, there are monographs devoted to a given
writer's interpretation of the Sermon or to that of a few selected
authors. In what follows we will attempt to briefly describe this
literature.

The work which comes nearest to a history of the interpretation
of the Sermon on the Mount is Harvey K. McArthur's Understanding
the Sermon on the Mount [see Bibliography]. In the Prologue, Mc-
Arthur gives a brief account of the literature on the Sermon from
the Didache to the present. He discusses the Sermon on the Mount
under four categories: the Mosaic tradition, the Pauline tradition,
the Eschaton, Ethics. In each section he refers to major interpreters of the Sermon in reference to these categories. In his fourth
chapter McArthur lists 12 approaches to the Sermon on the Mount:
(1) Absolutist, (2) Modification, (3) Hyperbole, (4) General Principles, (5) Attitudes-Not-Acts, (6) Double Standard, (7) Two Realms,
(8) Analogy of Scripture, (9) Interim Ethic, (10) Modern Dispensationalist, (11) Repentance, and (12) Unconditional Divine Will. Under each of these McArthur discusses writers who have been representative of these respective approaches.

Carl F. H. Henry in his chapter on the Sermon on the Mount

1

in Christian Personal Ethics follows a typology similar to that of
McArthur.   He refers to seven appraisals which have been made of
the Sermon and to representatives of each except for the "Reformed"
in which he develops his own views.   Henry's seven types are:
(1) Humanistic, (2) Liberal, (3) Dispensational, (4) Interim Ethic,
(5) Existential, (6) Anabaptist-Mennonite, and (7) Reformed.

August Tholuck in the introduction to Die Bergpredigt (i.e.,
Commentary on the Sermon on the Mount) has a section on "Exegetical Literature" in which he comments briefly on many commentaries on the Gospels and on Matthew, as well as on single works
on the Sermon on the Mount, the Beatitudes, and the Lord's Prayer,
from the Church Fathers to his own time.   His comments are very
brief and in most cases highly opinionated.

In Der Sinn der Bergpredigt (The Meaning of the Sermon on
the Mount), Hans Windisch criticizes "some recent interpretations"
of the meaning of the commandments and the problem of their practicability.   He deals primarily with Dibelius, Herrmann, and Bultmann.   Under his criticism of the "dogmatic solutions of the problem
of impossibility," Windisch treats Carl Stange and Gerhard Kittel.

In his essay, "The Sermon on the Mount," in the Interpreter's
Bible, Amos Wilder describes briefly the "chief conceptions that
have been held concerning the meaning and intention of the discourse."
He gives primary attention to the Reformation, the nineteenth century,
Schweitzer, and Dibelius.

James Langley's Th.D. thesis, "Critique of Contemporary In-
terpretations of the Sermon on the Mount," analyses the views of
Chrysostom, Augustine, Luther, Calvin, the Anabaptists, Tolstoy,
Herrmann, Stange, and Kittel.   The major portion of the thesis
examines and criticizes the interpretations of Schweitzer, Reinhold
Niebuhr, and C. H. Dodd.

In the first part of Tal Bonham's The Demands of Discipleship: The Relevance of the Sermon on the Mount, he criticizes
Schweitzer's view as "the interim evasion of the Sermon's relevance,"
and Dispensationalism as "the postponed evasion of the Sermon's
relevance."   In his fourth chapter Bonham attempts to identify the
most prominent modern interpretations of the Sermon's relevance
under the following headings: Salvation, Social reformation, Proclamation of perfection, External transformation, Internal transformation, Peace-of-Mind, Judgment.   He examines and discusses representative writers under each category.

Günther Bornkamm's essay "Die Gegenwartsdeutung der Bergpredigt" ("The History of the Exposition of the Sermon on the Mount")
makes only brief references to the interpretation of the Sermon in
Tolstoy, Marx, Ragaz, Weiss, Schweitzer, and Thurneysen.

In Chapter IV of Archibald Hunter's A Pattern for Life there
is a brief review of modern interpretations of the Sermon on the

Mount including Tolstoy, Schweitzer, Hermann, Kittel, Bonhoeffer.

Conrad R. Willard's Th.D. thesis, "The Sermon on the Mount
in the Writings of the Ante-Nicene Fathers from New Testament
Times to Origen," sets forth the comments of the Ante-Nicene Fathers on the Sermon on the Mount in a section by section commentary
form. He also criticizes Schweitzer's interim ethic and the modern
dispensationalist view, using H. A. Ironside as a representative.

Kaarle Laurila in Leo Tolstoi und Martin Luther als Ausleger
der Bergpredigt devotes 92 pages to Tolstoy's interpretation of the
Sermon on the Mount. He begins with a discussion of the religio-
centric character of Tolstoy's world view and proceeds to show how
Tolstoy's understanding of the Sermon led to his views on anti-mili-
tarism, anti-patriotism, universal brotherhood, and anarchism. Laurila's interpretation of Luther is briefer and more congenial. He
has a rather lengthy criticism of Tolstoy's views, especially on love
and nonviolence. In a brief concluding section Laurila examines the
thought of Emil Brunner and Carl Stange in reference to the Sermon
on the Mount.

In an article entitled "How Shall We Interpret the Sermon on
the Mount?," Irvin W. Batdorf examines the Sermon in reference
to eschatology and to its practicability in Windisch, Dibelius, and
Wilder.

Christian Krause has made a study of the Sermon on the Mount
in ecumenical thought since World War II. He attempts to present
a chronological development of ecumenical thought on the question of
the Kingdom of God and eschatology, of ethics and of the Sermon on
the Mount since World War II. Krause's examination of the available
material, primarily the volumes of reports and minutes of ecumenical
conferences, reveals that with few exceptions there has been little
direct critical confrontation with the Sermon on the Mount in the discussions on social ethics in the ecumenical movement. Direct work
on the Sermon in the ecumenical movement has been done primarily
by the study conferences in London (1946) and Bossey (1947) on the
theme "Biblical Authority for the Church's Social and Political Message Today."

Turning now to studies on individual interpreters of the Sermon
on the Mount, Adolf Holl, in Augustins Bergpredigtexegesis nach
seinem Frühwerk, discusses Augustine as textual critic of the Sermon on the Mount, his hermeneutical principles, and then treats
Augustine's exegesis of the Sermon.

Jeroslav Pelikan in the Introduction to The Preaching of Augustine; "Our Lord's Sermon on the Mount," includes sections on "Augustine's Exposition of the Sermon on the Mount" and "Augustine as
an Interpreter of the Sermon on the Mount."

Pelikan has also edited The Preaching of Chrysostom; Homilies
on the Sermon on the Mount. In the Introduction he has a section

on "Chrysostom as an Expositor of the Sermon on the Mount."

Studies on Luther are more numerous than for anyone else.
Georg Wünsch's Die Bergpredigt bei Luther is a substantial study
dealing with the relationship between Luther's interpretation of the
Sermon on the Mount and his views regarding the world, man,
property. Wünsch also discusses the early development of Luther's
thought on the Sermon on the Mount and the sources of his views.

As the title suggests, Harald Diem's Luthers Lehre von den
zwei Reichen untersucht von seinem Verstandnis der Bergpredigt aus
discusses Luther's interpretation of the Sermon on the Mount in relation to his teaching regarding the two kingdoms.

Hermann Beyer in his essay "Der Christ und die Bergpredigt
nach Luthers Deutung" examines Luther's views on the Sermon on
the Mount with special reference to its relationship to the Christian
life.

Erwin Mühlhapt is the editor of a series entitled Evangelien-
Auslegung, which consists of Luther's exposition of the Gospels.
One volume is Auslegung der Bergpredigt, which contains an intro-
ductory essay by Paul Althaus on Luther and the Sermon on the
Mount.

Calvin's approach to the Sermon on the Mount is described in
two works. One is Evangelische Radikalismen in der Sicht Calvins;
Sein Verständnis der Bergpredigt und der Aussendungsrede (Matth.
10), by Hiltrud Stadtlund-Neumann. The author deals with Calvin's
interpretation of Matt. 5:17-48, 6:19-34, 7:1-5 and in a brief concluding section, with his method of interpretation. The study is especially concerned with Calvin's differences with the Anabaptists and
other sectarian movements.

Hermann Schlingensiepen, in a Bonn dissertation, Die Auslegung
der Bergpredigt bei Calvin, concentrates on Calvin's treatment of
Christ as an interpreter of the Law and on the concept of love as
reflected in the Sermon on the Mount.

Ingred Engel has made a study of Friedrich Naumann and his
views on the Sermon on the Mount. The work by Engel was a Marburg dissertation entitled "Die Bergpredigt in den sozialen Spannungen
des 19. Jahrhunderts; Eine Untersuchung zu Friedrich Naumann."
With slight revision, Engel's thesis was published in 1972 with the
title Gottverständnis und sozialpolitisches Handeln; Eine Untersuchung
zu Friedrich Naumann.

Naumann, who left the Lutheran ministry in 1894 to enter politics, was a founder of the National Socialist Party and its first
president. He was an advocate of pan-Germanism. After the November Revolution in 1918, he became one of the founders of the
German Democratic Party. Throughout his career he attempted to

relate the Sermon on the Mount to his social and political views.
His understanding of the Sermon was significantly influenced by a
tour of Palestine in 1899. Naumann held the conviction that Jesus'
task was to improve the present world through his deeds and words.
This was the view of the Christian socialists in Germany who believed that the Gospel was a social message. His tour of Palestine,
however, convinced Naumann that Jesus was not a social reformer
and that it would not be right to derive a program of reform from
the Sermon on the Mount. While Naumann believed that Jesus' ethical teachings should be understood literally, they cannot be literally
fulfilled within our world and therefore they cannot any longer have
authority. These views were impressed upon Naumann through his
travels in the land where Jesus lived.

Ingrid Engel studies the development of Naumann's social and
political thought, especially in reference to his views on the Kingdom of God and the Sermon on the Mount. She concludes the work
with an analysis of the change in Naumann's thinking which resulted
from his travels in Palestine in 1899.

In the chapters which follow, an attempt is made to trace the
history of interpretation of the Sermon on the Mount from the patristic period to the twentieth century. From the extensive bibliographical material on the Sermon on the Mount I have attempted to discuss
those movements and authors which have made the most significant
contribution to this field. As the following bibliography shows, only
a small part of the material is included. In addition to this are the
many sermons, meditations, and popular works which relate the
Sermon on the Mount to the Christian life in its individual and social
dimensions. This essay and the accompanying bibliography substan-
tiate the fact that the Sermon on the Mount has been, and continues
to be, the most popular and most frequently discussed section of the
Bible.

2 THE ANTE-NICENE PERIOD

The immediate post-Resurrection period was a unique and crucial one in the history of the Church and in the development of
Christian thought. The initial dynamic and ecstatic breakthrough of
the post-Resurrection era had begun to wane. There was left, however, a set of ideas which had to be preserved and refined so that
further missionary and educational activity could be carried on.
There was a need for Christian witnesses who could recommend
their new faith to Jews and pagans and who could find common
terms of discourse in the interest of mutual understanding and per-
suasion.

But early Christianity also had to defend the faith against hos-
tile criticism and slander, and so the second century saw the rise
of the apologetic movement. It was necessary for these "apologists"
to defend the faith against a dual accusation. On the one hand,

Christianity was accused of being a danger to the Roman Empire and of undermining its structure. On the other hand, Christianity was seen as a nonsensical movement--a superstition mixed with philosophical fragments.

From the writings of the Ante-Nicene period it is evident that one of the most serious threats to Christianity was posed by innumerable Gnostic schools and sects of the first three centuries. A sharp dualism of matter and spirit characterized the Gnostics. Salvation came by knowledge (gnosis) which they sought in various and often bizarre combinations of Christianity, Hellenistic philosophy, and Oriental cult, magic, and myth. Instead of a gospel rooted in history and in human life, they concerned themselves with a wholly "spiritual" realm which was accessible through secret wisdom.

One of the most threatening of these Gnostic movements was associated with Marcion, a second-century Christian heretic, and against whom Tertullian wrote an apology. He was a bitter anti-Judaist and a foe of legalism. Salvation came by faith alone, but not faith in the God of the Old Testament who was a barbarous and false deity. It must be by faith in the God of Jesus Christ who is a God of love and mercy. Marcionism was a real danger to Christianity because its dualism denied a real incarnation. Moreover, this same dualistic typology undercut Christianity from its historic and spiritual roots in Judaism. The Old Law and the New were not part of a continuing drama of redemption; rather there was a radical discontinuity between the two.

This was something of the milieu of the post-Resurrection and Ante-Nicene period. And as might be expected, the writings from this period reflect the dynamic forces and tensions at work both within and upon the emerging Christian movement.

In its efforts to define and communicate the faith and to combat heresy, the Church's primary source of authority was the Scriptures of the Jewish Old Testament, and especially the Gospels and Epistles which recorded the events and the meaning of the life and work of Jesus. The Jewish Old Testament was upheld against Marcionites and Gnostics, but it was so interpreted as to make Jesus the fulfiller of Messianic prophecy. A New Testament was compiled from the writings of those who were eyewitnesses or their immediate companions, and it became a trustworthy record of the initial revelation. The Scriptures then became for the Early Church a source of inspiration and authority as they gradually formulated their creeds and as they defined the correct interpretations of the Scriptures and the Church's tradition.

No portion of the Scriptures was more frequently quoted and referred to by the Ante-Nicene writers than the Sermon on the Mount. The fifth chapter of Matthew appears more often in their works than any other single chapter, and Matthew 5-7 more frequently than any other three chapters in the entire Bible.

[Harold Smith, in Ante-Nicene Exegesis of the Gospels, 4 vols
(London: Society for Promoting Christian Knowledge, 1926), records
the comments of the Ante-Nicene Fathers on the Gospels. The sec-
tion on Matt. 5-7 with parallels in Luke in vol II covers pp 179-311.
There is an index of biblical texts in The Ante-Nicene Fathers, vol
X, A. Cleveland Coxe, ed (NY: Scribner's, 1899). The texts for
Matt. 5-7 are on pp 237-8. Conrad R. Willard's "The Sermon on
the Mount in the Writings of the Ante-Nicene Fathers from New
Testament Times to Origen," unpub ThD thesis, Central Theological
Seminary, Kansas City, KS, 1956, sets forth the comments of the
Ante-Nicene Fathers on the Sermon on the Mount in a verse by
verse commentary form.]

DIDACHE

One of the earliest extant post-biblical writings is the Didache,
or the Teaching of the Twelve Apostles, which may date from the
early part of the second century. It is a short early Christian
manual on morals and church practice and consists of 16 brief
chapters. Chapters 1-6 are a summary of Christian morality and
describe the "Two Ways"--the "Way of Life" and the "Way of
Death." This section includes quotations from the Sermon on the
Mount such as the Golden Rule in negative form, and those verses
relating to nonresistance, perfection, meekness. Chapter 8 on fasting and prayer makes reference to Matt. 6:5 on not "praying as the
hypocrites do." This chapter also contains the full text of the Lord's
Prayer.

JUSTIN MARTYR

Of the second-century Apologists perhaps the most important
was Justin Martyr. His best-known work is an Apology addressed
to the emperor Antonius Pius, the father of Marcus Aurelius. It
is referred to as the First Apology because there is an appendix
which is now commonly listed as a second apology. In the First
Apology Justin replies to the charges of immorality which have been
preferred against the Early Church. In chapters 15 and 16 he summarizes "some few of the doctrines which we have received from
Christ himself." Through both these chapters he quotes freely from
the Sermon on the Mount as examples of Christ's doctrine. These
include references to lust and adultery, divorce, love of enemies,
non-swearing, anxiety, prayer, false prophets.

IRENAEUS

Irenaeus was born either in Syria or in Asia Minor, probably
during the first half of the second century. He relates that in his
early youth he was associated with Polycarp, Bishop of Smyrna.
Irenaeus accompanied Polycarp when he was sent on a mission to
Marseilles in the south of Gaul. At Lyons Irenaeus became a dea-
con and later a presbyter. Of his works the chief one that remains
is his five books Against Heresies. In Book IV, chapters 12-13,

Irenaeus discusses the relationship between the New Law and the Old and refers especially to Matt. 5:21ff., where Jesus makes reference to what was said to the men of old and then to what he said. The thrust of Irenaeus' argument is that Jesus' message is not contrary to, nor is it an abrogation of past laws, but a fulfillment and extension of them. Moreover, such precepts as Jesus taught do not emanate from one who abolishes the Law, but from one who fulfils, expands and develops it in us (IV, 13, 4). Furthermore, Irenaeus also focuses on inward motives from which outward acts eventuate. Here he points to Jesus' words about lust and adultery, anger and murder. We must not only abstain from evil deeds but also from evil desires (IV, 13, 1). In IV, 16, 4 he says that the Gospel makes an advance beyond the morality of the Law. Referring to Matt. 5:22 where Jesus says that whoever says, "You fool!," shall be liable to the hell of fire, Irenaeus states that the Gospel's morality is superior because it shows that man is not only responsible for his deeds, but also his words.

TERTULLIAN

Tertullian was born in Carthage about the middle of the second century. At the age of about forty he became a Christian and soon after a priest in Rome or in Carthage. He was the first major writer to use Latin and is sometimes called the father of Latin theology. The range of his writings is quite diverse, and he wrote as an apologist and as an opponent of heresy. Among his numerous writings are five big books Against Marcion. It is from this work that we get most of our information about Marcion because Tertullian quotes his views in order to answer them.

In chapters 14-17 of Book IV Against Marcion Tertullian refers frequently to the Sermon on the Mount in his effort to refute Marcion's heresy. Tertullian uses several of the Beatitudes with their emphasis on blessing as a contrast to Marcion's god. Marcion's god has never given proof of his liberality by any preceding bestowal of minor blessings (IV, 14). Likewise when Jesus refers to the fathers who spoke well of the prophets, Tertullian charges Marcion's Christ of being a "turncoat." Now the destroyer, now the advocate of the prophets! (IV, 15). The defense of the prophets could not be consistent in the Christ of Marcion, who came to destroy them (IV, 15).

As with Irenaeus, Tertullian sees Christ as an extension and a continuation of the Law. Here too he is probably refuting Marcion's discontinuity between the Old and the New. In commenting on love of enemies and nonresistance Tertullian writes: "Thus, whatever [new provision] Christ introduced, he did it not in opposition to the Law, but rather in furtherance of it, without at all impairing the prescription of the Creator" (IV, 16).

ORIGEN

The most prolific of the Ante-Nicene writers was Origen, who
was born of Christian parents, probably in Alexandria, about 185.
Origen was primarily a biblical scholar. One of his works was a
commentary on Matthew which was divided into 25 books. Unfortunately, the first nine, with the exception of two fragments, are
lost. Book II which contained the Sermon on the Mount has only
one extant fragment. This is on the seventh Beatitude: Blessed
are the peacemakers [for English text of this fragment, see Origen's
Commentary on Matthew in The Ante-Nicene Fathers, vol IV, orig
suppl to the American ed, Allan Menzies, ed (NY: Scribner's,
1925), p 413].

From the foregoing survey of the Ante-Nicene literature it is
evident that the Sermon on the Mount was frequently quoted and referred to and that it was employed to define Christ's teaching and
doctrine and to answer and refute the charges levelled against the
early Christian community. But very early the Sermon on the
Mount also became a classic statement of Christian ethics. It af-
forded direction as to what a Christian should be and how he should
live. Conrad R. Willard in his thesis, "The Sermon on the Mount
in the Writings of the Ante-Nicene Fathers from New Testament
Times to Origen" [references are to this unpub ThD thesis, Central
Baptist Theological Seminary, Kansas City, KS, 1956], is confident
that the early Christians considered Jesus' teachings relevant and
applicable to their situation. After a careful search of the literature, Willard states that the idea that the ethics of the Sermon
were for some time in the future, when Christ would reign in person upon the earth, never once appears in their writings [p 124].
The moral authority of the Sermon on the Mount for the Ante-Nicene
writers is further underscored by Willard: "The strength of this
dissertation rests upon its presentation of the writings of the Post-
Apostolic Church Fathers, illustrating beyond all doubt that they
preached and taught and wrote as though the Sermon was valid for
them and the people to whom they preached" [pp 191-92].

3 CHRYSOSTOM

Chrysostom was born in Antioch ca. 345-347 although there is
some evidence that he may have been born in 354, the same year
as Augustine. In 386 he was advanced to the priesthood and for the
next twelve years he was the great preacher of Antioch. During
this period he delivered a series of "Homilies" on Genesis, Matthew,
John, Romans, Galatians, Corinthians, Ephesians, Timothy, and
Titus, which established his reputation as one of the greatest preach-
ers and biblical expositors. His sermons exemplify an eminent
combination of exegesis and practical application. However, unlike
Origen, Tertullian, and others, he opposed the allegorical method
of interpreting the Scriptures. Chrysostom is the typical example
of the Antiochene school of hermeneutics. The Antiochene school,

in contrast to the Alexandrian allegorical method, approached the
Scriptures in a more sober and restrained manner and interpreted
them more grammatically, historically, and literally.

Chrysostom's Homilies on the Gospel of St. Matthew represents
the oldest complete commentary on Matthew extant from the patristic
period. Thus the section on the Sermon on the Mount is likewise
the oldest and most thorough exposition from that period that is
available today.

As with his predecessors, so there is evidence in Chrysostom's
homilies on the Sermon on the Mount that he was an apologist. The
heretical dualistic views of the Gnostics and the Manicheans are his
concern. In his comments on the first verses of Matthew 5 Chrysostom's reference to Gnostic dualism is evident: "... and besides,
he stopped the shameless mouths of the heretics signifying by this his
care of both parts of our being, that he himself is the Maker of the
whole creation. Therefore also on each nature he bestowed abundant
providence, now amending the one, now the other" (XV. 1) [references
are to The Preaching of Chrysostom: Homilies on the Sermon on the
Mount, ed Jeroslav Pelikan (Philadelphia: Fortress Pr, 1973)]. Concerning Matt. 5:29: "If thy right eye offend thee, pluck it out, and
cast it from thee," Chrysostom says: "... therefore he hath given
these injunctions; not discoursing about our limbs;--far from it, --
for nowhere doth he say that our flesh is to be blamed for things,
but everywhere it is the evil mind that is accused. For it is not
the eye that sees, but the mind and the thought" (XVII. 3). Here by
implication he rejects the Gnostic-Manichean concept that the body is
evil and the mind and spirit are good. Chrysostom rather reverses
the situation and holds that it is the mind and thought that are the
root of evil rather than the bodily organs. In XV. 8 Chrysostom
refers to those who maintain that the Creator of the world and the
one who "makes his sun to rise on the evil and on the good, who
sends the rain on the just and on the unjust" is in some sense an
evil being. He further comments on those who say that the Father
to Christ was not the Creator. Of these he says: "Seest thou the
children of the devil, how they speak out of the fountain of their
father, alienating the work of creation from God ..." (XVI. 8).

Another dimension of Gnostic dualism, as we have seen, was
the divorce between the old covenant and the new. In contrast to
this discontinuity Chrysostom accepts the Old Testament. Regarding
Matt. 5:20 where Jesus says that unless one's righteousness exceed
the righteousness of the Scribes and Pharisees, he cannot enter the
Kingdom of Heaven, Chrysostom comments:

> And observe also here, how he commends the Old Law, by
> making a comparison between it and the other; which kind of
> thing implies it to be of the same tribe and kindred for more
> and less, is in the same kind. He doth not, you see, find
> fault with the Old Law, but will have it made stricter.
> Whereas, had it been evil, he would not have required more

of it; he would not have made it more perfect, but would
have cast it out.... So that from all considerations it is
clear, that not from any badness in itself doth it fail to
bring us in, but because it is now the season of higher precepts [XVI. 6].

In an even more pointed reference to the Gnostics and Manichaeans, he speaks about Jesus' coming not to destroy the Law but
to fulfill it. On this he says: "Now this not only obstructs the ob-
stinancy of the Jews, but stops also the mouths of those heretics,
who say that the old covenant is of the devil. For if Christ came
to destroy his tyranny, how is this covenant not only not destroyed,
but even fulfilled by him?" (XVI. 3). It is clear that for Chrysostom there is no break in the continuity of the Old and New Law.
Jesus' sayings did not repeal the former, but they were "a drawing
out, and filling up of them" (XVI. 4).

Another perennial problem which came into sharp focus during
the Reformation had to do with the applicability and relevance of
the Sermon on the Mount to the common life. Was it intended for
everyone, or was it a counsel of perfection applicable only to a
select few who took the way of asceticism? Or is the Sermon an
ethic only for a brief interim during which the messianic community
awaits the coming of the Son of Man? These questions will be discussed in more detail later. Chrysostom, while he does not discuss
these issues in any detailed or systematic fashion, does nevertheless
indicate his thinking about them.

The Sermon on the Mount begins with Jesus' disciples coming
to him and his teaching them. While it is to them that the Sermon
is initially addressed, nevertheless, Chrysostom says that it is directed to all through them (XV. 1). "For though it was spoken unto
them, it was written for the sake also of all men afterwards. And
accordingly on this account, though he had his disciples in his mind
in his public preaching, yet unto them he limits not his sayings, but
applies all his words of blessing without restriction" (XV. 2). However, there is some indication that Chrysostom drew the later distinction between those who take the "way of perfection" in contrast
to those who view Christ's teachings as being required of all Christians. The following quotation seems to reflect this view:

Let us not therefore suppose his injunctions are impossible:
for there are many who duly perform them, even as it is....
Whence it is manifest that even now there are many who
show forth the apostolical life.... Now as to the fact, that
there are many who have attained unto this, we might show it
even from those, who have practiced this self-denial even in
our generation [XXI. 5].

Here there is the possibility that Chrysostom is referring to the
monastic life. It remained, however, for a later period to heighten
and sharpen this distinction.

At several points in Chrysostom's homilies on the Sermon on the Mount his preference for a historical and more "literal" interpretation, as opposed to an allegorical, is apparent. In his commentary on the third Beatitude he rejects the interpretation of the earth as a figurative earth. "Some say a figurative earth, but it is not this, for nowhere in Scripture do we find any mention of an earth that is merely figurative" (XV. 5). The sharpest distinction between the literal and the allegorical methods of interpretation come in Chrysostom's exposition of the fourth petition of the Lord's Prayer. Origen and others maintained that the bread referred to in this petition could not be physical bread but was a figure for Christ or spiritual bread. Chrysostom's understanding of bread is literal. He says:

> But mark, I pray thee, how even in things that are bodily, that which is spiritual abounds. For it is neither for riches, nor for delicate living, nor for costly raiment, nor for any other such thing, but for bread only, that he hath commanded us to make our prayer. And for 'daily bread,' so as not to 'take thought for the morrow.' Because of this he added, 'daily bread,' that is, bread for one day [XIX. 8].

Chrysostom's homilies on the Sermon on the Mount represent a moderate and restrained method of exegesis. He cautions against allegorizing and employs a more literal and historical approach. Moreover, he is on the side of those who hold that the Sermon on the Mount is relevant and applicable to every Christian. Thus to this day his homilies are fine examples of the art of combining homiletics and hermeneutics.

4 AUGUSTINE

Augustine, born in 354, is without doubt one of the greatest and most influential Christian theologians. His influence was deeply impressed upon the medieval period, and his thought lay behind many of the motifs which came to the fore during the Reformation. Even today he remains an intellectual power and an acknowledged spiritual father. Paul Tillich said that Augustine's influence not only overshadowed the next thousand years but all periods ever since. He also acknowledged his own dependence upon Augustine, saying that his own theology was more Augustinian than Thomistic [Tillich, A History of Christian Thought, ed Carl E. Braaten (NY: Harper & Row, 1968), pp 103-4].

Much attention has been given to the leading themes in Augustine's philosophy and theology. These include: epistemology, doctrine of God, doctrine of man, election and predestination, Christology, Church and sacraments, and his theology of history. However, much less attention has been given to Augustine as a preacher and biblical exegete. For he was not only an outstanding philosopher and theologian but also a renowned preacher and interpreter of the

Scriptures. Augustine's great masterpieces--the Confessions, the
City of God, and On the Trinity are universally known. But his
works on the Gospels, on the Psalms, and on the Sermon on the
Mount have not been widely studied and commented upon. For our
purposes we are especially concerned with his commentary on the
Sermon on the Mount [the only full-length study of Augustine's The
Lord's Sermon on the Mount (De Sermone Domini in monte) is
Adolph Höll's Augustins Bergpredigtexegese nach seinem Frühwerk
(Vienna: Herder, 1960)].

De Sermone Domini in monte was one of Augustine's earlier
works and was probably written between 392 and 396. It is divided
into two books. The first book deals with Matthew 5 while the
second is on Matthew 6 and 7. As the bibliography shows, it exists
in a number of editions and has been translated into numerous languages. [It is interesting to note that Augustine is probably the
first to speak of Christ's Sermon as the "Sermon on the Mount";
however, this designation did not come into widespread use until
after the Reformation.]

Augustine begins The Lord's Sermon on the Mount by referring
to it as the highest standard of morality and as the perfect measure
of the Christian life. The passage reads as follows:

> If anyone piously and soberly considers the sermon which
> our Lord Jesus Christ preached on the mount, as we read
> it in the Gospel according to Matthew, I think that he will
> find in it, as regards the highest morals, the perfect meas-
> ure of the Christian life. We do not venture to promise this
> rashly, but conclude it from the very words of the Lord him-
> self. For the way this sermon is brought to a close makes
> it clear that all the precepts which have to do with shaping
> this life are in it ... he indicated--sufficiently, I think--
> that these words which he spoke on the mountain so perfectly
> shape the life of those who wish to live by them that such
> men are rightly compared to one who builds his house upon
> the rock. I have said this to make it clear that this sermon
> is filled with all the precepts by which the Christian life is
> formed [I. 1. 1; references are to The Preaching of Augus-
> tine: "Our Lord's Sermon on the Mount," ed Jeroslav Peli-
> kan (Philadelphia: Fortress Pr, 1973)].

From this opening passage and what follows, it is evident that
Augustine is convinced that the ethical content of the Sermon on
the Mount was not a moral code for a select few but was rather a
perfect rule and pattern for each Christian life. It was a standard
for every follower of Christ and in it one could find solutions to
the problems relating to human life and conduct.

In his discussion of the Beatitudes and the Lord's Prayer,
Augustine is intrigued by the symbolism of numbers, especially the
number seven which was regarded as a symbol of perfection and

wholeness. In 3. 10 Augustine suggests that the very number of
the Beatitudes should be carefully considered. He then elaborates
on the seven stages found in the seven Beatitudes. There are eight
Beatitudes, however, and Augustine's explanation of this is as follows:

> The eighth maxim returns, as it were, to the beginning, for
> it shows forth and commends what is complete and perfect.
> And so in the first and the eighth statements the Kingdom of
> Heaven is mentioned.... For indeed it is said, 'Who will
> separate us from the love of Christ: will tribulation or dis-
> tress, or persecution or famine, or nakedness, or peril, or
> the sword?' (Rom. 8:35). Seven in number, then, are the
> things which bring perfection; and the eighth illuminates and
> points out what is perfect, so that through these steps others
> might also be made perfect, starting once more, so to speak,
> from the beginning [1. 3. 10].

In 1. 4. 12 he further expands this interpretation:

> The eighth maxim, which returns to the beginning and de-
> clares the perfect man, is perhaps also signified by the cir-
> cumcision on the eighth day in the Old Testament, by the
> resurrection of the Lord after the Sabbath, which is surely
> the eighth and at the same time the first day, and by the
> celebration of the octave of the feast which we observe on
> the occasion of the regeneration of the new man, and by the
> number itself of Pentecost. For to seven multiplied seven
> times (which comes out forty-nine) an eighth is added, so to
> speak, so that the number fifty is completed and we return,
> as it were, to the beginning.

Though Augustine's sevenfold typology and his symbolism of
numbers appears strained and unduly superimposed upon the biblical
texts, nevertheless, this pattern affords him a method of relating
various parts of the Sermon on the Mount to each other and to correlate command and promise as expressed in the Old Law and the
New.

In his introduction to The Preaching of Augustine: "Our
Lord's Sermon on the Mount" [pp xvii-xix], Jeroslav Pelikan notes
another theme which he finds running through Augustine's interpretation of the Sermon on the Mount. This is a "great chain of being"--a concept well-known through Arthur O. Lovejoy's The Great
Chain of Being: A Study of the History of an Idea (Cambridge, MA,
1936). This theme occurs in 1. 2. 9 where the Kingdom of God is
viewed as so ordered that what is distinctive and superior in man
rules without resistance those other elements which are common to
us and the beasts. Again in 1. 12. 34 Augustine says that all na-
tures are beautiful in their order and by their degrees. Pelikan
states that this ordering of all being becomes in Augustine's exegesis
both a way of understanding the ethic of the Sermon and a weapon

against the Manichaeans [p xviii]. Against Manichaean asceticism
and dualism Augustine says that though our mind becomes tainted by
the desire of earthly things, earth itself, in its own nature and
order, is clean (2. 13. 44).

In this pattern of thought one can also discern the influence of
Neo-Platonism upon Augustine and his modification of its claims.
There was in Neo-Platonism a tendency to devalue the world and to
escape from it. Augustine rejected this disparagement toward the
world and saw the experience of the divine in everything. God is
the creative ground of the world in terms of love [on Augustine's
relationship to Manichaeism and Neo-Platonism, see Tillich, A History, pp 106-9].

Another area which needs to be discussed is Augustine's understanding of the relationship between the Old Law and the New in the
Sermon on the Mount. The most extensive treatment of this problem
is in Augustine's Reply to Faustus. Faustus was a renowned Manichaean leader who affirmed that acceptance of the New Testament
necessitated a repudiation of the Old Testament and its God. He
maintained that there was a break between the Old and the New Law
because Christ did not fulfill the Old Law but rather destroyed it.
The "dialogue" between Augustine and Faustus on this issue is in
Books XVII-XIX of the Reply to Faustus.

Faustus proceeded to offer every conceivable argument to support his claim that Christ destroyed the Law. Augustine refutes
each argument and says that Christ fulfilled the Law in at least six
different ways [for detailed discussion of these issues, see Harvey
K. McArthur, Understanding the Sermon on the Mount (NY: Harper,
1960), pp 26ff]. Among these ways were Jesus' fulfilling its Messianic predictions and his transforming its ceremonial aspects and
thus revealing their true significance. Augustine frequently resorts
to the idea that the Old Law prophesied and prefigured Christ. The
observances and rites prescribed by the Old Testament were symbolic in that they pointed to Christ. He says: "Besides, they
(Catholic Christians) see in Christ and the Church the fulfillment
of all the prophecies of the Old Testament, whether in the form of
actions, or of symbolic rites, or of figurative language" (XVII. 7)
[Augustine, Works, vol V, ed Marcus Dods (Edinburgh: T. & T.
Clark, 1872)]. Faustus had argued that since Christians do not observe many of the rites of the Old Testament, therefore it is evident that Christ destroyed the Law. Not so, said Augustine, because these Old Testament rites were only types of Christ, and
when he came he fulfilled them so that there is no longer any need
for Christians to observe them. Thus in XIX. 13: "Thus the
sacraments of the Old Testament, which were celebrated in obedience to the Law, were types of Christ who was to come; and when
Christ fulfilled them by his advent they were done away, and were
done away because they were fulfilled. For Christ came not to
destroy, but to fulfill." And again in XVIII. 4: "The things in the
Law and the Prophets which Christians do not observe, are only the
types of what they do observe."

So from the above it appears that Augustine was unwilling to admit that Christ set aside the Law and that he was eager to maintain the continuity between the Old and the New in view of Faustus' radical charge that Christ did indeed destroy the Law. However, in 1. 2 of The Lord's Sermon on the Mount the break between Old and New appears much sharper. Augustine speculates on the significance of Christ going up the mountain to deliver his sermon.

> If there is a question as to what the mountain signifies, it is well taken to mean the greater precepts of righteousness, for those which were given to the Jews were lesser. Yet, through his holy prophets and servants, one and the same God gave, according to a thoroughly ordered division of times, lesser precepts to a people who still needed to be bound by fear and through his Son gave greater precepts to a people who were now ready to be freed by love.

John J. Jepson concludes from this passage that Augustine is firmly convinced that the Lord intended to replace the Law of the Old Testament by a new one. For this reason he emphasizes the fact that the difference between the commandments of Sinai and those of the Sermon on the Mount is not only a difference of application and permanence but also of quality [Augustine, The Lord's Sermon on the Mount, tr John J. Jepson (Westminster, MD: Newman Pr, 1948), p 5]. This seeming difference in emphasis between the Augustine of the Reply to Faustus and the Augustine of The Lord's Sermon on the Mount represents an ambiguity which McArthur says has never been resolved. He, however, leans toward the view that Augustine basically regarded the New as an extension of the Old though implicit in it [McArthur, Understanding the Sermon, pp 30ff].

The range of Augustine's exposition of the Sermon on the Mount is marked by a tension between the theoretical and the practical, between the literal and the allegorical. Adolf Holl concludes that Augustine's Sermon on the Mount manifests a well-balanced relationship between exegetical exactness and theological depth; that his chief contribution to contemporary exegesis is not in his introduction of critical questions but in his theological interpretation, and that measured by the scholarly standards of his time, Augustine's significance cannot be disputed [Adolf Holl, Augustine Bergpredigtexegese nach seinem Frühwerk, p 66].

5 THE MEDIEVAL PERIOD

In speaking about the Middle Ages one is confronted with a two-fold temptation. On the one hand, he can characterize this period as a "Dark Age" replete with superstition, barbarism, gross inequality, exploitation by ecclesiastical and civil powers, etc. Or, on the other hand, he can view this period as the golden age of faith and as one of the high and creative hours in Western civilization.

The beginning of the Middle Ages is usually dated about 600 with the papacy of Gregory the Great. The so-called high Middle Ages with its great systems of theology and scholastics, its Gothic art, and its feudal life, come about 1200-1300. With the coming of the middle of the fifteenth century this monumental structure begins to disintegrate and new and fresh motifs appear which make possible the Renaissance and the Reformation.

Paul Tillich has suggested that there is one basic problem which one finds in all periods of the Middle Ages. It is that of a transcendent reality, manifest and embodied in a special institution, in a special sacred society, leading the culture and interpreting nature. He says that this is the perspective which enables one to understand the Middle Ages and that without it there is no understanding [A History of Christian Thought, p 134].

The medieval period was one of change in society, philosophy, theology, the church, and the understanding of the Christian life. Insofar as Christian ethics and the meaning of the New Law for the Christian life were concerned, a new view developed which was to have a far-reaching impact upon the medieval and post-medieval periods.

Thomas Aquinas in whom the scholastic synthesis came to its climax, and who can be called the "father of Catholic theology," wrote a "Treatise on Law" which comprises Questions 90-108 in his Summa Theologica, Part 2. 1. The most relevant sections which deal with issues raised in the Sermon on the Mount are Questions 107 and 108. In commenting on Christ fulfilling the Law, Aquinas said that the New Law fulfills the Old by supplying that which was lacking in the Old Law. He continues as follows:

> Now Christ fulfilled the precepts of the Old Law both in his works and in his doctrine. In his works, because he was willing to be circumcised and to fulfill the other legal observances, which were binding for the time being.... In his doctrine he fulfilled the precepts of the Law in three ways. First, by explaining the true sense of the Law. This is clear in the case of murder and adultery, the prohibition of which the Scribes and Pharisees thought to refer only to the exterior act: wherefore our Lord fulfilled the Law by showing that the prohibition extended also to the interior acts of sins. Secondly, our Lord fulfilled the precepts of the Law by prescribing the safest way of complying with the statutes of the Old Law. Thus the Old Law forbade perjury: and this is more safely avoided, by abstaining altogether from swearing, save in cases of urgency. Thirdly, our Lord fulfilled the precepts of the Law, by adding some counsels of perfection: this is clearly seen in Matt. 19:21 where our Lord said to the man who affirmed that he had kept all the precepts of the Old Law: One thing is wanting to thee: If thou wilt be perfect, go, sell whatsoever thou hast, etc. [Summa Theologica, Pt 2. 1, Ques 107, art 2].

In this passage Aquinas speaks of "precepts" and "counsels of perfection," a distinction which became basic in Catholic moral theology. This led to what is sometimes called the "double standard view" insofar as the observance of the New Law is concerned. Evangelical counsels as distinguished from moral precepts or commandments are advisory directives of Christ. They are given as guides which lead to a closer approximation to perfection and imitation of Christ himself. More specifically, the evangelical counsels have traditionally been associated with the virtues of poverty, chastity, and obedience. Obedience to the precepts or commandments is necessary for salvation, but the evangelical counsels are essential for perfection and they obtain more merit and favor with God. The classic definition of, and distinction between, the precepts or commandments and the counsels is in Part 2. 1, Question 108 article 4 of the Summa Theologica.

> The difference between a counsel and a commandment is that a commandment implies obligation, whereas a counsel is left to the option of the one to whom it is given. Consequently in the New Law, which is the law of liberty, counsels are added to the commandments, and not in the Old Law, which is the law of bondage. We must therefore understand the commandments of the New Law to have been given about matters that are necessary to gain the end of eternal bliss, to which end the New Law brings us forthwith: but that the counsels are about matters that render the gaining of this end more assured and expeditious.... Nevertheless, for man to gain the end aforesaid, he does not need to renounce the things of the world altogether: since he can, while using the things of this world, attain to eternal happiness, provided he does not place his end in them: but he will attain more speedily thereto by giving up the goods of this world entirely: wherefore the evangelical counsels are given for this purpose.
>   Now the goods of this world which come into use in human life, consist in three things: viz., in external wealth pertaining to the concupiscence of the eyes; carnal pleasures pertaining to the concupiscience of the flesh; and honors which pertain to the pride of life, according to I John 2:16: and it is in renouncing these altogether, as far as possible, that the evangelical counsels consist. Moreover, every form of the religious life that professes the state of perfection is based on these three: since riches are renounced by poverty; carnal pleasures by perpetual chastity; and the pride of life by the bondage of obedience.

For a further interpretation of these questions raised in the Sermon on the Mount we turn to Cornelius à Lapide who lived after the medieval period but who was securely rooted in its thought. Lapide, a voluminous biblical exegete, was born in Belgium in 1567. He taught Sacred Scripture for forty years, first at Louvain (1596-1616) and then at the Roman College (1616-1636). His exten-

tensive commentaries cover the entire Bible with the exception of
Job and Psalms [references that follow are to The Great Commen-
tary, vol I, tr Thomas W. Mossman (London: John Hodges, 1890)].
His commentary on Matt. 5-7 covers about 140 pages.

In commenting on Matt. 5:17 regarding Christ's statement
about fulfilling the Law, Lapide says that a part of this fulfillment
of the Law consisted of Christ's adding to things of precept evangelical counsels of perfection (p 212). In Matt. 5:48 Jesus says
that you must be perfect, as your heavenly Father is perfect.   Here
again Lapide speaks about precepts and counsels. He writes.

> You will ask whether this perfection be of counsel or of
> precept? I reply, partly of counsel, partly of precept.
> First, it is of precept that every believer in Christianity
> should endeavor to be perfect.... Hence we learn from this
> passage that all Christians are under obligation to be ad-
> vancing towards perfection according to their state and con-
> dition.... This perfection is of counsel so far as it extends
> itself to the observance, not only of commands, but of evan-
> gelical counsels, such as voluntary poverty, chastity, and
> religious obedience ... [pp 244-45].

Thus there develops out of the medieval period a new way of
understanding the ethic of the Sermon on the Mount. In the Sermon
and in the New Testament are to be found both precepts and evangelical counsels, and these in effect become two paths which lead to
salvation.

Prior to this period the New Law as expressed in the Sermon
on the Mount was understood as a way that applied to all Christians.
There were, however, certain passages in the Didache, in Chrysostom, and in Augustine which could be interpreted from the double
standard viewpoint. Before the Middle Ages the rigorous demands
of the Sermon on the Mount were largely seen as possibilities for
every Christian. But now these demands are precepts plus evangelical counsels which can be voluntarily chosen by those who would
aspire to perfection. The Sermon on the Mount together with such
Scriptures as Matt. 19:16-30 and I Cor. 7:38 become the bases for
the evangelical counsels of poverty, chastity, and obedience.

Lapide introduces still another dimension in his commentary
on the Sermon on the Mount. Not only are there evangelical counsels there but also dogma relating to the Trinity, the Incarnation,
the Church, and the Sacraments. In commenting on Christ's fulfilling the Law he says: "For Christ added to the Law precepts of
explicit belief concerning God the Three in One, and concerning
Christ's Incarnation, Passion, and Redemption" (p 216). And concerning Christ's words that not an iota, not a dot, will pass from
the Law until all is accomplished, Lapide writes: "All things, that
is, which have been spoken concerning me and my acts, my Church
and Sacraments in the Law and the Prophets" (p 214).

By the time of Lapide the Reformation had already occurred
and his commentary reflects his disagreement with such "absolu-
tists" as the Anabaptists who maintained that Christ's references to
non-swearing and nonresistance do not take away the right of defending ourselves when we are attacked by an enemy, but only forbids the desire of vengeance (p 234).

By the sixteenth century new views were abroad--views which
rejected the medieval exegetes and substituted other "evasions" of
the demands of the Sermon on the Mount in their stead. But there
were also "radical disciples" who took the Sermon on the Mount
literally and insisted on ordering their lives by it. To these movements we now turn.

6 MARTIN LUTHER

The chief source for Luther's views on the Sermon on the
Mount comes from a series of sermons on Matthew 5-7 which
were delivered in Wittenberg [references are to Luther's Works,
vol 21: The Sermon on the Mount, ed Jeroslav Pelikan (St. Louis:
Concordia Pub Hse, 1956)]. Knowledge about the evolution of these
sermons from the pulpit to the appearance of the finished commentary is sketchy, and this has caused some scholars to seriously
question their reliability. One cannot be sure whether the editor
or editors, whoever they were, did not take certain liberties with
the text of Luther's sermons as delivered. Jeroslav Pelikan suggests that there seems to be no warrant however for the extreme
skepticism of certain scholars regarding the reliability of this commentary. He says that there are many parallels throughout Luther's
works for most of the ideas and many of the terms that appear here
(p xxi).

In his preface to the commentary Luther sets the stage for
what is to follow. He intends to refute the false teaching of the
papists and the schismatics, especially with reference to the fifth
chapter of Matthew. Against these "perversions" Luther wants to
present the "true, pure, and Christian meaning" of these texts.
Moreover, he has no doubt that he has done so. To say the least,
Luther's language is direct and forthright and he leaves little doubt
as to whom he is speaking and what he is saying.

The wicked devil has managed so cleverly to twist and per-
vert, especially the fifth chapter, making it teach the exact opposite
of what it means. This chapter "has fallen into the hands of the
vulgar pigs and asses, the jurists and sophists, the right hand of
that jackass of a pope and his mamelukes." With their two standards of perfection they have made salvation dependent upon works
apart from faith. Thus, in the first place, Luther intends his commentary to be a polemic against the "squires, the jurists and sophists."

Luther's second group of "heretics" are the "new jurists and sophists"--the schismatic spirits and Anabaptists. "From their crazy heads they are making new trouble out of this fifth chapter." The papists go too far to the left and keep nothing of this teaching of Christ. But the others go too far to the right when "they teach miserable stuff" like it is wrong to own private property, to swear, to hold office as a ruler or judge, to protest or defend oneself, to stay with wife and children. The "schismatics" do not recognize any difference between the secular and the divine realm, much less what should be the distinctive doctrine and action in each realm. "From these horrible examples of both the papists and the schismatic jurists we learn and know what the devil has in mind, especially his intention to distort this fifth chapter of St. Matthew, and thereby exterminate pure Christian teaching" (pp 1-6).

Besides the papists and the schismatics, Luther levels sharp criticism against the Jews. He says that the target and object of the Sermon on the Mount was principally the Jews. They were devoid of mercy; they were lenient with regard to the Sixth Commandment; they found scriptural basis for hating enemies. Their teaching and life were both imperfect and wrong because they taught that they should love only their friends, and they lived accordingly. In commenting on Matt. 6:24, Luther says that this is a judgment of Christ upon greedy people, and primarily upon his Jews. Christ attacks the doctrine and the life of the Jews, to rebuke and reform their delusions and deeds (pp 30, 33, 67, 92f, 118f, 129, 186).

Luther's interpretation of the Sermon on the Mount and his polemic against the above "misconceptions" is centered to a large extent around his doctrine of "the two kingdoms." By his distinction between the secular and the divine realm Luther tries to maintain the validity of the Sermon on the Mount for all Christians without making the "mistakes" of the Catholics or the Anabaptists. One of the most explicit statements of this concept is found in Luther's comments on Matt. 5:38-42. "This text has also given rise to many questions and errors among nearly all the theologians who have failed to distinguish properly between the secular and the spiritual, between the kingdom of Christ and the kingdom of the world" (p 105). God rules the secular kingdom through secular authority and the spiritual kingdom through His Word. The Catholics confused the two kingdoms by assigning temporal authority to the pope, while the Anabaptists confused them by maintaining that the secular realm could be ruled with the Law of God, either the Ten Commandments or the Sermon on the Mount.

In his teaching about nonresistance Christ is not tampering with the responsibility and authority of the government, but he is teaching individual Christians how to live personally, apart from their official position and authority (p 106). This brings us to the question of the implication of the doctrine of the two kingdoms for the individual Christian. Luther distinguishes between the person and the office, for these two are present simultaneously in the same man. Thus it is permissible to go to court and lodge a complaint against injustice or violence as long as one does not have a false heart. A Christian may carry on all sorts of secular business with impunity--not as a Christian but as a secular person--while his heart remains pure in his Christianity, as Christ demands. This distinction between the person and the office is set forth clearly in the following passage:

> Thus when a Christian goes to war or when he sits on a judge's bench, punishing his neighbor, or when he registers an official complaint, he is not doing this as a Christian, but as a soldier or a judge or a lawyer. At the same time he keeps a Christian heart. He does not intend anyone any harm, and it grieves him that his neighbor must suffer grief. So he lives simultaneously as a Christian toward everyone, personally suffering all sorts of things in the world, and as a secular person, maintaining, using, and performing all the functions required by the law of his territory or city, by civil law, and by domestic law [p 113].

The above distinction enables a Christian not to resist any evil, but within the limits of his office, a secular person should oppose every evil. But the plain words of Christ remain: "Do not resist evil." Luther says that this injunction applies to the disciples of Christ, whom he is teaching about their personal lives, apart from the secular government. The resistance to evil, the administration of justice, and punishment should be left to the one who holds a position in the secular realm. As for the disciples, they should try to follow Christ's commands.

Another problem which arises with regard to the person and the office concerns the moral character of the person. Is the efficacy of the office enhanced or negated by the quality of the person's life? No, because the office is an order given by God, and it is not separated from His majesty. One must recognize the office as the order of God, in spite of the nature of the person. So the person may be good or evil, but the office is right and good since it does not belong to man but to God. The important and necessary thing is to distinguish between the office and the person. Just because one man is pious and twenty are wicked, you must not reject the office on account of the person. The test is not whether the person is righteous or not, but whether the tendency and purpose of the office is to praise and confirm the doctrine of faith in Christ and whether they harmonize with what he has spoken, commanded, and instituted. Whether an official is pious or wicked, neither detracts from the office nor adds to it. "We should always be guided by this certain standard, which should be applied to every kind of person, whether pious or impious, in office or out of office: Do the signs aim at praising Christ and advancing your faith?" (pp 277-80).

In a Postscript to The Sermon on the Mount, Luther turns to

the problem raised by the strong emphasis in the Sermon on works, merit, reward. He makes a sharp distinction between merit and grace. They are mutually exclusive so that when grace is being preached, certainly merit cannot be preached.

One must make a distinction between faith or being a Christian and its fruit. Christ in the Sermon on the Mount is saying nothing about how we become Christians, but only about the works and fruit that no one can do unless he already is a Christian and in a state of grace. The passages in the Sermon about reward and merit are simply intended to comfort Christians. Christians will have to endure poverty, suffering, and persecution because of their faith. The insistence upon grace alone must be preserved, and then terms like "merit" and "reward" can be given to the fruit that follows. Such a statement as Matt. 5:12 where Jesus says that your reward is great in heaven, does not apply to any confidence in our own works contrary to faith, but to the consolation of Christians and believers. Luther gives the following advice concerning the question of merit and grace:

> Learn to give this answer regarding the passages that refer to merit and reward: 'Of course I hear Christ saying (Matt. 5:3): "Blessed are the poor, for they shall have the Kingdom of Heaven"; and (Matt. 5:11, 12): "Blessed are you when you suffer persecution for my sake, for your reward is great in heaven." But by these statements he is not teaching me where to build the foundation of my salvation, but giving me a promise that is to console me in my sufferings and in my Christian life' [p 293; see pp 285-94 for entire Postscript].

Luther's treatment of the Sermon on the Mount is no mean accomplishment. He has promulgated the doctrine of justification by faith alone against the "works righteousness" of the "papists." On the other hand, with his doctrine of the two kingdoms, Luther maintains that a Christian can be a citizen of the Kingdom of God without renouncing his responsibility to the state. Thus he answers the "anarchism" of the "schismatics" with their literalistic approach to the Sermon on the Mount. Whether Luther is to be regarded as a "responsible realist" or an "acculturated compromiser" is an issue which continues to divide interpreters of the Sermon on the Mount.

7 HULDREICH ZWINGLI

Zwingli, who was the chief of the reformers in German-speaking Switzerland, was born in 1484. He was educated in Basel and later in Bern and Vienna. He became an admirer of Erasmus and by training and disposition was a humanist.

Zwingli gave more emphasis to the Gospel as law then did Luther. The New Law of the Gospel was valid not only for the

moral situation but also for the state, and one of Zwingli's central
principles was that the Law of the Gospel should be the basis of the
law of the state. Edward Peters points out [references are to Ulrich Zwingli: Selected Works, ed Peters (Philadelphia: Univ of
Pennsylvania Pr, 1972)] that by 1525 Zürich was fast becoming the
first urban theocracy of the Reformation (p xxii). It was, however,
Zwingli's insistence that there be this close cooperation with the
civil authorities which led to the rupture in his dealings with the
Anabaptists and the subsequent persecutions.

The Anabaptists came to feel that Zwingli's reform was too
conservative. But the precipitating factor was a Zürich cantonal
decree that all children must be baptized. This led in January
1525 to a public debate between Zwingli and the Anabaptists. Out
of this context there appeared in 1527 a tract containing statements
by the Anabaptists and Zwingli's refutation. The Anabaptist position
was probably that of Conrad Grebel and the Confession of Fatih
written by the Baptists of Bern (pp 123-25). This treatise was entitled "Refutation of the Tricks of the Baptists by Huldreich Zwingli."

In refuting the Anabaptists Zwingli deals with several issues
which are grounded in the Sermon on the Mount. These have to do
with the sword and nonresistance, judging, and swearing oaths. In
examining these issues, it becomes evident that there was a radical
disagreement between Zwingli and the Anabaptists and that he viewed
them as irresponsible biblical exegetes as well as threats to the social order. We have seen that Zwingli sought to relate the Law of
the Gospel to the laws of the state. The Anabaptists also dealt with
this issue, but they proposed a solution which would have undercut
the Zürich theocracy.

The first and fundamental issue on which Zwingli and the Anabaptists were inexorably divided was that of infant baptism. While
this question is related to the Sermon on the Mount in terms of the
nature of Christian discipleship and the tension between church and
state, between the Kingdom of Christ and the world, it is not my
intention to discuss the issue here. Rather let us turn to the questions of nonresistance, judging, and swearing oaths, all of which
are more directly related to Jesus' pronouncements in the Sermon
on the Mount.

Was it possible for Christians to wield the sword in view of
Christ's directives to love enemies and to offer no resistance to
evil? No, said the Anabaptists because the use of the sword is
outside the perfection of Christ. However, the Anabaptists held
that in the worldly order the magistry is necessary to restrain and
punish evil. But in the perfection of Christ the only "sword" to be
used is excommunication for the admonishing and exclusion of the
sinner. "Can a Christian use, or ought he to use, the sword
against evil for the defense of the good or from love? ... This
reply is therefore revealed to us unanimously: Christ teaches us
to learn from himself" (p 196).

Zwingli charges the Baptists with confusing the perfection of Christ with the perfection of Christians. He vehemently rejected the notion that Christians need no magistracy. Granted that a Christian will not omit things that should be done, and he will refrain from deeds that are not right. "But," Zwingli says, "it is our misfortune that among men we do not find so absolute perfection, and may not hope to find that all who confess Christ are wholly happy, as long as we bear about this domicile of the body" (p 197). He agrees with the Baptists that the sword is an ordinance of God outside the perfection of Christ and that wherever Christians do not arrive at perfection there is need for the sword. But Zwingli charges that the Baptists mean something else entirely, i.e., that "the heretical church of the rebaptized needs no sword, for it is within the perfection of Christ" (p 197).

A second question dealt with the matter of whether a Christian may pronounce or give judgment in secular matters in light of Christ's words about non-judging. Should they judge between force and force, strife and strife, in which the unfaithful differ?

Zwingli now resorts to a most interesting Christological interpretation by distinguishing between Christ's earthly mission and his office of divine judge and king. In his first coming Christ's mission was not to judge, but to save. He rejected the attempt to make him a king and there was no harshness about him. The error of the Anabaptists is that "they do not yet discriminate between Christ's omnipotence, providence and divinity, by which he ever governs all, and his mission which he performed here" (p 200). What the Anabaptists have done is to only see one side of Christ's mission and that side they have made into a law regarding nonjudgment. But Christ is now both judge and king. Thus Zwingli replies: "Let no one therefore judge. By no means. For that is to confuse divine and human law" (p 200).

The third question is that of swearing oaths. The Baptists on the basis of Christ's injunction in the Sermon on the Mount to swear not at all believed that this forbad all oath-taking by Christians. Zwingli engages in a lengthy and sophisticated refutation of the Baptists. He analyzes the Greek, Latin, and German words for "swear." His conclusion is that to swear to a sacred obligation is not prohibited by the Old Testament or by Christ's word. What Christ prohibits when he says, "Swear not at all," is swearing lightly or offhand. Here no mention occurs of the oath required by public authority. So the Anabaptists have confused the issue by forbidding all swearing when Christ was speaking only about flippant swearing in daily intercourse. In commenting on Jesus' words about your yea being yea and your nay, nay, Zwingli says: "There you have it. He does not speak about our oath; he does not touch upon the forum or court or magistracy, but only upon daily conversation in our familiar intercourse" (p 212).

Doubtless, Zwingli's attempt to relate the Law of the Gospel to the law of the state caused him to make such a vehement defense of oath taking against the Anabaptists. Zwingli believed that their real intention in rejecting oaths was to destroy the magistracy and its power. If the oath is abolished, then all order is overthrown. Moreover, swearing an oath to God can be an example of a man's faith and trust in God. An oath can be a divine thing, a sacred anchor to which we flee when human wisdom can go no further. Seen from this perspective Zwingli maintained that the oath can be an act of love toward the neighbor and is in keeping with the commandment to love God and the neighbor. "Who then will dare against all the authority of Scripture to deprive the people of God of the oath?" (p 210).

But after all his bitter charges against the Baptists and his defense of oaths, Zwingli's summation is remarkably libertarian. "To give in brief the sum of my opinion, I myself do not think an oath ought to be demanded, or can be demanded, without disturbing conscience, except when either all human attestation fails or the safety of a neighbor is gravely imperilled, and then only in case that in no oath that we take is the name of God blasphemed" (p 219).

8 JOHN CALVIN

The second of the great Swiss reformers was John Calvin, born in France in 1509. Because of persecution of the Protestants in France, Calvin moved to Geneva, where like Zwingli at Zürich, he established a theocracy. His best-known work is The Institutes of the Christian Religion [vol XX, The Library of Christian Classics, ed John T. McNeill (Philadelphia: Westminster Pr, 1960)], which became a primer for Protestants, and which has few equals in the area of systematic theology in terms of inclusiveness, conciseness, and order. Among Calvin's other writings was his Commentary on a Harmony of the Evangelists, Matthew, Mark, and Luke [vol I, tr William Pringle (Grand Rapids, MI: Eerdmans, 1949)], which is a source for our understanding of his interpretation of the Sermon on the Mount.

In Book II, chapters 7-11 of The Institutes Calvin deals with the Law and the relationship between the Old and the New Testaments. In chapter 8 Calvin discusses the Moral Law or the Ten Commandments, and he draws the antithesis between the Pharisees' and Jesus' respective interpretations of the Law as these are reflected in Matthew 5. The error of the Pharisees was that they believed that the Law was fulfilled as long as nothing was committed by way of outward works against the Law. Christ, however, reproved this error by declaring that an unchaste glance at a woman is adultery, and that anger in the heart and hatred are equated with murder. But this did not mean that Christ was another Moses, the giver of the Law of the Gospel, which supplied that which was lacking in the Mosaic Law. Christ did not add to the Law, but he only restored it to its integrity by freeing it and cleansing it from the falsehoods of the Pharisees (pp 373-4). Or as he says in the Commentary on a Harmony of the Evangelists: "We must not imagine Christ to be a new legislator, who adds any thing to the eternal righteousness of his Father. We must listen to him as a faithful expounder, that we may know what is the nature of the Law, what is its object, and what is its extent" (vol I, pp 283-4).

It is evident from both the Institutes and the Commentary on a Harmony of the Evangelists that Calvin's intent is to emphasize the unity of the Bible and the continuity between the Law and the Gospel. In his Commentary he writes:

> With respect to doctrine, we must not imagine that the coming of Christ has freed us from the authority of the Lav for it is the eternal rule of a devout and holy life, and must, therefore, be as unchangeable, as the justice of God, which it embraced, is constant and uniform.... Let us therefore learn to maintain inviolable this sacred tie between the Law and the Gospel, which many improperly attempt to break. For it contributes not a little to confirm the authority of the Gospel, when we learn, that it is nothing else than a fulfillment of the Law; so that both, with one consent, declare God to be the Author [vol I, pp 277-8].

As with Luther and Zwingli, Calvin criticizes the Anabaptist interpretation of the Sermon on the Mount. This is particularly evident in reference to oaths. Calvin says that the Anabaptists have blustered a great deal on the ground that Christ appears to give no liberty to swear on any occasion because he commands, Swear not at all. The Anabaptists are in error because they center their attention on a single word and do not understand the scope or context of Christ's saying. Swearing is not prohibited in all cases, for when there are just reasons to demand it, the Law not only permits, but expressly commands us to swear. Calvin concludes: "Christ, therefore, meant nothing more than this, that all oaths are unlawful, which in any way abuse and profane the sacred name of God, for which they ought to have had the effect of producing a deeper reverence" (Commentary, vol I, p 295). In the Institutes, Book II, chapter 8. 26, Calvin raises the question whether the Sermon on the Mount forbids oaths. Again, he criticizes the Anabaptists and proceeds to argue that the Bible permits and encourages certain types of oaths. He substantiates his claim with references to Paul, Abraham, Isaac, Jacob, Laban, Boaz, Obadiah. In a summary statement to this section Calvin says: "Thus I have no better rule than for us so to control our oaths that they may not be rash, indiscriminate, wanton, or trifling; but that they may serve a just need--either to vindicate the Lord's glory, or to further a brother's edification. Such is the purpose of this commandment of the Law" (Institutes, p 394).

Regarding Christ's words on nonresistance, Calvin maintains that there are certain cases in which resistance is permissible.

While Christ does restrain our hands, as well as our minds, from
revenge, Calvin believed that one could offer resistance without revenge. Thus: "... when any one has it in his power to protect
himself and his property from injury, without exercising revenge,
the words of Christ do not prevent him from turning aside gently
and inoffensively to avoid the threatened attack" (Commentary, vol
I, p 299).

Another issue that evolves from Calvin's teaching on nonviolence is that of law-suits. In light of Christ's words, "If any one
would sue you and take your coat, let him have your cloak as
well...," are law-suits forbidden? No, because these words are
not to be taken literally.

> None but a fool will stand upon the words, so as to main-
> tain, that we must yield to our opponents what they demand,
> before coming into a court of law: for such compliance
> would more strongly inflame the minds of wicked men to
> robbery and extortion; and we know, that nothing was farther
> from the design of Christ.... Hence we conclude, that
> Christians are not entirely prohibited from engaging in law-
> suits, provided they have a just defence to offer.... But
> we must remember what I have already hinted, that we ought
> not to quibble about words, as if a good man were not per-
> mitted to recover what is his own, when God gives him the
> lawful means. We are only enjoined to exercise patience,
> that we may not be unduly distressed by the loss of our
> property, but calmly wait, till the Lord himself shall call
> the robbers to account [Commentary, vol I, 299-301].

In the foregoing discussion Calvin attempts to counteract the
literalism and the "ethical radicalism" of the Anabaptists, and thus
he appears to compromise the directives of Christ. While the Anabaptists may have caused Calvin to overstate a position of accommodation and compromise, the doctrine of the Schoolmen presented
the opposite reaction.

In Book II, chapter 8. 56 Calvin criticizes the concept of the
"evangelical counsels." He writes:

> These commandments--'Do not take vengeance; love your
> enemies,' which were once delivered to all Jews and then to
> all Christians in common--have been turned by the School-
> man into 'counsels,' which we are free either to obey or not
> to obey. What pestitential ignorance or malice is this!...
> Either let them blot out these things from the Law or recog-
> nize that the Lord was Lawgiver, and let them not falsely
> represent him as a mere giver of counsel [Institutes, p 419].

Calvin quotes with approval Chrysostom's contention that Christ's
teachings regarding love of enemies reveal them clearly to be not
exhortations but imperatives. He also notes that every one of the

Church Fathers regarded these as actual commandments, and that
even in Gregory the Great's time this was still the case. Why then,
Calvin argues, do the Schoolmen regard Christ's teachings as being
a burden too heavy for Christians? At this point Calvin becomes
the theologian of grace. Christ's demands are indeed hard and difficult for us in our feebleness. However, it is in the Lord and
through his grace that we act virtuously. To be a Christian under
the Law of Grace does not imply unbridled license outside the Law,
but it means that one is engrafted in Christ by whose grace we are
free from the curse of the Law, and by whose Spirit we have the
Law engraved upon our hearts (see Institutes, pp 420-1).

So Calvin moves back and forth between the "errors" of the
Schoolmen and the Anabaptists, and thereby he appears to be contra-
dictory and inconsistent. He is wrestling with one of the perennial
issues regarding the Sermon on the Mount, viz. how are its ethical
imperatives related to Christian existence in both its personal and
social dimensions?

Hiltrud Stadlund-Neumann has written about Calvin's interpretation of the Sermon on the Mount especially in relation to the Anabaptists [Evangelische Radikalismen in der Sicht Calvins; Sein Verstandnis der Bergpredigt und der Aussendungsrede (Matth. 10) (Neukirchen-Vluyn: Neukirchener Verlag des Erziehungsvereins, 1966)].
He concludes that Calvin's views must be seen in their historical
and theological context. Calvin was interested in furthering the
newly-won Reformation, but at the same time he wanted to counteract the "ethical radicalism" of the Anabaptists. In this process
Stadlund-Neumann says that there was the danger of one-sidedness
on both sides. Calvin in his eagerness to resist the synergism he
discerned in the Anabaptists, leaned toward an ethical indifferentism
in reference to the Sermon on the Mount. The Anabaptists, on the
other hand, manifested a works-righteousness position. His conclusion is that in their attempt to correct each other, they needed to
be corrected (p 149).

The main-line Reformers whom we have now discussed, each
held a view of the church which regarded it as being continuous
with society. Therefore the demands of the Sermon on the Mount
had to be interpreted so that the state and the social order could
be maintained. For Christians were not only responsible to "follow
Jesus," but also to maintain order and administer justice.

The Reformation gave birth to another group who maintained
that the Reformers had not gone far enough and that indeed the Reformers needed to be reformed. It is their vision and their understanding of the Sermon on the Mount that we must now consider.

9   THE ANABAPTISTS

Ernst Troeltsch in his well-known contrast between the "sect-

type" and the "church-type" says that the sects take the Sermon on
the Mount as their ideal and that they lay stress on the simple but
radical opposition of the Kingdom of God to all secular interests
and institutions [The Social Teaching of the Christian Churches, vol
1, tr Olive Wyon (London: Allen & Unwin, 1931), p 332]. Troeltsch's sect-type corresponds with H. Richard Niebuhr's "Christ
against culture" typology. Niebuhr remarks that the Mennonites
have come to represent the "Chirst against culture" attitude most
purely, since they not only renounce all participation in politics and
refuse to be drawn into military service, but follow their own distinctive customs and regulations in economics and education [Christ
and Culture (New York: Harper, 1951), p 56]. The Anabaptists,
who are a classic example of the sectarian and Christ against culture position, found their authority and dynamic in the teachings of
Jesus, especially the Sermon on the Mount.

"Wiedertäufer" (Anabaptists) was originally a term of reproach
because they wanted to "baptize over again." Subsequently it has
come to be a comprehensive designation of various groups on the
Continent who in the sixteenth century refused to allow their children to be baptized and reinstituted the baptism of believers. Their
views on baptism, their insistence that the church and the state be
separate, their rejection of oaths and violence, caused them to become the object of derision, persecution, and martyrdom.

Among the groups that have been included under the Anabaptist
designation are: Thomas Münzer and the Zwickau prophets; the
Swiss Brethren; Hutterites; Melchoirites or Hoffmanites; Mennonites.
These groups are diverse, and too often in the past the whole of
Anabaptism has been judged on the basis of the revolutionary, anti-
nomian, and apocalyptic excesses of Münzer, the Zwickau prophets,
and the Melchoirites. However, in recent decades, thanks to the
diligence and quality of Mennonite as well as non-Mennonite scholarship, a more balanced and objective view has emerged. This trend
locates the genius of Anabaptism, not in Münzer or the other apocalyptic movements, but in the Swiss Brethren and especially in Menno Simons and the Mennonites. Now the view is widely held that
the Anabaptists represented an extension of the Reformation and
that the free church tradition is an outgrowth of this "left wing of
the Reformation." Moreover, the separation of church and state,
the insistence that religion and life are inexorably related, are
values which emerged from the Anabaptist tradition. Harold S.
Bender suggests that the "Anabaptist vision" includes three major
points of emphasis: a new conception of the essence of Christianity
as discipleship; a new conception of the church as a brotherhood;
and a new ethic of love and nonresistance ["The Anabaptist Vision,"
in The Recovery of the Anabaptist Vision, ed Guy F. Hershberger
(Scottdale, PA: Herald Pr, 1957), p 42]. Bender states further
(p 43) that for the Anabaptists the great word was not "faith" as it
was with the reformers, but "following" (Nachfolge Christi).

Perhaps the sharpest point of cleavage between the Anabaptists

and the Reformers centered around their respective views on the
relationship of the Christian to the state. The Anabaptist position
emerged from their interpretation of the teachings of Jesus, especially the Sermon on the Mount, and their understanding of the
Kingdom of God. John S. Oyer suggests that the fundamental antagonism between the Zürich reformers and the Anabaptists stemmed
from their differences in emphasis on the Sermon on the Mount.
Oyer feels that for Zwingli the Sermon on the Mount was incidental
while for the Anabaptists it was central. Consequently, Zwingli interpreted their emphasis as an attempt to replace civil authority
with the authority of the love ethic in a Christian community ["The
Reformers Oppose the Anabaptist Theology," in The Recovery, ed
Hershberger, pp 207-8].

          The traditional Anabaptist position holds that the church and
the state must be separate since the church consists only of the
saints while the state is concerned with everyone in the community.
The state was ordained because of sin, but the church was created
for the saved. According to the Anabaptist view, true Christians
must have nothing to do with the state. But this is not anarchism
because the state has been ordained of God on account of sin and to
restrain sin. However, the "saints" can take no part in it, and it
should be left to be administered by "sinners." Thus the Anabaptists withdrew from political life, and as Roland H. Bainton states:
"... the separation became all the more marked because the ethic
of the Sermon on the Mount was taken literally and made incumbent
upon all Christians" [The Reformation of the Sixteenth Century (Boston: Beacon Pr, 1952), p 100; this work provides one of the best
treatments of Anabaptism in English, with inciteful comparisons of
the Anabaptists, the Reformers, and the Catholics].

          Johannes P. Bachmann has made a notable study on the Ser-
mon on the Mount in the interpretation of the Enthusiasts and of
Luther. He prefers to use the term Schwärmer (enthusiasts) rather
than Anabaptists. He centers much of his analysis on the Hutterites
as a prototype of the Anabaptist movement. Regarding the differences between the Enthusiasts and Luther, Bachmann writes: "I am
inclined to draw the conclusion that the basic principle of interpretation must be seen in the difference between the world and the
Christian community" ["The Sermon on the Mount in the Interpretation of the Enthusiasts and of Luther," STM thesis (Union Theological Seminary, New York, 1961), p 50]. Quoting from the Hutterian
Chronicle, Bachmann states that for Hutter the order of government
is not within the realm of Christ's perfection. The government is
necessary, as we need daily bread. It is disciplinarian since most
people cannot be ruled by the Word of God. But the Christian is
forbidden to participate in government because the use of force is
forbidden in the Sermon on the Mount. Such commands as "Love
your enemies," "Forgive us our debts," "Judge not, that you be not
judged," make participation in government difficult to the extent
that a Christian cannot hold a government office [Die älteste Chronik
der Hutterischen Brüder, pp 307, 300; quoted in Bachmann thesis,

pp 18-9, 28]. Thus Bachmann concludes: "The Enthusiasts nor-
mally recognize the governmental power. But they confine it to the
levying of taxes and the sentencing of evildoers. Obedience often
is refused when the government demands anything which is 'against
God'" (pp 17-8).

The Anabaptist relation to the state is integrally related to
their understanding of the Kingdom of God. Robert Friedmann,
writing about the Kingdom theory of the Anabaptists, says that their
view of the Kingdom implies a new set of values which are best illustrated in the Sermon on the Mount. Love, forgiveness, self-sur-
render, hating not even one's own persecutors are values so radically different that they seem paradoxical and unrealizable to an unre-
generate mind. These values point to a different dimension than
that of the secular and the worldly. The Anabaptists were highly
suspicious of the values of this world because they believed that they
were citizens of another kingdom whose norms ran counter to those
of the world ["The Doctrine of the Two Worlds," in The Recovery,
ed Hershberger, p 111]. Menno Simons, in speaking about the Kingdom of Christ, wrote: "This Kingdom is not a Kingdom in which
they parade in gold, silver, pearls, silk, velvet, and costly finery,
as is done by the haughty, proud world.... But in the Kingdom of
all humility not the outward adorning of the body, but the inward
adorning of the spirit is sought with zeal and diligence" ["Foundation of Christian Doctrine," in The Complete Writings of Menno
Simons, tr from Dutch Leonard Verduin, & ed John Christian Wen-
ger (Scottdale, PA: Herald Pr, 1956), p 217].

The Kingdom ideal of the Anabaptists was one that related to
life and to this world and not only to the world to come. They
found in the teachings of Jesus a "new law" which was to be followed and taken with ultimate seriousness. In Jesus' words: "But
I say to you," the Anabaptists saw something great and new. These
were the commands of Jesus himself and not merely a clarification
of the Law. They were to be obeyed and followed. Clarence Bauman points out that for the Anabaptists the proclamation of Jesus
was an ethic of obedience which admitted one to the Kingdom of
God. In the antitheses of the Sermon on the Mount they found what
man must do if he would follow Jesus. The problem whether the
ethic of Jesus was possible or impossible was unfamiliar to the
Anabaptists. They believed that the spirit of God empowered the
believers to be obedient to Christ. Moreover, Bauman says that the
Kingdom of God was not only an ideal but also a method by which
the ideal could be realized. For the Anabaptists the Kingdom was
not first of all an entity at the end of time but an immanent reality.
The future coming of the Kingdom of God did not deter the Anabaptists from centering their attention on the righteousness of that Kingdom in the midst of the present world [Gewaltlosigkeit im Täufertum
(Leiden: E.J. Brill, 1968), pp 309-10]. Harold S. Bender succinct-
ly summarizes the above discussion:

The Anabaptist vision was not a detailed blueprint for the re-

construction of human society, but the Brethren did believe
that Jesus intended that the Kingdom of God should be set up
in the midst of earth, here and now, and this they proposed
to do forthwith. We shall not believe, they said, that the
Sermon on the Mount or any other vision that Jesus had is
only a heavenly vision meant but to keep his followers in tension until the last great day, but we shall practice what he
taught, believing that where he walked we can by his grace
follow in his steps ["Anabaptist Vision," in The Recovery, ed
Hershberger, p 54].

Besides the issue of infant baptism, the points of sharpest
cleavage between the Anabaptists and the civil authorities related to
military service and the swearing of oaths. In both areas they
found in the Sermon on the Mount authority for their views.

Pilgrim Marpeck, a South German Anabaptist leader, speaking
of Matt. 5, said: "All bodily, worldly, carnal, earthly fightings,
conflicts, and wars are annulled and abolished among them through
such law ... which law of love Christ ... himself observed and
thereby gave his followers a pattern to follow after" [quoted by
Bender, "Anabaptist Vision," in The Recovery, p 51]. Menno
Simons, after quoting Matt. 5:43-48 on love of enemies, said: "Behold this is the voice of Christ. All those who are his sheep will
hear his voice" ["Blasphemy of John of Leiden," in The Recovery,
p 44]. Referring again to Matt. 5, Menno leaves no doubt about
his absolute rejection of force and violence:

> Peter was commanded to sheath his sword. All Christians
> are commanded to love their enemies; to do good unto those
> who abuse and persecute them; to give the mantle when the
> cloak is taken, the other cheek when one is struck. Tell
> me, how can a Christian defend Scripturally retaliation, re-
> bellion, war, striking, slaying, torturing, stealing, robbing
> and plundering and burning cities, and conquering countries?
> ["Reply to False Accusation," in The Recovery, p 555].

Just as with the teachings of Jesus regarding nonresistance
and love of enemies, so the Anabaptists took literally the command
of Jesus concerning oaths. His injunction, "Swear not at all," was
to be obeyed without exception. Menno Simons points to the Anabaptist martyrs who refused to swear an oath even though it meant
death for them. He writes:

> That yea is Amen with all true Christians is sufficiently
> shown by those who in our Netherlands are so tyrannically
> visited with imprisonment, confiscation, and torture; with
> fire, the stake, and the sword; while with one word they
> could escape all these if they would but break their yea and
> nay. But since they are born of the truth, therefore they
> walk in the truth, and testify to the truth unto death, as may
> be abundantly seen in Flanders, Brabant, Holland, West

Friesland, etc. ["Confession of the Distressed Christians,"
in The Recovery, p 521; see also pp 518-9].

In the Sermon on the Mount the Anabaptists found a law or a
charter for the true Christian life, and their chief concern was to
pattern their lives after the teaching and example of Jesus even
though the price was martyrdom. To a great degree, the "Anabaptist vision" is encompassed in the words of Hans Denck: "To
know Christ truly is to follow him daily in life."

10   PROTESTANT SCHOLASTICISM TO PROTESTANT LIBERALISM

PROTESTANT SCHOLASTICISM

In the post-Reformation period there developed a movement
which is often referred to as "Protestant orthodoxy" or "Protestant
scholasticism." The dynamic and spontaneity of the Reformation
was arrested by a concern for correct dogmatic opinion and whether
or not particular formulations were true to Luther or Calvin. Theological statements came to be identified with truth and took priority
over the experience of faith. Ethics subsequently declined sharply,
and the Sermon on the Mount and its moral implications were neglected. Or the Sermon on the Mount was seen as driving men to
despair because of their sin and their inability to follow its precepts
and thus preparing the way for salvation by grace alone.

THE PURITANS

In the late sixteenth and the seventeenth centuries another
Protestant outlook known as Puritanism arose in England and New
England. Most of the Puritans came out of the Calvinistic tradition,
and they attempted to make the Bible the sole guide for faith and
life. True to their Calvinist heritage, they held firm beliefs about
the sovereignty of God and predestination. Moreover, the Puritans
demanded express scriptural warrant for all the details of public
worship, and this led them to oppose many practices in the Church
of England. For example, they objected to rings at weddings,
kneeling before the altar at the Lord's Supper, the sign of the cross,
special dress and vestments by the clergy, organs in churches, and
crosses on steeples. The church needed to be purified of these
"popish" vestiges. Other characteristics of the Puritans were their
emphasis on preaching and upon rigid standards of conduct, especially in regard to Sunday observance and amusements. While they produced a number of works on casuistry, the Puritans did not add any
significant contribution to the history of interpretation of the Sermon
on the Mount.

Denominationally, the Puritans comprised primarily Presbyterian, Congregational, and Baptist groups. But perhaps the most
distinctive of the movements related to Puritanism were the Quakers.

THE QUAKERS

The Quakers were started by George Fox in the middle of the
seventeenth century. Like the Anabaptists, they objected to oaths
and war, and found the scriptural basis for their position mainly in
the Sermon on the Mount.

Fox was often brought into court and even imprisoned for his
refusal to swear an oath. On one such occasion in 1665 when he
was in prison, a Dr. Cradock came with a great company and asked
Fox what he was in prison for. His reply was as follows:

> 'I told him, "for obeying the command of Christ and the
> apostle in not swearing." But if he being both a doctor and
> a justice of the peace, could convince me that after Christ
> and the apostle had forbidden swearing, they commanded
> Christians to swear, then I would swear. "Here was the
> Bible," I told him, "he might if he could show me any such
> command." The Doctor quoted the text, "Ye shall swear in
> truth and righteousness." "Ay, it was written so in Jere-
> miah's time, but that was many ages before Christ command-
> ed not to swear at all; but where is it written so, since
> Christ forbade all swearing? I could bring as many in-
> stances for swearing out of the Old Testament as thou, and
> it may be more; but of what force are they to prove swear-
> ing lawful in the New Testament, since Christ and the apostle
> forbade it?"' [Thomas Hodgkin, George Fox (Boston: Hough-
> ton, Mifflin, 1896), pp 37-8].

In 1675 William Penn wrote A Treatise of Oaths in which he
presented "several weighty reasons why the people called Quakers
refuse to swear." In this work Penn appeals to Jesus' statement
on oaths in the Sermon on the Mount to buttress his argument. In
the latter part he has a lengthy section containing selections, or
"numerous testimonies of Gentiles, Jews, and Christians, both Fathers, Doctors, and Martyrs," on oaths. These span the period
from antiquity to Penn's time and form a "history of doctrines" on
oaths [for these "testimonies" see The Select Works of William
Penn, vol II, 4th ed (London: Wm Phillips, Geo Yard, 1825/repr,
NY: Kraus, 1971/), pp 46-127; for another example of Penn's ap-
peal to Matt. 5:33-37 to refute oaths, see Ibid, vol III, p 509].

Perhaps the most eminent and articulate Quaker apologist and
theologian was Robert Barclay, born in Scotland in 1648. In his
Apology Barclay prefaces a rather lengthy discussion of oaths by
quoting Matt. 5:33-37 and James 5:12. "Considering the clarity of
these words, it is really remarkable that anyone who professes the
name of Christ can pronounce an oath with a quiet conscience....
If anyone had tried to frame a blanket prohibition of anything, could
he make it more embracing than these strictures against swearing
under any circumstance?" [Barclay's Apology in Modern English,
ed Dean Freiday (Alburtis, PA: Hemlock Pr, 1967--dist Friends Book

Store, Philadelphia, pp 412-3; for the entire discussion on oaths,
see pp 412-24].

The second area in which Quakers found support in the Sermon on the Mount concerned nonresistance and war. In "Primitive
Christianity Revived in the Faith and Practice of the People Called
Quakers" Penn wrote: "We also believe that war ought to cease
among the followers of the Lamb, Christ Jesus, who taught his disciples to 'forgive and love their enemies,' and not to war against
them and kill them ..." [Select Works, vol III, p 510].

Barclay in his Apology holds the same uncompromising position as Penn. In a section on "Revenge and War," he develops an
apology for peace by dealing with various arguments against his position by reference to the Sermon on the Mount and other scriptural
passages as well as to the Church Fathers. After quoting Matt.
5:38-48 Barclay states:

> Indeed, the words themselves are so clear that I find no
> need to illustrate or explain them. It is easier to reconcile
> the greatest of contradictions, than it is to reconcile these
> laws of our Lord Jesus Christ with the wicked practice of
> war. They are plainly inconsistent. Who can reconcile 'Do
> not resist one who is evil' with the injunction that evil must
> be resisted by force? Or, 'If someone slaps you on the
> right cheek, turn and offer him your left' with 'strike again?'
> Or, 'Love your enemies' with pursuit of them by fire and
> sword? Or, 'Pray for those who persecute you' with visit-
> ing fires, imprisonment, and even death itself upon those
> who not only do not persecute you, but who are earnestly
> concerned for your eternal and temporal welfare?
>   Whoever has found a way to reconcile these things must
> also have found a way to reconcile God with the devil, Christ
> with Antichrist, light with darkness, and good with evil. If
> this is impossible, as indeed it is, it is also impossible to
> reconcile war and revenge with Christian practice. Men only
> deceive themselves and others when they try unreservedly to
> do such an absurd and impossible thing [Barclay's Apology,
> ed Freiday, p 425].

Barclay is convinced that war is absolutely unlawful for those who
would be disciples of Christ. While Jesus teaches us to love our
enemies, war teaches us to hate and destroy them.

In addition to their position on oaths and war, the Quakers
found in the Sermon on the Mount injunctions which undergirded
their emphasis upon simplicity. Like the Anabaptists, the Quakers
were literalists in their interpretation of the Sermon on the Mount.
Here were directives which were to be explicitly followed by those
who claimed to be disciples of Christ. Moreover, to this day they
are recognized in the wider Christian community for their commit-
ment to peace and service.

GERMAN PIETISM

The development of a scholastic Lutheranism marked by fixed
dogma and intellectual conformity led to the Pietistic movement in
Germany. Its two best-known leaders were Philipp Jakob Spener
and August Hermann Francke. Against the scholastic tendencies,
Pietism asserted the primacy of feeling in Christian experience, the
active participation of laity in the life of the church, and a sharp
cleavage between the Christian and the world. Spener and Francke
organized small groups who met in private homes to cultivate their
faith especially through common Bible study. They sought for new
life and renewal as they read and studied the New Testament.

The Pietistic movement did not produce any official doctrinal
writings nor any principles which could be acknowledged as consti-
tuting the essence of Pietism. The literature was primarily private
and devotional in nature. While the Pietists did not write any trea-
tises on the Sermon on the Mount, one must believe that it occupied
a central place in their study of the New Testament. Moreover,
their approach to the Christian life was consistent with a number of
motifs in the Sermon on the Mount. Among these were their intense
earnestness, an insistence that the Christian faith must have practical consequences, and antagonism toward worldliness.

Another significant contribution of the Pietists was in the area
of practical benevolence. In 1695 Francke began a school for poor
children, and in 1698 he established his famous Orphan House which
had 134 children at the time of his death.

The Pietistic movement has had an extensive impact upon
Lutheranism. It was influential in the founding of such groups as
the Moravians, the Methodists, and the German Baptists from whom
today's Brethren groups have come. The universities of Halle and
Tübingen became centers of Pietism, and such well-known figures
as Immanuel Kant and Friedrich Schleiermacher reflected elements
of pietistic upbringing and learning.

JOHN WESLEY

In England the counterpart to German Pietism was Wesleyanism
or Methodism. By the latter part of the seventeenth century the impetus of the English Reformation had largely been spent. The Church
of England had settled into a state of security. Moreover, rational-
istic tendencies had made deep inroads into the Church. The religious milieu was so permeated by rationalism and natural religion
that it did not seriously touch people's hearts or lives. The resur-
gence of new religious vitality resulted from the labors of a few
men, the chief of whom were John Wesley, Charles Wesley, and
George Whitefield.

John Wesley was born in 1703, the son of an Anglican priest
of high church leanings. He was a distinguished student at Oxford,

and while there he became the leader of a group which met to deep-
en their lives through study and discipline. Later Wesley was sent
to Georgia as a missionary. While crossing the ocean he was deeply impressed by a group of Moravians who manifested a serene faith
in the midst of a terrible storm. The Georgia adventure did not
produce the results Wesley had hoped for, and he returned to England. Though he was an Anglican priest he did not experience fulfillment and the spiritual certainty he desired. But one evening upon reluctantly attending a religious meeting in Aldersgate Street, his
life was changed and he "felt his heart strangely warmed" and that
he trusted Christ and him alone for his salvation.

Wesley was in agreement with the Reformation doctrine of
justification by grace alone, but he added another dimension by his
emphasis on the life of experienced grace, zealous moral endeavor,
and growth toward perfection. Through justification God forgave
sins and brought redemption. But sanctification was the process of
growth initiated by justification. As Christ became real in a person's life he would grow in grace and this would manifest itself in
his conduct and his works. Perhaps the most characteristic mark
of Methodism was its insistence that the Christian grows in grace
and increasingly manifests the perfect qualities of Christ.

With this background let us now turn to Wesley's interpretation
of the Sermon on the Mount. Among Wesley's collected discourses,
thirteen are given to the Sermon on the Mount, and these form a
sizeable commentary. He deals with the entire Sermon, with the
exception of Matt. 5:21-48.

Wesley believed that the Sermon on the Mount was given to all
mankind alike, and is a description of the whole of religion. It is
a full prospect of the Christian life as it ought to be (Sermon XXI,
intro. secs. 5-7) [references are to Wesley's Works, 3d ed, vol V
(London: John Mason, 1829); the 13 Discourses on the Sermon on the
Mount cover pp 247-433]. The Sermon on the Mount is by the Son
of God who came from heaven and is showing us the way to heaven
(Sermon XXI, intro. sec. 3). Being free from the findings of later
critical, biblical scholarship, Wesley believed that Jesus delivered
the Sermon as a unified and systematic public address. Moreover,
it was perfect in method and each part harmonized with the others.
Consequently, it set forth exactly what our Lord intended for us to
know. Wesley divided the Sermon on the Mount into three distinct
branches, the first of which was Matt. 5, the second, Matt. 6, and
the third, Matt. 7 (Sermon XXI, sec. 10).

Beginning with the Beatitudes, Wesley held that in them our
Lord lays down the sum of all true religion in eight particulars.
He combined two interpretations which some held to be mutually exclusive. There were those who regarded the Beatitudes as succes-
sive stages which a Christian takes in his journey to the promised
land. Others said that they belong at all times to every Christian.
"And why may we not allow both the one and the other?" Wesley

asks. If we begin at the lowest of these gifts and move on up the
scale to the highest, it does not mean that we relinquish the lower
as we progress but that we add to and build on the foundation which
is laid. The Beatitudes form a progression toward perfection.
Real Christianity always begins in poverty of spirit, and goes on in
the order set forth in the Beatitudes until the Christian is made
perfect (Sermon XXI, part I, sec. 1). Perfection then is an end
toward which a Christian progresses, and the quality of the perfect
life is set forth in the Beatitudes. They are the genuine religion
of Jesus Christ and reflect the picture of God insofar as He is imi-
table by man. Wesley describes the Beatitudes in rapturous terms,
and the essence of the Wesleyan movement is perhaps nowhere better described than in these words:

> What beauty appears in the whole! How just a symmetry!
> What exact proportion in every part! How desirable is the
> happiness here described! How venerable, how lovely the
> holiness! This is the spirit of religion; the quintessence of
> it. These are indeed the fundamentals of Christianity. O
> that we may not be hearers of it only! ... Nay, but let us
> steadily 'look into this perfect law of liberty, and continue
> therein.' Let us not rest, until every line thereof is tran-
> scribed into our own hearts. Let us watch, and pray, and
> believe, and love, and 'strive for the mastery,' till every
> part of it shall appear in our own soul, graven there by the
> finger of God; till we are 'holy as He which hath called us
> is holy, perfect as our Father which in heaven is perfect!'
> (Sermon XXIII, part III).

In the first branch of the Sermon on the Mount (Matt. 5)
Jesus sets forth the ethical principles of true religion, those inward tempers contained in spiritual holiness which pervades the
soul. In the second branch (Matt. 6) our Lord gives practical application of that contained in the first. He shows how all our actions may be made holy, and good, and acceptable to God, by a
pure and holy intention (Sermon XXVI, intro. sec. 1).

But purity of intention does not relate only to such religious
actions as prayer, fasting, and almsgiving. It has a wider reference and must be applied in our ordinary business (Sermon XXVIII,
sec. 1). Religion is not merely private; it has communal and social dimensions. But the Sermon on the Mount sets boundaries for
our business. Jesus said that we are not to lay up treasures on
earth, but in heaven. Commenting on Matt. 6:19-23 Wesley said:
"In our business we are to attempt to succeed only to the extent
that we are enabled to meet our financial obligations, to provide
adequately for ourselves and for our family; but beyond this we
dare not go" (Sermon XXVIII, secs. 11-12). Here Wesley charts
a course between asceticism and unrestrained freedom of enterprise.
He is dealing with the tension of being in the world but not of it.

Finally in the third branch (Matt. 7) our Lord proceeds to

point out the most common and most fatal hindrances of the holiness
described in the preceeding two branches. Among these are the
dangers of judgment, of hypocrisy, of false prophets. But you will
know them by their fruits. "We are to know the worth of any doctrine and of any life by the fruit that it produces, by the effects it
has for moral power and goodness in the character and disposition
of men" (Sermon XXII, part III, secs. 1-4).

In the latter part of the third branch Jesus exhorts us by
various motives, to break through all, and secure that prize of our
high calling (Sermon XXX, sec. 1). This branch concludes with a
final parable of the two builders. Wesley urges everyone to dili-
gently examine on what foundation he builds, whether on a rock or
on the sand. He then lists entities built on sand: my orthodoxy,
or right opinion which I have called faith; a set of notions I suppose
more rational or scriptural than others have; on my belonging to "so
excellent a Church, reformed after the true Scripture model, blessed
with the purest doctrine, the most primitive Liturgy, the most apostolic form of government." These may be helps to holiness; but
they are not holiness itself (Sermon XXXIII, part III, sec. 1). The
foundation upon which one must build is Jesus Christ. It is when
our affections proceed from a living faith in God through Jesus
Christ that they are good and acceptable to God. The way to holiness and perfection as set forth in the three branches of the Sermon on the Mount has to do not so much with externals as with inward intention and moral earnestness. Or as Wesley put it: "Let
thy religion be the religion of the heart. Let it lie deep in thy in-
most soul" (Sermon XXXIII, part III, sec. 12).

11 PROTESTANT LIBERALISM

    The term "Protestant Liberalism" or "Liberal theology" is a
somewhat broad designation for a range of religious thought origi-
nating in the nineteenth century and reaching its zenith in this coun-
try in the decades preceding World War II. It was unified less by
specific doctrines than by a temper of mind and certain common
motifs. Among these were the authority of Christian experience,
confidence in man and his future, the centrality of Jesus Christ,
social idealism, the attempt to reconcile Christ and culture.

    Another significant development of the liberal period was the
rise of biblical criticism. The Bible was subjected to the same
rigorous analysis as any other literature. As a result, many views
concerning the Bible which were accepted as inviolate were subjected
to doubt or outright rejection. The decisive issue concerned the
significance and authority of the Bible. Acceptance of the results
of biblical criticism meant the abandonment of the view that the
Bible was an infallible record of divine revelation to men.

    In regard to the person of Christ the way was now open to
clear away the "husks" and get to the "real kernel." This was the

period of the search for the "real Jesus" or the "historical Jesus."
The "real Jesus" had been enshrouded in the grave clothes of dogma
and orthodoxy, and he needed to be set free. Thus it was common
to draw a distinction between the religion about Jesus and the religion of Jesus. It was upon the latter that liberal theology focused
its attention.

Another tendency was to either ignore or significantly rein-
terpret certain biblical events and concepts. For instance, the
miracle stories were often rejected or else rationalized. Jesus'
teaching about the future aspects of the Kingdom of God was mini-
mized. The tendency was to emphasize the Kingdom as being within
man and/or to equate it with the ideal society toward which history
was moving.

The theological scene of the nineteenth century was dominated
by two figures--Friedrich Schleiermacher (1768-1834) and Albrecht
Ritschl (1822-1889). Both had a profound impact on liberal theology
and both were influenced by the philosophy of Immanuel Kant.

In his Critique of Pure Reason, written in 1781, Kant limited
knowledge to the experienced world--the world of phenomena. Behind
the phenomena lies reality which is not accessible to our perception.
Therefore claims to knowledge must be limited to the experienced
world, shaped by the rational structures of mind. Kant's views undercut any claims to knowledge of God through "pure reason." Likewise Kant attacked the traditional proofs of God's existence.

But religion can yet be established on a sound basis. It still
has to do with reason, but of a different sort than "pure reason."
Its basis must be "practical reason." Kant developed this view in
the Critique of the Practical Reason on 1788. While absolute knowledge of reality is unattainable by "pure reason," nevertheless, man
is conscious of a feeling of moral obligation. There is a "categori-
cal imperative"--a moral oughtness that is universal. This moral
law within is man's noblest possession, and all his action ought to
be based on the universal law of duty and morality which is the law
of the self and the universe.

It was the first Critique that influenced Schleiermacher. He
held that religion though related to reason and ethics was not determined by them. The essence of religion was a unique realm of
experience--the experience of one's absolute dependence upon God.
For Ritschl it was the second Critique that was most significant for
opening a new possibility of recapturing the insights of the Reformation. He repudiated metaphysics and was a sharp critic of Pietism.
Religion is related to experience but it is essentially moral in nature. Thus Ritschl's theology is often referred to as the "theology
of moral values."

Ritschl regarded Christianity as an ellipse with two foci, rather
than a circle with one center. One focus was justification and rec-

onciliation. The other was the Kingdom of God. Justification and
reconciliation have to do with forgiveness of sin and the redemptive
work of Christ. The Kingdom of God is the organization of humanity
through action inspired by love. "The Christian idea of the Kingdom of God denotes the association of mankind--an association both
extensively and intensively the most comprehensive possible--through
reciprocal moral action of its members, action which transcends all
merely natural and particular considerations" [The Christian Doctrine
of Justification and Reconsiliation, 2d ed, tr H. R. Mackintosh, A.
B. Macaulay (Edinburgh: T. & T. Clark, 1902), p 284].

One of Ritschl's positive contributions was his rediscovery of
the centrality of the Kingdom of God. His close identification of the
Kingdom of God with a social ethical ideal was a central emphasis
of liberalism and was to have a pronounced effect upon the development of the "social gospel" in Protestantism.

Ritschl made a significant impact upon the theology of the latter part of the nineteenth and the early twentieth centuries--so much
so, that one can speak of a "Ritschlian school." Perhaps the two
most outstanding members were the eminent Berlin church historian,
Adolf von Harnack, and the Marburg theologian, Wilhelm Herrmann.

ADOLF VON HARNACK

In the winter semester of 1899-1900 Harnack delivered a series
of lectures at Berlin which were published under the title Das Wesen
des Christentums [references are to Eng ed, What Is Christianity?
tr Thomas B. Saunders (NY: Harper & Row, 1957)]. As the title
suggests, Harnack proposed to delineate what was truly essential in
Christianity. His intention was to clear away the husks so that the
kernel could be exposed. Behind the changing forms of Christianity
there is that which is unchanging and which is valid for all time.
The place to look for this permanent element is in the Synoptic Gospels; for they contain the plain picture and content of Jesus' teaching.
But one must be careful not to confuse the framework in which the
Gospel is presented with that which is essential. In the Synoptic
Gospels one reads about miracles, demons, and the catastrophic end
of the world, but these are not central to Christianity.

The essence of Christianity is to be discerned in the personality of Jesus and in his teaching. The teaching of Jesus may be
grouped under three heads. Each is of such a nature as to contain
the whole, and hence can be exhibited in its entirety under any one
of them. These are: the Kingdom of God and its coming; God the
Father and the infinite value of the human soul; the higher righteousness and the commandment of love (p 51).

In reference to the Kingdom of God, Harnack recognized that
in the Gospels there is the idea of two kingdoms--of God and of the
devil—and that at some future time the devil would be defeated and
God would reign. Jesus shared this view with his contemporaries;

he grew up with it and retained it. But if one wants to know what
the Kingdom of God and its coming meant for Jesus, he must read
and study the parables.

> The Kingdom of God comes by coming to the individual, by
> entering into his soul and laying hold of it.... It is the rule
> of the holy God in the hearts of individuals.... From this
> point of view everything that is dramatic in the external and
> historical sense has vanished; and gone, too, are all the ex-
> ternal hopes for the future.... It is not a question of angels
> and devils, thrones and principalities, but of God and the
> soul, the soul and its God [p 56].

As we shall see later, it was this immanent view of the Kingdom of God which was rejected by Weiss and Schweitzer. Rudolf
Bultmann, writing from this later eschatological perspective, said
of Harnack: "Harnack somehow never clearly saw nor understood
the eschatological character of the appearance of Jesus and of his
preaching of the imminent advent of the Kingdom of God" (p x).

Jesus' teaching on the higher righteousness and the commandment of love shows conclusively that the Gospel is an ethical message. He severed the connexion between ethics and external forms
and ritual. "In all questions of morality he goes straight to the
root, that is, to the disposition and the intention" (p 71). That is
the meaning of the higher righteousness. It is that which will
stand when the depths of the heart are probed. Harnack relates
the higher righteousness to the Sermon on the Mount as follows:
"A large portion of the so-called Sermon on the Mount is occupied
with what he says when he goes in detail through the several de-
partments of human relationships and human failings as to bring the
disposition and intention to light in each case, to judge a man's
works by them, and on them to hang heaven and hell" (p 72). The
moral principle can finally be reduced to one root and to one mo-
tive--love. It can take the form of love of the neighbor or of the
enemy.

Though Jesus freed morality from all alien connections which
included public religion, nevertheless, there is a point where religion and morality combine. In view of the Beatitudes it may best
be described as humility. Jesus made love and humility one. Humility has a religious dimension because it is characterized by re-
ceptivity, by the expression of inner need, by prayer for God's
grace and forgiveness. It is the opening of the heart to God. In
the Beatitudes religion and ethics are joined because the poor in
spirit and those who hunger and thirst after righteousness are also
the peacemakers and the merciful. In these four Beatitudes one
discerns the nature of the higher righteousness. In a succinct summary statement Harnack writes:

> In thus expressing his message of the higher righteousness
> and the new commandment of love in these four leading

thoughts, Jesus defined the sphere of the ethical in a way in
which no one before him had ever defined it. But should we
be threatened with doubts as to what he meant, we must steep
ourselves again and again in the Beatitudes of the Sermon on
the Mount. They contain his ethics and his religion, united
at the root, and freed from all external and particularistic
elements [pp 73-4].

WILHELM HERRMANN

Wilhelm Herrmann was born in 1846. He studied at Halle
where he lived for two and a half years in the home of Friedrich
August Tholuck. There he came in contact with Martin Kähler and
met Albrecht Ritschl who significantly influenced his thought. In
1889 Herrmann became a professor at Marburg where he remained
until his retirement in 1916. He was a renowned teacher and among
his students at Marburg were Karl Barth and Rudolf Bultmann.

Like Harnack, Herrmann interpreted Jesus' concept of the
Kingdom of God as being a present and inner reality. Thus he said
that Jesus must have meant that the beginning of the Kingdom of
God is given to men in the stirrings of such righteousness and such
trust or religion in their hearts. Jesus took seriously the language
of the Old Testament and understood the Kingdom of God as the rule
of God. But this rule of God man may see and experience. Above
all, the Kingdom of God is the rule of God in man's own heart
[Herrmann, Systematic Theology, tr Nathaniel Micklem, Kenneth A.
Saunders (NY: Macmillan, 1927), p 46].

But Herrmann emphasizes another side of Jesus' world view,
and in this he anticipates Weiss and Schweitzer. Jesus held a view
of the world that left him no concern for the future of human society.
For him the world was near an end and he saw the beginning of its
destruction approaching. The final judgment was at hand, and his
aim was to prepare souls for this coming glory. Therefore Jesus'
teachings are colored by this eschatological outlook. This situation
raises a two-fold barrier for us. In the first place, we do not share
Jesus' standpoint and are not greatly affected by the idea that the end
of the world is approaching. Secondly, circumstances in which we
see the promise of a better future, were to Jesus harbingers of ruin.
We are in the position that we do not feel ourselves face to face with
the end of the world, but are confronted with innumerable social obligations. Therefore Jesus' admonition not to be anxious cannot be
taken literally because of the different type of world we live in.

We are delivered from this dilemma through the findings of historical research and modern biblical knowledge. And this is a great
gain because it frees us from trying to take the Catholic monastic
way toward perfection and also from the enthusiastic Protestant followers of Leo Tolstoy.

If then the words of Jesus be understood as due to his mental

outlook, they will not obscure the fact that the pursuit of
power and possessions, as protected by law, is a moral obligation. Unless in particular circumstances, love requires
us to sacrifice these things, it is our moral duty to do battle
for the conditions under which we exist on earth [Adolf Harnack & Wilhelm Herrmann, Essays on the Social Gospel, tr
G. M. Craik (London: Williams & Norgate; NY: Putnam,
1907), p 211].

The upshot of Herrmann's view regarding Jesus' utterances,
especially those in the Sermon on the Mount, is that we cannot possibly comply with them because we do not share his conception of
the universe. If this is the case, are we to conclude that Jesus'
teachings are irrelevant for us? Or how does the Sermon on the
Mount relate to us? In his Ethik [(Tübingen: J. C. B. Mohr, 1901)],
Herrmann says that there are three possible ways of interpreting the
Sermon on the Mount. First, we may regard Jesus' teachings in
the Sermon as exaggerations set forth in a moment of passion.
Secondly, they are new and more rigid laws to regulate human behavior. Thirdly, they cannot be seen as rules that have general
validity and are applicable in every situation, but they are demands
that may come into force at any given moment (p 132). Their
meaning lies in the fact that Jesus wishes to open the way for a
right disposition (Gesinnung) within. The term "Gesinnung" is one
of Herrmann's key categories in his Ethik [see especially pp 126-
42]. To try to obey the Sermon on the Mount as general rules
would divert us from following Jesus. Such a way would shut us
off from his living mind and his mysterious greatness. The teachings of Jesus are illustrative of a new set of mind and of the will,
a disposition grounded in Jesus' person and power. At the end of
a paper read by Herrmann at the Evangelical Social Congress at
Darmstadt in 1903 we have a good summary of his "Gesinnungs-
ethik":

> We must accept the directions of Jesus, neither as enforced
> and arbitrary laws, nor yet as mere outbursts of emotion,
> but as the effulgence of his mind. They are not cords he
> has wound about us, but clues to direct us to freedom....
> Least able, however, to understand the true force of the
> moral ideas of Jesus--the unity of his mind--are the num-
> bers of religious people who are practically tied to the prin-
> ciple of pharisaic morality, according to which certain rules
> may teach us the nature of the good, and a will that is
> ready to be bound by them may be accounted good. Yet
> even among all these, every one will at length understand
> his thoughts, who draws so near to the person of Jesus that
> he is conscious of his power to deliver, and becomes free
> for service as he was [Harnack & Herrmann, Essays on the
> Social Gospel, pp 224-5].

12 FRIEDRICH AUGUST THOLUCK

In 1826 Tholuck became professor at Halle University where
he remained until his death in 1877, except for a short appointment
as embassy chaplain at Rome from 1827-1829. At Halle Tholuck
was influential in imparting a pietistic and evangelical emphasis to
both students and faculty. He was the author of a number of commentaries on various biblical books. His most learned and elabor-
ate exegetical work was Die Bergpredigt [references are to Eng ed,
Commentary on the Sermon on the Mount, tr R. Lundin Brown
(Edinburgh: T. & T. Clark, 1869)] originally published in 1833.
There are few if any expositions of the Sermon on the Mount more
scholarly and extensive than Tholuck's. This classic nineteenth-
century work has not had its twentieth-century counterpart. Tholuck
was a noted linguist, and this is evident in Die Bergpredigt since
Hebrew, Greek, and Latin references abound. His acquaintance with
the relevant writings of the Church Fathers, of the medieval period,
and of his immediate predecessors and contemporaries is truly remarkable. Tholuck's characteristic method of interpretation is to
examine a given passage linguistically and historically, and in so
doing to make his own interpretation of its meaning and significance.
Die Bergpredigt is, in addition to its exegetical significance, a sec-
tion-by-section history of interpretation of the Sermon on the Mount.

Tholuck's approach to the Sermon on the Mount is not that of
the detached critical scholar. Rather he is an evangelical apologist
who is concerned about the relation of the Sermon on the Mount to
the evangelical doctrine of salvation. The demands set forth in the
Sermon can be attained through faith in Christ, but he only partially
alludes to this in the Sermon itself. Though the work of redemption
was only to be unveiled by the completed work of Christ, nevertheless, the Preacher of the Sermon on the Mount is himself this redeemer in person. Allusions to Christ the redeemer are unmis-
takable. Thus those Beatitudes which speak of spiritual poverty,
of hunger and thirst after righteousness, point to him who invites
men to himself because his yoke is easy and his burden light. And
if Christ requires a righteousness beyond that of the Scribes and
Pharisees, does this not presuppose a faith in him through whom
strength is given to fulfill what he requires? "Christ could not
have designated his coming as the fulfillment of all the Messianic
expectations, had he come only to increase the demands of the Law,
without also giving an increased measure of strength" (p 41).

Tholuck believes that the Sermon on the Mount was addressed
primarily to the Disciples and secondarily to the people. Christ's
object in giving the Sermon was to exhibit himself as the fulfiller
of the Law and to enunciate the magna charta of his new kingdom
(p 14). Moreover, the Sermon on the Mount seems to be the counterpart of the lawgiving on Mount Sinai. It sets forth the Law of
Moses in a wider and deeper aspect.

In the eight Beatitudes Tholuck sees an ethical order. The

first four are of a negative character in that they express the spiritual desire which marks participation in the Kingdom of God. The
three following are positive and set forth the attribures of character
required in members of the Kingdom. The eighth shows how the
world will react toward members of the Kingdom. The Beatitudes
are essentially identical because each of them comprises all spiritual blessings. One must not view them as a progression from one
stage to another which excludes the rest, or in advancing to one,
leaves the others behind.

Consistent with his high Christology, Tholuck proposes another
hermeneutical explanation which is especially relevant to the Beatitudes. In analyzing Christ's sayings we dare not assume that no
other meaning is implied in his words than one within the compass
of his hearers and familiar to them. Many of Christ's sayings far
transcended the limits of the occasion on which they were given and
embraced the whole future of the Kingdom of God. They went beyond the thought range of his contemporaries and possessed a dimension which would be measured only by him and by posterity.
But it does not follow that Christ speaks only to posterity. While
he went beyond the sphere of vision of his hearers, he had points
of contact with those to whom he spoke. Thus the interpreter must
hold in dialogue both the temporal and trans-temporal dimensions of
Christ's teachings. The first Beatitude illustrates the foregoing
principle. To his hearers the idea of the poor was no new idea
since those who gathered round him were from the lower classes.
The idea of physical poverty is carried over into the sphere of
poverty of the spirit, and those poor are pronounced blessed who
are also sensible of their spiritual poverty (pp 65-6, 71).

Matt. 5:21-48 with its antitheses between the Mosaic Law and
the "New Law" of Christ presents difficulties for the interpreter insofar as their contemporary relevance is concerned. Here Tholuck
introduces another hermeneutical principle which holds that the spiritual, and not the literal, interpretation is the true one. Since the
spirit of an author is expressed by means of the word and the letter,
the interpreter must naturally begin there. But there is a grada-
tion here which one dare not ignore. The letter is important as an
element in the word, the word as a member of the sentence, the
sentence as a part of the organic whole. Consequently, in order to
understand the word one must gain an understanding of the whole
work, and the correctness of the interpretation of a sentence and
an isolated clause must be determined by the consistency of that interpretation with the idea of the whole word. Tholuck believed that
it was the departure from this hermeneutical principle that was responsible for "false, merely literal, and hence unscriptural" views
of such commands as those in verses 28, 34, 39-42. This errone-
ous exegesis was to be found principally in the Quakers. This is
why they have rejected oaths and resistance to evil. Such literal
obedience doubtless arises from reverence for Christ's words, but
it fails to realize that clinging to the particular lowers the general,
and veneration of the letter leads to a depreciation of the spirit.

So the sayings of Christ, especially in this section of the Sermon
on the Mount, must be interpreted according to the whole scope of
Christian doctrine, according to the spirit of Christ (pp 163-5).

In the Sermon on the Mount the Lord's mode of address is
that of the popular orator. The language is not that of the school
nor of the lawyer. Hence it is faulty for us to make minute distinctions and to take the letter of what he says in a strict literal
sense, and to press it unduly. Christ is using examples and is
speaking figuratively; and example is seldom of universal force, a
figure has seldom universal application. The Sermon on the Mount
is a striking model of example and figure, and in order to interpret it correctly one must not "wander from the green meadows of
a lively and spiritual interpretation into the barren tracts of scholastic abstractions" (pp 165-6).

Though Tholuck's "spiritual interpretation" of the Sermon on
the Mount avoids literalism, it is open to charges of relativism and
subjectivism. Thus Tholuck writes: "The popular orator gives
forth his utterance in concise and terse language, trusting to the
common sense of his hearers as his interpreter, which with intui-
tive skill curtails or supplements his sayings, according as the intention of the speaker and the connection of the discourse require"
(p 165). At any rate, Jesus' words about oaths and nonresistance
cannot be taken as absolute prohibitions. In the circumstances in
which we are actually placed, the use of the oath is necessarily con-
ceded in certain cases (p 253). And as for the commands in verses
39-42, they are to be regarded as only concrete illustrations of the
state of mind and heart required--as extreme cases, which no doubt,
under certain circumstances, may occur (p 269).

The passage of time has not altered the significance of Tholuck's Die Bergpredigt. It is an admirable synthesis of exegetical
and historical scholarship, and is a rich source for any serious
study of the Sermon on the Mount.

13 SØREN KIERKEGAARD

Kierkegaard was a gadfly and an irritant to the prevailing
thought patterns of the nineteenth century, and it was only in this
century that he came to be recognized as the creative genius he
was. With his insistence that truth is subjectivity and his penetrating insights into the meaning of existence, Kierkegaard has
exerted a profound influence upon twentieth-century philosophy and
theology, as well as such areas as art, literature, psychology. In
his description of selfhood, the concept of anxiety occupied a central place. Consequently, Jesus' admonition about not being anxious, and his description of the birds and the lilies in the Sermon
on the Mount motivated Kierkegaard to write three separate interpretations of Matt. 6:24-34.

The first of these, Hvad vi laere af lilerne paa marken og af

himmelens fugle (What We Learn from the Lilies of the Field and
the Birds of the Air) was published in 1847 and consists of three
discourses. The first discourse is entitled: "To Be Satisfied with
the Fact of Being Human."

The lilies one is asked to consider are not rare, potted
plants, but those which, though uncared for, grow in profusion.
They succeed without striving. They are beautiful without assistance. If the lily could speak to an anxious person would it not say:
"Why do you thus wonder at me? Should not the fact of being human be equally as glorious?... Should what is true of poor me not
be true of the fact of being human, which is the marvel of creation?"
[The Gospel of Suffering and the Lilies of the Field, tr David F.
Swenson, Lillian M. Swenson (Minneapolis: Augsburg Pub Hse,
1948), p 176; references are to this ed]. In this first discourse
Kierkegaard tells one of his charming parables. It is about the lily
and the bird. There was once a lily which stood alone near a little
brook. It was beautiful, carefree, and happy. One day a little bird
visited the lily and kept returning. Instead of rejoicing in the lily's
beauty the bird emphasized its own freedom and the lily's bondage.
The bird told stories about other places where unusually magnificent
lilies grew in great abundance. Such brilliant scenes surpassed all
description, and the bird tried to humiliate the lily and to question
by what right it was really called a lily in comparison with such
magnificence.

The lily became troubled and was no longer satisfied with itself. It began to lament why it was not born in another place under
different circumstances and why it was not born an imperial lily because the bird had said that the imperial lily was the most beautiful
of all lilies.

Finally the lily and the bird agreed that the next morning a
change should take place. Early the next morning the bird came
and with its beak began to cut away the soil from the lily's roots.
When this was accomplished, the bird took the lily under its wing
and flew away. The intention was that the bird would take the lily
where the magnificent lilies bloom and plant it there. But on the
way the lily withered (pp 178-81).

Kiekegaard says that the lily is the human and that from the
lily we learn to be satisfied with the fact of being human, and not
to be disturbed about the distinctions between man and man. "All
worldly concern is at bottom due to the fact that a man is not satisfied with the fact of being human, that by means of the comparison
he anxiously desires to be different" (p 184).

This same theme is illustrated by another parable. A stock
dove lived in a forest. On a nearby farm lived some tame doves.
The stock dove frequently exchanged thoughts with a pair of the
tame doves. One day the tame doves talked about the necessities
of life. The stock dove reported it had no worries because it let

each day carry its own troubles. The tame doves said that their
future was assured by the grain stored by the rich farmer. Thereupon the stock dove began to worry about its future and like the
farmer began to gather provisions. Eventually the stock dove decided to join the tame doves and flew into the barn. But at night
when the farmer locked the dovecote, he at once discovered the
strange dove. The next day he killed it. As with the lily, Kierkegaard says that the stock dove is man and that anxiety is man's sin
(pp 188-91).

In the second discourse Kierkegaard turns attention to "The
Glory of Our Common Humanity." Man's glory consists of his being created in the image of God. The fact that man is spirit is his
invisible glory. The bird has no worldly care for the necessities
of life because it lives only in the moment and has no consciousness of eternity. But with man the situation is otherwise. His
anxiety is grounded in the juncture of the temporal and the eternal
in man's consciousness. "The temporal and the eternal can pain-
fully touch one another in numerous ways in the human consciousness, but one of the contacts at which the man particularly winces
is the care for the necessities of life" (p 215).

Another mark of the glory of our common humanity lies in
man's capacity to work. Work is the perfection of the human and
through working, the human resembles God, who also works.

In the final discourse Kierkegaard deals with "The Happiness
of Our Common Humanity Consists in First Seeking the Kingdom of
God." He extends the analogy of man and nature. The life of nature is brief, melodious, blooming, but every moment is characterized by the prey of death, and death is the stronger. The blessedness of being a man and that which distinguishes him from nature
is man's capacity for choice. Lilies and birds have no choice, but
man does. "For it is indeed true that the one happiness still consists in choosing rightly, but the choice itself is still the glorious
condition" (p 228). Moreover, man must choose between God and
the world--between God and Mammon. This choice cannot be evaded,
and it has eternal consequences.

Man is called to seek first God's Kingdom which is the name
of the eternal happiness which is promised to the human and before which the beauty and peace of nature pale and disappear. God's
Kingdom is righteousness. It is both "above the heavens" and
"within you." "God's Kingdom is still that which is to be sought
first, but which shall also endure through all eternities to the last"
(p 236).

In 1848 Kierkegaard published Christelige taler [references are
to Christian Discourses, tr Walter Lowrie (London: Oxford Univ Pr,
1940)]. Part I consists of a commentary on Matt. 6:24-34 and is
entitled "The Anxieties of the Heathen." Kierkegaard contrasts the
heathen and the Christian by drawing analogies from the lilies and

the birds and examines these differences under the following headings: the anxiety of poverty, the anxiety of abundance, the anxiety
of lowliness, the anxiety of highness, the anxiety of presumption,
the anxiety of self-torment, the anxiety of irresolution, fickleness,
disconsolateness [for a discussion of each of these "anxieties," see
pp 17-93].

From the lilies and the birds we learn to know the anxieties
of the heathen which the lilies and the birds do not have even though
they have corresponding needs. But the lilies and birds likewise
show us that the Christian should receive God's gifts and have no
anxiety for the morrow. This is to be a Christian, which, of
course, these lesser creatures can never be (pp 13-5).

The third work, Lilien paa Marken og Fugeln under Himlen
(The Lilies of the Field and the Birds of the Air), was written in
1848 and published in 1849. Three lessons are to be learned from
the lilies and the birds--silence, obedience, and joy.

To be silent is an art; it is to seek first the Kingdom of God.
Silence is also the mood of prayer. As the true man of prayer becomes more earnest in his praying, he has less and less to say and
in the end becomes silent. He had supposed that to pray is to
speak; he learned that to pray is not merely to be silent but to hear
(Christian Discourses, p 323).

The second instruction is obedience which is set forth in "No
man can serve two masters." The lilies and the birds exemplify
unconditional obedience and are united in perfect unity. Man is to
learn from them how to be absolutely obedient. It was man's sin
which (by not willing to serve one master, or by willing to serve
another master, or by willing to serve two or many masters) disturbed all the beauty of the world. Man's sin of disobedience created a discord in a world where everything was good and harmonious (Christian Discourses, p 346).

Finally, from these creatures of nature man can learn joy.
The lilies and the birds are unconditionally joyful and are joy itself.
And yet they also have sorrow because all of creation is subjected
to corruption. But in spite of this, the lilies and birds are joyful.
The key to joy is to cast all our care upon God, entirely, absolutely, as the lilies and birds do. What they do unconsciously man
must learn to do consciously. Then it is that man can make this
prayer of joy: "Thine is the kingdom and the power and the glory,
for ever and ever. Amen" (pp 347-56).

In these three expositions on Matt. 6:24-34 one discerns quite
clearly several Kierkegaardian motifs. However biblically grounded
they are, they expose Kierkegaard's existential thought. Man's existence is characterized by the necessity of choice before God, is
marked by anxiety, and is fulfilled by a "leap of faith" which is
made possible by the grace of God. Such is the nature of the Ser-

mon on the Mount. It is not an objective discussion of truth, but
is more like a finger that continues to point at the existing believer
before God.

14 LEO TOLSTOY

Tolstoy is perhaps best known as a great novelist who wrote
War and Peace and Anna Karenina. But he was also a moralist and
social reformer and an absolutistic interpreter of the Sermon on the
Mount. His career was stormy and controversial. Because of his
unorthodox views he was excommunicated from the Orthodox Church
in 1901. After 1877 he renounced his literary ambitions and turned
increasingly to religious and social critical themes. His religious
and political anarchism finally led to a break with his family who
would not follow the life he wanted to live. Just before his death
in 1910 Tolstoy left home in search of a refuge where he could live
quietly and come closer to God.

In Ispoved' (My Confession), written in 1878-79, Tolstoy poign-
antly relates his religious pilgrimage. He tells of the moral and
spiritual suffering he endured in searching for answers to the meaning of existence. He attempted to maintain a rational approach, but
he found little help in the writings of philosophers, theologians, and
scientists which he systematically examined. Finally, Tolstoy turned
away from his circle of the rich and learned and began to cultivate
the acquaintance of the believers among the poor, the simple and
unlettered. It was among these peasants that he found the clue to
life and experienced a "conversion." He describes this "awakening"
as follows:

> I began to examine closely the lives and beliefs of these peo-
> ple, and the more I examined them, the more did I become
> convinced that they had the real faith, that their faith was
> necessary for them, and that it alone gave them a meaning
> and possibility of life.... I began to love these people. The
> more I penetrated into their life, the life of men now living,
> and the life of men departed, of whom I had read and heard,
> the more did I love them, and the easier it became for me
> to live. Thus I lived for about two years, and within me
> took place a transformation, which had long been working
> within me. What happened with me was that the life of our
> circle, --of the rich and the learned, --not only disgusted me,
> but even lost all its meaning. All our acts, reflections, sci-
> ences, arts, --all that appeared to me in a new light. I saw
> that all that was mere pampering of the appetites, and that
> no meaning could be found in it; but the life of all the work-
> ing masses, of all humanity, which created life, presented
> itself to me in its real significance. I saw that that was life
> itself and that the meaning given to this life was truth, and
> I accepted it [My Confession, vol XIII The Complete Works
> of Count Tolstoy, tr Leo Wiener (NY: AMC Pr, 1968), pp 59-
> 61].

In 1881-1882 Tolstoy wrote Soedinenie i perevod chetyrekh Evangelii (The Four Gospels Harmonized). After making a study of the New Testament he concluded that the whole Christian tradition is contained in the four Gospels. In composing his harmony, Tolstoy translated the Gospels from the Greek. He included the Gospel of John since his aim was not historical, philosophical, or theological. His main intent was to find the meaning of the teaching. Previous harmonies were all equally unsuccessful because they were harmonized on a historical basis. Tolstoy differentiates his harmony from the previous ones as follows:

> I leave the historical meaning entirely alone, and harmonize only in the sense of the teaching. The harmonization of the Gospels on this basis has this advantage, that the true teaching represents, as it were, a circle, of which all the parts determine their mutual significance, and for the study of which it is immaterial from what place we begin. In studying in this manner the Gospels, in which the historical events of Christ's life are so closely connected with the teaching, the historical consecutiveness appeared quite immaterial to me, and for the historical consecutiveness it made no difference to me which harmonization of the Gospels I took as my basis [The Four Gospels Harmonized and Translated, vol I Complete Works, p 18].

As for the central teaching of the Sermon on the Mount in Tolstoy's Four Gospels Harmonized, it can be summarized in five rules.

> Having warned his hearers that he did not destroy the Law, but only gave a few additional little rules, the fulfillment of which gives the Kingdom of God, Jesus expresses these five rules, namely: Be not angry; commit no adultery; swear not; go not to law; war not. Jesus says, Here are five rules, but they all come down to one. This rule is, What you would that others should do to you, do you to others. This rule takes the place of the former Law [vol I Complete Works, p 272; these five rules, with their fulfillment in the Golden Rule, are elaborated upon, pp 287, 299-300].

Tolstoy's most extensive exposition of the Sermon on the Mount is found in V chem moía viera (My Religion), written in 1884. This is an autobiographical work in which Tolstoy seeks to systematize his religious beliefs. From his childhood Tolstoy was most impressed with the teachings of Christ concerning love, meekness, humility, self-renunciation, and retribution of evil with good. But he found that the Orthodox Church was more concerned with dogmas than with the above teachings, and this confused and repelled him.

> What repelled me from the church was the strangeness of the church dogmas, and the recognition and approval given by the church to persecutions, capital punishment, and wars, and the mutual rejection of various creeds; but what shattered my

confidence in it was that indifference to what to me seemed
to be the essence of Christ's teaching and the bias for what
I regarded as inessential [My Religion, vol XVI Complete
Works, p 8].

The solution to his doubts Tolstoy found in the Gospels, especially the Sermon on the Mount. He believed that nowhere did
Christ give so many moral, clear, intelligible rules as in the Sermon on the Mount. "As I read these rules, it seemed to me that
they had special reference to me and demanded that I, if no one
else, should execute them" (My Religion, p 10). A new world
opened before Tolstoy when he came to the realization that verses
38 and 39 of Matt. 5 were the key to the whole. These verses
about nonresistance to evil causes everything which had been dark
to become clear. He understood for the first time that the center
of gravity of the whole thought was in the words, Do not resist evil,
and that what follows is only an explanation of the first proposition.
The concept of nonresistance now filled Tolstoy's horizon, for he
had discovered the key which unlocks everything.

The first thing that startled Tolstoy after he experienced this
"rebirth" was the contradiction between nonresistance and the courts.
"The courts do not forgive, but punish; they do not do good, but
evil, to those whom they call enemies of society" (My Religion,
p 25). Thus it turns out that Christ himself must have rejected
the court system.

After a further apologetic section on nonviolence, Tolstoy discusses in detail (My Religion, pp 63-94) the five commandments
which he had elaborated upon more briefly in The Four Gospels
Harmonized and Translated. With this he concludes his exposition
of the Sermon on the Mount in My Religion.

The fullest treatment of Tolstou's concept of nonviolence is
in Tstarstvo Bozhie vnutri vas [The Kingdom of God Is Within You,
vol XX Complete Works] written in 1893. It is here that he levels
his harshest criticism against the state and other social institutions.
In a word, Tolstoy's religious and political anarchism are most evident here. Tolstoy accuses the Orthodox Church of being preoccupied with creeds, sacraments, theologies, the worship of persons
and images and neglecting good works. For Tolstoy it is an either-
or choice--either the Sermon on the Mount or the creed. He
writes:

> The Sermon on the Mount, or the symbol of faith: it is im-
> possible to believe in both. And the churchmen have chosen
> the latter: the symbol of faith is taught and read as a
> prayer in the churches; and the Sermon on the Mount is ex-
> cluded even from the Gospel teachings in the churches, so
> that in the churches the parishioners never hear it, except
> on the days when the whole Gospel is read [p 78].

This same sharp distinction between theology and ethics is evident
in the following:

> The churches are confronted with a dilemma--the Sermon on
> the Mount, or the Nicene Creed--one excludes the other: if
> a man sincerely believes in the Sermon on the Mount, the
> Nicene Creed, and with it the church and its representatives,
> inevitably lose all meaning and significance for him; but if a
> man believes in the Nicene Creed, that is, in the church,
> that is, in those who call themselves its representatives, the
> Sermon on the Mount will become superfluous to him. And
> so the churches cannot help but use every possible effort to
> obscure the meaning of the Sermon on the Mount and to at-
> tract people to itself [Kingdom of God, vol XX Complete
> Works, p 87].

As in The Four Gospels and in My Religion, Tolstoy refers
to Christ's five commandments in the Sermon on the Mount. He is
convinced that though they express an eternal ideal, nevertheless
men can to a degree reach them in our time (Kingdom of God, p
104).

The Sermon on the Mount not only stands in opposition to the
established church, but also to the state. He writes:

> Christianity in its true meaning destroys the state.... For
> every sincere and serious man of our time it is quite obvious
> that true Christianity--the teaching of humility, of forgiveness
> of offenses, of love--is incompatible with the state, with its
> magnificence, its violence, its executions, and its wars. The
> profession of true Christianity not only excludes the possibili-
> ty of recognizing the state, but even destroys its very founda-
> tions [p 242].

So Tolstoy has equated nonviolence with the essence of Christianity and has viewed it as an ideal which is possible both for individuals and society. For him the Sermon on the Mount (and especially the command of nonviolence) was a law binding on all men
and bringing all human institutions under judgment.

In the beginning of The Kingdom of God Is Within You Tolstoy
addresses those (especially within the church) who had criticized My
Religion. He challenges them to answer a series of questions.
These are the questions he deals with in the rest of his work, but
they also give us a good summary of his interpretation of the Sermon on the Mount. There can be no doubt that for Tolstoy the answer to these questions is unequivocal and uncompromising. These
are his questions: Did Christ actually demand from his disciples
the fulfillment of what he taught in the Sermon on the Mount? And
if so, can a Christian, remaining a Christian, go to court, taking
part in it and condemning people, for seeking in it defense by
means of violence, or can he not? Can a Christian, still remaining

a Christian, take part in the government, using violence against his neighbors, or not? And the chief question, which now, with the universal military service, stands before all men, --can a Christian, remaining a Christian, contrary to Christ's injunction, make any promises as to future acts, which are directly contrary to the teaching, and, taking part in military service, prepare himself for the murder of men and commit it? (Kingdom of God, p 35).

15 CONSISTENT ESCHATOLOGY

JOHANNES WEISS

As we have observed, the influence of Kantian philosophy led liberal theology to closely identify Christianity with the experiential and the ethical. While both Harnack and Herrmann acknowledged the eschatological aspect of Jesus' teaching about the Kingdom of God, nevertheless they believed it could best be defined as the rule of God in the hearts of men. Ritschl's view of the Kingdom tended to be more socially oriented. It concerned man's working with Jesus to realize the moral life in society. At any rate, as the nineteenth century drew to a close, there was widespread agreement that the Kingdom of God was both immanent in individual religious experience and was to be gradually realized as an ideal society within history.

In 1892 there appeared a modest-sized volume entitled Die Predigt Jesu vom Reiche Gottes (Jesus' Proclamation of the Kingdom of God), by Johannes Weiss. This work was to have a profound impact upon liberal theology and upon subsequent interpretations of Jesus and his teachings. Rudolf Bultmann recalls how Julius Kaftan in his lectures on dogmatics in Berlin said, "If Johannes Weiss is right and the conception of the Kingdom of God is an eschatological one, then it is impossible to make use of this conception in dogmatics" [Bultmann, Jesus Christ and Mythology (NY: Scribner's, 1958), p 13].

Weiss had been a student of Ritschl (who was also his father-in-law). Through his studies in theology and the New Testament, Weiss came to reject the prevailing opinions of liberal theology regarding the Kingdom of God. The view of the Kingdom of God which he found in the Gospels was at variance with that of Ritschl and the Ritschlians. It was not primarily an ethical entity which could be described in terms of religious experience nor could it be equated with the gradual development of the good society. Rather, for Jesus, the Kingdom of God was an apocalyptic and eschatological event which God would soon consummate. The Disciples were to pray for its coming, but men could do nothing to establish it. Not even Jesus could do this. Only God could, and He must take control. In the meantime Jesus had to battle the devil and to prepare his followers to await and prepare for the Kingdom through repentance, humility, and renunciation [Jesus' Proclamation of the King-

dom of God, tr Richard H. Hiers, David L. Holland (Philadelphia:
Fortress Pr, 1971), pp 129-30]. Weiss perhaps best summarized
the basic differences between himself and his liberal contemporaries
concerning the Kingdom of God in these words: "The Kingdom of
God as Jesus thought of it is never something subjective, inward,
or spiritual, but is always the objective messianic Kingdom, which
usually is pictured as a territory into which one enters, or as a
land in which one has a share, or as a treasure which comes down
from heaven" (Jesus' Proclamation, p 133).

This then was Jesus' view of the Kingdom of God insofar as
historical scholarship could determine it. But this did not answer
the question as to how the church should subsequently understand
the Kingdom. Weiss was intent upon letting the historical data
speak for itself, and in so doing he ruptured the harmonious relationship that had existed between contemporary New Testament exegesis and systematic theology. He had broken with the New Testament exegetes, but he still found Ritschlianism to be the best theological alternative. Weiss was willing to accept the findings of historical criticism, but he was not willing to make them his own nor
to insist that the church in all times had to adhere to Jesus' interpretation of the Kingdom. For Weiss the liberal view of the Kingdom of God was probably the best for the Christianity of his time.
Like Schweitzer, he found that Jesus' concern for an eschatological
kingdom had little if anything to say about modern ethical issues.
We do not share Jesus' eschatological outlook. Weiss writes: "We
no longer pray, 'May grace come and the world pass away,' but we
pass our lives in the joyful confidence that this world will evermore
become the showplace of the people of God" (Jesus' Proclamation,
p 135).

But if we cannot get ethical directives from the historical
Jesus with his apocalyptic vision, we can still rely upon the guidance
of the exalted Christ, "who were he among us today, would lead us
in reorganizing the world according to the ideas which God reveals
to us through history" [Weiss, Die Nachfolge Christi und die Predigt
der Gegenwart (Göttingen: Vandenhoeck & Ruprecht, 1895), p 164;
quoted in Intro, Jesus' Proclamation, p 23]. But there are also
hints in the synoptic Gospels as to what Jesus might do were he to
reappear among us. He would not simply repeat the Sermon on the
Mount nor wait quiescently for the coming of the Kingdom of God.
Rather, he would work for its realization in history and would encourage us through our preaching and instruction to do all we can
to awaken it. [For a detailed discussion of Weiss' Die Predigt
Jesu vom Reiches Gottes and its relationship to various contemporary and subsequent biblical, ethical, and theological issues, see
Introd to Jesus' Proclamation, pp 1-54.]

ALBERT SCHWEITZER

Weiss was soon joined by a formidable ally in the person of
Albert Schweitzer. He used the term konsequente Eschatologie

("consistent" or "thorough-going" eschatology) to set forth the view
that the whole of Jesus' public work is to be explained by his eschatological beliefs.   Schweitzer acknowledged his agreement with
Weiss, but Weiss had not gone far enough.   Schweitzer writes:

> So toward the end of the century the view which sees an es-
> chatological character in the preaching of Jesus and his Mes-
> sianic self-consciousness begins to make headway, as de-
> veloped by the Heidelberg theologian, Johannes Weiss, in a
> book written with wonderful clarity, The Preaching of Jesus
> Concerning the Kingdom of God.   Scientific theology cher-
> ishes, nevertheless, in secret the hope that it will not, after
> all, have to admit everything that Weiss propounds.   In re-
> ality, however, it has to go even further than he, for he
> comes to a stop halfway.   He makes Jesus think and talk es-
> chatologically without proceeding to the natural inference that
> his actions also must have been determined by eschatological
> ideas [Out of My Life and Thought, tr C. T. Campion (NY:
> Holt, 1949), p 48].

According to Schweitzer, the Jesus presented in the Gospels
was not the historical Jesus of nineteenth-century liberal theology--
a Jesus who was a high-souled teacher of morality who sought to
establish the spiritual reign of God in men's hearts and thus induce
a reign of justice on earth.   Rather, he is a stranger and an enig-
ma to our time, an unworldly, apocalyptic figure who "comes to us
as one unknown, without a name."   Jesus shared the eschatological
and apocalyptic world-view of late Judaism.   The Kingdom which he
announced was not to be founded and realized in the natural world
by himself and his followers, but was to be expected as coming with
the almost immediate dawn of a supernatural age.   The imminence
of the Kingdom and the urgency of the hour is seen in Matt. 10
where the mission of the Twelve is recorded.   Matt. 10:23 is for
Schweitzer one of the key verses in his interpretation of Jesus:
"... for truly, I say to you, you will not have gone through all the
towns of Israel, before the Son of Man comes."   [Schweitzer's position is described more comprehensively in my "The Problem of
the 'Historical Jesus' from Schweitzer to Bultmann," unpub STM
thesis, Lutheran Theological Seminary, Gettysburg, PA, 1964, pp
28-75.]

   Schweitzer's well-known characterization of the Sermon on the
Mount is that of "interim ethics."   These radical and uncompromising teachings were given in that brief interim before the Eschaton
in order to prepare the Disciples for the advent of the Kingdom.
The ethics of the Sermon on the Mount are therefore the ethics of
repentance.   The new morality which detects the spirit beneath the
letter of the Law equips one to enter into the Kingdom of God.
The Beatitudes reflect the same point of view.   They define the
moral disposition which justifies admission into the Kingdom.   Thus
Schweitzer says:

As repentance unto the Kingdom of God the ethics also of the
Sermon on the Mount is interim ethics. In this we perceive
that the moral instruction of Jesus remained the same from
the first day of his public appearance unto his latest utterances, for the lowliness and serviceableness which he recommended to his disciples on the way to Jerusalem correspond
exactly to the new moral conduct which he developed in the
Sermon on the Mount: they make one meet for the Kingdom
of God.... Whosoever at the dawning of the Kingdom is in
possession of a character morally renovated, he will be found
a member of the same. This is the adequate expression for
the relation of morality to the coming Kingdom of God [The
Mystery of the Kingdom of God, tr Walter Lowrie (NY: Dodd,
Mead, 1914), pp 97, 99].

Jesus' understanding of the Law is likewise viewed from the
perspective of "consistent eschatology." Schweitzer describes
Jesus' attitude toward the Law as a sort of detached indifference.
He did not declare himself either for it or against it. He felt no
obligation to declare it binding or non-binding. This was of no
practical importance for Jesus. His real concern was the new
morality, not the Law. It was holy and inviolable only insofar as
it pointed the way to the new morality. Consequently, Jesus assumed that the Law would come to an end at the beginning of the
Messianic Kingdom. Both Jesus and John the Baptist demanded repentance and an absolute and inward ethic, instead of meticulously
observing the minute details of the Law. This was the most obvi-
ous line of conduct in light of the nearness of the coming Kingdom.
They had no reason to attack it because they knew that it would pass
away with the coming of the Kingdom. After quoting Matt. 5:17-18,
"Think not that I have come to abolish the Law and the Prophets;
I have come not to abolish them but to fulfill them. For truly, I
say to you, till heaven and earth pass away, not an iota, not a dot,
will pass from the Law until all is accomplished," Schweitzer concludes: "Jesus thus clearly affirms that the Law is only valid until
the beginning of the Kingdom of God. How, indeed, could he have
held that it would retain its validity for the men of the resurrection,
the partakers of the Kingdom" [The Mysticism of Paul the Apostle,
tr William Montgomery (NY: Seabury Pr, 1968), p 190].

In the last of the Beatitudes (Matt. 5:11-12) Jesus pronounces
blessing upon those who are persecuted because their reward will
be great in heaven. Schweitzer says that it is generally believed
that when Jesus speaks of persecution which his disciples shall encounter, he is predicting what they must endure when they are left
alone after his death. But this is totally false, for when he speaks
like this he is referring to the affliction which his followers must
bear with him before the dawn of the Kingdom. Consequently, the
last Beatitude rightly proclaims that the Disciples have reason to
rejoice and be exceeding glad, for in what they must endure is
revealed their right to membership in the Kingdom of God. While
they are still afflicted by the power of this world their reward is

already prepared in heaven [Mystery of the Kingdom of God, pp 219-20].

        Let us finally turn to Schweitzer's interpretation of the Lord's Prayer. In this prayer Jesus teaches the believers to ask for nothing else than the content of the Kingdom of God. It is under such forms as the hallowing of God's name, the rule of his will upon earth, forgiveness of sins--with the addition of a petition for deliverance from "temptation." "Temptation," Schweitzer says, refers to the pre-Messianic Tribulation. However, the fourth petition, "Give us this day our daily bread," seems to be at variance with the eschatological perspective. It seems to break entirely from the theme of the rest of the Prayer. Moreover, it appears to contradict the sayings which follow about taking no thought for eating and drinking (Matt. 6:25-34). In Matt. 6:33 Jesus says that they should concern themselves only with the Kingdom of God. How then, Schweitzer asks, is it conceivable that, amid these petitions for the one thing needful, Jesus should bring in one which gives expression to the forbidden anxiety about earthly needs?

        At this point Schweitzer analyzes the Greek words in the fourth petition and finds that they mean: "Our bread, the coming [future] bread, give us this day." He concludes:

        The natural translation 'Our bread, the Coming bread, give us today' makes sense of the fourth petition and, in fact, exactly the sense which is required to fit in with the remaining petitions. Like these it asks for one of the blessings of the coming Kingdom of God; in this case, the food of the Kingdom.... The petition therefore means: The future food of the Kingdom of God, give us even today. In other words: Let Thy Kingdom immediately come, in which we shall eat the food of the Messianic feast [Mysticism of Paul, p 240].

        Truly Schweitzer was a towering figure, and though his consistent eschatology is excessive, there is a logical consistency about it that enabled him to explain far more of the words and deeds of Jesus than liberal theology had been able to do. Eschatology has come to occupy a central place in contemporary theology. Likewise, after Weiss and Schweitzer, no one can any longer study and interpret the Sermon on the Mount without coming to grips with the eschatological issue. Archibald M. Hunter says of Schweitzer: "Nevertheless, his excesses should not blind us to the great services he rendered scholarship. Two things he did. He compelled scholars to face squarely the problems of eschatology and to produce better solutions of them than he had done. And second, he put the life of Jesus in its true setting" [The Works and Words of Jesus (Philadelphia: Westminster Pr, 1950), p 13].

16 DISPENSATIONALISM

The period following the American Civil War until the beginning of the twentieth century was one of marked upheaval and change. This was the time of industrialization and the beginning of urbanization. Moreover, Darwin's theory of evolution presented a serious threat to traditional theological views concerning the authority of the Bible and the nature of man. Protestant liberalism attempted to affect a rapprochement between the "abiding truths and the changing categories." However, those of a more conservative bent were not so ready to accept these innovations. They were intent upon defending and preserving "the faith once and for all delivered to the saints."

Out of this milieu there developed the Bible and prophetic conference movement which sought to defend the Bible as the inerrant and infallible Word of God and to relate it both to present and future happenings. This movement developed its own distinctive norms or biblical interpretation, and from it emerged a hermeneutical scheme which has come to be known as dispensationalism. The basic rationale of dispensationalism is that sacred history is divided into a number of dispensations--usually seven, in each of which God deals with man on a different basis.

Most critics of dispensationalism regard it as a modern movement which began with John Nelson Darby and the Plymouth Brethren in the nineteenth century. Those who hold the dispensationalist view resent the notion that dispensationalism is recent, unorthodox, or separatist. They acknowledge their dependence upon Darby. However, they hold that neither Darby nor the Brethren originated the concepts involved in the system. They merely systematized motifs which go back to the Church Fathers. Justin Martyr, Irenaeus, Clement of Alexandria, Augustine, Pierre Poiret, John Edwards, Isaac Watts are regarded as forerunners of contemporary dispensationalism [for more detailed discussion of its origins see Charles C. Ryrie's competent apology for dispensationalism, Dispensationalism Today (Chicago: Moody Pr, 1965), pp 65-78].

The year 1909 is an important date in the development of dispensationalism because of the publication of The Scofield Reference Bible [NY: Oxford Univ Pr, 1909], which represents the classic expression of the movement in America. Scofield occupies a position of prominence and authority second to none among dispensationalists. C. Norman Kraus speaks of "Scofield's synthesis" and says of him:

> Scofield's significance in American dispensationalism lies in the fact that he sought to put the more tenuous theological concepts into concrete outline form.... If we ask whether he represents a development in dispensationalism which is vital to the larger theological picture, the answer is no.... His predecessors were the innovators, the radicals; he has become the conservative, the scholastic [Dispensationalism

in America: Its Rise and Development (Richmond: John Knox Pr, 1958), pp 129-30; the book is a good balanced view of the movement by a non-dispensationalist].

Before turning to the dispensationalist interpretation of the Sermon on the Mount, it is necessary to describe its "theology of history" as set forth in the dispensations. First, however, one must define "dispensation." Scofield's definition, in his Reference Bible, is widely accepted and can be regarded as the classic one: "A dispensation is a period of time during which man is tested in respect of obedience to some specific revelation of the will of God" (p 5). In the Introduction to the Reference Bible he says: "The Dispensations are distinguished, exhibiting the majestic progressive order of the divine dealings of God with humanity, 'the increasing purpose' which runs through and links together the ages, from the beginning of the life of man to the end of eternity."

The number of dispensations varies, but generally seven is regarded as the "correct" number. [For a description of modern dispensational outlines, see Kraus, Dispensationalism in America, pp 25-44.] Again let us use Scofield's scheme as our model. He says that the Scriptures divide time, which is the period from the creation of Adam to the "new heaven and a new earth" of Rev. 21:1, into seven unequal periods which are usually called "dispensations" (Eph. 3:2), although they are also called "ages" and "days." These periods are characterized by some change in dealing with mankind, or a portion of mankind, in respect to the questions of sin and man's responsibility. Scofield suggests that five of these dispensations have been fulfilled and that we are probably living toward the close of the sixth. The seventh, and last, is before us.

These seven dispensations are as follows: (1) Man Innocent, which extended from the creation of Adam to the expulsion from Eden; (2) Man under Conscience, from the Expulsion through the Flood; (3) Man in Authority over the Earth, after the Flood to Babel; (4) Man under Promise, from Abraham to Egyptian bondage; (5) Man under Law, from Wilderness of Sinai to the dispersion of the Jews which still continues; (6) Man under Grace, begun by the sacrificial death of Christ. The first event in the closing of this dispensation will be the descent of the Lord from heaven, when sleeping saints will be raised and, together with believers then living, caught up "to meet the Lord in the air: and so shall we ever be with the Lord" (I Thess. 4:16-17). Then follows the brief period called "the great tribulation." After this will occur the personal return of the Lord to the earth in power and great glory, and the judgment which introduces the seventh and last dispensation. (7) Man under the Personal Reign of Christ. After the purifying judgments which attend the personal return of Christ to the earth, he will reign over restored Israel and over the earth for one thousand years. This is the period commonly called the Millennium. The seat of his power will be Jerusalem, and the saints, including the saved of the dispensation of grace, viz., the Church, will be associated with him

in his glory. Satan is "loosed a little season" and gathers the nations to battle against the Lord and his saints. The great "white
throne" is set, the wicked dead are raised and finally judged, and
then come the "new heaven and a new earth"--eternity begun [C. I.
Scofield, Rightly Dividing the Word of Truth (NY: Fleming H. Revell,
1907), pp 13-8].

The problem to which we now turn concerns the relationship
of the Sermon on the Mount to the dispensational pattern. [For
critical studies from a non-dispensational, evangelical perspective,
see Tal D. Bonham, The Demands of Discipleship; The Relevance
of the Sermon on the Mount (Pine Bluff, AR: Discipleship Book Co,
1967), pp 55-80; Carl F. H. Henry, Christian Personal Ethics
(Grand Rapids, MI: Eerdmans, 1957), pp 286-92; for a defense of
the dispensationalist view, see Ryrie, Dispensationalism Today, pp
105-9.] Perhaps the most frequent criticism of the dispensational
interpretation of the Sermon on the Mount centers around the question of the Sermon's contemporary relevance. Bonham characterizes
the dispensational viewpoint as "the postponed evasion of the Sermon's relevance," and Henry states that "there is no secure ground
for postponing the relevance of the Sermon on the Mount to a future
eschatological age."

Are these charges valid? Let us examine some of the dispensational interpretations of the Sermon on the Mount. In Scofield's
notes on the Sermon on the Mount in The Scofield Reference Bible
we read:

> The Sermon on the Mount has a twofold application: (1)
> Literally to the Kingdom. In this sense it gives the divine
> constitution for the righteous government of the earth. When-
> ever the Kingdom of Heaven is established on earth it will be
> according to that constitution.... The Sermon on the Mount
> is pure law, and transfers the offense from the overt act to
> the motive.... The Sermon on the Mount in its primary ap-
> plication gives neither the privilege nor the duty of the
> Church [pp 999-1000].

Scofield's analysis and that of those who followed him is based
on several presuppositions. For one, the Sermon on the Mount is
identified with law and does not contain the Gospel. The dichotomy
between law and gospel is well expressed by Donald Grey Barnhouse. He points out that as Christians we do not get a lamb and
have it killed on an altar by a priest, nor do we follow literally
other ceremonialism of the Law. These demands of the Law were
fulfilled by the death of Christ, and we are now free from them.
This is precisely the case with certain passages in the Sermon on
the Mount. Any attempt to apply them to our present-day civilization will end in confusion. So Donald Grey Barnhouse says:

> The offer of the Kingdom as made in the Sermon on the
> Mount is now definitely past. The age of grace runs its

course. We are not to make the mistake of trying to force
the Sermon on the Mount to a literal fulfillment today. It
will be fulfilled literally, but not until the age in which we
live comes to its close and the Lord Jesus shall be dealing
once more with his people Israel [His Own Received Him Not
(NY: Fleming H. Revell, 1933), pp 38, 40-1].

Barnhouse, in keeping with Scofield's views, discerns a specific example of the absence of grace in the Sermon on the Mount
in the petition on forgiveness in the Lord's Prayer. We pray for
an imperfect forgiveness because our forgiveness is conditioned upon
our readiness to forgive, and such forgiveness comes from a "sinful heart." But in the "grace" section of the New Testament there
is another prayer which rises from a "thankful heart that feels and
knows the grace of God." It is Eph. 4:32: "And be ye kind one to
another, tenderhearted, forgiving one another, even as God for
Christ's sake hath forgiven you." Barnhouse concludes: "But in
the days when he spoke, when law yet reigned, and grace had not
come into effect there could be no such full forgiveness from God"
[His Own, p 49]. (Scofield, in commenting on Matt. 6:12, says:
"This is legal ground. Cf. Eph. 4:32, which is grace. Under law
forgiveness is conditioned upon a like spirit in us; under grace we
are forgiven for Christ's sake, and exhorted to forgive because we
have been forgiven" [Reference Bible, p 1002].)

William L. Pettingill reflects this same cleavage between law
and gospel when he writes: "You will search in vain in Matthew
for a statement of the Gospel of the Grace of God" [Simple Studies
in Matthew (Harrisburg, PA: Fred Kelker, 1910), p 11]. In a later
reference, Pettingill rejects the liberal emphasis upon the teachings
of Jesus and their neglect of Paul. He states: "The Sermon on the
Mount is not the way of salvation for the sinner.... The Sermon
on the Mount is pure law, and the Christian is not under law, but
under grace" [Simple Studies, pp 57-8].

Lewis Sperry Chafer is an influential interpreter of dispensationalism and has written a seven-volume systematic theology.
Commenting on the Sermon on the Mount, he says:

The treatment of this discourse by writers of the past and
present often reveals the extent of their comprehension of
the present divine economy under grace. Apparently, the
root difficulty is the failure to recognize what is rightfully
a primary and what is rightfully a secondary application of
this teaching. When the primary application is given to this
Scripture, it is usually on the supposition that the Church is
the Kingdom and therefore passages related to the Kingdom
are addressed to her. Let it be dogmatically asserted at
this point that those who hold such views either have failed
to recognize the hopeless, blasting character of the law
which this discourse announces and from which the Christian
has been saved, or they have failed to comprehend the pres-

ent position and perfection of Christ which is the estate of
every believer. Apparently the two great systems--law and
grace--become so confused that there could be no order of
thinking [Systematic Theology, vol V (Dallas: Dallas Seminary
Pr, 1948), p 97; for additional exposition of Chafer's interpretation of the Sermon on the Mount, see "The Teachings
of Christ Incarnate," Bibliotheca Sacra 108 (1951), 391-413].

For Chafer, the rules of human conduct are not to be found in the
Sermon on the Mount which is for the future age. The rules of
conduct for the present age appear in the Gospel of John, the Acts,
and the Epistles of the New Testament [Systematic Theology, vol V,
p 98].

From the above it is evident that dispensationalism finds no
"church truth" in the Sermon on the Mount but law directed primarily to the future Kingdom. Consequently, a second presupposition logically follows. The Sermon on the Mount does not apply to
the "church age"--the dispensation of grace, but to the coming kingdom age. Barnhouse asks: "When will the Sermon on the Mount
become effective?" His answer: "It will take the personal return
of the Lord Jesus Christ, coming not as the meek and lowly Savior,
but as the Lord of power and glory, to enforce righteous principles
upon the earth" [His Own, pp 45-6]. Pettingill and Chafer present
the same views. Pettingill asks a question and gives his answer.
"If, then, the Sermon on the Mount be neither the way of life for
the sinner, nor the rule of life for the believer, what is it? The
answer is that the Sermon on the Mount is the code of laws of the
Kingdom of Heaven, which Kingdom, though for the time being rejected and held in abeyance, will one day be set up on the earth"
[Simple Studies, p 58]. And Chafer: "It therefore stands as well
founded that the Sermon on the Mount both by its setting in the context and by its doctrinal character belongs for its primary application to the future kingdom age" [Systematic Theology, p 99].

A study of dispensationalist writing gives one the preponderant
view that the Sermon on the Mount is future oriented. However,
this is not wholly the case. Since the Sermon on the Mount is a
part of the inspired Word of God, like all Scripture, it is applicable
to believers in this age. Scofield points out that there is a beautiful moral application to the Christian because it always remains
true that the poor in spirit, those who mourn, the meek, the merciful will be blessed [Reference Bible, p 1000]. Following Scofield,
Pettingill says that we shall find many eternal principles expressed
in the Sermon on the Mount. These are set forth in several of the
Beatitudes as Scofield had shown. But Pettingill makes another interesting comment about the relevance of the Sermon on the Mount.
He states that the Sermon is of great value, and one reason for its
value is that we who are now members of Christ's body, the Church,
are destined to reign with Christ over the Kingdom. "Therefore we
ought to have lively interest in the Laws of the Kingdom" [Simple
Studies, p 59]. Chafer says that a secondary application of the

Sermon on the Mount to the Church means that lessons and principles may be drawn from it. He immediately qualifies this statement by saying that as a rule of life, the Sermon on the Mount is addressed to the Jew before the cross and to the Jew in the coming Kingdom, and is therefore not now in effect [Systematic Theology, p 97].

Charles C. Ryrie, in a spirited defense of dispensationalism against its opponents, maintains that the dispensationalist does recognize the relevance and application of the teachings of the Sermon to believers today regardless of how much nondispensationalists want to make him say otherwise. But the primary fulfillment of the Sermon and the full following of its laws are applicable to the Messianic Kingdom. This position, Ryrie feels, is in keeping with other conservatives' interpretation of Scripture. He says further that the dispensationalist in no way disregards the importance of the ethical teachings of the Sermon for today, and it gives proper recognition to the ultimate purpose of the Sermon [Dispensationalism Today, pp 107-8].

Ryrie concludes his Sermon on the Mount apology as follows:

> Thus the dispensational interpretation of the Sermon on the Mount simply tries to follow consistently the principle of literal, normal, or plain interpretation. It results in not trying to relegate primarily and fully the teachings of the Sermon to the believer in this age. But it does not in the least disregard the ethical principles of the Sermon as being not only applicable but also binding on believers today [p 109].

The dispensational interpretation of the Sermon on the Mount has produced lively debate in fundamentalist, evangelical, and liberal circles. Whether Ryrie's judgment, expressed above is an acceptable conclusion, will doubtless provide "ammunition for subsequent campaigns."

17 CARL STANGE

Carl Stange (1870-1959) was educated at the universities of Halle, Göttingen, and Leipzig. He was a professor of systematic theology at the universities of Königsberg, Greifswald, and Göttingen. As an interpreter of Luther, Stange emphasized the theocentric character of his thought in opposition to the ethical idealism of the Ritschlians. He also made significant contributions to the discussion of philosophy, ethics, and dogmatics.

Stange's interpretation of the Sermon on the Mount appears in a lengthy essay entitled "Zur Ethik der Bergpredigt" which was published in volume 2 of Zeitschrift für systematische Theologie in 1924 (page references are to this essay). He states that the Sermon

sets forth the ethical ideal of Jesus. Stange manifests a close affinity with Wilhelm Herrmann in his emphasis upon the inner intention (Gesinnung) instead of the outward act. This was the basic
difference between Jesus and the Pharisees because they believed
that the exact observance of the Law was the way to perfection,
while Jesus held that the observance of the Law was worthless if
it did not represent the fruit of the intention (pp 38-40). Kant's
concept of the good will is in keeping with the intention of the Sermon on the Mount. Our moral consciousness shows us a value
which transcends all the values--the absolute value of the good intention (p 41). Thus the ethic of Jesus and the Sermon on the
Mount is a Gesinnungsethik--an ethic of the good Gesinnung.

The Pharisaical ethical system found a more widespread expression in the medieval church with its veneration of saints, its
monasticism, its sacramentalism, and its indulgences. Stange proceeds to analyse and criticize the Catholic "double standard" view
with its precepts and evangelical counsels. The problem with Catholicism was that though it rightly recognized that the commands
of Jesus were impossible for men to keep, it held that a select
group could obtain special merit through their fulfillment. But in
this view they ran counter to the spirit of the Sermon on the Mount
(pp 44-8).

A second, but equally false, interpretation of the Sermon on
the Mount is Tolstoy's. For him the real problem was, How can
we make the culture Christian? How can we attain a Christian society? How can we reform the culture in keeping with the guidelines of the Sermon on the Mount? But, according to Stange, this
is not the problem of Jesus. While Tolstoy had a widespread influence upon his time and while he served to sharpen men's consciences,
his failure was that he concentrated on the outward fulfilling of Jesus' demands. In this he was in the same sphere as Catholicism.
Tolstoy was right that the Sermon on the Mount applied to all men,
rather than to a select few. But he erred in believing that everyone could fulfill the commands of Jesus. In this respect the Catholic
Church had a much deeper insight than Tolstoy because it held that
the mass could not keep the demands of the Sermon on the Mount.
Tolstoy displayed a childlike optimism in believing that man by himself could do the good if he only knew it (pp 48-56).

The optimistic ethical idealism which followed the tradition of
Kant declared: You can because you ought. But Stange says that
the essence of the moral problem is not the ideal of action but the
conversion of the will. Man's destiny is determined not by the political and economic spheres, but by the transformation of the will.
The ethical demand does not give one the strength to do good, but
it shows us our inability to do the good. Consequently the formula:
You can because you ought, must be replaced by another: You
ought, but you cannot (pp 56-9).

For Stange the purpose of the Sermon on the Mount is to make

one conscious of his sin and his inability to do the good. It is not
the concept of the ideal which is at the center of the Christian ethic,
but the idea of sin, conversion, and confession. The humanistic
ethic is the ethic of the ideal while the Christian ethic is the ethic
of the consciousness of sin (p 63). The ethic of Jesus heightens
one's ethical self-comprehension. Consequently, it leads from imperative to judgment, from ideal to penitence (p 64). Therefore the
transformation of the will and of the intention is brought to the center of the ethical discussion. So the last word of moral consciousness is consciousness of our sins. It is at this point that we discern the sharpest cleavage between Jesus' ethic and ethical idealism
(p 67).

But consciousness of sin points beyond judgment and penitence
to consciousness of, and communion with, God. Wherever consciousness of sin is awakened, there faith in God is alive. When
we reach the highest degree of ethical understanding, we come to a
consciousness of God. The ethical life process leads to communion
with God (p 69).

For Stange the solution to the problem posed by the Sermon
on the Mount is Christological. Jesus' preaching about penitence
is integrally related to his messianic consciousness. He has a communion with God that he makes possible for us. Fellowship with
God is grounded in the presence of Jesus, and this is the prelimin-
ary condition which makes the fulfillment of his commands a possibility (pp 70-1). The fundamental character of Jesus' proclamation
was not ethics, but his reference to God (p 73). It is through the
life of God that we find the realization of the good. The way to the
good is for man the way to God (p 74).

The ethics of Jesus arises from his God consciousness.
Therefore one understands Jesus' ethic only when he considers the
God consciousness above the ethical consciousness. Only in setting
the God consciousness over the ethical consciousness does the
moral life attain its completion (p 74).

Stange's interpretation of the Sermon on the Mount has been
criticized by Hans Windisch because it is a "purely theological solution" which neglects questions of form and origin. Windisch is
more in sympathy with Tolstoy because he believes that Tolstoy's
insistence upon the literal fulfillment of Jesus' commands represents
a return to the original meaning of the teaching. While Stange offers an attractive theological interpretation of the Sermon on the
Mount, Windisch questions whether it reflects the Sermon's actual
intention. One positive observation which Windisch makes is that
Stange seeks a solution to the problem raised by the ethics of the
Sermon on the Mount within the Sermon itself [The Meaning of the
Sermon on the Mount, tr S. MacLean Gilmour (Philadelphia: Westminster Pr, 1951), pp 61, 118, 59].

Kaarle S. Laurila summarizes Stange's position as one which

maintains that the demands of the Sermon on the Mount are unreal-
izeable by natural man. The Sermon convincingly shows us that we
are incapable of following Jesus' commands apart from a total conversion of the will or a new birth which is accomplished by God
through the Holy Spirit. "In this sense," Laurila says, "is the way
of men to the good the way to God." This, however, still does not
deal adequately with practical implications of the Sermon on the
Mount.

Laurila feels that Stange's answer to the dilemma raised by
the Sermon is that we must have the intention in every circumstance to act in accordance with the demands of Jesus, insofar as
this is possible in this imperfect, evil world. But it appears to
Laurila that this is the same answer that has been given before and
that Stange does not adequately resolve the issue [Leo Tolstoi und
Martin Luther als Ausleger der Bergpredigt (Helsinki: Suomalainen
Tiedeakatemia, 1944), p 92].

18 GERHARD KITTEL

Gerhard Kittel (1888-1948) was a professor of New Testament
at Kiel, Leipzig, Greifsward, Tübingen, and Vienna. He concentrated on the Jewish background of the New Testament and concluded
that the Jewish element prevailed over the Hellenistic in the composition of the New Testament books. He is perhaps best known as
the editor of the voluminous and monumental Theologische Worter-
buch zum Neuen Testament (1933-).

In his interpretation of the Sermon on the Mount, Kittel stands
close to Stange and they are often mentioned together. His essay
"Die Bergpredigt und die Ethik des Judentums" appeared in 1925 in
Zeitschrift für systematische Theologie, volume 2 (page references
are to this essay). With slight revision, this essay was incorporated in Die Probleme des palästinischen Spätjudentums und das
Urchristentum (1926).

As the title of Kittel's essay suggests, he explores the relationship between the Sermon on the Mount and the ethics of Judaism.
He is convinced that the ethics of Jesus have their roots in Judaism
and Old Testament piety. Kittel proposes the thesis that there is
not a single one of Jesus' ethical teachings of which it could be
said, a priori, that it has any claim, as an individual precept, to
absolute originality (p 577). The basic difference between Jesus and
the rabbis is not in the novelty of the former's demands, but in the
absolute intensity of Jesus' ethics and in his concentration upon the
religious dimensions of morality in contradistinction to ritualism and
an ethic tied to nationalism. The demand of Jesus is an absolute
one. What he commands, he does so unqualifiedly (pp 579-82).
The Sermon on the Mount with its absolute demands, has significance not because it provides us with a practical program for the
ideal development of mankind. Rather it belongs to the very essence

of its demand that men do not fulfill it, and cannot fulfill it, as
long as they live as sinful men in a sinful world. It is no accident
that the Beatitudes were placed at the beginning of the Sermon. The
demand that follows was not to be fulfilled in all its detail by men
who prided themselves on their human achievement but by the poor
in spirit, those who hunger and thirst after righteousness (pp 583-4).

How shall one understand the Sermon on the Mount with its
"absurd, paradoxical, and exaggerated demand?" Kittel suggests
that it originates in the self-consciousness of Jesus and by his mission. Moreover, it is the rule of God. This accounts for its absoluteness and uncompromising character (pp 584-5).

Kittel criticizes those who in the last 150 years separated the
teaching of Jesus from his person. If Christianity is reduced to the
ethical maxims of the Sermon on the Mount, a paradox will remain
because the "key has been lost" to a resolution of their absurd and
despairing absoluteness. Or if the absolute demands of the Sermon
on the Mount are compromised so that they appear as everyday
morality, one must understand that they are as different from
Jesus' demands as earth and heaven (p 589).

The Sermon on the Mount represents a demand that cannot be
fulfilled. The Torah and every other human law had only one pur-
pose--to be fulfilled and to improve the world. But the purpose of
the Sermon on the Mount is altogether different. It pulls down and
it can only shatter. In a word, its last end and only purpose is to
shatter and lay bare man's great ethical need. But this is not the
final story because the cross of Christ is a correlate to the demand
of Jesus. The Gospel exposes our neediness and sinfulness, but it
also points to the reality of forgiveness and grace. Thus for Kittel, the ultimate fulfillment of the paradox posed by the Sermon on
the Mount is in the authority of Christ (pp 590-1).

Hans Windisch provides a succinct summary of Kittel's approach to the Sermon on the Mount:

> In all this Kittel emphasizes again that the theological prob-
> lem of the imperative of the Sermon on the Mount leads to
> the conviction that ethical idealism has collapsed. In the
> second place, he maintains with great energy that there is
> a connection between the singularity and absoluteness of the
> ethical paradoxes of Jesus and the singularity and absolute-
> ness of his person. In his hands the problem of the Ser-
> mon on the Mount passes over into the Christological prob-
> lem. Finally, he finds the solution, to which the Sermon
> itself points, in the Pauline doctrine of the cross [The Mean-
> ing of the Sermon on the Mount, tr S. MacLean Gilmour
> (Philadelphia: Westminster Pr, 1951), p 61].

19 HORACE MARRIOTT

In his introduction to The Sermon on the Mount Marriott states
that he has endeavored to write a fairly complete treatise on the
Sermon on the Mount which combines critical, exegetical, and expository elements. A large part of the book deals with textual and
source analysis and with parallels and affinities to the Sermon on
the Mount in pre-Christian Jewish literature, and these aspects are
probably Marriott's most significant contributions to Sermon on the
Mount scholarship. Applying the methodology of the "Synoptic Problem" he reconstructs the Greek Q text of the Sermon on the Mount,
and this is a unique feature of his study.

In examining the place of the Sermon on the Mount in the
teaching of Jesus, Marriott sees a number of limitations in the Sermon. It presents a very partial expression of his teaching. The
claim that the Sermon on the Mount expresses the substance of
Jesus' teaching, or at least of all his ethical teaching, is far from
the truth. There is a dearth of doctrine in the Sermon as there
are no predictions of the Passion and Resurrection, no teaching
about Christ's relation to the forgiveness of sin, no trinitarian understanding of the relationship between Father and Son, no teaching
about the Holy Spirit, the Church, or the Sacraments. As for eschatology, there is no explicit announcement of Christ's second coming,
nothing about signs which precede it, or the duty of being watchful
in view of its approach, and there is silence as to a catastrophic
coming of the Kingdom. In the area of ethics, Marriott finds that
there is no teaching on love to God or on love to Christ, no reference to voluntary self-sacrifice for others, nothing about Sabbath observance and the traditions of the Jews. Marriott concludes that
the Sermon on the Mount is clearly neither a doctrinal nor an eschatological discourse. While it does not cover the whole field of Jesus' teaching, it is preeminently ethical in character [The Sermon
on the Mount (London: Society for Promoting Christian Knowledge,
1925), pp 206-9; page references are to this work].

As seen above, Marriott regards the eschatological influence
upon the Sermon on the Mount as minimal. In reaction against the
Interim Ethic concept, Marriott writes:

> That eschatology should enter into his teaching was inevitable,
> for it is inseparable from religious ethics. But to maintain
> that it was the center of gravity of his whole message, and
> that ethics were only subsidiary and incidental, is to traverse
> the plain testimony of the Gospel records [p 237].

His minimizing of eschatology is further substantiated by the claim
that the Sermon on the Mount is essentially representative of Jesus'
earlier teaching and that there is ground for thinking that eschatology entered less into Jesus' thought than at a later time. Marriott says that it is hardly without significance that the Gospels assign a great ethical discourse to the earlier part of his ministry,

and a great eschatological discourse (Mark 13) to the closing days
of his earthly life (pp 223, 238-9).

In reference to Jesus' absolute commands regarding oaths and
nonresistance, Marriott observes that the general tenor of Christ's
teaching is to enunciate broad principles of conduct and to leave it
to men to determine for themselves the precise application of those
principles to particular cases. Thus it would be out of harmony
with the general character of Jesus' teachings if we accepted these
precepts as precise and binding rules. Marriott concludes that
Jesus did not intend these startling injunctions to be taken as universally binding rules. This does not mean that under no circumstances will we act in literal accord with them, but only that we
need not feel under obligation to do so (p 254).

In his concluding section Marriott deals with the relevance of
the Sermon on the Mount to contemporary social problems. He
lists such areas as war, the divorce of ethics from religion, external good behavior and conformity to conventional standards in
contrast to inward integrity, an optimistic view of man's progress,
international relations, race, Christian union. The general spirit
of the age is too worldly and materialistic to constitute a complete
and satisfying ideal. Consequently, the Sermon on the Mount contains a relevant message for this age because it provides the corrective of its errors, the redress of its imperfect and inadequate
aims and ideals, and the true and only way along which it can proceed towards a solution of its many and great problems (pp 261-6).

20 HANS WINDISCH

Without question one of the most important and thorough twentieth-century studies of the Sermon on the Mount is Hans Windisch's
Der Sinn der Bergpredigt which was first published in 1929 as volume 16 of a series called "Untersuchungen zum Neuen Testament,"
of which Windisch himself was editor. A second edition appeared
in 1937. The English translation by S. MacLean Gilmour is from
the second German edition and is entitled The Meaning of the Sermon on the Mount [Philadelphia: Westminster Pr, 1951; page references are to this work].

Windisch begins by analyzing two post-World War I trends in
German New Testament scholarship. One resorts to historical criticism and tries as much as possible to free itself from all dogmatic and all modernizing theological influences. The other view
attempts to produce a "theology," a synthesis of history and theology, of history and metaphysics, or of history and philosophy of
history (p 17). Windisch proposes that these two areas must be
delineated and that one must learn to distinguish between historical
and theological exegesis and to make clear where the one ends and
the other begins. For Windisch the methodology of the historical
interpreter is basic and primary. Therefore, he states the purpose

of his book as follows: "The purpose of what follows is to show,
with reference to an especially important document of the New Testament, the Sermon on the Mount, what historical and critical exegesis, has taught us to see" (pp 18-9).

   In the first chapter Windisch deals with the relationship of the
Sermon on the Mount to eschatology. Two facts emerge with respect to the problem of eschatology. First, the Sermon on the
Mount, like all the speeches in Matthew, is conditioned by eschatological expectation. But secondly, the Evangelist has forced a
good deal of material into this framework that originally was entirely unaffected by eschatological beliefs. The Sermon on the
Mount is conditioned in its entirety by eschatology. It is eschatological legislation, but it is also radically religious legislation.
Consequently, such designations as "interim ethic" and "exceptional
legislation" are inadequate. "The radicalism of the Sermon on the
Mount is not dependent on the imminence of the final revelation, or
on the accidental brevity of the interim, but on the essential circumstance that the event for which one must prepare is the rule of
God; that the summons comes from God who now, by the mouth of
Jesus, demands something utter and absolute" (p 29).

   Thus Windisch is not a "consistent eschatologist," for though
eschatology is a primary foundation of the Sermon on the Mount
there are parts which are non-eschatological. Among these are:
the sayings about the salt and the light; the logion about sacrifice
in Matt. 5:23f; the saying about spiritual adultery; the prohibitions
of divorce, of oaths, and of revenge; the command to love one's
enemies; the saying about the eye; the logion about two masters; the
saying about the mote and the beam; the assurance that prayer will
be heard; and the Golden Rule (p 30). This leaves the following
passages which are dominated by eschatology: the Beatitudes; the
sayings concerning the Kingdom in Matt. 5:19-20; the second saying
with reference to reconciliation in verses 25f (if it is to be understood as an eschatological parable); the sayings about hindrances in
verses 29f; the Lord's Prayer; the logion about storing up riches;
the saying about passing judgment in chapter 7:1f; the pericope of
the two ways in verses 13f; the warning about the Final Judgment
in verses 21-23; and the concluding parables (p 37).

   The relationship between the eschatological and the non-eschatological elements in the Sermon on the Mount can be understood as
two currents of the Synoptic proclamation brought together by Jesus.
One current is purified and radicalized wisdom teaching; the other
is the prophetic-eschatological proclamation of salvation and judgment. Windisch concludes: "It is characteristic of the Sermon on
the Mount that its radicalisms are fed from both streams; but in the
main they issue from the religious wisdom of Jesus. Both the wisdom and the eschatology in Jesus' teaching are heightened to radical
demand, and this fact is one of the most important in accounting for
the combination of these two forms of proclamation that originally
were essentially foreign to one another" (p 40).

In chapter II Windisch turns to the meaning of the commandments and the problem of their probability and comes to his main
thesis. He begins by discussing modern interpretations of the Sermon on the Mount. Among them are Wilhelm Herrmann, Martin
Dibelius, Rudolf Bultmann, each of whom have "modernized" the
teachings of Jesus by viewing them through Kantian and eschatological lenses. Of these tendencies Windisch writes: "We can sum-
marize the essence of this whole approach as follows: It always
presupposes a spiritual orientation that, from the very outset, determines the judgment that is passed on the gospel sayings" (p 55).

But there is another solution which is equally erroneous--the
Paulinizing or dogmatic. Carl Stange and Gerhard Kittel are the
two exponents of this position. For Stange the purpose of the Sermon on the Mount is to compel the hearer to pass a judgment of
condemnation upon himself. The Sermon on the Mount leads from
imperative to judgment, from ideal to penitence. For Kittel the
Sermon exposes man's moral dilemma and throws him into despair.
The situation opens the way for a Christological solution. The
cross of Christ is a correlate to the Sermon's demands. Kittel's
solution is in the Pauline doctrine of the cross. Windisch says that
both Stange and Kittel seek to provide a purely theological solution
to the problem of the Sermon on the Mount. Their interpretation
rests upon two theological axioms: the demands of the Sermon on
the Mount are an adequate representation of the will of God and
therefore are absolutely obligatory; and we cannot fulfill them. A
solution is to be found only by means of divine intervention. In the
one instance this saving revelation is said to be contained within
the Sermon itself; in the other, it has to be discovered elsewhere
in the New Testament (p 61).

Having exposed the inadequacies of these idealistic and theological interpretations, Windisch is now ready to set forth the results of historical exegesis. The essence of his view is that the
Sermon on the Mount is essentially a collection of commandments
and that these are practicable in the sense that Jesus expected them
to be obeyed as a condition of salvation. The commands have an
immediate, practical purpose and they are to be followed if the disciple relationship is to be maintained. The Sermon on the Mount is
an explication of the will of God as it applies to us. The Evangelist wants to portray Jesus as a new lawgiver who intends to both
fulfill the Mosaic Law and to improve upon it. Windisch says that
we begin by establishing the fact that any radical and consistent rejection of "legalism" is foreign to the extant sayings of Jesus. By
"legalism" he understands a doctrine of the relation of the religious
man to his God that is determined largely by commandment and by
obedience to commandment (p 73). The teaching of Jesus in Matt.
5 is not an ethic of repentance, as Stange held, not is it to be understood as Jesus' bringing a new attitude but not a new law. This
antithesis is false because these imperatives are to be understood
as commandments whose practicability is everywhere assumed
though occasionally the difficulty of carrying out a given command
may be stressed.

In light of these results, Windisch sees a clear picture of the
social ethic of the Sermon on the Mount and indeed the whole ethical
teaching that Jesus had in mind. It has no political reference whatever although it can have political and social implications. It is related to a man's neighbor, brother, enemy, and judge, but not to his
fellow countryman, fellow citizen, superior, employer, or governor.
It is individualistic in the sense that it envisions encounters of man
with man. Community, economic, and national organization, and
the ethical relationships therein entailed, are not considered in the
Sermon on the Mount or elsewhere in Jesus' ethical teaching. The
entire social ethic of the Sermon on the Mount is articulated in individual sayings that are to be understood literally and interpreted
literally (pp 122-3).

In his third chapter, "Christ and His Attitude to Judaism in
the Sermon on the Mount," Windisch makes some observations about
the Christology of the Sermon on the Mount. He believes that Jesus
lays claim to four Christological prerogatives: (1) the authoritative
interpreter of the Law; (2) a new legislator; (3) a prophet, though in
the main only one who renews and makes more compelling the message of his predecessors; (4) the future judge of the world (p 126).
Thus the Christ of the Sermon on the Mount presents himself as an
expositor of the Law, legislator, prophet, future world judge, and
Lord of the new religious community. But beyond these specifically
Messianic functions, the Christology of the Sermon on the Mount
does not go. The doctrine of salvation set forth in the Sermon is
pre-Christian and pre-Pauline. Windisch thinks it can perhaps best
be described as "liberal Jewish Christian" (p 130). Windisch can
find no basis in the Sermon on the Mount for Christ the redeemer.
However, he says that the basis for the Pauline-Johannine Christology can be found there in germinal form. The Messianic view of
Jesus in the Sermon on the Mount was one of his authority as teacher, as prophet, and his prospective authority as world judge. Such
a vision led to the formation of the church and also fomented opposition to the synagogue and its authorities (pp 138-9).

After further discussing the relationship between Jesus and
Judaism, Windisch states that the Sermon on the Mount, despite its
pre-Pauline character, is a manifesto of the Christian Messiah in
which the gulf between the Christian community and the orthodox
synagogue is already evident. One can see the cross looming in
the background of the Sermon, not the cross as a symbol of God's
saving grace (this has no relationship to the Sermon on the Mount),
but the cross as a symbol of the verdict that Sadducean and Pharisaic Judaism had to reach with regard to Jesus. He had under-
mined the Torah and repudiated the Halakah. He showed no respect
for the authority of the rabbis and even seemed to place himself
above Moses. The claim of such a man to be Messiah had to be
branded as false and blasphemous, and he himself had to be crucified and exterminated as a deceiver and as a danger to the people
(p 152).

Thus, contrary to Stange and Kittel, Windisch presents the

view that Christ the redeemer and the Pauline view of salvation are
absent from the Sermon on the Mount. Moreover, one finds no trace
in the Sermon of the resurrection and exaltation of Christ and of the
energizing power of the Spirit which were the foundation stones upon
which the disciples built the new religious community.

In his final chapter Windisch proposes a theological exegesis of
the Sermon on the Mount and in so doing he covers many of the
themes in the previous sections. He emphasizes again his main thesis that the Sermon on the Mount consists of commands which are to
be obeyed. Windisch describes Tolstoy and many Baptists as representatives of these who regard the Sermon as a binding authority.
They cannot simply be dismissed as "fanatics" or "sectarians." In
one of the most forceful defenses of his thesis, Windisch writes:

> If this is what they are, then Jesus himself was a fanatic
> and the founder of a sect. The unmistakable conclusion of
> our exegesis is that such people have correctly understood
> the Sermon on the Mount. The Sermon intends to proclaim
> commands. It presents demands that are to be literally un-
> derstood and literally fulfilled. Polemic against 'fanatics' is
> to a large extent polemic against the Sermon on the Mount
> and criticism of Jesus himself [p 172].

Though Windisch sets forth a theology of the Sermon on the
Mount, his real affinity is with "historical criticism." He concludes his book with a comparison of the respective methodologies
of theological and historical criticism. Theological exegesis seeks
to discover the "permanent value" of Scripture, the meaning of
Scripture for our time. But it is subject to frequent changes because of the changing intellectual and spiritual climate. Moreover,
it is also unstable because the tradition it works with is not uniform or unequivocal. Therefore theological exegesis is always relative and partial. Consequently, in reference to the Sermon on the
Mount, historical exegesis must precede, parallel, and stand over
against all theological interpretations. The task of historical exegesis is to transcend change and flux and to reach back into the
past, the static, and the fixed. It is clear that for Windisch historical exegesis must serve as the corrective of every attempt to
extract a theology from, or impose a theology upon, the Sermon on
the Mount. That is, historical exegesis must oppose all dogmatizing
and modernizing reinterpretations of the Sermon on the Mount. Windisch's concluding sentence leaves no doubt where his real interest
lies. "That is the function of historical exegesis, and it only can
truly explain the meaning of the Sermon on the Mount" (p 213).

Windisch's interpretation of the Sermon on the Mount is open
to a number of objections. Does he not detach and isolate the Sermon on the Mount too much from the rest of the Synoptics and the
New Testament? Isn't his distinction between historical and theological exegesis too sharp and artificial? Does he claim for historical exegesis an "objectivity" which is unwarranted and even im-

possible? However, in spite of these and other criticisms, Windisch has dealt in a forthright and scholarly manner with most of the fundamental problems related to the Sermon on the Mount. His work will continue to be one of the outstanding landmarks on the terrain of Sermon on the Mount interpretation.

21 AN IMPOSSIBLE POSSIBILITY

Among the "theological giants" of the twentieth century, Reinhold Niebuhr stands with the tallest. Probably no other American theologian has had so profound an impact upon his time as has Niebuhr. His work on theological anthropology is among the most penetrating and insightful in Christian history. His many writings on the relationship between Christian theology and politics have extended his influence far beyond the Christian community. He is acknowledged to be not only a great theologian but also a renowned political theorist and philosopher of history.

Niebuhr, however, never constructed a "system" of theology. His theological methodology can perhaps best be described as dialogical. Theological reflection was not an ivory tower discipline, but evolved out of the context of polemical encounter with his opponents. Theology was a response to the "heresy" of "the liberal culture of modernity, " of pacifism, of secular idealism, of utopianism, etc.

In 1932 Niebuhr's epochal Moral Man and Immoral Society [NY: Scribner's, 1932] was published. This work left a profound impact upon American theology, comparable to Barth's Der Römerbrief upon Continental theology. It was concerned with the problem of power, and its most basic contention was that a sharp distinction must be drawn between the moral and social behavior of individuals and of social groups, national, racial, and economic; and that this distinction justifies and necessitates political policies which a purely individualistic ethic must always find embarrassing [Moral Man, p xi]. It may be possible to establish just relations between individuals by moral and rational suasion and accommodation, but in inter-group relations this is virtually impossible. Relations among groups must always be predominantly political rather than ethical. While unselfishness is the highest moral ideal of the individual, the highest moral ideal of society is justice. Societies must strive for justice even though they must use resistance and coercion. Such means will offend the sensitive moral spirit, and while these two moral perspectives are not mutually exclusive, and the contradiction between them is not absolute, they are not easily harmonized.

Thus there is a conflict between religious and political morality. The religious ideal expressed in its purest form, as in the Sermon on the Mount, has nothing to do with the problem of social justice. It makes disinterestedness an absolute ideal without reference to social consequences.   "Pure religious idealism does not concern itself

with the social problem"; "Nothing is clearer," Niebuhr writes, "than
that a pure religious idealism must issue in a policy of nonresistance
which makes no claims to be socially efficacious. It submits to any
demands, however unjust, and yields to any claims, however inordi-
nate, rather than assert self-interest against another" [Moral Man,
pp 263, 264]. Such a course, Niebuhr insists, must always result
in policies which, from the political perspective, are quite impossible. One can easily appreciate the shockwaves Niebuhr's Moral Man
and Immoral Society produced in "the liberal culture of modernity,"
for he undercut some of its most cherished ideals and long-held presuppositions.

        Niebuhr levelled some of his sharpest polemic against pacifism.
He made a distinction between the classical, non-political Anabaptist
position and modern pacifism which advocated the renunciation of
force in the relations between nations. The former kept before the
Christian community the ultimate norm of an impossible ideal without claiming that it could be a political strategy. The latter, however, tended to make the gospel of nonviolence a substitute for the
New Testament position of nonresistance. Pacifism was another indication of the political irrelevance of Christian liberalism. Paci-
fists with their desire for purity of ideals and their distaste for the
requirements of justice in a morally ambiguous world, evaded the
messiness of politics and contracted out of history.

        In 1935 An Interpretation of Christian Ethics, which was orig-
inally presented as the Rauschenbusch Memorial Lectures in the
Colgate-Rochester Divinity School, was published [NY: Harper]. Niebuhr's essential concern in this work is how one relates the radical
ethic of agape to viable norms of ethical discrimination in the historical order. Many of the same themes in Moral Man and Immoral
Society recur, but Niebuhr now begins to move more in the direction
of a theological anthropology which culminated in his magnum opus,
The Nature and Destiny of Man.

        The ethic of Jesus as set forth in the Sermon on the Mount
does not deal with the immediate moral problem of every human
life--the problem of arranging some kind of armistice between various contending factions and forces. Nor does it have anything to
say about the relativities of politics and economics and the necessary balances of power which exist and must exist in even the most
intimate social relationships. The absolute perfectionism of Jesus'
ethic sets itself uncompromisingly not only against the natural self-
regarding impulses, but against the necessary prudent defenses of
the self, required because of the egoism of others. "It does not
establish a connection with the horizontal points of a political or
social ethic or with the diagonals which a prudential individual ethic
draws between the moral ideal and the facts of a given situation.
It has only a vertical dimension between the loving will of God and
the will of man" [An Interpretation, p 39]. Or as Niebuhr says
elsewhere: "The injunctions 'resist not evil,' 'love your enemies,'
'if ye love them that love you what thanks have you?' 'be not anx-

ious for your life, ' and 'be ye therefore perfect even as your Father
in heaven is perfect, ' are all of one piece and they are all uncompromising and absolute" [Christianity and Power Politics (NY: Scribner's, 1940), p 8].

Jesus' ethic is not, however, an "interim ethic, " but there is
an eschatological element in it and basis for it. The ethical demands made by Jesus cannot be fulfilled in man's present existence.
Their final fulfillment is possible only when God transmutes the
present chaos of this world into its final unity [An Interpretation,
pp 55-6].

An Interpretation of Christian Ethics contains the famous chapter, "The Relevance of an Impossible Ethical Ideal. " The love
commandment which is the essence of Jesus' ethic is not a simple
possibility but an impossible possibility. The ethic of agape is impossible to fulfill in our historical existence. It is revealed and il-
lumined through Christ and the Cross. "Christ is the revelation of
the very impossible possibility which the Sermon on the Mount elaborates in ethical terms" (p 120). Christ surpasses the limit of
man's moral possibilities and this can reduce man to despair. But
the paradox is that Christ is both our hope and our despair. Christ
and the Cross reveal not only the possibilities but the limits of human finitude. Consequently, repentance becomes the gateway into
the Kingdom of God for those who no longer place their confidence
in purely human possibilities. "It is out of such despair, 'the godly
sorrow which worketh repentance, ' that faith arises" (p 121).

It is in this context that we discern "the relevance of an impossible ethical ideal. " While the law of love and the Sermon on
the Mount are impossibilities, nevertheless, they offer immediate
possibilities of a higher good in every given situation. An impossible ethic always presents us with an ultimate norm that transcends
the range of possible achievements. But such a norm also makes
possible the kind of searching criticism of both intention and action
that provides the impetus for the highest moral creativity. [For
an admirable treatment of Niebuhr's thought in a primarily biblio-
graphic work, see Nathan A. Scott, Jr., Reinhold Niebuhr (Minneapolis: Univ of Minnesota Pr, 1963).]

22   C. H. DODD

For the distinguished New Testament scholar, C. H. Dodd,
there are two concepts which are central in the interpretation of
New Testament ethics. One is "realized eschatology"--the idea
that with the coming of Jesus the Kingdom of God was realized.
Jesus spoke about the presence of the Kingdom in such terms as
"The Kingdom of God has come upon you." The other concept is
the "kerygma"--the existence of a primitive and constant element in
the New Testament presentation of Christianity consisting of the
saving acts of God in history, particularly in the death and resurrection of Christ.

The ethical teaching (didaché) of the New Testament is embedded in the context of the kerygma which consists of a report of historical facts and an explanation of their religious significance. Dodd discerns a pattern in the New Testament regarding the relationship between kerygma and didaché. Those who responded to the proclamation became members of the community, the Church. They were then instructed in the ethical principles and obligations of the Christian life. Thus the order of approach was first proclamation and then moral instruction, first kerygma, then didaché [Dodd, Gospel and Law (NY: Columbia Univ Pr, 1951), pp 8-24; for detailed analysis of the kerygmatic content, see Dodd, The Apostolic Preaching and Its Developments (Chicago: Willett, Clark, 1937), pp 1-49].

The Sermon on the Mount represents the most detailed compilation of didaché and consists of moral maxims drawn from the teaching of Jesus for the guidance of Christians. It is not a sermon at all, but "a highly articulated and systematic presentation of the main features of the Christian ethical system" [Gospel and Law, p 6]. Dodd thinks that the structure of the Matthaean version of the Sermon on the Mount may have been influenced at some stage by a form of catechetical instruction, if it is not based directly upon it. In the Lucan version, however, traces of the catechetical scheme are much more difficult to discern [Dodd, More New Testament Studies (Manchester: Manchester Univ Pr, 1968), pp 17-8].

The ethical teaching of the early Church was set in the context of the kerygma. This resulted in a transformation of the ethical ideas because they were defined by the Gospel as it was contained in the kerygma. Dodd suggests that there are four points where the Christian ethic of the New Testament betrays such direct dependence upon the Gospel. One of these is Christian eschatology which was an essential element in the Gospel as it was contained in the primitive kerygma. Its essence is found in Mark's succinct summary, "The time is fulfilled, and the Kingdom of God is upon you" (Mark 1:15). "The gospel of primitive Christianity is a gospel of realized eschatology" [Apostolic Preaching, p 147].

This belief influenced the ethical ideas of early Christianity in two ways. First, the note of impending catastrophe was strong; and since the world seemed temporary, only values which were abiding were worthy of attention. Such a mood resulted in a moral earnestness and a sober sense of responsibility. It enabled one to contemplate the ultimate ethical demand as the absolute claim of God.

Secondly, as the expectation of an immediate end of the world faded under the impact of facts, the church came to a new appreciation of what had already happened. The great expectation was already realized, and because of what Christ had done and what he had suffered, the heights and depths of human nature were laid bare [Gospel and Law, pp 25-32].

The Sermon on the Mount and the teachings of Jesus must
therefore be understood in relation to the kerygma, and a central
element of the kerygma is the proclamation that "The Kingdom of
God has come upon you"--that the Eschaton has been realized. In
The Parables of the Kingdom [NY: Scribner's, 1961] Dodd defines
realized eschatology as follows: "Here then is the fixed point from
which our interpretation of the teaching regarding the Kingdom of
God must start. It represents the ministry of Jesus as 'realized
eschatology,' that is to say, as the impact upon this world of the
'powers of the world to come' in a series of events, unprecedented
and unrepeatable, now in actual process" (p 35). A further elabora-
tion of the relation of Jesus' ethics to the Kingdom of God is seen
in History and the Gospel. Dodd says that Jesus' ethical teaching
is no system of general casuistry, nor yet an "interim ethic" for a
brief and special period in history. He continues:

> It is the absolute ethic of the Kingdom of God, the moral
> principles of a new order of life. The implied major prem-
> ise of all his ethical sayings is the affirmation 'The Kingdom
> of God has come upon you:'--The Kingdom of God has come
> upon you, therefore love your enemies that you may be sons
> of your Father in heaven.... The Kingdom of God has come
> upon you, therefore take no thought for your life, but seek
> first his Kingdom. The Kingdom of God has come upon you,
> therefore judge not, for with what judgment ye judge, ye
> shall be judged, in the judgment which is inseparable from
> the coming of God in his Kingdom. The teaching of Jesus
> is not an ethic for those who expect the speedy end of the
> world, but for those who have experienced the end of this
> world and the coming of the Kingdom of God [History and the
> Gospel (NY: Scribner's, 1938), p 125].

In an essay, "The Ethics of the New Testament" [in Moral Principles of Action, ed Ruth Nanda Anshen (NY: Harper, 1952)], Dodd
says (p 553) that the total teaching of Jesus is primarily concerned
with one theme: "The Kingdom of God is at hand;" "The Kingdom
of God has come upon you" (Mark 1:15, Matt. 12:28, Luke 10:9).

While Dodd's chief emphasis is upon realized eschatology, he
does not question Jesus' use of apocalyptic language. He says that
there remains a certain tension in Jesus' teaching between "other
worldliness" and "this worldliness." This is represented by the apparent contradiction between the prayer, "Thy Kingdom come," and
the declaration, "The Kingdom of God has come upon you." Furthermore, almost all parts of the New Testament express the tension
between: the Kingdom of God will come; it has come: Christ has
come; Christ will come [The Parables, p 167; Gospel and Law, p
28]. But Jesus used apocalyptic imagery as a series of symbols
standing for realities which the human mind cannot directly appre-
hend. And the fact that history has not yet been consummated leads
men to think and speak in terms of futuristic imagery and categories. There can be little doubt that Dodd stands at the opposite

pole from Schweitzer insofar as their respective understanding of
Jesus' teachings is concerned. Dodd expresses the priority of "realized eschatology" over "consistent eschatology" in this cogent passage: "In the New Testament the apocalyptic symbolism of the Old
recurs freely, but with a profound difference. The divine event is
declared to have happened" [Apostolic Preaching, pp 145-6].

Many interpreters find a definite eschatological element in the
Beatitudes. Dodd acknowledges this also, but it is in the "background." Thus he writes:

> It is true that the blessings assured to the various types all
> have 'eschatological' associations, or, to use language nearer
> to that of the Gospels, are functions of the Kingdom of Hea-
> ven, or of God.... But all would be entirely consistent with
> the idea of a Kingdom which already was present.... Any
> idea of a Kingdom yet to come by way of a catastrophic sud-
> denness is in the background [More New Testament Studies,
> p8].

There remains the question of the relevance of Jesus' teachings, especially those in the Sermon on the Mount. Dodd thinks
that they were intended as a Law. The principal body of Jesus'
ethical sayings found in the Sermon on the Mount is so placed in
Matthew as to suggest a parallel with the promulgation of the Law
of Moses from Mount Sinai. Moreover, the parallelism is further
evidenced by the antitheses between the Old Law and the New in the
Sermon. Dodd believes that Matthew represented Jesus as the King
who promulgates a New Law for his subjects. Consequently, there
is reason to believe that the ethical precepts of Jesus are intended
to constitute a Law. It is also significant that the Sermon on the
Mount ends with a parable which in Dodd's view leaves no doubt
that Jesus' precepts are to be obeyed. Dodd concludes: "It appears, then, that we shall not be far wrong in taking the Sermon
on the Mount as Matthew represented it--namely, as the New Law
which supersedes the Law of the Old Testament--the Law of the
Kingdom of God. That, I believe, is the sense in which any rea-
sonable reader would understand the Sermon upon an unprejudiced
reading of it [Gospel and Law, pp 62-5].

But Jesus' ideal will never be completely realized by men in
this world. Nevertheless, it is clear that it can be realized in
some measure upon every level of human action. Dodd says that
we are not concerned with a precise and limited definition of rules
of behavior, but with "the quality and direction of action which shall
conform with the divine standard." This quality and this direction
may be present from the lowest level of achievement to the most
saintly. But at whatever level, the precepts are obligatory. However, at no level will they ever by completely fulfilled. Therefore,
they will always represent a challenge for us ["Ethics...," in Moral
Principles, ed Anshen, p 558].

In international relations it may be neither possible nor desirable for nations to act like the man who turns the other cheek. But even at this level, human action is wrong unless it partakes of this quality of patient and unselfish respect for the other party, no matter how objectionable the situation. Likewise, the aim must be in the direction of overcoming evil with good. Without this frame of reference, actions are not only wrong but ultimately disastrous. Dodd affirms the universal relevance of Jesus' ethic when he observes: "The Law of Christ, we conclude, is not a specialized code of regulations for a society with optional membership. It is based upon the revelation of the nature of the eternal God, and it affirms the principles upon which His world is built and which men ignore at their peril" [Gospel and Law, p 81].

23 DIETRICH BONHOEFFER

Bonhoeffer's Nachfolge (English version The Cost of Discipleship) is a classic on the meaning and implications of Christian discipleship. Karl Barth, referring especially to the opening sections, said that it is by far the best that has been written on the subject [Eberhard Bethge, Dietrich Bonhoeffer, tr Eric Mosbacher, Peter & Betty Ross, Frank Clarke, Wm Glen-Goepel; ed Edwin Robertson (NY: Harper & Row, 1970), p 372]. Its authority is enhanced by the author's quality of life. For whenever one gives his life for his faith, his words gain the authority of his example.

Nachfolge grew out of lectures which Bonhoeffer gave while directing the seminary at Finkenwalde between 1935 and 1937. It is divided into three sections: Grace and Discipleship; The Sermon on the Mount; and The Church of Jesus Christ and the Life of Discipleship. It is with the second section that we are particularly concerned in this study.

William Kuhns has called Nachfolge Bonhoeffer's angriest book --possibly his one "angry" book [In Pursuit of Dietrich Bonhoeffer (London: Burns & Oates, 1967), p 81]. In order to understand Bonhoeffer's "anger" one must be aware of the German political situation. This was the period of Hitler's rise to absolute power. Persecution of the Jews was raging. Criticism of the regime from any quarter, including the church, was quickly squelched. Church organization, ritual, and theology continued, but the prophetic quality of the faith was wanting. Bonhoeffer was convinced that Germany could be saved only through a genuine return to Christian discipleship and to the Christian faith.

Bonhoeffer's interest in the Sermon on the Mount antedated the publication of Nachfolge by a number of years. Bethge states that there can be no doubt that the book owes its impetus and pungency to a preoccupation with the Sermon on the Mount dating back to a time long before 1935 [Bethge, p 369].

Between 1933 and 1935 Bonhoeffer administered two German pastorates in London. Among his sermons was a series on the Sermon on the Mount. Unfortunately these sermons have not survived, although sixteen of the others preached in London have. In April 1934 Bonhoeffer wrote to E. Sutz:

> Please write and tell me some time what you say when you preach about the Sermon on the Mount. I am working on this now--trying to keep it extremely simple and straightforward, but it always comes back to keeping the commandment and not evading it. Discipleship of Christ--I'd like to know what this is--it is not exhausted in our concept of faith. I am setting to work on something I might describe as an essay--this is a first step [quoted in Bethge, p 376].

As early as 1927 Bonhoeffer expressed interest in Christian communities that could be expressions of discipleship. In 1935 a community, later known as "the House of Brethren," was realized at Finkenwalde. In a letter to his brother, Karl Friedrich, in January 1935, Bonhoeffer wrote:

> I think I am right in saying that I would only achieve true inward clarity and sincerity by really starting work on the Sermon on the Mount. Here alone lies the force that can blow all this stuff and nonsense sky-high, in a fireworks display that will leave nothing behind but one or two charred remains. The restoration of the Church must surely depend on a new kind of monasticism, having nothing in common with the old but a life of uncompromising adherence to the Sermon on the Mount in imitation of Christ. I believe the time has come to rally men together for this [quoted in Bethge, p 380].

Bonhoeffer's interpretation of the Sermon on the Mount differs from most scholarly studies in that there is no recourse to philology, archaeology, and historical criticism. He does not deal with the usual problems raised by criticism of the Gospels such as the composition of the Sermon, eschatology, etc. His interest lay in another direction. His intention was to reassert the validity of "faith alone" and "grace alone" by restoring to them their concreteness in the life of discipleship. Interpreting the Sermon on the Mount can too easily become a substitute for "doing it." Thus Bonhoeffer says: "To deal with the word of Jesus otherwise than by doing it is to wrong him. It is to deny the Sermon on the Mount and to say No to his word. If we start asking questions, posing problems, and offering interpretations, we are not doing his word ..." [The Cost of Discipleship, tr R. H. Fuller (NY: Macmillan, 1949), p 168].

Our task is "to do" the Sermon on the Mount, to relate it to the concrete problems of life. More important than the critical questions are the ones which ask what Christ is asking of us today and what his will is for us today. In Ethics Bonhoeffer writes: "It

is evident that the only appropriate conduct of men before God is
the doing of His will.   The Sermon on the Mount is there for the
purpose of being done (Matt. 7:24ff.).   Only in doing can there be
submission to the will of God" [Ethics, tr Neville H. Smith, ed
Eberhard Bethge (NY: Macmillan, 1955), p 166].

A number of interpreters have dealt with the question of whether The Cost of Discipleship does not depart significantly from Luther's emphasis upon sola fide and sola gratia.   Bethge says that in
1928, when he was in Barcelona, Bonhoeffer had still read the Sermon on the Mount in the traditional Lutheran way, whereby to understand it literally was to make it into a law, and that law was
abolished in Christ.   Bethge notes further that while Bonhoeffer
was in America he had grown less sure of this interpretation, and
in his university seminar of 1932 he had dealt with the relationship
between faith, commandment, and obedience along the lines of The
Cost of Discipleship.   Bethge concludes that Bonhoeffer did not intend to question the complete validity of Luther's soteriology, but
rather to reassert that validity by restoring its concreteness here
on earth (pp 375-6, 372).

William Kuhns believes that Bonhoeffer's insistence on obedience as the ineluctable consequence of faith reached beyond Luther's
dictum sola fide and that Bonhoeffer's theology of obedience is clearly a theology of action.   But Kuhns makes another significant observation: "Obviously, the Church's condition demanded an emphasis of
this kind: only action could save the day, and Bonhoeffer realized
that the traditional Lutheran formulation had generally encouraged
passivity" [In Pursuit, pp 86-7].

Bonhoeffer had received his grounding in Luther from Reinhold
Seeberg and Karl Holl at Berlin.   Both Bethge and Kuhns agree that
he never departed from this tradition, even though he gave it a new
accent.   His "deviation" from Luther must be viewed within the political and ecclesiastical context of the early 1930's in Germany.

In his exposition on the Sermon on the Mount Bonhoeffer is not
formulating a new "works righteousness," but he is uniting moral
exhortation with doctrinal discussion.   No one reading his work on
the Sermon on the Mount can miss its predominant Christological
character.   Moreover, the Christological interpretation of Scripture
was one of the familiar marks of Luther's theology [for discussion
of the Christological character of The Cost of Discipleship, see John
A. Phillips, Christ for Us in the Theology of Dietrich Bonhoeffer
(NY: Harper & Row, 1967), pp 95-105].

Bonhoeffer's Christological interpretation of the Sermon on the
Mount is evident in his exposition of the Beatitudes.   He writes:

> Having reached the end of the Beatitudes, we naturally ask
> if there is any place on this earth for the community which
> they describe.   Clearly, there is one place, and only one,

and that is where the Poorest, Meekest, and most sorely
Tried of all men is to be found--on the cross at Golgotha.
The community which is the subject of the Beatitudes is the
community of the crucified. With him it has lost all, and
with him it has found all. It is the cross which makes the
Beatitudes possible [The Cost of Discipleship, p 97; all references following are to this book].

The section on Matt. 5:17-20 on the Law and its fulfillment is
entitled "The Righteousness of Christ." Bonhoeffer says that between the disciples and the better righteousness demanded of them
stands the Person of Christ who came to fulfill the law of the Old
Covenant. This, says Bonhoeffer, is the fundamental presupposition
of the whole Sermon on the Mount (p 105).

The basic theological orientation of Bonhoeffer's exposition of
the Sermon on the Mount centers around the themes of justification
and sanctification. He is attempting to relate faith to man's historical situation and to see its implications for the Christian life.
One must "follow Jesus" and must be in "fellowship with the Crucified." But this is possible only within the context of grace. It is
the Cross that enables man "to do" the Sermon on the Mount. These
themes recur again and again in Bonhoeffer's "The Sermon on the
Mount."

Let us see further how Bonhoeffer relates the above motifs to
the Sermon on the Mount. Jesus' sayings about oaths reflect his
concern for absolute truthfulness. Our ability to be truthful is only
possible through the power of the cross. Bonhoeffer says:

> It is only because we follow Jesus that we can be genuinely
> truthful, for then he reveals to us our sin upon the cross.
> The cross is God's truth about us, and therefore it is the
> only power which can make us truthful. When we know the
> cross we are no longer afraid of the truth. We need no
> more oaths to confirm the truth of our utterances, for we
> live in the absolute truth of God [p120].

As for Jesus' words about nonresistance, Bonhoeffer says that
the cross is the only justification for this precept, for it alone
makes possible a faith in the victory over evil which will enable
men to obey this command. Likewise, to love one's enemies takes
us along the way of the cross and into fellowship with the Crucified.
The more we walk this road, the more certain we are of the victory of love over the enemy's hatred (pp 125, 129).

Matt. 5 closes with Jesus' demand for perfection as the heavenly Father is perfect. The 6th chapter ends on the note of freedom from anxiety. The followers of Jesus are perfected through
suffering in the fellowship of the cross. The perfect are the blessed
of the Beatitudes. As for freedom from anxiety, only those who
follow Christ and know him personally are delivered from the thrall-
dom of anxiety about material things (pp 135, 153).

It is Bonhoeffer's Christological perspective which resolves the
tension as to whether the precepts of the Sermon on the Mount are
to be taken literally or figuratively. The question of the literal
versus the figurative interpretation cannot be answered. Either way,
we cannot evade the basic issue, i. e., whether we will obey. Jesus
does not impose intolerable restrictions on his disciples. "So far
from imposing on them an intolerable yoke of legalism, he succours
them with the grace of the Gospel" (pp 114-5).

Bonhoeffer's interpretation of the Sermon on the Mount represents a balance and tension between faith and works, gospel and law,
and as such, it is open to challenge and criticism from both ex-
tremes. It must be viewed against the background of the German
church's struggle with Nazism. Consequently, the themes of obedience, following Christ, fellowship with Christ, doing the Sermon on
the Mount, are more predominant than they might have been in
more "normal" times. On the other side, the themes of grace, the
cross, the Gospel, give ample evidence that Bonhoeffer did not follow his eminent, next-door neighbor, Adolf von Harnack, who found
only the "Father" and not the "Son" in the Gospels.

Bonhoeffer's comments on the parable of the builders which
concludes the Sermon on the Mount provides a good summary of his
interpretation.

> Humanly speaking, we could understand and interpret the
> Sermon on the Mount in a thousand different ways. Jesus
> knows only one possibility: simple surrender and obedience,
> not interpreting it or applying it, but doing and obeying it.
> That is the only way to hear his word. But again he does
> not mean that it is to be discussed as an ideal, he means
> really putting it into practice.
>
> ... The only proper response to this word which Jesus brings
> with him from eternity is simply to do it. Jesus has spoken.
> His is the word, ours the obedience. Only in the doing of it
> does the word of Jesus retain its honor, might and power
> among us. Now the storm can rage over the house, but it
> cannot shatter that union with him, which his word has cre-
> ated [p 168].

24 MARTIN DIBELIUS

In addition to Hans Windisch, there is a second notable twentieth-century interpreter of the Sermon on the Mount--Martin Dibelius. In 1937 Dibelius delivered the John C. Shaffer Lectures at
the Yale Divinity School. Returning to Germany, he revised the
manuscript and it was published as The Sermon on the Mount [NY:
Scribner's] in 1940.

Since the Sermon on the Mount is so central for the Christian
way of living and for Christian ethics, it is necessary to get a clear

understanding of it with the aid of theological scholarship. However,
before this can be done, one must approach it philologically and historically.

Dibelius was one of the original exponents of Form Criticism,
and he employs its methodology in his study of the Sermon on the
Mount. Consequently, he begins with the purpose of the Evangelist
in composing the Sermon and his reasons for assigning it to its
familiar place in his Gospel. Dibelius feels that it is significant
that Matthew placed the Sermon on the Mount in the most prominent
place in his book. Before narrating the incidents in Jesus' life he
wanted to present Jesus' message. In the mind of the first Christians the Sermon on the Mount was a summary of Jesus' teaching.
Dibelius writes: "The Sermon on the Mount has a programmatic
character. It is programmatic first of all for the record of Jesus'
life and work providing the best example of his teaching, an impressive illustration of his manner of addressing men and a wonder-
ful indication of his power to teach the people as one having authority and not as the Scribes" [The Sermon, pp 16-7; all page references are to this work].

To call the Sermon on the Mount a "sermon" is a misnomer,
because as Dibelius believes, it is not a real discourse which was
"preached" by Jesus on a single occasion. "It is quite clear that
Jesus did not speak in this way, and that he spoke these various
words at a variety of occasions" (p 16). The elements in the Sermon on the Mount are mostly individual sayings brought together to
form separate groups, e.g., the Beatitudes, the new commandments, and the parables of the builders. Each group is complete
in itself and has no visible connection with the other groups. Matthew ignored chronology and historical order, and according to Dibelius his intention was to make the Sermon on the Mount a divine
law which should govern the communities of his time. Dibelius
summarized the method of Form Criticism and its application to the
Sermon on the Mount as follows:

> It is important for the understanding of our Lord's message
> that we should be aware of this method. Form Criticism
> ventures to go back to those small units of which Jesus'
> teaching consists, to detach them from their framework and
> to study their original meaning. Such units of tradition are
> the elements of which the Sermon on the Mount is composed.
> It is a summary of characteristic sayings whose historical
> occasion we do not know. They were brought together by the
> early tradition within the communities in order to form a
> kind of Christian law. Since this was their purpose the
> Evangelists added other sayings of our Lord to the collection
> which existed in the days of Q, thus completing or explaining
> the older tradition [pp 42-3].

The primary category used by Dibelius in describing the Sermon on the Mount is the "pure will of God." Jesus proclaims in an

absolute way the pure will of God. Though we are indebted to
Schweitzer for his eschatological interpretations of the Gospels, the
Sermon on the Mount is not an interim ethic, valid only for the
period before the end of the world. These commandments were
given for eternity because they represent the will of the eternal
God. They are God's actual demands upon men at all times and
for all time (pp 51, 98-9).

The eschatological dimension is very central in Dibelius' view.
He is convinced that all of Jesus' teachings have an eschatological
background. The Beatitudes which introduce the Sermon on the
Mount bear witness to its eschatological orientation. They promise
the Kingdom of God to the disinherited and to those without hope.
While it is true that some sections of the Sermon on the Mount do
not reflect an eschatological expectation, nevertheless, all of Jesus'
sayings must be viewed within the context of his prophetic call to
repentance because "the Kingdom of Heaven is at hand." This eschatological interpretation of the Sermon on the Mount enables us to
understand its radical and absolute demands. Jesus was oriented
toward the Eschaton and was intent on proclaiming the pure will of
God without regard to the circumstances of everyday existence.
Thus Dibelius says: "The Sermon on the Mount, on the whole, is
a collection of radical, absolute commands and sayings. They are
radical and absolute because the man who uttered them did not consider the circumstances of our life and the conditions of this world.
He looks only to the coming world, the Kingdom of Heaven" (p 65).
This means that even those passages which in isolation appear to be
no more than proverbial sayings or maxims are transposed to a
higher level. They become part of the Law of the coming Kingdom
and present God's demand in the time of crisis.

As for Jesus' interpretation of the Old Testament Law and of
Jewish piety, Dibelius states that he maintained that one must go
farther than the words of the Law. The fulfillment of the written
commandments is not enough. Whoever centers his attention on
God and His Kingdom instead of the wording of the Law will deepen
the significance of the commandments and expand their validity. Dibelius summarizes the relationship between Christ and the Law thus:
"Christ has brought with him not the revelation of a new law but the
message of the Kingdom. Its purpose is to transform men, and a
transformed humanity will be able to do more than men did under
the government of the old Law.... Thus, in proclaiming the absolute will of God, Jesus speaks not as a legislator, but as God's
ambassador in the last hour" (p 78).

The question of Jesus and the Law raises a Christological
problem. Who is this one who speaks with divine authority? What
is the importance of the Sermon on the Mount in relation to Jesus'
Messiahship? Dibelius' solution of this problem is related to his
Form critical methodology. He makes a distinction between the
time in which Jesus lived and the time when the sayings were collected, i.e., between the situation before Easter and the situation
after Easter.

Before Easter Jesus was regarded by his followers as the
personal embodiment of the coming Kingdom. His healings and his
words were signs of the heavenly Kingdom. Indeed, he inaugurated
the new age.

After Easter the situation was completely changed. The Christian community was born by the conviction that God raised Jesus
from the dead and that the exalted Christ will return and bring from
heaven the divine Kingdom. Consequently, Jesus' commandments assume the status of a new law. The Christians feel that Christ has
instructed them to live in accordance with these sayings. They are
no longer proclamations of the will of God in all its radicalism, but
rules of conduct for the life within the communities and are adapted
to the conditions of this life. This situation occurred because the
words of the Sermon on the Mount had been spoken by the Messiah,
the Christ, the Lord, the Son of God.

Dibelius summarizes the changed situation before Easter and
after Easter as follows:

> As regards the sayings of the Sermon on the Mount we may
> state that before Easter they were words of Jesus spoken to
> reveal God's will, and that after Easter these sayings were
> collected to be a rule of conduct for the Christian communi-
> ties. During his lifetime the sayings of Jesus were intended
> to serve as signs of the Kingdom of Heaven. Collected and
> brought together in a slightly elaborated form in the summary
> called the Sermon on the Mount, the sayings became rules by
> which the Christians were to prepare themselves for the
> membership in that Kingdom and for a life 'in Christ' mean-
> while. Before Easter the simple words which we read in
> the Sermon on the Mount had more value than precepts of
> the sages, because the man who uttered them was a warrant
> of the Kingdom of Heaven, the personal embodiment of all
> faith and hope. His sayings were for his listeners judgment
> and a promise in the name of God. After Easter they be-
> came the law which the heavenly Lord has given [pp 102-3].

Having dealt with the exegetical and historical questions, Dibelius in his final chapter is ready to speak to the question of the
Sermon on the Mount's relation to the world of today. Too much
Christian theology becomes preoccupied with practical considerations without developing a clear understanding of the meaning of the
biblical record. Dibelius avoids this error by putting off practical
conclusions until the end of his study.

Dibelius returns to his contention that Jesus proclaims the
pure will of God. He does so by giving some radical examples of
what God demands, but he does not set forth the application of
these demands to this world. This would be impossible because
the conditions of this world are not the conditions of God's Kingdom.
Moreover, practical details would only be relevant and applicable
for a short time because the world is constantly changing.

How then are we to understand the contemporary relevance of
the Sermon on the Mount? If we view it as an ideal of religion or
of ethics, it is remote from modern life and cannot be fulfilled on
earth. "The Sermon on the Mount is not an ideal but an eschatological stimulus intended to make men well acquainted with the
pure will of God" (p 135). It speaks of God's eternal will and not
of human and worldly conditions. While we cannot perform its demands in their full scope, we are able to be transformed by it.
"The most important thing is that the Sermon on the Mount be effective in the hearts of Christians.... The Christian Law does not
demand of us that we do something but that we be something" (p
137). We should not seek in the Sermon on the Mount authoritative
decisions concerning the social issues of today. Even if Jesus had
discussed some of these, he would have treated them in the historical and political context of his time. Nevertheless, Dibelius
thinks that we have in the Sermon on the Mount a standard by which
to solve such problems because all these questions of our daily life
are to be decided by Christians as men who are responsible to God
alone, and who know the pure will of God from the Gospel. The essence of Dibelius' answer to the Sermon on the Mount's practical
relevance is perhaps best expressed in the following quotation:

> This, then, is what the Sermon on the Mount demands--that
> Christians should live on their own responsibility before God.
> God's will came to expression not in systems which are ap-
> plicable only to certain periods and to certain parts of the
> world. God's will is revealed in our own midst by signs,
> the most perceptible of which are the sayings of the Sermon
> on the Mount. The conditions of this world are not amenable
> to the Kingdom of God and it is not our task to found this
> Kingdom. Rather our task is to perform signs, not the signs
> described in the Bible, but signs of our own time--to perform
> them as individuals, as communities, as churches, and if
> possible as nations.... The only presupposition here is the
> transformation of man. A community of men who by their
> belief and their conduct proclaim God's will is and would be
> the most convincing witness of God's Kingdom [pp 137-8].

25 LEONHARD RAGAZ

Leonhard Ragaz was born in 1868 and studied at Basel, Jena,
and Berlin. He served as pastor in several Swiss villages and was
a pastor and school teacher in Chur before becoming pastor in
Basel in 1902. In 1908 he became a professor of systematic and
practical theology in Zürich. Ragaz became increasingly active in
the religious socialist movement in Switzerland and he and Hermann
Kutter were prominent leaders. In 1921 he left his professorship
and also withdrew from the church "in order to serve Christ in
freer air," without being bound by state, church, and society. In
an autobiographical account of his spiritual development, Ragaz reports that his study of Marx's Das Kapital made a powerful and
"religious" impression upon him. It was Christoph Blumhardt,

however, whose theology and social concern made the strongest impact upon him. Ragaz's understanding of discipleship (Nachfolge)
led him to pacifism and to voluntary poverty--ideals which he saw in
Tolstoy and St. Francis. But he is perhaps best known for his prophetic insistence that religion must have a social dimension and must
provide a stimulus for the revolution of the world [for brief autobi-
ography of Ragaz's spiritual development, see Markus Mattmüller,
Leonard Ragaz und der religiöse Sozialismus Bd I (Zollikon: Evangelischer Verlag, 1957), pp 240-6].

Shortly before his death in 1945 Ragaz published Die Bergpredigt Jesu [Bern: Verlag Herbert Lang, 1945]. His first chapter
designates the Sermon on the Mount as "the magna charta of the
Kingdom of God." The central category of Ragaz's theological
thought is the Kingdom of God, and he acknowledged his indebtedness
to Ritschl. But whereas Ritschl neglected the eschatological dimension of the Kingdom, Ragaz understood the Kingdom as both present
and future. It represented not only an immanent, but also a transcendent reality.

A second term which is central to Ragaz's interpretation of
the Sermon on the Mount is "revolution." He charges that the Sermon has been misinterpreted as being utopian or a fantasy, and it
has become too closely identified with bourgeois morality. It is not
a bourgeois morality nor a utopia or fantasy. Moreover, it is not
a summation of rules. Rather it is realistic and something quite
uniform and simple. It is the way of God in opposition to the world,
religion, and ethics. The Sermon on the Mount is the unprecedented
message of the revolution of the world by God [Die Bergpredigt, pp
7-9].

In 1944 Ragaz published Die Gleichnisse Jesu. He believed
that the parables of Jesus and the Sermon on the Mount comple-
mented each other and belonged together. The parables speak about
the Kingdom of God while the Sermon on the Mount speaks about
discipleship. But both these emphases belong together and both are
related to the revolution of the world. Ragaz says that Die Bergpredigt Jesu is not a historical-exegetical study for theologians and
biblical scholars. Rather it is intended as a powerful stimulus.

Beginning with the Beatitudes, Ragaz believes that the complete
renovation of the world, which the Kingdom of God signifies, is
splendidly and at the same time concisely set forth in the eight
Beatitudes. It is the first Beatitude, however, which Ragaz considers fundamental to the rest--indeed to the entirety of the Sermon
on the Mount. He prefers the Lucan text which says, Blessed are
the poor, for yours is the Kingdom of God. Thus at the beginning
of the Sermon on the Mount, as with the entire Gospel of the Kingdom of God, stand the poor. Moreover, the idea of poverty is not
understood by the world because it runs counter to the world's
ideals. But if one would inherit the Kingdom, he must become
poor before God. Property and possessions, the "spiritual" no less

than the material, are opposed to this concept. In reference to material poverty, Jesus is not referring to utter destitution. It is rather to be understood in the sense of "proletariat," and this term points to the higher meaning of poverty (Armut). Not only the first Beatitude, but all of them, point away from the world to God. This is their simple, deeper, and powerful meaning. They point to the revolution of the world by God which is the Kingdom of God [Bergpredigt, pp 13-6; Ragaz, Die Bibel: Eine Deutung Bd V (Zürich: Diana Verlag, 1949), pp 38-9].

For Ragaz the Sermon on the Mount stands in radical tension and opposition to the world. This is especially apparent in Jesus' saying that one cannot serve God and mammon. The Kingdom of God is in opposition to religion, power, and mammon. Mammon or money is responsible for the great differences between persons which are evidenced by class strife. Moreover, it leads to strife and war in both private and social life. Capitalism, which is the modern collective form of "mammonism," is at the root of imperialism, militarism, class wars, and world wars. Ragaz refers frequently to St. Francis as one who embodied the ideal of poverty and who turned against the god of mammonism. It is mammonism which is the root cause of the care or anxiety against which Jesus warns. But in the revolution symbolized by the Sermon on the Mount mammonism will be defeated through the poverty of the Kingdom of God. Ragaz writes:

> The 'poverty' of the Sermon on the Mount is not an institution, but a principle, not a new form, but a new atmosphere, which arises out of the revolution of Christ. It is the overcoming of mammonism through the Kingdom of God, and the new society of man. For this the whole Christian community must pioneer. But it must go out from there and penetrate the world, and this is the world revolution that is now coming [Bergpredigt, p 149; see pp 132-49 for the whole discussion].

The Kingdom of God is in opposition to mammonism, but also to violence and power. Ragaz is convinced that Jesus' teachings about reconciliation and nonresistance forbid both war and capital punishment. But he is reluctant to make a law of these teachings in the way Tolstoy did. Jesus' word is no law but a way of freedom for the sons and daughters of God. Jesus is not speaking against the form of violence, but against the principle of violence. When Jesus speaks about turning the other cheek or going the second mile, he is not laying down a literal rule, but rather a principle or symbol. His teaching about nonviolence is a symbol of what one's attitude and conduct should be in the face of violence [Ragaz, Von Christus zu Marx--von Marx zu Christus (Hamburg: Furch Verlag, 1972), p 168; Bergpredigt, pp 55, 78-85].

A predominant note in Ragaz's interpretation of the Sermon on the Mount is that its emphasis is social and political as well as in-

dividualistic. The Sermon is the magna charta of private life, but
it is also the order of life of the Kingdom of God and as such it applies to political life. The "individualism" of the Sermon on the
Mount must be seen within the context of the Kingdom of God. Like
the prophets, Jesus proclaimed social justice as a constituent of the
Kingdom. While one should be cautious in speaking of "social" in
the contemporary sense, nevertheless, the entire Gospel as a whole
is a social gospel. To give the Sermon on the Mount an exclusively
individualistic interpretation is to distort it because it, as well as
every basic principle of the Gospels, has a social meaning [examples
of Ragaz's emphasis upon the social dimension of the Gospels are:
Bergpredigt, pp 48, 55, 128, 146; Die Bibel: Eine Deutung, p 128;
Die Gleichnisse Jesu, p 15].

       While Ragaz speaks of the Kingdom of God as present and fu-
ture and while he says that it will be realized through God's power,
he believes that it will come to this world and men will behold the
new revolution. Ragaz says that the essential message of the Bible
is the Kingdom of God for the world and its coming to the earth.
Moreover, the outlines of this new order are closely akin to socialism. "In the Kingdom of God the whole of socialism is contained."
In the message of the Kingdom of God the truth of Christianity and
the truth of socialism are intimately related. The new heaven of
Christianity and the new earth of socialism are joined in the message of the Kingdom so that it is difficult to distinguish the one from
the other [Von Christus zu Marx, pp 190-202]. Ragaz's attempt to
relate socialism and Christianity and his vision of the revolution of
the Kingdom of God has led to the charge that he has equated socialism with the Christian Gospel. Whatever one's judgment of Ragaz
may be, he cannot miss his prophetic concern. His writings represent a Weckruf to a new order of existence in which "the kingdoms
of this world shall become the Kingdom of our Lord and of His
Christ."

       But finally it is the Sermon on the Mount which is fundamental
to Ragaz's theology and social ethics. The Sermon transcends every
Christology, dogmatic, ethics, religion, and even Christianity. It is
this freedom from every theology and religion which makes it the
great sign of the revolution of the world as well as of ethics and
religion. While the Sermon on the Mount is not the last and only
form of the message of the Kingdom of God and while we may read
too much into it, nevertheless, the whole of the Gospel, and even
Christ himself, must be understood in terms of the Sermon on the
Mount [Bergpredigt, pp 193-4].

26 THE MANSONS

       While the two well-known British New Testament scholars,
T. W. Manson and William Manson, have not written any monographs on the Sermon on the Mount, they have discussed it in a
number of their writings. Of the two, William Manson has written

more extensively on the Sermon on the Mount, and we will turn to
him first.

WILLIAM MANSON

William Manson's basic approach to the religious and absolute
ethic of Jesus expressed in the Sermon on the Mount is that it must
be interpreted within the context of grace. The Sermon begins with
the theme of gospel or grace in the Beatitudes. The fact that the
Kingdom of Heaven is promised to the poor, the sorrowful, the hun-
gry, the persecuted, is clear evidence of Jesus' emphasis upon the
note of grace. But this is true not only of the Beatitudes; it characterizes the entire Sermon. Manson observes: "Here clearly, as
the forefront position of the Beatitudes indicates, it is in grace that
the Christian revelation begins, and it is on grace that it rests--a
point which must not be overlooked in the constructing of any part
of the Matthew-Sermon" [Jesus the Messiah (Philadelphia: Westminster Pr, 1946), p 116].

But now a question arises when we inquire about the qualifica-
tions of spirit which the inheritors of the Kingdom are seen to exhibit. Do the blessed possess antecedent virtues or excellences of
character? or do they win or acquire on their own the Kingdom of
God? Or are we dealing here with a doctrine of predestination
whereby Jesus promises the Kingdom to the predestined elect? Manson rejects the above alternatives and comes to what he regards as
the "real core of the whole matter." Jesus in the Beatitudes is
characterizing and pronouncing as blessed not those who possess antecedent states or qualities of character but those who exhibit certain responses or reactions when the Gospel of the Kingdom is presented to them. The sense of need, the sorrow, the humility, the
soul hunger of the Beatitudes are results produced by the gospel-
message. In other words, Jesus regards the Gospel itself as the
true reagent which brings out the basic character of the individual
[Wm Manson, Jesus and the Christian (London: James Clarke, 1967),
pp 53-4].

A second problem which Manson raises concerns Jesus' demand
of "righteousness" as defined in the section on the Law (Matt. 5:21-
48). The movement from the grace of the Beatitudes to the moral
requirement of what follows expresses the true order of things.
The coming of the Kingdom of God implies the apprehension of both
God's love or grace and His moral requirement. In the section on
the Law Jesus is speaking to those who already know him through
the Gospel, and whom he now means to perfect in holiness. For
Jesus it is the Gospel which produces the ethic. The ethic is response to God's forgiveness, love, and holiness. Manson writes:

'I say unto you, Love your enemies, and pray for them that
persecute you; that you may become sons of your Father who
is in heaven.' Love, as here presented, is the highest thing
that men are taught of God, and what Jesus is formulating is

not an abstract ideal of righteousness per se, but the life to
which men are called in response to the redeeming love of
God and as sons of God, sharers in His spirit [Jesus the
Messiah, p 125].

This brings us to the problem of the Sermon on the Mount's
practicality and possibility of achievement. Manson suggests that
the question of what is possible is not the first question which we
need to ask. Rather, our first question must be, What is the will
of God? This was the motive which inspired Jesus at every point
of his teaching. Moreover, this is the only possibility if we are
ever to know God. Only by being confronted by the will of God can
we know the radical nature of any truly religious experience--peni-
tence, grace, the forgiveness of sins, hope, blessedness, life [Jesus
and the Christian, p 56; Jesus the Messiah, pp 130-1]. But this is
not a principle for contemplation, but for action. The teaching of
Jesus is meant to be applied. But we must recognize that even the
best life will fall short of the ultimate ideal, and it may be imprac-
ticable for organized society within the structure of its function.
Nevertheless, only an absolute ideal has the capacity to inaugurate
and sustain repentance, or supply a norm whereby society can be
judged in reference to its direction and goals.

However, there remains the problem of the social relevance
of such absolute ideals as nonresistance to evil, giving to all who
ask, and the abjuring of worldly cares and interests. Manson suggests that these seem to set up not an impossible, but an anarchic
ideal of conduct. These commandments have the intention of revealing what perfect trust in God and love to man really mean with
regard to the spirit of our actions. When we confront the necessity
for public justice, good government, and the defense of the weak
against the strong, we will find that the absolute demands of Jesus
are not easily applicable to these areas. To follow his commandments literally would overthrow the foundations of law and order,
and defeat the good which the state exists to serve. It would appear un-Christian to press the Christian absolute upon orders of
life which stand outside of the powers of the Kingdom of God. Manson concludes:

But so long as the Kingdom of God only intersects our mun-
dane existence, and does not fill the whole sphere of it,
there will be limits to what can be demanded of the state in
its name, and to what can be set up as definition of social
duty. What the Christian ethic does here is not to provide
a law for society, but to create a tension in its midst which
cannot but have transforming results. The Kingdom of Heav-
en is as leaven. Thus indirectly, not directly, politics and
law, the social and the economic ordering of life, and the
principles governing our international relations all come at
last under the sign of the Kingdom which Jesus revealed
[Jesus the Messiah, p 133].

In one of his earliest works Manson defines the character of
Jesus' ethic as the Law of the Kingdom of God and sets it in the
context of grace without which we cannot fathom its "practicality."
He says:

> If the ethic of Jesus is high, if it cannot be woven together
> with the ways of the world, it is because it is the law of the
> Kingdom of God, and needs to be envisaged in that new con-
> text of grace, resource and power. Because it is the law
> of the Kingdom of God, it cannot simply be added like a
> piece of new cloth on to the old fabric of the world's life,
> or be poured like new wine into old bottles. It is in itself
> destructive of the old forms and fashions. It needs to cre-
> ate new institutions and moulds for itself. It exists, first
> and last, in a Divine context of redemptive and regenerative
> forces. If we take it out of that context or if we forget
> what that context means, we need not wonder if it seems
> impracticable [Wm Manson, Christ's View of the Kingdom of
> God (London: James Clarke, 1918), pp 116-7].

T. W. MANSON

T. W. Manson's most sustained discussion of the Sermon on
the Mount is in his Ethics and the Gospel [NY: Scribner's, 1960] in
the chapter, "Jesus and the Law of Moses." As the context suggests, he is interested in Jesus' understanding of the Jewish Law of
his day, and Manson believes that there is no better focusing point
for such a study than the Sermon on the Mount.

Accepting the familiar four-source analysis of the Synoptics,
Manson cautions against viewing the Evangelists as "literary hacks"
who produced gospels by stringing other people's work together.
They were genuine composers and were endowed with the same creative capacity as poets, musicians, or artists.

He proceeds to outline the modern critical position as stated
by Dibelius in The Sermon on the Mount. He digresses from Dibelius' conclusion that the Sermon on the Mount is made up by combining single sayings which Jesus uttered on various occasions to
different people. This is only true to a degree because there are
sections of the Sermon, e.g., in chapter 5, where there is a systematic treatment of a number of commandments in the Jewish Law.
This is not a collection of separate sayings, but likely comes from
Jesus himself as he dealt with these commandments at once and not
in a series of separate sayings. The same is true for chapter 6
where there is a collection of three sayings about various kinds of
religious observances.

Manson states that the first task is to understand what the
Sermon as a whole and as it stands is trying to say. He feels that
Windisch's analysis has been the most fruitful in this regard.

The opening verses of Matt. 5 show that the Sermon on the Mount is addressed to the disciples and not to mankind in general. Thus we dare not glibly conclude that the Sermon can be simply accepted and applied in such areas as politics and economics. It does not deal directly with these wider social areas. "The Sermon is not saying: 'This is how men in general should live if they really want to build the Kingdom of God on earth.' It is saying: 'This is how you who are in the Kingdom of God must live if your citizenship is to be a reality'" [Ethics..., p 51].

Manson suggests that the new life described in the Sermon on the Mount is divided into three main sections, and that this division is based upon an ancient maxim in the Pikē Aboth, the Sayings of the Fathers, which is a popular part of rabbinic literature. There we are told that the world rests upon three pillars: the Law, the worship, and the "imparting of kindnesses."

The Sermon on the Mount takes these fundamentals of Judaism and restates them as fundamentals of the New Israel living under the New Covenant. According to Manson the basic divisions of the Sermon are: the New Law (5:17-48), the New Standard of Worship (6:1-34), and the New Standard of Corporate Solidarity (7:1-12) [Ethics..., p 52].

After briefly discussing each of the above sections, Manson concludes that the Sermon on the Mount does in the main give a fair picture of Jesus' attitude to, and his understanding of, the Jewish spiritual heritage. Much in the Sermon is paralleled in Jewish sources. However, the Sermon on the Mount takes the best and deepest things in Judaism and adds to them the still deeper insights of Jesus which are in essence the things embodied in his messianic ministry.

Manson suggests that Jesus' summation of the New Law is in the commandment: "Be ye perfect as your heavenly Father is perfect." The ultimate standard is God Himself, but the actual content of the Law shows that knowledge of the Father is through the Son. Jesus' words, "But I say to you," point to him as the bearer of authority. Moreover, Jesus' instruction in the Sermon on the Mount is paralleled in his conduct. The Sermon on the Mount is not a sermon that says, "Do as I say and not as I do." It is this integrity and standard of conduct that Jesus demands of his followers. They must not merely keep free from evil, but they must show in their lives a positive quality akin to the goodness of God. The challenge of "Be ye perfect ..." is to produce words and deeds of a quality like that which we see in Jesus, and to follow him.

27 AMOS N. WILDER

In his essay on the Sermon on the Mount in The Interpreter's

Bible, Wilder first discusses its literary and historical analysis and
then its interpretation and relevance.

In analyzing the sources and comparing the Sermon in Matthew
and in Luke, Wilder concludes that a previously existing source containing a discourse of Jesus underlies the Sermon as reported in
Matthew and Luke. This discourse began with the Beatitudes, urged
the love of enemies and nonresistance, warned against judging, and
concluded with the saying concerning the tree and its fruits and the
final parable of the builders ["The Sermon on the Mount," The Interpreter's Bible, vol VII (NY: Abingdon-Cokesbury, 1951), p 158].

The material common to Matthew and Luke makes up a little
less than half of the total content of the Sermon. In the remainder
there are two rather fully elaborated sections for which there is little or no parallel in Luke. The first is Matt. 5:17-48 which consists of six contrasts between Jesus' teaching and that of contemporary interpreters of the Law. The second, Matt. 6:1-18 consists
of three contrasts regarding religious practice. Thus Matthew is
apparently using material which Luke did not know or chose not to
use. Wilder feels that it is more likely that this material came to
Matthew independently. He concludes:

> The picture of the composition of the great discourse is then
> the following: Matthew has taken the sermon source repre-
> sented in Luke 6 as his framework, finding in it his begin-
> ning (the Beatitudes) and ending (the parable of the builders).
> In this framework he has incorporated his two sequences
> (roughly, Matt. 5:17-37 and 6:1-18) and other lesser units of
> various provenance, no doubt himself supplying a certain
> number of the connecting transitions ["The Sermon," in In-
> terpreter's Bible, p 159].

Another special feature of Matthew is his interest in the relation of the Gospel to the Law or the Tradition. Wilder believes
that the Sermon on the Mount reflects the varied impulses within
the early Christian community as they dealt with the question of its
relationship to the Jewish Law. Wilder writes:

> Matthew has more or less consciously set Jesus over against
> Moses as a new lawgiver. The New Law for the church is
> set over against the Old Law of God's people, not as abolish-
> ing but fulfilling it.... It follows that Matthew conceives of
> this teaching as having a rather concretely legislative char-
> acter.... Emphasis moreover is laid on obedience, per-
> formance, good works ["The Sermon," p 160].

Wilder is very cognizant of the eschatological context of the
teachings of Jesus. Jesus believed that the new age was imminent--
the Kingdom of God was "at hand." His ethics were the ethics of
the Kingdom. This, however, seemingly does not account for Jesus'
silence regarding social questions such as civic and political life

and responsibility. Wilder says that Jesus was speaking to a group
which was largely a simple rural and small-town society ["The Sermon," p 162]. While Jesus spoke as a phophet and a teacher, he
went beyond the prophets and the wise men because of his consciousness that the Kingdom was drawing nigh. Indeed he was the bearer
of the Kingdom of God, its voice and agent. His ethics is that of
the new age and the new covenant. The Sermon on the Mount is directed to those who have already begun to enter into the new age and
who have begun to share its new powers.

     Jesus' eschatological viewpoint in no sense reduces his ethics
to a relatively unimportant position. His expectation of an early
end of the present order does not imply that his ethical teaching
was an interim ethic relevant only to an emergency situation. It
can best be described as an ethic of the present Kingdom of God or
a new covenent ethic. Wilder says:

> Thus the ethic is not an interim ethic. It is not even a re-
> pentance ethic in the sense that it calls for 'fruits worthy of
> repentance,' i.e., conduct evidencing the changed disposition.
> Rather, it can be best designated as an ethic of the present
> Kingdom of God or a new-covenant ethic. It is not primarily
> an ethic for the relations and conduct of the future transcen-
> dental Kingdom. Nor is it a Kingdom ethic in the sense that
> its practice would admit to the Kingdom nor that it would
> 'build' the Kingdom. It is a Kingdom ethic in the sense that
> it represents the righteousness of those living in the days of
> the new covenant and empowered and qualified by the recon-
> ciliation and redemption of that age [Eschatology and Ethics
> in the Teaching of Jesus, rev ed (NY: Harper, 1950), pp 160-
> 1].

     The eschatological context of Jesus' ethic does not divorce it
from historical-political realities. The eschatological element is the
counterpart and overtone of the historical element. Creative eschatology constitutes a body of myth which bears immediately upon the
present situation. Mythopoetic language is indispensable in expressing
faith's deepest insights. What cannot be expressed in immediate and
realistic terms, can only be adequately conveyed by the imaginative
terms of faith, in the case of Jesus' ethics, by eschatological categories. Eschatological terminology must be viewed as a mythopoetic
way of underlining the urgency and ultimacy of what Jesus is doing
in the present. It is this activity that determines not only Jesus ur-
gent call to personal discipleship but also the general ethical principles in the Sermon on the Mount [Eschatology, pp 56, 161-7].

     How shall we understand the modern relevance and interpreta-
tion of the Sermon on the Mount? Jesus' teachings in the Sermon
were conditioned by special circumstances and a special outlook.
They did not constitute a set of laws, nor were they general principles of universal application. Consequently, we face a task of reinterpretation. We must see that most of the drastic ethics of Jesus

had their origin in the personal situation of Jesus' ministry. Our
reinterpretation must have a biographical background. Thus Wilder
writes: "We recover, then, an historical, a biographical setting
for the so-called ethical absolutes. Their generality of application
vanishes, the interim aspect vanishes. They are occasional utterances to particular persons which the sacred records have lifted
out of the obscurity of their original moment" [Eschatology, p 192].

Since Jesus' utterances did not constitute a set of laws, we
are free to apply them to our own situation. The Christian of today will be guided, not by any single saying of Jesus, but by his
whole life and teaching, bearing in mind the disparity between his
situation and ours. With the guidance of the Holy Spirit and the experience and counsel of other Christians, he will be in a position to
deal with specific choices. Christians will differ in their responses;
some will feel called to bear costly witness while others will not
feel so obligated. At any rate, it is evident that whenever the Sermon on the Mount is taken seriously, there will be conflicts with
current social standards and values. Let us conclude with these observations of Wilder:

> Even where the Christian is not led to break with the pat-
> terns and institutions in which he is involved, he will be con-
> stantly testifying against them in word and deed. The gospel
> and the church represent an invasion of the world by the
> power and grace of God. There cannot but be collision and
> costly witness here. Thus those who seek to live by the in-
> sights and directives of the Sermon on the Mount will consti-
> tute a continual ferment in society, breaking out here and
> there in open defiance and non-cooperation. That is the
> meaning of the figures of the salt, the light, and the leaven
> ["The Sermon," Interpreter's Bible, p 164].

28 ARCHIBALD M. HUNTER

In his characteristic concise and lucid style, A. M. Hunter
has written A Pattern for Life, which is an exposition of the Sermon on the Mount. Beginning with a source analysis of the Sermon,
Hunter believes that it gathers together sayings of Jesus that were
uttered on many different occasions. It is a composite of fragments
from perhaps twenty discourses. Following B. H. Streeter's four-
source analysis of the synoptic Gospels, Hunter says that it is probable that Luke's Sermon on the Plain represents the Sermon as it
stood in Q. Matthew incorporated both the Q and the L Sermons
plus other Q sayings paralleled elsewhere in Luke. Hunter concludes further that Matthew had the needs of catechumens in mind
when he composed the Sermon. These teachings of Jesus showed
how God meant the men of the Kingdom to live. They served as a
summary and design of life in the Kingdom of God [A Pattern for
Life (Philadelphia: Westminster Pr, 1953), pp 11-4; page references
are to this book].

The style of the Sermon on the Mount is poetical, pictorial, and proverbial. Thus Hunter believes that we should steer clear of a too-literalistic interpretation of the Sermon. A distinction between mandata and exempla may be helpful. Mandata are moral imperatives stating deep, broad principles; exempla are illustrations of these principles in action. "Resist not evil" and "swear not at all" are imperatives stating principles. In the former Jesus is stating the principle of non-vindictiveness in personal relations, not non-resistance to evil in any and every circumstance. In the latter, he is calling for absolute sincerity in speech, not prohibiting oaths in all circumstances. To confound the letter with the spirit, as the Anabaptists, the Quakers, and Tolstoy have done, is to land oneself in absurdity (pp 15-20).

There are three qualities which make the Sermon on the Mount unique and that show the originality of Jesus as a moral teacher: its insight into essential morality, its inwardness, and its universality.

Jesus had the genius to go to the heart of the moral question-- to obedience to God out of a pure heart. He internalized morality, saying that good fruit comes only from a good tree. The Sermon on the Mount is catholic in its scope, transcending all exclusiveness and particularism. This is exemplified by the Lord's Prayer which is devoid of anything narrow and nationalistic (pp 24-6).

In a chapter on the Sermon and the Gospel, Hunter refutes the Liberal tendency that identified the Sermon on the Mount with the essence of Christianity. Likewise, he criticizes the point of view which imagines the Sermon to be a collection of plain, practical rules for right living which are a simple possibility and which are relatively devoid of theology. In the New Testament Hunter discerns a two-fold pattern--one theological, the other ethical: the Gospel which the apostles preached; and the Commandment, growing out of the Gospel, which they taught to those who accepted the Gospel. This pattern is evident in a typical Pauline epistle. It begins with some aspect of the Gospel and concludes with a "practical" section setting forth the moral standards required of believers. Just so, the sayings of Jesus in the Sermon on the Mount represent not Jesus' "Gospel" but his "Commandment." They are his design for living in the Kingdom (pp 100-3).

Hunter finally examines the Sermon on the Mount and the ethic of Jesus. There are four theses about the ethic of Jesus: (1) it is a religious ethic; (2) it is a disciples' ethic; (3) it is a prophetic ethic; and (4) it is an unattainable ethic.

Jesus' ethic is religious in that it is rooted and grounded in the "good News" of the Kingdom of God. This means that it is an eschatological ethic but not an interim ethic as Schweitzer believed. Schweitzer read the Gospels in such a way that he ignored those passages which imply that the Kingdom has already come. Contrary to Schweitzer, Hunter believes that Jesus spoke of the Kingdom as a present reality in his ministry, and not as an impending catastrophe. Following the understanding of C. H. Dodd, Hunter writes: "The difference is that we find the key to the Gospels in 'realized,' not in 'futurist,' eschatology" (pp 106-8).

The ethic of Jesus is essentially a disciples' ethic. It was addressed to the Twelve and to that immediate wider community of Jesus' followers. "It was given as a way of life for the men of the Kingdom, not for mankind at large." We must remember this when we consider the questions of the Sermon's relevance and practibility today. Jesus' teaching primarily concerns committed Christians. Moreover, we Christians are not invited to rise to these heights in our own strength (pp 108-10).

Hunter's third thesis states that the Sermon on the Mount is prophetic and not legal. The teachings of Jesus are not in keeping with our usual understanding of laws. Laws are formulated on calculations as to how most men may be expected to behave. It would be useless to enact laws which would pressure people to be saints. But this is precisely what the Sermon on the Mount does. Consequently, it is contrary to our definition of laws.

But it deviates from our understanding of laws in another respect. A court can judge an overt crime that has been committed, but (though it attempts to) it cannot deal with men's intentions and inward disposition. As an example, Jesus' statement that everyone who is angry with his brother shall be in danger of the judgment, puts judgment out of the reach of any human tribunal. Only God can do that.

Therefore, we cannot regard Jesus as a second Moses nor the Sermon on the Mount as a new code of laws.

> He does not traffic, as the legalist does, in rules and regulations to cover every conceivable act of conduct. He lays down deep and far-reaching principles. He enunciates the ideals and aims that ought to govern the lives of men who are living in that new order of grace which he calls the Kingdom of God. In short, the teaching of Jesus as we have it in the Sermon resembles 'a compass rather than an ordnance map; it gives direction rather than directions.' It is a design, not a code, for life in the Kingdom [pp 110-2].

If the ethic of Jesus is unattainable, how can it have any practical relevance? As a design for living, the Sermon on the Mount tells us the following: (1) the kind of people we ought to be; (2) the influence we ought to exert in the world; (3) the way in which, as Christians, we ought to behave socially; (4) the kind of worship we ought to render; (5) the attitude we ought to have towards earthly and heavenly treasures; and (6) the manner in which we should treat our fellowmen.

Hunter does not subscribe fully to those, who like Kittel and
Stange, view the Sermon as showing us our sense of failure and
despair and thus preparing us for the saving message of the Cross.
However, he says that we are not asked to scale the heights of the
Sermon in our own unaided strength: we are offered the continuing
presence, through the Spirit, of him who promised, "Lo, I am with
you alway."

The Sermon also gives us stimulus and guidance for the Christian life. Its standards and principles need to be before us in making
decisions and resolving moral dilemmas. "In the last resort, the
way in which a man will respond to the demand of Jesus will depend
on his own conscience (which the Sermon will greatly sensitize and
sharpen), the guidance of the Spirit, and the shared wisdom of his
fellow-Christians." In conclusion, Hunter returns once more to the
Sermon as "Design for Life." "Though we, no more than the first
disciples, can ever hope to reach the ideal in this fallen world, we
are summoned day by day, with the help of the Spirit to make the
effort. For it is Design for Life in the Kingdom of God" [pp 113-6].

29 JOHN WICK BOWMAN

In The Gospel from the Mount [Philadelphia: Westminster Pr,
1957] Bowman says that he is endeavoring to popularize interpretations of the Sermon on the Mount that were given to students over a
period of some thirty years. Roland W. Tapp, a former student and
research colleague, assisted Bowman in the preparation of the book.
In spite of the author's claim, this is not a popular work, but makes
a contribution to Sermon on the Mount research. While an overall
thesis is not readily discernible, nevertheless this study approaches
the Sermon on the Mount with creative and sometimes unique insights.

Bowman believes that the Beatitudes in Matthew represent an
original Aramaic poem in two stanzas of four verses each. The
main theme of the Sermon on the Mount is grace or gospel, and not
law. This appears in the Beatitudes where the blessings are con-
ferred by God alone upon man. As a whole, the Beatitudes announce
God's blessing upon certain stages attained in the development of the
personality of the Christian pilgrim on the upward way.

Bowman's emphasis upon grace is evident in his summary
statement regarding the first "stanza" of the Beatitudes (Matt. 5:3-6).
He writes:

> ... in stanza one of the Beatitudes it is intended that we ob-
> serve the moral or spiritual progress of a single individual
> adjudged as representative of the 'sons of the Kingdom.' The
> stages of that progress are, successively, first, an awakening
> to one's state of inadequacy and moral poverty in the light of
> the Gospel of the Kingdom (Matt. 4:23), however imperfectly

this Gospel be understood at first; secondly, the determination to 'turn' to God in repentance, accompanied by the assurance of divine forgiveness; thirdly, the adoption of a constant attitude of trust in God alone, together with a sense of progressive achievement in the acquisition of the 'land' (Kingdom); and finally, the earnest longing to acquire the total 'righteousness' which constitutes 'salvation' for man [The Gospel, pp 35-6].

The ideas in the first four Beatitudes which comprise the first stanza were taken from the prophetic writings of the Old Testament where they abound in profusion. They are not an "interim ethic" applicable to a limited period under ideal conditions, but rather a normal series of reactions on the part of men to situations arising in a very imperfect world and likely to prove normative for such situations as long as time lasts [Bowman, "An Exposition of the Beatitudes, " J of Bible & Religion 15 (1947), 166].

When we turn to the second "stanza" of the Beatitudes (Matt. 5:7-10), we are in a different milieu. Now the positive note replaces the negative, and the apparent feeling of emptiness gives way to the portrayal of the richness of a personality capable of making a vital contribution to the life and uplift of mankind. In his article on the Beatitudes cited above, Bowman offers the unique observation that the second stanza's structure and content are derived in toto from Psalm 85:10:

Mercy and Truth are met together;
Righteousness and Peace have kissed each other.

This conclusion, which he develops further, simplifies both the exegetical and critical problems of the second stanza ["An Exposition, p 166; for further discussion of this relationship, see Bowman, "Travelling the Christian Way--The Beatitudes, " Review & Expositor 54 (1957), 388-92]. The four Beatitudes of this "stanza" provide a basis for the understanding of the remainder of the Sermon on the Mount. Indeed the remainder of the Sermon constitutes Jesus' own interpretation of each of the Beatitudes of this "stanza" in turn. Thus the Beatitudes assume a central and decisive position in Bowman's analysis of the Sermon.

Let us see how these Beatitudes relate to the remainder of the Sermon. Matt. 5:7 constitutes a social ethic of which "mercy" like to God's is the ruling principle and without which men have no right to expect God's mercy to apply to them. Matt. 5:21-48 is Jesus' exposition and interpretation of this Beatitude dealing with social ethics.

Matt. 5:8 pictures true religion of a purified people who are worthy to enter into the temple of God and to enjoy his fellowship. Similarly all of Matt. 6 is concerned with Jesus presentation of true religion.

Matt. 5:9 concerns evangelism or the making of peace through
the gospel of peace, while 5:10 represents the acquisition of that
righteousness which is the true image of God and which is at once
salvation for man and his chief end.   Matt. 7 deals extensively with
the acquisition of that righteousness which constitutes salvation for
man and is the proper theme of evangelism [The Gospel, pp 37-43].

The remainder of Bowman's study is a working out of the
above themes from Matt. 5:21 through chapter 7.   He has provided
his own translation of the Sermon, and this adds a note of novelty
and freshness.   Another notable aspect of Bowman's work is his
frequent references to the rabbinical tradition and its relation to the
Sermon on the Mount.

30   CARL F. H. HENRY

Carl F. H. Henry is one of the best-known and most articulate
spokesmen of American evangelicalism.   In his Christian Personal
Ethics [Grand Rapids, MI: Eerdmans, 1957; page references are to
this work] there is a section on the Sermon on the Mount in which
he discusses seven interpretations of the Sermon [see above, p 1-2].
The last of these is the Reformed for which Henry himself is an
apologist.

Henry begins by referring to a major tenet of Reformed theology, viz., the unity of the divine covenant with man.   God's revelation does not change as time passes nor does it contradict itself.
God's ethical norms are constant and authoritative for all men at
all times in all places.   The moral law expressed in Scripture
forms an organic unity.   Matt. 5:17-20 substantiates this view and
determines the approach to the entire Sermon on the Mount.   Jesus
did not revise or negate the Mosaic Law but declared that it is
eternally valid.   His ethic and the Old Testament ethic are in harmony and represent a basic continuity.   "The Sermon brings into
clear relief the eternal oneness of the Law" (p 310).

Proceeding from this basis, Henry gives evidence of the points
of continuity between the Sermon on the Mount and the Decalogue.
There are direct references or allusions to each of the Commandments in the Sermon on the Mount with the exception of the sabbath
commandment.   But this does not mean that we can dismiss the
sabbath commandment as belonging to the ceremonial law alone and
therefore as wholly abrogated by Jesus.   Nowhere does Jesus abolish the Sabbath, and there is no question of its validity on the basis
of God's command.   Thus, without question, biblical ethics exempli-
fies a fundamental unity and continuity.   Henry concludes: "If we
turn to the ethical teaching of Jesus as a whole we find, even if in
summary form, remarkable evidence of Jesus' assertion of the permanent validity of the Commandments....   The ethic of Eden and
the ethic of Sinai and the ethic of the Mount of Beatitudes and the
ethic of future judgment of the race stand in essential unity and
continuity" (p 315).

The above view, however, does not exclude the unique contribution that Jesus brought to Hebrew-Christian ethics. While Jesus had
the highest respect for the Law, he did advance beyond it. Henry
says: "He assigns to himself the right to criticize the Law itself,
not in the sense of destroying it, but of fulfilling it by bringing out
its inner moral demand and by exhibiting its higher intent" (p 316).
This advance is also evidenced by Jesus' intense inward emphasis.
He emphasizes the spirituality of the Law and looks behind words
and actions to the very thoughts and intentions of the heart. But he
goes beyond this. He regards himself as the climactic disclosure
of Old Testament revelation. He stands at the center of the Sermon on the Mount in a way in which Moses never stood related to
the Old Testament Law. He claims the right to interpret the Law
because he bears an authority which transcends and is independent
of the Law.

This brings us to the question of the place of grace in the
Sermon on the Mount. Henry says that grace is to be found in both
the Decalogue and the Sermon, and the two revelations differ in degree, not in kind. Both were given by the Redeemer-God. But
though there is grace in the Sermon on the Mount, one does not find
the doctrine of the cross nor substitutionary atonement there. Moreover, the Sermon makes no judgment as to the possibility of its
fulfillment in man's present condition. The note of grace is mar-
ginal in the Sermon on the Mount, but the Sermon is pointing toward
it and may be the "last step" before its proclamation.

A final theme with which Henry deals is the contemporary
relevance of the Sermon on the Mount. Both the Reformed and the
Anabaptist traditions recognize the validity of the Sermon as a rule
of practice for the regenerate believer who shares in God's redemptive grace. They differ, however, on the question of the applicability of the Sermon to all ethical relationships. The Anabaptists maintain that the Sermon is an authoritative norm for both
group and personal relationships, while the Reformed tradition confines its significance to personal relations. The Sermon on the
Mount is a guide in the person-to-person sphere and in the immediate "one-and-one" neighbor relationships, but it does not deal with
the believer's broader social relationships. Contrary to the Anabaptist view, the Reformed view does not find in the Sermon on the
Mount normative statements about public oaths or war. As Henry
says: "The Sermon gives an individualistic articulation of ethics--
dealing with my relations to the person at my side, and not with the
larger question of my duty to social groups in the order of economics and politics, or to humanity as a whole" (p 324).

Based on his Reformed hermeneutic, it is evident that Henry
does not regard the Sermon on the Mount as a complete ethical
norm that is applicable to all situations. The Sermon does not
contain the whole of Christian ethics. Consequently, it must be
supplemented by the Epistles and other biblical teaching where the
ethical problem is set forth in broader dimensions. It is in the
Epistles of Paul and Peter that we move beyond the one-to-one re-

lationship and see the implications of Christian ethics for state,
community, and economic relations. In a word, any Christian social ethics, as well as personal ethics, must be formulated in view
of the whole of biblical revelation. This does not mean that the
Sermon on the Mount is diminished because it remains the most
comprehensive ethical discourse of Jesus. Henry concludes:

> It contains the character and conduct which Jesus commends
> to his followers, the demand which the nature and will of
> God make upon man, the fundamental law of the Kingdom,
> and the ideal and perfect standard. It is the ultimate formu-
> la of ethics for which ideal human nature was fashioned by
> creation and is destined in eternity. Fallen nature is justi-
> fied in Christ in conformity to it, and redeemed nature ap-
> proximates it by the power of the indwelling Spirit of God
> [p 326].

31 JOACHIM JEREMIAS

Jeremias' Die Bergpredigt [The Sermon on the Mount, tr
Norman Perrin (Philadelphia: Fortress Pr, 1963); page references
are to this ed] is a small but significant contribution to Sermon on
the Mount interpretation. He begins with the question of the meaning of the Sermon on the Mount and discusses three of the answers
that have been given. The first is the perfectionist conception
which holds that in the Sermon Jesus tells his disciples what he requires of them. He lays before them the will of God as it should
determine their way of life. Jeremias points to Hans Windisch as
one who set forth this position with ruthless honesty. For Windisch
the Sermon on the Mount is as much an obedience ethic as that of
the Old Testament. It is law and not gospel. His conclusion was
that the Sermon stands fully in the context of the Old Testament
and of Judaism. Jeremias differs with Windisch in that he believes
that there are fundamental differences between the demands of Jesus
and the ethic of late Judaism. Furthermore, Jeremias states that
Jesus was not a teacher of the Law, or a preacher of wisdom like
that of some of his contemporaries. Instead his message went beyond the bounds of late Judaism.

A second answer to the meaning of the Sermon on the Mount
is that of Lutheran orthodoxy which claims that it is an impossible
ideal. Its high demands lead us to despair, because we realize that
they cannot be fulfilled. Indeed this was Jesus' intention. He wanted to confront his hearers with the realization that it was impossible
to fulfill the demands of God by their own strength. He wants to
lead them through their experience of failure to despair of themselves. Consequently, the Sermon on the Mount drives men to the
cross as the way out of their dilemma. It is praeparatio evangelica.
Jeremias' criticism of this position is that it is a misreading of the
Sermon because nowhere is there a clear statement upon which such
a theory could be built. Rather, the astounding fact is that

Jesus expected that his disciples would do what he commanded. His
teachings apply to everyone who is a follower of Christ. The conclusion of the Sermon on the Mount makes this especially clear.

A third understanding of the Sermon on the Mount is that it is
an interim ethic--a view set forth especially by Weiss and Schweitzer
[see Section 15, "Consistent Eschatology," for discussion of this
view]. Jeremias is more sympathetic with this view than the former
two because all of Jesus' preaching is directed to the Eschaton, and
the dynamic of eschatology lies behind every word of his. However,
this view is too extreme because Jesus is not a fanatical enthusiast
whose ethic is an expression of anxiety in the face of imminent catastrophe. Rather, the dominating thing for Jesus is something quite
different. It is knowledge of the presence of salvation. The decisive accent is not on human effort, but upon the fact that the salvation of God has come. Thus Jesus did not proclaim an exceptional
law relevant for a brief interim, but his words have validity not only
until the Eschaton, but also after it (Mark 13:31).

In his second chapter Jeremias deals with the origins of the
Sermon on the Mount by means of literary and Form criticism.
After comparing the Matthaean and Lucan versions of the Sermon,
he concludes: "We have, therefore, in the Sermon on the Mount, a
composition of originally isolated sayings of Jesus. . . . These isolated sayings were first gathered together in the form of an Aramaic
Sermon on the Plain, out of which the Greek Sermon on the Plain in
Luke and the Greek Sermon on the Mount in Matthew have in turn
developed" (p 17).

The interpretation of the Sermon on the Mount which Jeremias
develops more fully than anyone else is that in its present form it
is an early Christian catechism. He begins by referring to C. H.
Dodd's observation about kerygma and didaché in the earliest Christian preaching [see Section 22]. Jeremias believes that the Sermon
on the Mount as a whole, together with the Epistle of James, is the
classical example of an early Christian didaché. But what was the
purpose for which this didaché was composed? What was its "Sitz
im Leben?" Jeremias concludes that the sayings of Jesus in the
Sermon on the Mount were composed on the basis of perenetic considerations, and that its original function was in catechetical instruction for the pre-baptized, or in post-baptismal instruction for the
newly-baptized. "In Luke (6:20-49) this catechism is designed for
Gentile Christians and in Matthew (chapters 5-7) for Jewish Christians" (p 23).

If one grants that the Sermon on the Mount is an early Christian catechism, then a further deduction must be made. It was preceded by something else. "It was preceded by the proclamation of
the Gospel; and it was preceded by conversion, by a being over-
powered by the Good News" (p 23). Jeremias believes that it is
only with this presupposition that we can rightly understand the individual sayings of Jesus. Every word of the Sermon on the Mount

was preceded by something else, and the example of Jesus stands behind all his teachings. This means that the Gospel preceded the demand. Or to state it better: "The sayings of Jesus which have been brought together in the Sermon on the Mount are a part of the Gospel" (p 30).

The above presupposition also enables us to understand the radical demands of the Sermon on the Mount. Jesus' call to discipleship is directed to those for whom the power of Satan has already been destroyed by the Gospel, and who already are members of the Kingdom of God and radiate its reality.

The incompleteness of the Sermon can also be understood in this context. The teachings of Jesus collected in the Sermon on the Mount are not a complete compendium for Christian discipleship. Rather they are symptoms, signs, examples, of what is implied when the Kingdom of God breaks into the world which is still under sin, death, and the devil. The new life of the disciple should point to the reality of the Kingdom's presence and should testify to the world that the Kingdom of God is already dawning.

Finally, referring to the triad with which he began, Jeremias summarizes his interpretation of the Sermon on the Mount as follows:

> The sayings of Jesus which have been collected in the Sermon on the Mount are not intended to lay a legal yoke upon Jesus' disciples; neither in the sense that they say: 'You must do all this, in order that you may be blessed' (perfectionist conception); nor in the sense: 'You ought actually to have done all of this, see what poor creatures you are' (theory of the impossible ideal); nor in the sense: 'Now pull yourself together; the final victory is at hand' (interim ethic). Rather, these sayings of Jesus delineate the lived faith. They say: You are forgiven; you are the child of God; you belong to the Kingdom. The sun of righteousness has risen over your life. You no longer belong to yourself; rather, you belong to the city of God, the light of which shines in the darkness. Now you may also experience it: out of the thankfulness of a redeemed child of God a new life is growing. This is the meaning of the Sermon on the Mount [p 34].

32 HARVEY K. McARTHUR

McArthur's Understanding the Sermon on the Mount [NY: Harper, 1960] is one of the more significant recent studies. He says that his primary purpose is to deal with the basic practical, historical, and theological problems raised by a thoughtful reading of the Sermon on the Mount. The book is especially noteworthy for its historical examination of the Sermon's interpretation. McArthur deals with the relation of the Sermon on the Mount to four areas:

the Mosaic tradition, the Pauline tradition, the Eschaton, ethics.
In each section he examines the historical precedents before giving
his own conclusions.

What was the relation of the ethic in the Sermon on the Mount
to that proclaimed by the Mosaic tradition in Judaism? McArthur
answers the question by four contentions: (1) Jesus abrogated some
aspects of the Pentateuch; (2) he advanced beyond other sections and
represented a legitimate development out of the Mosaic tradition;
(3) at many and perhaps most points, the ethic of Jesus was paralleled by some of his contemporaries; and (4) the total impact of
Jesus' ethic differed significantly from that of his contemporaries.

Jesus' ethic differed from that of his contemporaries in four
particulars: (1) he eliminated the nonessential and concentrated on
the essential more drastically than did his contemporaries; (2) he
was unique in the consistently radical character of his demands; (3)
the ethic of Jesus was not for an already established society but for
heroic individuals and for the New Community which was to consist
of such individuals; and (4) he differed from his contemporaries in
the personal authority claimed by his handling of the ancient traditions [for full discussion of the above conclusions, see McArthur's
Understanding the Sermon, pp 26-57; following page references are
to this book].

A second problem concerns the Sermon on the Mount and the
Pauline tradition. There seems to be a different emphasis in the
Sermon on the Mount than there is in Paul. The Sermon appears
to expound a religion of works, a religion of character, or in some
sense, a religion of human achievement. The Pauline emphasis on
grace seems to be at variance with this. McArthur addresses himself especially to the Liberal distinction between the religion of Jesus
and the religion about Jesus. Much of the "Quest of the Historical
Jesus" presupposed that behind the Christ of the creeds one could
recover a much simpler faith, that of Jesus himself. McArthur's
alternative to Harnack and liberal Protestantism is that while there
is a gulf between the Sermon on the Mount and the Pauline tradition, the Christian faith includes both the Sermon itself and the religious faith which arose in response to the Sermon and the remainder of Jesus' ministry, his death and his resurrection. In the light
of this perspective the Christian community affirms three things:
(1) that while the Sermon may not have presupposed Rom. 1-8 the
Christian community does make this presupposition; (2) that the demands of God can be fulfilled only where there has been a prior
transformation of life by God's grace and Spirit; and (3) that this
transformation has occurred through and because of the life, ministry, teaching, death and resurrection of Christ. McArthur suggests
that the Sermon may originally have been proclaimed without any
thought of certain distinctively Pauline doctrines. However, today
the Christian community must understand it in the framework of the
total faith that emerged in response to these events (pp 78-9).

McArthur suggests further, that after Schweitzer and Bultmann, it is more difficult to make the distinction between the "religion of Jesus" and the "religion about Jesus." If Schweitzer's consistent eschatology is taken seriously, then Jesus must be seen as
an apocalyptic figure whose thought is far from simple or intelligible.

Bultmann, with his Form critical methodology, his demythologi-
zation, and existential interpretation, suggests that we can gain very
little historical information about Jesus from the Gospels. The Gospels already represent the kerygma of the early Christian community
so that the "religion of Jesus" is indeed the "religion about Jesus"
(pp 152-3).

McArthur's third concern is the Sermon on the Mount and eschatology. Did Jesus, as Schweitzer believed, expect history to
come to a swift close? If so, what effect did this expectation have
on his ethics? In the Sermon on the Mount an interim ethic? Can
and should the eschatology of Jesus be translated into modern terms,
as Bultmann believes? McArthur's conclusions may be summarized
in three statements: both eschatological and non-eschatological sanc-
tions appear in the Sermon on the Mount; the imminence of the Eschaton is nowhere stressed in the Sermon, though the Evangelist may
have assumed that his portrayal of the general pattern of Jesus'
thought supplied this emphasis; and the character of the ethic is nowhere explicitly conditioned by the eschatological expectations, although the silence of Jesus with respect to the problems of social
order may have been due, in part, to his expectation of the Eschaton (pp 80-104, 155-8).

In his final chapters McArthur deals with the question of the
Sermon's relevance. In what sense is it a possibility for the Christian life? He outlines twelve approaches that have been taken to the
ethic of the Sermon on the Mount [see above, p 1]. Of these, six
are of primary value. They are: the absolutist, hyperbole, general
principles, attitudes-not-acts, repentance, and unconditional divine
will views.

McArthur suggests that a different order may help bring out
the significance of these principles. The absolutist insight correctly
affirms that the commands are to be taken seriously and that they
constitute an inescapable demand upon us. Such an understanding
leads to repentance, to the turning of one's life to God. But repentance is not an end in itself. One must turn again to the Sermon
on the Mount with the question of how he shall live. The Sermon
does not supply a detailed answer, but it indicates the direction in
which a life committed to Christ will move. An element of hyperbole will be recognized, but it will not alter the Sermon's radical
demands. It must also be understood that the specific injunctions
are not as important as the general principles which they reveal.
The Christian must remember that Jesus was primarily concerned
with attitudes, not acts, although attitudes which do not produce acts
are unreal. Finally, the Christian must see that the Sermon pro-

claims the unconditioned divine will and must himself accept the responsibility of adjusting its precise details to fit the human situations
confronted (p 148).

Another way to describe the ethic of the Sermon on the Mount
is to say that Jesus reached out to the limits of human possibility,
exploring what life would be like for an individual wholly dedicated
to God rather than to himself and to the usual prudential considerations. The life committed to the Spirit of God and to His love is
the final goal. The details of the Sermon on the Mount are markers
on the way to that goal.

> Our eyes need to be opened to what 'love' may mean in vari-
> ous situations, or whither the guidance of the Spirit will lead
> us. This is the function of the Sermon on the Mount....
> But the concrete commands of the Sermon are great land-
> marks along the way. They reassure us when we have read
> the compass aright, and they trouble us when we twist the
> reading of that compass to our own advantage. Let us read
> and reread the Sermon until our hearts and wills and minds
> are steeped in its atmosphere. Then let us live with courage
> but with humility [pp 159-60].

33 W. D. DAVIES

With few exceptions, W. D. Davies' The Setting of the Sermon
on the Mount [Cambridge, Eng.: Cambridge Univ Pr, 1964; page
references are to this work] has been acclaimed for its great learning and erudition. Reviewers have generally praised Davies' extensive knowledge of Judaism. This is a massive and learned study
which is not easy reading. Neither is the continuity of the argument easily discerned or followed. A subsequent volume, The Sermon on the Mount, consists of lectures delivered at the Protestant
Episcopal Theological Seminary, Alexandria, Va. These lectures
enabled Davies "to set forth in a more accessible and brief form
the main lines of the argument in The Setting of the Sermon on the
Mount."

Davies' intention is to illuminate the setting of the Sermon on
the Mount by means of critical historical analysis. Thereupon he
takes up the place of the Sermon in Matthew's Gospel, in Jewish
messianic expectation, in contemporary Judaism, in the early
Church, and in the ministry of Jesus.

As for the setting of the Sermon on the Mount in Matthew,
Davies concludes that the Sermon is the "law" of Jesus, the Messiah
and Lord, but Matthew avoids the express concept of a New Torah
and a New Sinai. He regards Jesus as a teacher of righteousness,
but avoids designating him "a New Moses" (p 108).

In reference to Jewish messianic expectation, Davies finds

that there was ambiguity in the Jewish expectation of the Messiah and that this ambiguity has invaded Matthew's presentation of the Messianic era. Moreover, Matthew's picture of Jesus fulfills only a part of those varied expectations (pp 187-90).

In his chapter on the setting of the Sermon on the Mount in contemporary Judaism, Davies discusses Gnosticism and the Dead Sea Sect. He finds no point in Matthew where a direct encounter with Gnosticism is reflected. Anti-Gnosticism was not the reason for Matthew's emphasis on the ethical teachings of Jesus. So we cannot assume that Gnosticism particularly determined Matthew's thought and caused him to construct the Sermon on the Mount (p 207) [also see Davies, The Sermon on the Mount (Cambridge, Eng.: Cambridge Univ Pr, 1966), p 76]. As for Qumran, the Sermon on the Mount shows traces of the sectarian influence. But according to Davies, this material was utilized by the Evangelist in the dialogue which particularly concerned the Church of his day, that between Pharisaism and Christianity. He concludes:

> The sectarians had been given a rigid interpretation of the
> Law, by the Teacher of Righteousness, which was designed to
> lead to perfection. There is every reason to believe that
> Jesus offered an interpretation of the Law which was set
> over against this, his radicalism standing over against that
> of Qumran. But when Matthew constructed his 'Sermon' he
> utilized the tradition of the teaching for his own purposes--
> to set the Christian ethic not over against Qumran but over
> against Pharisaic Judaism, the ethic of the New Israel over
> against that of the Old.... [W]hatever the sectarian influ-
> ences on Matthew may have been, it would be unwise to look
> in their direction for the key to Matthew and, especially, the
> Sermon on the Mount [p 255].

Following the section on the Dead Sea Sect, Davies turns to a lengthy discussion of Jamnia, and it is here that he finds the key to the setting of the Sermon on the Mount. He writes:

> We are now able to sum up our treatment of the structure of
> the Sermon on the Mount. We cannot certainly connect it
> with the discussion and activity at Jamnia, but the possibility
> is a real one that the form of the Sermon on the Mount was
> fashioned under their impact. It is our suggestion that one
> fruitful way of dealing with the Sermon on the Mount is to
> regard it as the Christian answer to Jamnia. Using terms
> very loosely, the Sermon on the Mount is a kind of Christian,
> mishnaic counterpart to the formulation taking place there.
> It is not our intention to deny other formative influences on
> Matthew. But neither Gnostic nor 'sectarian' pressures are
> sufficient to account for the massive elevation of the teach-
> ing of Jesus in the Sermon on the Mount. Apart from the
> internal demands of the Christian community, it was the
> necessity to provide a Christian counterpart to 'Jamnia' that
> best illumines this [p 315].

The setting of the Sermon on the Mount in the early Church is
assessed in relation to Paul, the Q document, other New Testament
writings, etc. Davies believes that Paul had access to a tradition
of the words of Jesus which constituted for him part of the "law of
Christ." Paul like Matthew appealed to these as authoritative.
Moreover, both Paul and Matthew viewed the Exodus as a prototype
of the greater redemption accomplished by Christ. Paul shared
with Matthew a common understanding of Christ and his words.
"Thus the Sermon on the Mount would not have appeared to Paul as
an alien importation into the faith. Like Matthew, Paul too can
speak of a law of Christ, partly, at least, composed of Jesus'
words" (p 366). This law of Christ or Law of the Messiah, as
Davies calls it, provides a bridge between the first century and the
second. Davies rejects the frequent suggestion that the Christianity
of the New Testament is a religion of grace while that of the second
and later centuries is one of law. As we move from the first-century Church to that of the second there is no break that separates
them. Rather, "the Law of the Messiah" provides a continuity between these communities (p 414).

Finally, Davies deals with the Sermon's setting in the ministry of Jesus. The words of the Sermon on the Mount ultimately
lead us back to the one who uttered them, and they are themselves
kerygmatic. But we dare never view the event of Christ as an ab-
straction divorced from life. Nowhere is the Gospel set forth without moral demand. Likewise, nowhere is morality understood apart
from the Gospel. The teachings of Jesus in the Sermon on the
Mount are the astringent protection against any Christological interpretation in other than moral terms. Despite Matthew's editorial-
ization, the moral demand of Jesus persists in the Sermon on the
Mount (pp 433-5).

In a brief concluding statement, Davies returns to the tension
between gospel and law. The Sermon on the Mount in its setting
spans the arch of grace and law. It joins the "works righteousness" of James and the Pauline "justification by grace alone." "Its
opening, the Beatitudes, recognizes man's infinite need for grace,
his misery; its absolute demand recognizes man's infinite moral
possibilities, his grandeur" (p 440).

Truly, the scope and scholarship of Davies' work is most impressive. However, one must be sympathetic with Samuel Sandmel's
comment that Davies has chosen to write on the setting instead of
the content of the Sermon on the Mount, thereby selecting location
and form over content. For Sandmel this is a tragedy that a great
scholar has by choice written a book that is tangential, and falls
short of central significance [Theology Today, vol 23 (July 1966),
293-4].

34 JEWISH INTERPRETATIONS

CLAUDE G. MONTEFIORE

The chief sources presenting Montefiore's views on the Sermon on the Mount are The Synoptic Gospels, published in 1909 and considerably revised in 1927, and Rabbinic Literature and Gospel Teachings, published in 1930. He presented the latter as "a sort of supplement" to his Commentary on the Synoptic Gospels and supplied the Rabbinical parallels to the Gospels of which there were few in his Commentary [Montefiore, Rabbinic Literature and Gospel Teachings (NY: KTAV Pub Hse, 1970), p xxxv; given as RL in following page references].

Montefiore was a prominent exponent of "Liberal Judaism" and this perspective is very evident in both the above works. In the Preface to The Synoptic Gospels he speaks of his point of view as follows:

> My book does not pretend to learning. If it were not for my special point of view, I should have no justification to write upon the Gospels at all.... If it be asked: 'Why then do you venture to throw your work at the public?' I can only reply that the peculiar point of view to which I have alluded has, I hope, made my book of some interest and use to a few persons, both within and without my religious community.... This 'peculiar point of view' is that of a Liberal Jew who has not found his profound attachment to Liberal Judaism inconsistent either with a high appreciation of the lives and teachings of many of the ancient Rabbis ... or with a similar high appreciation of the character and teachings of Jesus ... [Montefiore, The Synoptic Gospels, vol I, 2d ed (NY: KTAV Pub Hse, 1968), p ix].

In a Note at the end of volume II of The Synoptic Gospels Montefiore refers again to his "peculiar point of view" and adds that he probably holds a higher view of the greatness and originality of the teaching of Jesus than is common among Liberal Jewish writers [p 670; vol II--only--of Synoptic Gospels will appear as SG in following page references]. Montefiore was convinced that his approach enabled him to treat the classic sources of Judaism and Christianity as no one before him had done. Thus he believed that he could serve as a "bridge" between these two traditions.

In The Synoptic Gospels Montefiore begins the section on the Sermon on the Mount by stating that the Sermon is not a summons to repentance, or a proclamation of the imminence of the Judgment and of the Kingdom. It seems to be intended for those who have already accepted the call and message of Jesus, and are ready for his most developed teaching. Moreover, it is not a sermon with which Jesus was likely to have started his career as a teacher, but rather one in which he summed it up (SG p 27).

In his subsequent discussion of the Sermon on the Mount, Montefiore departs from this initial non-eschatological estimate and reflects a position close to the "consistent eschatology" of Weiss and Schweitzer. In commenting on the Beatitudes, Montefiore says that Jesus doubtless believed that the Kingdom was coming very soon--during his lifetime or soon after his death. He saw himself as its herald, and it might be said that in a sense the Kingdom had already begun. Montefiore quotes Weiss with approval on his suggestion that the higher righteousness of Jesus was intended for men who were soon to appear before the judgment seat of God. The Sermon on the Mount is spoken from the point of view of inevitable crisis and the expected near end of the world (SG pp 35, 54).

This eschatological outlook accounts for the fact that the Sermon contains no program for the improvement of this world and its institutions. The Sermon gives us no answer to our social questions, nor how to organize the society of later ages.

> It has no thought of a human race who are to live upon the earth for centuries upon centuries, but it is spoken to a small band of men who are to turn their backs upon earthly matters, and to expect and prepare for a new 'heavenly' order.... To the question, 'How are we best to order the life of mankind?', we receive no answer; what is answered is the question which an earnest and tender conscience must always put to itself: 'What must I do to be saved?' [SG p 54].

Commenting on Jesus' teaching on nonresistance (Matt. 5:38-42), Montefiore emphasizes the individualistic vs. the social aspects of the Sermon on the Mount. Jesus was not thinking about public justice, the order of civic communities, the organization of states, but only how the members of his religious brotherhood should act towards each other and towards those outside their ranks. Public justice was outside his purview. There was no need for such concern because the old order was approaching a catastrophic end. Nonresistance is not to be taken literally and does not apply to the work of the police or defensive war. In these spheres, Montefiore thinks, the injunction is wholly inapplicable and false. "Jesus did not bother his head about the state." He is not thinking of the state, but only of the individual. Jesus is thinking about private injuries, not of public justice or public wrong-doing. His concern is not so much about the wrong-doing as it affects the wrong-doer, but as to what is the sufferer's right attitude concerning it (SG pp 70-5, RL p 52).

Montefiore's views on Jesus' teaching about divorce and oaths are noteworthy. Jesus' extreme attitude toward divorce is untenable and objectionable. However, his implied attack upon the inferiority of women in Oriental society, and upon the unjust power of divorce given to men, was of the highest importance and value (SG p 67). As for oaths, Montefiore believes that Jesus forbad all oaths of every kind and on every occasion for the disciples and members of

the coming Kingdom. He agrees with the Quaker interpretation on
oaths and feels that they have been the true interpreters. Jesus,
however, goes beyond the Rabbis because there is no ordinance or
injunction in Rabbinical literature never to swear or take an oath
(SG p 68, RL p 50).

One of Montefiore's major concerns, of course, is the relationship of the Sermon on the Mount to the Old Testament and to
Rabbinic literature. One parallel between the Sermon and the Old
Testament relates to Jesus on the "mountain." Montefiore feels
that this recalls Moses on Sinai and that Matthew wants to contrast
the two Laws: the one old, imperfect and transitory; the other new,
perfect and definitive. The Law of Jesus fulfills the Law of Moses
and the teaching of the prophets (SG p 29). In Matt. 5:17-20 there
are three instances of fulfillment of the same character. It consists in entirely prohibiting what had previously been restricted only,
and in requiring to be observed absolutely and universally that which
previous legislation had enjoined to be observed only within limits.
Montefiore concludes, however, that in spite of the "antitheses" in
the Sermon on the Mount, Jesus had no deliberate intention of teaching a new religion or a new "righteousness" (SG pp 50, 55).

Montefiore points out that it is very common in books on
Christian theology to speak of the imperfect or transitional or pre-
paratory morality and religion of the Old Testament as compared
with the perfect, permanent, or absolute morality and religion of
the Gospel and the Sermon on the Mount. But Judaism has developed on its own lines so that some of the "imperfections" in the Old
Testament are corrected in later literature, quite independently of
the Gospels. Many Christians would regard such passages as Matt.
5:28, 6:4, or 7:5 as splendid additions to, or perfections of, the
Old Testament. However, to many Jews they seem less so because
they are already familiar to them in their own tradition (SG pp 126-
7).

On the whole, Montefiore takes a very positive and congenial
attitude toward the Sermon on the Mount. However, in commenting
on Matt. 6:1-4 where Jesus refers to the hypocrisy practiced in the
synagogues, Montefiore writes: "It is this constant suggestion of
moral and religious inferiority in Judaism as such, which, be it
remembered, is a word that connotes, not a dead religion of 1900
years ago, but a living religion of today--it is this which no doubt
makes us sometimes throw stones and exaggerate in turn" (SG p
95). Referring to other specific passages in the Sermon on the
Mount, Montefiore says:

>   As regards the moral and religious teaching of the Sermon
>   on the Mount, the liberal Jew can by no means subscribe to
>   every word of it, or regard it as perfect and permanent.
>   Passages such as 5:22 and 7:14 are objectionable; they are
>   as 'imperfect and transitional' as many a passage in the Old
>   Testament. Passages such as 5:20, 34, 38-42, need qualifi-

cation and restriction. The theology of a passage such as
7:7 is open to considerable question. We must bring our
critical judgment to bear upon the Sermon on the Mount as we
must bring it to bear upon the Pentateuch. In some respects
we have advanced beyond both [SG p 127].

In comparing the Sermon on the Mount with Rabbinic teaching,
Montefiore states that on the whole the latter is more sober and
less enthusiastic than the teaching of the former. But the Rabbis
considered consequences more than Jesus. They were more practical and had more common sense, if less genius. Comparing the
religion of the Rabbis to that of the Beatitudes, Montefiore says that
the Rabbinic teaching is more comprehensive but also somewhat less
concentrated, intense and passionate (SG p 74, RL p 2). Montefiore
refers to several passages in the Sermon which are "purely original"
since they do not harmonize with, or are not easily paralleled by,
Rabbinic sources. They are mainly: 5:10-12, 32, 38-48, 6:6, 18,
33. "But though not very numerous, they are of immense importance and significance, and mostly of a high greatness and nobility"
(SG p 127) [for reference to uniqueness of 5:48 see RL p 110].

As we have seen, Montefiore has a high regard for the Sermon on the Mount, and he views it as a "meeting-ground" for Jew
and Christian. One reason for this possibility is the absence of the
Christological element in the Sermon. Montefiore finds that it contains no article of faith concerning the person of its giver; nothing
about his Messiahship; no word about his divinity. Consequently,
one can live in the spirit of the Sermon on the Mount, and yet, like
every Jew from Jesus' day to this, need not "acknowledge any Man
as our religious 'Lord'." Furthermore, the Sermon on the Mount
makes a rapprochement between Jew and Christian possible because
it contains nothing which is essentially antagonistic to Judaism.
There are abundant parallels in Rabbinic literature for most of its
utterances. "The highest spirit of the Old Law is in harmony with
the purest statement of the New" (SG pp 125, 126). Montefiore expresses his overall view and appreciation of the Sermon on the
Mount as follows:

> And yet it may perhaps be urged that the originality and
> greatness of the Sermon does not lie in any particular part
> of it. They lie in the whole. How much of it may go back
> to Jesus must be always uncertain. That the Sermon has
> grown from smaller groups and separate sayings is most
> probable. But it remains for all time a religious document
> of great nobility, significance, and power [SG p 127].

GERALD FRIEDLANDER

With Gerald Friedlander we confront a man of different tem-
perament from Montefiore. While Montefiore was conciliatory in
his evaluation of the Sermon on the Mount, Friedlander is polemical
and apologetic. Indeed, he takes particular issue with the views of

Montefiore expressed in The Synoptic Gospels. In 1911 he published
The Jewish Sources of the Sermon on the Mount [NY: KTAV Pub Hse,
1969; page references are to this work], which was intended, in the
first place, as a contribution to comparative theology. He attempts
to describe the relationship between Christianity and Judaism by
means of comparison and contrast. To limit the scope of his in-
quiry he confines himself to the Sermon on the Mount. The teaching
of the Sermon must be compared not only with the Old Testament
and its Rabbinic glosses preserved in the Mishna, Tosephta, Gemara,
Midrashim, and Targumin, but also with Jewish Hellenic literature,
which includes the Septuagint, the Apocrypha, Philo, and the Apocalyptic writings. Friedlander regards his attempt to read a few
chapters of the New Testament in the light of contemporary Jewish
thought as a novel venture. He says that he has endeavored to ana-
lyze the Sermon and to trace its sources, so far as they are dis-
coverable (pp xxxvii-xxxviii).

The tone of Friedlander's work is polemical, and this has led
T. W. Manson to remark: "Friedlander's main thesis is that any
good in the Sermon on the Mount can be paralleled from Jewish
sources, and that nothing that cannot be paralleled from Jewish
sources is any good" [Manson, Ethics and the Gospel (NY: Scribner's,
1960), p 57]. Let us consider a few of Friedlander's statements
which may give credence to Manson's evaluation. Friedlander acknowledges the lofty tone of the Beatitudes but then adds that we
should not forget that all that they teach can be found in Isaiah and
the Psalms. "Israel finds nothing new here. The Jew rejoices to
think that such fine teaching is common to Judaism and Christianity."
Concerning Jesus' teaching on divorce, Friedlander says that Judaism
has again nothing to learn from this negative teaching. Regarding
almsgiving, Friedlander writes: "The Sermon on the Mount does
well to impress on the generous the need of secrecy in their almsgiving, but it has nothing to offer which is not found in the teaching
of the Scribes and Pharisees." As for the Lord's Prayer, he says
that it is merely an adaptation of nine verses of Ezekiel (Ezek. 36:
23-31). He adds: "This should finally settle the question as to the
originality of the Lord's Prayer. It is taken, we have seen, from
the Old Testament, and therefore can lay no claim whatsoever to
originality." Friedlander at the conclusion of his study says that
four-fifths of the Sermon on the Mount is exclusively Jewish. He
also declares that "In our opinion this Pharisaic teaching is infinite-
ly superior to that of the Gospel" (pp 23, 59, 107, 165, 266, 214).

Friedlander is more outspoken than Montefiore on the "unfair
treatment of the Pharisees" in the Sermon on the Mount and in the
Gospels in general. Commenting on Matt. 5:20, Friedlander writes:
"Here the Gospel denies the possibility of the Pharisees or Scribes
being able to enter into the Kingdom of Heaven. Their righteousness is sin, only the new and higher righteousness of Jesus will
enable his disciples to enter into the coming Kingdom" (p 35).
Christian writers generally know little about the Jewish literature,
and they are naturally influenced by the New Testament picture of

the Pharisee. Friedlander states that the New Testament view is
one-sided, and it is neither charitable nor just. "The New Testament has drawn a prejudiced, untrue, and unfair picture of the
Pharisees" (p 36).

In a lengthy discussion of Matt. 6:19-34, Friedlander discerns
an "unJewish asceticism." Over against Jesus' renunciation of
"mammon" and the view that wealth is tainted, the Jewish Scriptures
declare that gold and silver belong to God (Hag. 2:8). In Judaism
there was no desire to renounce money, or to refuse to utilize it in
a good and proper manner. At this point Judaism rejects the Gospel teaching. Wealth is one of Christianity's many deadly sins. But
this has no parallel in Judaism. "Christianity is not of the world--
Judaism is of the world.... Judaism is not 'a religion,' it is life"
(pp 180-1).

This same spirit of asceticism and renunciation is reflected in
Jesus' teaching about having no care or anxiety. The absolute faith
in Providence, unaccompanied by any effort on man's part, in 6:33,
is not a Jewish doctrine because man is placed on earth to labor
(Cf. Gen. 3:19 and 2:15). "There is nothing in the Psalms or any
other book of the Old Testament which teaches us to have no care,
but we are reminded to trust in God alone, for He is mighty to
save" (p 196).

Another cleavage between Judaism and the Sermon on the
Mount relates to Jesus' teaching about nonresistance in 5:38-42.
Friedlander says that the spirit of abnegation and self-denial that
sacrifices individuality and personal freedom is alien to Jewish
teaching. There are times when a Jew can and should overcome
evil by good, but justice cannot be forgotten in an attempt to fulfill
the divine law of love. In his private life man must renounce revenge, but in public life a different law obtains. Justice requires
that wrong should be resisted. It must be emphasized that Judaism
forbids the exercise of revenge. "Judaism, unlike Christianity (as
taught in the Sermon on the Mount), recognizes the duty of fighting
against evil. It repudiates the 'higher and newer' law, 'resist not
evil'" (pp 67-8).

Friedlander is far more reluctant and negative in his evaluation
of the "unique" parts of the Sermon on the Mount than is Montefiore.
Among Jesus' original teachings are: nonresistance, "asceticism,"
and having no care for worldly things. In his section on Jesus'
teaching about almsgiving, Friedlander says: "If Jesus, in the Sermon on the Mount, said anything new, it was that the old Jewish
public worship should cease and be replaced by private devotions in
one's inner chamber" (p 111).

Friedlander rejects Montefiore's contention that the Sermon on
the Mount could be the ideal meeting-ground and bond of union between Jew and Christian. Judaism prefers to adhere to the old
paths instead of embracing the new Law of the Gospel. Gentiles

have been unwilling to accept the "heavy yoke" of God's Kingdom
(i.e., the Torah). Instead they have taken up the "easy yoke" of
the Gospel. But no Jew could possibly admit the claims of Jesus
which involve his right to abrogate the Divine Law, his power to
forgive sins, the efficacy of his vicarious atonement, and his ability
to reveal God the Father of man to whomsoever he will. Underlying these claims is the belief in his divinity and unique divine
sonship. Consequently, the most positive thing that Friedlander can
say about Jesus and the Gospels and Christianity is that they have
been of the greatest benefit to non-Jewish people in the same way
that Mohammed, the Koran, and Islam have been. As for the Sermon on the Mount, "This is not to condemn the teaching of the Sermon. It has its part to play in the religious training of the world"
(pp 264-5).

35 AFTERWORD

The foregoing survey of the history of interpretation of the Sermon on the Mount reveals many approaches and attempted solutions
to its critical and ethical problems. While the critical and historical questions are of special interest to New Testament scholarship,
the problem of the Sermon's application and contemporary relevance
strikes a more universal note. What is the Sermon on the Mount's
"answer" to such basic ethical questions as: What ought I to do
and be? Around what center of value should I orient my life? In
what sense, if any, can the "individualistic" demands of the Sermon
on the Mount be applicable to the interrelationships between ethnic,
racial, economic, religious, and national communities? Dietrich
Bonhoeffer said that the question of the Sermon on the Mount always
comes back to keeping the commandment and not evading it. How
right he was! After one has explored the critical issues with erudition and exactitude, and after one has set the Sermon on the Mount
in its "correct" theological perspective, the question of the Sermon's
relevance still confronts us. Like a "hound of heaven" it tracks us
down the days and years and will not let us evade or escape its
radical demands.

For the Christian community the Sermon on the Mount is authoritative because it is a part of the New Testament. Its position
is further enhanced because it comes from the lips of Jesus. Furthermore, behind the words is the person of Jesus the Christ. The
quality of life set forth in the Sermon on the Mount is embodied in
the life style of Jesus. He who announced the advent of the Kingdom
of God exemplified the "ethics of the Kingdom."

In the classical Christian creeds and in the thought of the
most eminent Christian theologians, there has been a tendency to
subordinate the "Jesus of history" to the "Christ of faith." Or to
put it another way, the "word of the cross" has overshadowed Jesus' words about discipleship and the qualities needful for citizenship in the Kingdom. There is a gospel song that says of Jesus:

"He the great example is and pattern for me." That is a partial
Christology, but it points to a dimension too often neglected and
evaded.

According to each of the Gospels, Jesus' initial word to his
disciples was, "Follow me." This call to discipleship is addressed
to each Christian, and it is in the Sermon on the Mount that one
finds guidelines and directives for discipleship. The Christian life
is not only a gift of grace, grounded in the cross and resurrection
of Christ, but a summons to follow him. Discipleship involves a
pattern of living described in the Beatitudes--meekness, mercy, purity of heart, peacemaking. It includes integrity and truthfulness so
that one's "yes is yes" and "no, no." One is called upon to endure
evil and suffering rather than to inflict them upon others. There
must be a simplicity and singleness of purpose centered in God's
Kingdom rather than in mammonism.

The Sermon on the Mount's radical demands cannot be evaded
by understanding them as a summons to repentance and as a preparation for the word of grace. They are not an interim ethic given in
a time of imminent crisis, but now no longer relevant. Nor dare
we assign their application and relevance to the future kingdom which
will be realized after the Second Advent. Rather, the Sermon on the
Mount has a contemporary relevance in that it presents us with
goals toward which we are constrained to move and with standards
of judgment by which every decision and action must be evaluated.

Thus we are called upon to make the attempt to "follow Jesus"--to do what he commands. This is a vital dimension of Christian discipleship. But all our efforts, no matter how inspired and
inspiring, will fall short of the ideal. The "sin which so easily be-
sets us" will find us not doing the good we want and doing the evil
we do not want. Jesus' towering demand, "You, therefore, must be
perfect, as your heavenly Father is perfect," will remain for us an
"impossible possibility" as long as we participate in human existence. Sheer human will and effort will experience frustration when
confronted with the Sermon on the Mount's commands.

The lofty ethic of the Kingdom which Jesus proclaimed from
the mount and his exemplary life will continue to captivate and in-
spire us. But if he is only a master teacher and the great example, he becomes our despair rather than our hope because we cannot measure up to him. But through his death and resurrection
God's grace is mediated to us. Forgiveness, acceptance, and love
are extended to us so that discipleship is an act of responsive obedience to the one who is model and example but also savior and lord.

Christian discipleship implies our attempt to "do" the Sermon
on the Mount, but our doing is also a gift of grace. The Pauline
paradox of "I, yet not I, but the grace of God" persists in reference to the Sermon on the Mount. Throughout the history of Christian doctrine the paradoxical tension between synergism and grace

has never been resolved.   The Sermon on the Mount is not a new
law which we must keep to gain salvation.   But neither dare we ignore and neglect its demands since we are saved by "grace alone."
It is along this continuum that we must take our place with the realization that the paradox will always remain.

The Christian community continues to be inspired and chal-
lenged by those who see in the Sermon on the Mount a pattern for
living.   There have always been those who believed that the teachings of Jesus must lead to a life of costly witness and that "following Jesus" implied "entering the narrow gate" and taking the "hard
way" which "leads to life."   For some this has meant a commit-
ment to simple living, a rejection of oaths, and a conscientious attempt to be nonresistant.   Without these witnesses the church would
be greatly impoverished.   For they continue to act as light and salt
and leaven in a church and in a world which too easily embrace
mammonism, war, racism, classism, so that the tension between
Christ and culture is relaxed and they tend to become indistinguish-
able.

One of the most difficult problems relating to the Sermon on
the Mount concerns its relevance as a social ethic.   There is widespread agreement that the commands of the Sermon have an individualistic or person to person reference.   How can social groups exist
without resisting evil and exercising judgment?   How are they to
"turn the other cheek" and "go the second mile?"   How is it possible
for them to take no thought and to reflect no anxiety about tomorrow?   Such hard realities caused Luther to propose his theory of
the "two kingdoms."   Likewise it led the Anabaptists to the conviction that a "true Christian disciple" could not participate in state-
craft and the civil order.   Reinhold Niebuhr, perhaps more pro-
foundly and convincingly than anyone else, argued that the moral op-
tions open to individuals are usually impossible for social groups to
realize.   Nation states, for example, cannot exist in a "fallen world"
by following literally the Sermon on the Mount because they are involved with the competing and sometimes dichotomous claims of love
and justice.

How then can we view the contemporary relevance of the Sermon on the Mount?   The Sermon's teachings will lead some to take
the way of radical discipleship without regard for social and political
implications.   Their witness will constantly remind us of the temptation to make our peace with the mores of a secular culture, to compromise our convictions prematurely, to seek our own advantage first
rather than the Kingdom of God.   The "Christ against culture" position has been a stimulus for renewal in Christian history and must
continue to be so.

But there are other Christians who will become deeply involved
in the arenas of politics and economics where radical discipleship
becomes an "impossible possibility."   But the ideals of the Sermon
on the Mount are still relevant.   On the justice-injustice continuum

there are gradations and degrees. The Christian whose decision-making and activity are informed by the Sermon on the Mount will ever seek to realize the highest levels of justice and "love" in any given situation. While the choices are never black and white-- wholly good vs. wholly evil--nevertheless, the "shade of grey" is crucial. The Christian's task is to seek to move social structures toward more humaneness, more responsiveness to the common good. In a word, his goal is to renew and transform our political, economic, and social communities so that they will increasingly reflect and conform to the Kingdom.

Schweitzer called the Sermon on the Mount an interim ethic and he maintained that Jesus' whole life and ministry was conditioned by eschatology. While most interpreters reject his extreme conclusions, few would deny that the Sermon has an eschatological reference. It is an "interim ethic" in that it is for those who live in "the time between the times." Our noblest moral efforts will not be sufficient to "build the Kingdom." In the face of the Sermon on the Mount's radical demands, we will experience frustration and failure. It is the gift of hope which makes the effort possible. Hope assures us that the Kingdom in which we participate and whose signs we behold, however dimly, will one day be realized. To seek first the Kingdom and to be obedient to its commands is an act of hope--that the time is coming when the kingdom of the world shall become the Kingdom of our Lord and of His Christ, and he shall reign for ever and ever!

Part II

BIBLIOGRAPHY

FOREWORD

An extraordinarily satisfying and meaningful hobby of Dr. W. Harold Row is set forth in the following pages. It is seldom that one's hobby or major extra-professional interest is so central to one's life task. Yet in the case of Harold Row there can be no doubt that his interest over many decades in the Sermon on the Mount deepened his faith for the many tasks that he performed as Executive Director of the Brethren Service Committee, which later became the Brethren Service Commission.

Harold, as he was known to thousands of his warm friends and admirers, left no stones unturned in his effort to find various versions of the Sermon on the Mount, and annotations, commentary and sermons relating thereto. Thus the Sermon on the Mount was to him not only an inspired literature but a literature of ever-widening meaning and of deepening insights.

His collections included discoveries in many libraries, churches, and repositories of religious literature in many countries, from the United States to the Soviet Union.

Many of us recall with deep satisfaction the sermons that he himself preached on the Sermon on the Mount, in which the inspiration and fruit of his study were invariably reflected.

The following pages are worth thoughtful study both for their spiritual value and as clues to Harold's devotion to a major theme of undying interest.

Andrew W. Cordier
President Emeritus
Columbia University

127

SERMON ON THE MOUNT TEXTS

[Bible. New Testament.]* English. Selections. 1899.
The Sermon on the Mount and other extracts from the New Testament; a verbatim translation from the Greek, with notes on the mystical or arcane sense by J. M. Pryse. New York: E. B. Page, 1899.

English. Selections. Wycliffe. 1902
The Sermon on the Mount and other passages from Wyclif's translation of the Bible. Boston: Directors of the Old South Work, 1902.

Gospels. English. Selections. Authorized. 1955.
The Sermon on the Mount and other sayings of Jesus.
Mount Vernon, N.Y.: Peter Pauper Press, 1955.
Decorated by Valenti Angelo.

Matthew I-VII. Mbundu of Benguella. 1889.
Mateo la Marko. Matthew, ch. I-VII and Mark, translated by W. M. Stover. Benguella: West Central African Mission, 1889.

_____. Nupe. 1860.
The first seven chapters of the Gospel according to St. Matthew, in Nupe. Translated by the Rev. Samuel Crowther. London: B. and F. B. S., 1860.

Matthew IV, 23-VIII, 1. English. 1861.
The Sermon on the Mount. Illuminated by W. and G. Hudsley. Illus. by Charles Rolt. Chromolithographed by W. R. Timms. London: 1861.

_____

*As in the classificatory hierarchy of, for example, a library catalog card, the following entries will all be understood to begin with the elements "Bible. New Testament."

_____. English. Authorized. 1955.
The Sermon on the Mount. Introduction by Norman
Vincent Peale. Wood engravings by John De Pol. Cleve-
land: World Publishing Co., 1955.

Matthew V. Algonkin. 1873.
[Cuoq, Jean Andre]
Chrestomathie algonquine. Paris: Maisonneuve et Cie,
1873.

_____. English.
The beginning of the New Testament translated by Wil-
liam Tyndale, 1525; facsimile of the unique fragment of the
uncompleted Cologne edition; with an introduction by Alfred
W. Pollard. Oxford: Clarendon Press, 1926.
Contains chapter V of Matthew in the versions of Tyndale,
MDXXXV, the Great Bible, MDXXXIX, the Geneva Bible,
MDLX, the Bishops Bible, MDLXXII, the Jesuit version,
Rheims, MDLXXXII, the Authorized version, MDCXI.

_____. _____. 1822.
Sermon and catechism for children. Printed by J.
Carey. York: 1822.

_____. _____. 1905.
The Beatitudes from the Sermon on the Mount. Harting,
Petersfield, Hampshire: Pear Tree Press, 1905.
200 copies printed by James Guthrie. Written out by
Percy J. Smith. Drawings by James Guthrie.

_____. _____. 1938.
Saint Matthew; chapter five of the Gospel according to
Saint Matthew. Chepstow, Eng.: Tinturn Press, 1938.

Matthew V, 1-11. Algonquin. 1873.
Fragments de chrestomathie de la langue algonquine.
Les huit beatitudes, Saint Mathieu, ch. V. Paris: 1873.

_____. English. 1868.
The Beatitudes of Our Lord, with parallel passages.
Six illuminations. London: T. Nelson and Sons, 1868.

_____. _____. 1905.
The Beatitudes from the Sermon on the Mount. Writ-
ten out by Percy J. Smith. Drawings by James Guthrie.
Harting, Petersfield: Pear Tree Press, 1905.

————. ————. Authorized. 1951.
The Beatitudes from the Sermon on the Mount. Written
out by Betty Althea Bunn, and printed in black and colour, as
a souvenir of the Festival of Britain. Bognor Regis, Sussex:
Mermaid Press, 1951.

————. ————. 1971.
The Beatitudes. Nine cards illuminated in gold and col-
ours. London: S. P. C. K., 1871.

Matthew V-VII. Polyglot. 1819.
Die Bergpredigt unsers Herrn und Heilandes Jesus
Christus. In deutscher, englischer und französischer
Sprache. Pyrmont: Uslar, 1819.

————. ————. 1860.
Our Blessed Lord's Sermon on the Mount in English, in
Tamil, in Malayalam, in Kanarese, and in Telugu; in the
Anglo-Indian character, with a vocabulary, minute grammati-
cal praxis and inflexional tables; by the Rev. G. U. Pope.
Madras: Gantz Brothers, 1860.
Oriental texts in parallel columns with two columns to
a page; English text at foot of the page.

————. American Indian sign language. 1880.
The Sermon on the Mount in the Indian sign-talk. Illus.
Fort Smith, Ark.: 1890.

————. Assamese. 1837.
Sermon on the Mount in Asámese. 1837.

————. Basque. 1831.
Sermon sur la montagne, en grec et en basque, pré-
cédé du paradigme de la conjugaison basque, par m. Fleury de
Lécluse. Toulouse: Vieusseux, 1831.

————. Bemba. 1906.
Fyebo fya kwa Yesu Klistu pa Lupili. Matthew V., VI.,
and VII. Mu Chi-Bemba. London: B. and F. B. S., 1906.

————. Bengali. 1035.
The Sermon on the Mount. 2d ed., enl., with extracts
on relative duties, in English, and Bengali in the Roman
character. Calcutta: 1835.

————. Braille. 1854.
Our Lord's Sermon on the Mount. Printed in embossed

(Matthew V-VII.)

characters for the use of the blind. Bristol: Asylum for
the Blind; London: Chapman and Hall, 1854.

_____. Canarese. 1869.
The Sermon on the Mount. 3rd ed. Mangalore: Basel
Mission Press, 1869.

_____. Danish. 1964.
Jesu bjergpraediken; Mattaeus-evangeliet, kap. 5-7.
København: Scripta, 1964.
225 copies printed plus 28 copies marked A-Å.

_____. _____. 1966.
Bjergpraediken. Mattaeus-evangeliet, kapitlerne fem til
syv. Efter aut. overs. af 1948. Vignetter af Harry W.
Holm. Eiler Eilentsers Bogtrykkeri, 1966.

_____. Dutch. 1945.
De Bergrede. 's-Gravenhage: E. Wattez, 1945.

_____. _____. 1968.
De bergrede. Naschrift van W. K. Grossouw. Den
Haag: Bert Bakker/Daamen, 1968.

_____. English. 1783.
The New-England Psalter; or Psalms of David. With
the Proverbs of Solomon, and Christ's Sermon on the Mount.
Being a proper introduction for the training up children in the
reading of the Holy Scriptures. Boston: T. and J. Fleet,
1783.
A number of subsequent editions by various printers
were published.

_____. _____. Authorized. 1845.
The Sermon on the Mount; Gospel of St. Matthew chap-
ters V., VI., VII. Illuminated by Owen Jones. London:
Longman, 1845.

_____. _____. 1854.
The Sermon on the Mount; Gospel of St. Matthew. Illuminated by F. Lepelle de Boi Gallais. London: 1854.

_____. _____. 1861.
The Sermon on the Mount. Illuminated by Samuel
Stanesby. London: John Field, 1861.

(Matthew V–VII. English.)

—————————. 1861.
        The Sermon on the Mount. Illuminated by Ward G.
Audsley. Illustrated by C. Rolt. London: Day and Son,
1861.

—————————. 1885.
        The inaugural address of the Kingdom of Heaven: being
a translation, by C. B. Seymour, of the Sermon on the
Mount, with a running comment and notes. Louisville, Ky.:
J. P. Morton, 1885.

—————————. 1885.
        The Sermon on the Mount. Illus. Introduction by the
Right Rev. the Lord Bishop of Ripon. London: Hodder and
Stoughton, 1885.

—————————. Authorized. 1886.
        The Sermon on the Mount. Boston: Roberts Brothers,
1886.
        Ornately illustrated.

—————————. 1893.
        The Sermon on the Mount in Burnz's pronouncing print.
New York: Burnz and Co., 1893.
        The object of this print is to present the pronunciation
        of English words as clearly and exactly as possible,
        without change of spelling. "Printed especially for Sun-
        day schools and missions, and for teaching illiterates
        and foreigners."

—————————. Miles. 1899.
        The Teaching of Jesus today. The Sermon on the Mount
rendered from the Greek into simpler English by Eustace H.
Miles. London: Grant Richards, 1899.

—————————. Authorized. 1900.
        The Sermon on the Mount. Wausau, Wis.: Philosopher
Press, 1900.
        Made into this book by Helen Bruneau Van Vechten,
        with decorative embellishment after the designs of
        Agnes Bassett.

—————————. 1908.
        The Sermon on the Mount, from the translation author-
ized by King James, A.D. 1611; together with the Revised

(Matthew V-VII.   English.)

version of A.D. 1901.   New York: Duffield, 1908.

_____.   _____.   Authorized.   1909.
The Sermon on the Mount.   Introduction by Rev. J.
Edgar Park.   Boston: Pilgrim Press, 1909.
Meditations by Rev. Park precede text.

_____.   _____.   1911.
The Sermon on the Mount.   Designed, written out, and
illuminated by Alberto Sangorski, including a miniature taken
from the painting "The light of the world" by Holman Hunt.
Printed on double leaves folded in Chinese style; title and
text within illuminated borders.   London: Chatto and Windus,
1911.

_____.   _____.   Authorized.   1913.
The Sermon on the Mount.   Portland, Me.: T. B.
Mosher, 1913.
900 copies published on Kelmscott handmade paper and
50 copies on Japan vellum.

_____.   _____.   1917.
The Sermon on the Mount.   San Francisco: J. H.
Nash, 1917.
Text within gold-lined ornamental border.   200 copies
printed.   Decorations by Roy F. Coyle.

_____.   _____.   1921.
The Sermon on the Mount.   Printed for the Book Club
of California by J. H. Nash.   San Francisco: 1921.
Text in red, blue, and black, within green double line
border.   300 copies printed.

_____.   _____.   Authorized.   1924.
The Sermon on the Mount.   San Francisco: Grabhorn
Press, 1924.
Colored illustrations.   190 copies printed.   Designs by
Stafford Duncan.

_____.   _____.   _____.   1926.
The Sermon on the Mount as told by St. Matthew.   San
Francisco: J. H. Nash, 1926.
Text in double columns within colored ornamental
borders.   Decoration and initials by William N. Wilke.
Unbound, in green paper folder.

(Matthew V-VII.   English.)

_____ .   1927.
Christ's Sermon on the Mount. Birmingham, Eng.:
Birmingham School of Printing, 1927.

_____ .   Authorized. 1930.
The Sermon on the Mount, from the Gospel of St.
Matthew.   Flancham, Bognor Regis, Sussex: Pear Tree
Press, 1930.
    200 copies printed.

_____ .   1930.
The Sermon on the Mount: the simple words of Jesus
Christ as told by his disciple, St. Matthew.   Printed for
Edward L. and Estelle Doheny by J. H. Nash.   San Fran-
cisco: 1930.

_____ .   Authorized. 1934?
The Sermon on the Mount: the simple words of Jesus
Christ as told by his disciple, St. Matthew.   Printed for
Edward L. and Estelle Doheny by John Henry Nash.   San
Francisco, 1934?

_____ .   1935.
The Sermon on the Mount; being the fifth, sixth, and
seventh chapters of the Gospel according to St. Matthew in
the King James version of the Holy Bible.   New York:
Golden Cross Press, 1935.
    110 copies of this edition of the Sermon on the Mount
    have been designed and hand illuminated by Valenti An-
    gelo and printed by Edmund R. Thompson at Hawthorn
    House, Windham, Connecticut, December, 1935.

_____ .   1935.
The Sermon on the Mount.   Drawings by Horace J.
Knowles.   London: Ivor Nicholson and Watson, 1935.

_____ .   1935.
The Sermon on the Mount; King James' version, the
Gospel according to St. Matthew.   Restatement as given
from the heavens for life guidance to Pallas Parma.   San
Francisco: Grabhorn Press, 1935.
    100 copies printed.

_____ .   1937.
The Sermon on the Mount.   Oxford: B. Blackwell, 1937.

(Matthew V-VII.   English.)

Printed on double leaves folded in Chinese style; title
and text within illuminated borders; initials.   Designed,
written out, and illuminated by Alberto Sangorski; includes a miniature taken from the painting "The light of
the world" by Holman Hunt.

_____. _____. 1938.
The Sermon on the Mount, from the Gospel according
to St. Matthew.   Privately printed for the Monastery Hill
Bindery. Chicago: 1938.
2000 copies printed.

_____. _____. 1940.
The Sermon on the Mount, by Our Lord Jesus Christ
as told by St. Matthew.   Eugene, Ore.:   University of Ore-
gon, John Henry Nash Fine Arts Press, 1940.
Designed by John Henry Nash.   In double columns;
within line borders.

_____. _____. _____. 1942.
The Sermon on the Mount from the Gospel according to
St. Matthew.   Printed for Holiday House of New York by the
Monastery Hill Press. Chicago: 1942.

_____. _____. _____. 1943.
The Sermon on the Mount, chapters V, VI, and VII of
the Gospel of Matthew from the Authorized Version of the
Holy Bible. Chicago: Basic Books, 1943.

_____. _____. _____. 1946.
The Sermon on the Mount.   Everett Shinn illustrated
ed. Philadelphia, Toronto: John C. Winston, 1946.

_____. _____. _____. 1950.
The Sermon on the Mount, being the fifth, sixth, and
seventh chapters of the Gospel according to St. Matthew in
the King James version of the Holy Bible.   Bronxville, N.Y.:
Press of Valenti Angelo, 1950.
50 copies, designed, printed and illuminated by Valenti
Angelo.

_____. _____. _____. 1952.
Excerpts from Christ's Sermon on the Mount according
to the Gospel of St. Matthew.   Lexington, Va.:   C. Harold
Lauck, 1952.

(Matthew V-VII.   English.)

—————————. ————————. . 1959.
—————— The Sermon on the Mount. New York: American Bible
Society, 1959.

—————————. ————————. . 1968.
—————— The Sermon on the Mount, being the fifth, sixth, and
seventh chapters of the Gospel according to St. Matthew in
the King James version of the Holy Bible. Chicago: Monastery Hill Bindery, 1968.
      Design, typography, and production by Norman W.
      Forgue. Text within blue and white borders.

—————————. ————————. 1972.
—————— The Sermon on the Mount. Port Moresby: Bible Society in Australia, 1972.

—————————. ————————. Paraphrases. 1724.
—————— A paraphrase upon Our Saviour's Sermon on the Mount.
London: J. Knapton, 1724.

—————————. ————————. ————————. 1855.
—————— Christ's Sermon on the Mount in verse; with analytical
divisions and explanatory notes. By R. A. London:
Wertheim and Macintosh, 1855.

—————————. ————————. ————————. Jobson. 1864.
—————— A metrical version of the Sermon on the Mount. By
D. Wemyss Jobson. Melbourne: H. T. Dwight, 1864.

—————————. ————————. ————————. Kimball. 1871.
—————— The Sermon on the Mount translated into English verse.
2nd ed. New York: A. D. F. Randolph, 1871.

—————————. ————————. ————————. Findlay. 1920.
—————— The Sermon on the Mount, with a paraphrase. By J.
Alexander Findlay. London: J. A. Sharp, 1920.

—————————. ————————. ————————. Scher. 1954.
—————— The Master-speech: the Sermon on the Mount; a nonsectarian interpretation of Matthew 5-7, with questions and
answers for study. New York: Exposition Press, 1954.

—————————. ————————. ————————. Jordan. 1964.
—————— Practical religion or the Sermon on the Mount and the
Epistle of James in the Koinonia "Cotton Patch" version.

(Matthew V-VII. English.)

Americus, Ga.: Koinonia Farm, 1964.

_____ . _____ . Phonetic. 1904.
Krist's Sermun on the Mount together with The prodig'l,
a poem, speld az spōk'n bi Judson Jōnz. Klēvland, Mine-
sota: J. Jōnz, 1904.

_____ . _____ . Shorthand. 1846.
The Sermon on the Mount; Matthew, ch. 5, 6, 7. In
phonography, written in an easy style for learners. London:
Isaac Pitman; Bath: Phonetic Institution, 1846.

_____ . _____ . _____ . 1848.
Christ's Sermon on the Mount in phonography. Pre-
pared by S. P. Andrews and A. F. Boyle. New York:
Andrews and Boyle, 1848.

_____ . _____ . _____ . 1866.
The Sermon on the Mount. Lithographed in the cor-
responding style of phonography, by James Butterworth.
London: F. Pitman, 1866.

_____ . _____ . _____ . 1866.
The Sermon on the Mount. Lithographed in the re-
porting style of phonography, by James Butterworth. London: F. Pitman, 1866.

_____ . French. 1822.
Le Sermon de Notre Seigneur Jésus Christ sur la
Montagne, extrait de l'Evangile selon Saint-Matthieu, chapi-
tres IV, V, VI et VII. Paris: 1822.

_____ . _____ . 1940.
Le Sermon sur la montagne. Paris: Societe religieuse
des Amis (Quakers), 1940.

_____ . _____ . 1962.
Le Sermon sur la montagne. G. L. M., 1962.

_____ . _____ (Guernsey). 1884.
The Sermon on the Mount and the Parable of the Sower,
translated into the Franco-Norman dialect of Guernsey from
the French of Le Maistre de Sacy by George Métivier, to
which is added a Sark version of the Parable of the Sower.
Edited, with parallel French and English versions, by John
Linwood Pitts. Guernsey: Guille-Allès Library, 1884.

(Matthew V-VII.)

_____. Gã. 1826.
Jesu Biergpradiken, oversat i det accraiske Sprog.
Med nogle Tillaeg af Luthers Lille Catechismus. Kiøbenhavn:
Forlagt i det Kongelige Vaisenhuses Bogtrgkkeri, 1826.
Translated by P. W. Wrisberg.

_____. Gahuku. 1972.
Gosohaq oko moloko ituni gapo. Canberra: Bible Society of Australia, 1972.

_____. Gari. 1972.
Nina turupatu a Iesu ta na vungavunga. Canberra:
Bible Society in Australia, 1972.

_____. German. Bolten. 1768.
Die Bergpredigt in einer neuen Über-setzung, von
Johann A. Bolten. Hamburg: 1768.

_____. Luther. 1887.
Die Bergpredigt unseres Herrn und Heilandes Jesu
Christi. Salzburg: Dieter. geb. m. Goldschnitt, 1887.

_____. 19-?
Die Bergpredigt Jesus Christi. Leipzig: Insel-Verlag,
19-?
Written by Graily Hewitt. 300 copies printed.

_____. Luther. 1911.
Die Bergpredigt Jesu Christi in der Lutherschen
Übersetzung. Leipzig: B. Behrs Verlag, 1911.

_____. 1914.
Die Bergpredigt. Illustriert von Eugen Burnand. Re-
produktionen des Original-Kartons zu den Glasmalereien für
die Kirche zu Herzogenbuchsee (Schweiz). Vorwort von Lasch.
Basel: Ernst Finckh Verlag, 1914.

_____. 1919.
Die Bergpredigt deützsch. Vuittemberg: 1522; Berlin:
Grandussche Verlags-Buchhandlung, 1919.
225 copies printed.

_____. 1921.
Die Bergpredigt. Offenbach am Main: Ernst Engel,
1921.

(Matthew V-VII. German.)

Printed on vellum; rubricated by hand. Unbound, un-
stitched; in cloth folder. Initials and ornaments drawn
and cut by Hans Schreiber.

_____. _____. 1922.
Die Bergpredigt. Evangelium Matthäi, 5-7. Frankfort
am Main: Hausdruckerei der Scriftgiesserei D. Stempel, 1922.
300 copies printed. Initials and ornaments drawn and
cut by Hans Schreiber.

_____. _____. Müller. 1936.
Deutsche Gottesworte; aus der Bergpredigt verdeutscht
von Ludwig Müller. 3. und 4. unveränderte Aufl. Weimer/
Thüringen: Verlag Deutsche Christen, 1936.

_____. _____. 1951.
Die Bergpredigt. Mit Holzschnitten von Rudolf Nehmer.
Berlin: Evangelische Verlag-anstalt, 1951.

_____. _____. 1952.
Auf den Felsen gebaut. Die Bergpredigt, Matth. 5-7.
Hrsg. von der Pressestelle der Evangelisch Lutherischen
Kirche in Thüringen. Jena: Wartburg Verlag, 1952.

_____. _____. 1955.
Die Bergpredigt Jesu Christi. Stuttgart-Weil im Dorf:
Ernst-Engel-Presse, 1955.

_____. _____. 1956
Die Bergpredigt. Wurzburg: Noack, 1956.

_____. _____. Paraphrases. 1771.
Die Bergpredigt Jesu, nach einer freien Übersetzung
in Versen. Zurich: Orell, 1771.

_____. _____. _____.
Die Bergpredigt unsers Herrn und Heilandes Jesu
Christi. In Versen. Strassburg: Heitz, n.d.

_____. Gothic and German. 1881.
Ulfilas Aivaggeljo thairh Maththaiu K. V-VII. Heraus-
gebeben von August Schäfer. Wildshut: 1881.

_____. Gothic. 1924.
Die gotische Bergpredigt, in Sievers, Eduard Wilhelm,

(Matthew V-VII.)

compiler and editor. Deutsche Sagversdichtungen des IX-XI
Jahrhunderts. Heidelberg: 1924, 164-73.

_____. Greek and English. 1834.
First lines in Greek; or, the Sermon on the Mount, exhibited both in Greek and English characters: with an inter-
linear translation. By Thomas Foster Harham. London: J.
Souter, 1934.

_____. Guaraní. 1888.
Edición bi-lengual guaraní y español de El sermón de
Jesu-Cristo en la montaña. Londres: Sociedad Biblica Bri-
tánica e Estrangera, 1888.

_____. Gujarati. 1854.
Sermon on the Mount with comments. Bombay: 1854.

_____. Hindustani. 1834.
The Sermon on the Mount. 2d ed., enl., with extracts
on relative duties, in English, and Hindustani in the Roman
character. Calcutta: Baptist Mission Press, 1834.

_____. Hiri Motu. 1972.
Iesu ia haroro ororo dekenai. Canberra: Bible Society
in Australia, 1972.

_____. Hungarian. 1948.
Hegyi Beszéd, mely írva taláható Máté evangyélioma.
5. 6. es 7. részében. Ford. Károli Gáspár. Budapest:
Ref. Traktátus Váll, 1948.

_____. Judaeo-Spanish. n.d.
... הבשורה על פי מת', פרשה ה'–[ז']
no title page; no date.

_____. Karen. 1857.
The Sermon on the Mount. Bghai Karen. Translated
by Francis Mason. Maulmain: American Mission Press,
1957.

_____. Kongo. Richards. 1891.
Nlongolo kua Kikongo. 1891.

_____. Latin. 1953.
Sermo Domini in Monte. Verona: Officina Bodoni, 1953.
100 copies printed.

Texts   141

(Matthew V-VII.)

———. Latin and French. 1953.
Sermo Domini in Monte. Verona: 1953.
50 copies printed. Composée en caractères Zeno de
Giovanni Mardersteig. Vellum.

———. Magi. 1972.
Oro de obasa. Port Moresby: Bible Society in Australia, 1972.

———. Motu. 1972.
Iesu na ororo ai e haroro. Port Moresby: Bible Society in Australia, 1972.

———. Nunggubuyu. 1972.
Najesus waniyambini marlandhirringindirriy. Canberra:
Bible Society in Australia, 1972.

———. Pidgin English. 1972.
Jisas i autim tok antap long mounten. Port Moresby:
Bible Society in Australia, 1972.

———. Pushtu. 1884.
The Sermon on the Mount. Lithographed. Lahore:
1884.

———. Seneca. Harris. 1829.
Christ hagonthahninoh nonodagahyot. Printed for the
American Tract Society by D. Fanshaw. New York: 1829.
Translated by T. S. Harris and J. Young. English
and Seneca on opposite pages. Bound with Young,
James, fl. 1820-29. Gainoh ne nenodowohga neuwahmuh-
dah.

———. Sindhi. 1883.
The Sermon on the Mount. Lithographed. Karachi:
1883.

———. Spanish and Tzeltal. 1951.
Sk'op Jesus la schol ta wits. El Sermon del monte
(Mateo 5-7). Cuernavaca: Tip. Indigena, 1951.

———. Suau. 1972.
Oea tupi eai guguiana. Port Moresby: Bible Society
in Australia, 1972.

(Matthew V-VII.)

_____. Tulu. 1900.
The Sermon on the Mount. Madras: Auxiliary to the
B. and F. B. S. Mangalore, 1900.

_____. Turkish. 1860?
The Sermon on the Mount. Constantinople: 1860?

_____.   . 1863.
The Sermon on the Mount with commentary. Constantinople: 1863.

_____. Umon. 1895.
Göspel Mark udid görö weni Jisus ugat age okput ibibi.
Age görö Umön. Mark's Gospel and the Sermon on the Mount
in Umön. Translated by Ebenezer Deas. Edinburgh: National Bible Society of Scotland, 1895.

_____. Zulu. 1860?
Enkulumo e ze shunyaelo nko Yesu Kristi e Nkosi e tu
e Ntabeni, Mattheu V. VI. VII. Ze penduloe nke nkulumo ea
ba ka Zulu (nko J. Allison). Pietermaritzburg: D. D. Bu-
chanan, 1860?

Matthew VI. English. Authorized. 1960?
The sixth chapter of St. Matthew containing the Lord's
prayer. New York: Hammer Creek Press, 1960?
65 copies printed. Decorations by Valenti Angelo. In
addition to above, 20 copies were printed on Arches
hand-made paper for the artist and printer.

SERMON ON THE MOUNT CRITICISM, INTERPRETATION, SERMONS, MEDITATIONS, ETC.

Aanby, Sigurd S. Bergprekenen med forklaringer. Til støtte ved undervisningen i middelskolens avgangsklasse. Oslo: Dybwad, 1926.

Abel, F. M. "Coup d'oeil sur la Koiné." Revue biblique 35 (1926) 5-26.

Abernathy, A. R. "A Study of the Sermon on the Mount." Review and Expositor 18 (1921) 193-201.

Achelis, Ernest C. Die Bergpredigt nach Matthäeus und Lucas exegetisch und kritisch untersucht. Bielefeld: Velhagen & Klassing, 1875.
An exhaustive study considered for many years a standard work.

Adams, Frank D. Did Jesus Mean It? Boston: Universalist Publishing House, 1923.
Prayers and study questions.

Adeney, Walter F. "Sermon on the Mount," in Hastings, James, ed. A Dictionary of Christ and the Gospels. vol. 2. New York: Charles Scribner's Sons, 1908, 607-12.

Ahlberg, Adolf. Bergspredikans etik. De nyare tolknings-försöken. Stockholm: Diakonistyrelsen, Bokförlag, 1930.
A scholarly treatment of the ethics of the Sermon on the Mount.

Ahlberg, P. V. Jesu bergspredikan enligt Matteus' evangelium 5.-7. kapitlen. Med text samt inledning och förklarande anmärkningar. Laxsjö: Författaren, 1927.

Aicher, Georg. "Mt. 5, 13: Ihr seid das Salz der Erde?"
Biblische Zeitschrift 5 (1907) 48-59.

Allen, Charles L. The Sermon on the Mount. Westwood,
N. J. : Revell, 1966.
    A popular interpretation relating the Sermon on the
Mount to the Christian Life.

Allen, Erastus D. The Spirit of Christ's Sermon on the
Mount. St. Louis: 1921.
    Brief popular treatment.

Allen, Isaac N. Reflections on Portions of the Sermon on
the Mount. Intended Principally for Soldiers. London:
Society for Promoting Christian Knowledge, 1848.
    Meditations.

Allen, J. P. The Sermon on the Mount. Nashville: Broadman Press, 1959.
    Questions designed for group study and discussion.

Allgeier, A. "Die Crux interpretum im neutestamentlichen
Ehescheidungsverbot. Eine philologische Untersuchung zu
Mt. 5, 32, und 19, 9" in Reverendissimo Patri Iacobo
Mariae Vosté. Roma: Saluta del Grillo, 1943, 128-42.

Allstrom, Elizabeth C. Truly I Say to You. Woodcuts by
Mel Silverman. New York: Abingdon, 1966.
    Juvenile.

Andrén, Victor. Jesu Bergspredikan. Tre föredrag.
Uddevalla: Krykliga forbundet, 1937.

Andrews, Charles F. The Sermon on the Mount. London:
George Allen & Unwin, 1942; New York: Macmillan,
1942; Toronto: Nelson, 1942; New York: Collier Books,
1962.
    Various topics such as the Kingdom of God, the Beati-
tudes, the Law of Love are emphasized. Sermon on the
Mount is a description of the good life.

Archer, E. Wallace. "Matthew V. 39." Expository Times
42 (1930-31) 190-91.

Arendzen, J. P. "Ante-Nicene Interpretations of the Sayings
on Divorce." Journal of Theological Studies 20 (1919)
230-41.

Arenson, Adolf. Die Bergpredigt. Berlin: Philosophisch-
theosophischer Verlag, 1914.
An address which interprets the Sermon on the Mount
from a theosophical point of view.

_____. Bergspredikan. Norrköping: Forlagsfören, 1914.
(See his Die Bergpredigt)

Arndt, Friedrich. Die Bergpredigt Jesu Christi. Siebenzehn
Betrachtungen in der Trinitatiszeit 1837 gehalten. 2 Bd.
Magdeburg: W. Heinrichshofen, 1838-1839.

Arnold, Eberhard. Salt and Light; Talks and Writings on the
Sermon on the Mount. Rifton, N.Y.: Plough Publishing
House, 1967.
The founder of the communities of the Society of
Brothers (Bruderhof) views the Sermon on the Mount as
relevant in its unconditional absoluteness to the Christian
life. Deals with such issues as hopes for a peaceful
world, the attitude of the heart in man's relationship to
his fellow man, man's relationship to material goods,
money, property, man's attitude to the question of power.

Asmussen, Hans. Die Bergpredigt. Eine Auslegung von
Matth. Kap 5-7. Gottingen: Vandenhoeck & Ruprecht,
1939.
Verse by verse commentary with practical emphasis.

Atkins, Gaius G. From the Hillside. Boston: Pilgrim
Press; London: Independent Press, 1948.
Popular exposition.

Augsburger, Myron S. The Expanded Life: the Sermon on
the Mount for Today. New York: Abingdon, 1972.
The Beatitudes are interpreted as an outline for the
Sermon on the Mount. They form a series of themes
which make up the Sermon. Each Beatitude is projected
into the Sermon to see how Jesus himself interpreted its
meaning. The nature of discipleship is emphasized by relating the Beatitudes to our total life pattern.

Augustin, George. "Soyez parfaits comme votre Père
céleste (Matth. 5, 17-48)." Bible et vie chrétienne 19
(1957) 85-90.

Augustine, Saint. Augustinus zur Bergpredigt. Eingeleitet
und übertragen von Albert Schmitt. St. Ottilien: Eos-

Verlag, 1952.
(See his De Sermone Domini in Monte. Book II, 1494)

_____ . Commentaire sur le Sermon de la Montagne.
Trad. de l'abbé Devoille. Rio de Janeiro: Au siège
central de l'église positiviste du Brésil, 1905.
(See his De Sermone Domini in Monte, 1494)

_____ . Les Commentaires de St. Augustin, sur le Ser-
mon de Nostre Seigneur sur la Montagne. Trad. Pierre
Lombert. Paris: A. Pralard, 1683; Paris, F. et P.
Delaulne, 1701.
(See his De Sermone Domini in Monte, 1494)

_____ . Commentary on the Lord's Sermon on the Mount,
with Seventeen Related Sermons. Trans. Denis J. Ka-
vanagh. New York: Fathers of the Church, 1951; Washington, D.C.: Catholic University of America Press, 1963.
(See his De Sermone Domini in Monte, 1494)

_____ . Divi Aurelii Augustine, ... de Sermone Domini
in monte secundum Matthaeum libri duo. Parisiis: apud
viduam M. Durand, 1669.
(See his De Sermone Domini in monte, 1494)

_____ . Divi Aurelii Augustine liber de Agone christiano.
De Sermone Christi in monte habito. Coloniae: U. Zell,
ca. 1472; Pellechet: 1571.
(See his De Sermone Domini in monte, 1494)

_____ . Expositio beati Augustini de Sermone Domini in
monte. Parisiis: per U. Gering et B. Rembolt, 1494;
Paris: 1502; Pellechet: 1506.
A commentary in two Books. Book I is an interpretation of Matthew 5 in which Augustine seeks to answer the
question of the true meaning of the Sermon on the Mount.
Book II deals with Matthew 6-7, and he emphasizes especially prayer, centering around an interpretation of the
Lord's Prayer. Augustine regards the Sermon on the
Mount as a perfect pattern of the Christian life and a
standard for every Christian. This work is a significant
contribution to the history of ethics and moral theology.

_____ . The Lord's Sermon on the Mount. Trans. John
J. Jepson. Westminster, Md.: Newman Press; London:
Longmans, Green, 1948.
(See his De Sermone Domini in monte, 1494)

_____. The Preaching of Augustine, "Our Lord's Sermon on the Mount." Edited and with an introd. by Jaroslav Pelikan. Trans. Francine Cardman. Philadelphia: Fortress Press, 1973.
(See his De Sermone Domini in monte, 1494)

_____. The Sermon on the Mount Expounded, and The Harmony of the Evangelists. Trans. by William Findlay and S. D. F. Salmond. Edinburgh: T. & T. Clark, 1873.
(See his De Sermone Domini in monte, 1494)

_____. De sermone Domini in monte libros duos. Turnholti: Typographi Brepols Editores Pontificii, 1967.
(See his De Sermone Domini in monte, 1494)

_____. De sermone Domini in monte secundum Matthaeum libri duo. Migne, Jacques P., comp. Patrologiae cursus completus. Series Latina 34. Parisiis: 1861, 1229-1308.
(See his De Sermone Domini in monte, 1494)

Azibert, L'abbé. "Le sermon 'in monte' selon S. Matthieu (V, VI, VII); in 'loco campestri' selon S. Luc (VI. 20-49)." Revue biblique 3 (1894) 94-109.

Bachmann, Johannes P. "The Sermon on the Mount in the Interpretation of the Enthusiasts and of Luther." STM thesis. Union Theological Seminary, New York, 1961.

Bacon, Benjamin W. "The Order of the Lukan 'Interpolations.' II. The Smaller Interpolation, Lk. 6:20-8:3." Journal of Biblical Literature 36 (1917) 112-39.

_____. The Sermon on the Mount; Its Literary Structure and Didactic Purpose. New York: Macmillan, 1902.
One of the early exponents of biblical higher criticism in the United States applies the "new science" to the Sermon on the Mount. A significant, scholarly work.

_____. "The 'Single' Eye." Expositor 8th ser. 7 (1914-A) 275-88.

Bäumlein, W. "Die exegetische Grundlage der Gesetzgebung über Ehescheidung." Theologische Studien und Kritiken 30 (1957) 329-30.

Bahnsen, Wilhelm. Das Christenthum der Bergpredigt, in Predigten dargelegt. Berlin: Hermann Peters, 1889. Sermons.

Baillie, Donald M. "The Sermon on the Mount." Expository
Times 39 (1927-28) 443-47.

Baker, Abijah R. A Question Book on the Topics in Christ's
Sermon on the Mount. 3 vols. Boston: Graves and
Young, 1863.

Balmforth, Ramsden. Spiritual Agnosticism and the Sermon
on the Mount in Relation to Problems of Social Recon-
struction. London: Daniel, 1921.
    The author emphasizes the ethical interpretation of the
Sermon on the Mount in contradistinction to the ecclesiastical, theological, or intellectual. A pronounced emphasis upon the practicality of the Sermon and its relevance to social problems.

Baltensweiler, Heinrich. "Die Ehebruchsklauseln bei
Matthäus." Theologische Zeitschrift 15 (1959) 340-56.

Barclay, William. The Old Law and the New Law. Edinburgh: Saint Andrew Press, 1972.
    A popular treatment of the Ten Commandments and the
Sermon on the Mount. Intended for study and discussion.

Barnette, Henlee. "The Ethic of the Sermon on the Mount."
Review and Expositor 53 (1956) 23-33.

Barth, Fritz. Die Grundsätze der Bergpredigt und das Leben
der Gegenwart. Basel: Helbing & Lichtenhahn, 1899.
Brief essay.

Barton, George A. "The Meaning of the 'Royal Law,' Matt.
5: 21-48." Journal of Biblical Literature 37 (1918) 54-65.

Bartsch, Hans W. "Feldrede und Bergpredigt. Redaktionsar-
beit in Lukas 6." Theologische Zeitschrift 16 (1960) 5-18;
auch in: Entmythologisierende Auslegung. Hamburg-
Bergstedt: 1962, 116-24.

Bassermann, Heinrich. De loco Matthaei capitis V, 17-20
commentatio exegetica, critica, historica theogorum
jenensium ordini.... Jenae: apud Hermannum Dabis,
1876.
    A detailed and scholarly commentary on Matthew 5:17-
20.

Bassi, Domenico. L'etica christiana nel Discorse della Mon-

tagna. Firenze: Felice Le Monnier, 1935.
Sermon on the Mount is divided into sections with each
chapter a commentary on one section. Question of ethics
is central.

Batdorf, Irwin W. "How Shall We Interpret the Sermon on
the Mount?" Journal of Bible and Religion 27 (1959) 211-
17.

Bates, Walter G. Our Lord's Great Sermon. New York:
Hobson Book Press, 1945.
Sermons and meditations.

Bauer, Johannes Baptist. "De coniugali foedere quid edixerit
Matthaeus? (Mt 5, 31f.; 19, 3-9)." Verbum Domini 44
(1966) 74-78.

_____. "'Quod si sal infatuatum fuerit' (Mt. 5, 13; Mc.
9, 50; Lc. 14, 34)." Verbum Domini 29 (1951) 228-30.

Bauer, W. "Das Gebot des Feindesliebe und die alten
Christen," in Aufsätze und kleine Schriften. Tübingen:
J. C. B. Mohr, 1967, 235-52.

Baumann, Franz. Leitlinien zur Lebensgestaltung. Eine
Auslegung der Bergpredigt. Zürich: Gotthelf-Verlag,
1965.
Meditations, with emphasis on the relevance of the
Sermon on the Mount for life.

Baumgarten, Otto. Bergpredigt und Kultur der Gegenwart.
Tübingen: J. C. B. Mohr, 1921.
Commentary which emphasizes post-World War I prob-
lems in light of the Sermon on the Mount.

_____. Der Krieg und die Bergpredigt. Berlin: C. Hey-
mann, 1915.

Bavinck, Johan H. Het licht des levens. Magelang: 1934.
Meditations.

_____. Tjahja kahidoepan atawa satoe pengoendjoek djalan
pada kaslametan jang kekal. Disalin ka dalam bahasa
Melajoe rendah oleh: saorang Tasik. Batavia: Dikeloear-
kan oleh Maleische Chr. Lectuur Vereeniging, 1936; Djakarta: B. P. Kristen, 1947 (1950).
(See his Het licht des levens)

Beckett, Thomas A.   Sermon on the Mount.   London: H. R.
Allenson, 1909.

Beguiristain, Santos.   El sermón de la montaña.   Madrid:
Marsiega, 1963.

Beijer, Erik.   "Gudsrikets rättfärdighet."   Svensk teologisk
kvartalskrift 18 (1942) 89-111.

_____. Kristologi och etik in Jesu Bergspredikan.
Stockholm: Diakonistyrelsen Bokförlag. 1960.
A scholarly analysis which treats the history of interpretation of the Sermon on the Mount and its relationship
to ethical and Christological questions.

_____. "Til Bergspredikans etik.   En litteraturöversikt.
Domprosten och förste teologie professorn teologie doktor
Erik Stave.   In piam memoriam, " in Svensk exegetisk
årsbok II.   Uppsala: Wretmans boktryckeri A.-B., 1937,
200-26.

Berger, R.   "Die Magna Charta der Gottesherrschaft."
Theologisches Jahrbuch (1967) 113-23.

Die Bergpredigt.   2. Aufl. Unterweise mich, Herr, nach
Deinem Wort. Gruppenarbeit unter Jugendlichen über
Bibel und Kirche.   5. Hrsg. von Carl Ernst Sommer.
Frankfurt am Main: Anker-Verlag, 1966.

Die Bergpredigt, nach Inhalt und Zusammenhang.   Ein
exegetisch-homiletischer Versuch.   Gütersloh: C. Bertelsmann, 1881.

"Die Bergpredigt und das positive Recht."   Gewalt und Ge-
waltlosigkeit.   Protokoll der Wochenend-Studientagung von
5.-7. Dez. 1952 im Heim der Evangelischen Akademie
Schloss Assenheim/Oberhessen: 1952.

De Bergrede.   Afzonderlijke uitgave uit de bijbelverklaring,
bewerkt naar Lange's Bibelwerk.   Zuid-Beyerland: L.
Rijsdijk, 1865.

De Bergrede.   In de nieuwe vertaling op last van de Neder-
landsch Bijbelgenootschap door de daartoe benoemde com-
missie bewerkt en in de Statenvertaling van 1657.   Met
een inleiding door L. J. van Holk.   Naarden: In den
Toren, 1941.

Berguer, Georges. Le Sermon sur la montagne qui est
comme le porche d'entrée de l'évangile portant gravés au
fronton, 3 mots: vous êtes heureux! Genève: Labor et
Fides, 1944.

Beyer, Hermann W. Der Christ und die Bergpredigt
nach Luthers Deutung. Munchen: C. Kaiser Verlag,
1935.

Beyer, Karl. Jesu als Lehrer. Präparationen zu den
Gleichnissen und der Bergpredigt. Hilfsbuch, Methodisches,
für den evangelischen Religionsunterricht. 6. Bd. Berlin:
Prausnitz, 1914.

Beyschlag, Karlmann. "Die Bergpredigt bei Franz von Assisi und Luther." Theologische Literaturzeitung 11 (1953)
688f.

_____. Die Bergpredigt und Franz von Assisi. Güters-
loh: C. Bertelsmann, 1955.
    Contains four sections: (1) Exegesis; (2) Analysis of
early Franciscan literature; (3) The Sermon on the Mount
in St. Francis of Assisi; (4) A comparison of the Sermon
on the Mount in Francis and Luther.

Biebericher, T. "Christus en het eudaimonisme, naar
aanleiding van Matth. VI. 1-5." Theologische studien 28
(1910) 24-31.

Bierbaum, Athanasius. Die Bergpredigt. 20 Abhandlungen
für Exerzitien und Monatskonferenzen vor Ordensleuten.
Werl: Franziskus-Druckerei, 1936.

Bietz, Arthur L. Truths for Eternity. Nashville: Southern
Publishing Assn., 1952.
    Meditations.

Bischoff, Erich. Jesu und die Rabbinen: Jesu Bergpredigt
und "Himmelreich" in ihrer Unabhängigkeit vom Rabbinis-
mus. Leipzig: J. C. Hinrichs, 1905.
    A scholarly treatise which maintains that Jesus'
words in the Sermon on the Mount are earlier than
the rabbinic parallels and that his concept of the Kingdom of God has a deeper meaning than the Old Testament parallels.

Blaauw, August F. H.   Jezus Christus in de Bergrede, ver-
geleken met Jezus Christus in het overige Nieuwe Testament.   Groningen: R. J. Schierbeek, 1870.
Scholarly monograph.

Blackall, Ofspring.   Practical discourses upon our Saviour's
Sermon on the Mount.   London: Printed by W. B. for
Thomas Ward, 1717-18.
Sermons.

Blackwood, Andrew W.   "The Sermon on the Mount for Today."   Union Seminary Review 41 (1929-30) 162-78.

Bläser, Pedro.   "Actitud de Jesús frente al Divorcio (Mt. 5,
27-42)."   Revista biblica 17 (1955) 78-80.

_____.   "Actitud de Jesús frente al Matrimonio (Mt. 5,
27-32)."   Revista biblica 17 (1955) 37-39.

_____.   "La vocación de los discípulos (Mt. 5, 13-16)."
Revista biblica 16 (1954) 119-21.

Blair, Edward P.   Leader's Guide to the Study of the Sermon on the Mount.   Nashville: Abingdon, 1968.
A study manual for the United Methodist Church's
Quadrennial Emphasis Bible Study 1968-1972.   Each of the
eight study sessions outlines objectives and suggestions for
reaching these objectives as well as how to prepare for
each session.   Emphasis is upon the relation of the Sermon on the Mount to living the Christian life.

Blair, James.   Our Saviour's Divine Sermon on the Mount,
Contained in the Vth, VIth, and VIIth Chapters of St.
Matthew's Gospel, Explained: and the Practice of It
Recommended in Divers Sermons and Discourses.   4 v.
London: Printed for J. Brotherton and J. Oswald, 1740.
Pub. in 1722-23 in 5 v.

Blomqvist, Rudolf.   Bergspredikan och vår kristendoms tre
första huvudstycken med en undervisares uppteckningar.
För hem och skola.   Visby: Författaren, 1939.

Blumhardt, Johann Christoph.   Die Bergpredigt Jesu.   Stutt-
gart-Hohenheim: Hänssler, 1969.
Brief book of meditations by the founder of Bad Boll
center.   Evangelical and pietistic accent.

Blunt, A. W. F. "The Sermon on the Mount." Expository
Times 39 (1927-28) 545-50.

Boardman, George D. Studies in the Mountain Instruction.
New York: D. Appleton, 1880 (1901).
Fourteen lectures.

Böcher, O. "Wölfe in Schafspelzen. Zum religionsgeschicht-
lichen Hintergrund von Matth 7:15." Theologische Zeitschrift 24 (1968) 405-26.

Boehmer, Julius. Die Bergpredigt. Neu verdeutscht und kurz
erklärt für das Bedürfnis der Gegenwart. Wernigerode:
Die Aue, 1926.

Börger, J. De Bergrede. Verzamelde redevoeringen.
's-Gravenhage: Orion, 1927.

Bogdashevskiĭ, D. Blazhenstva Gospodni. Kiev: 1907.

Bohmerle, Theodor. Das Glückseligkeitsreich. Eine Auslegung des Evangeliums Matth. 5-7. Langensteinbach:
Bibelheim Bethanien, 1921.

Boice, James M. The Sermon on the Mount. Grand Rapids:
Zondervan, 1972.
        A detailed examination of Matt. 5-7 from an evangelical
perspective. The Sermon on the Mount is a summons to
a new life and not a legalistic system of morality. It
shows us the absolute necessity of the new birth.

Bone, Harry, and Van Dusen, Henry P., and Cherrington,
Ben M. Ten Studies in the Sermon on the Mount. New
York: Association Press, 1926.
        Study questions. Contains a paraphrase of the Sermon
on the Mount by G. R. H. Shafto.

Bonham, Tal D. The Demands of Discipleship; the Relevance of the Sermon on the Mount. Pine Bluff, Ark.:
Discipleship Book Co., 1967.
        A historical survey of the history of interpretation of
the Sermon on the Mount with an emphasis on its relevance. Among other interpretations, Bonham deals with
the views of literalism, premillenialism, and dispensationalism.

_____. "A Study of the Relevance of the Sermon on the

Mount in Matthew 5-7." Th. D. thesis. Southwestern
Baptist Theological Seminary, 1963.

Bonhoeffer, Dietrich. The Cost of Discipleship. London:
SCM Press, 1948 (1959); New York: Macmillan, 1949
(1959).
(See his Nachfolge)

_____. The Extraordinariness of the Christian Life; a
Bible Study of the Sermon on the Mount. New York: Na-
tional Student Christian Federation, 1964.
Contains the section on the Sermon on the Mount from
The Cost of Discipleship. (See his Nachfolge).

_____. Nachfolge. München: C. Kaiser Verlag, 1937
(1967).
A classic work on the meaning of Christian discipleship
by the renowned theologian and martyr. The second and
longest section of the book is an exposition of the Sermon
on the Mount and the Christian life.

_____. El precio de la gracia. Trad. José L. Sicre.
Salamanca: Sigueme, 1968.
(See his Nachfolge)

_____. Le prix de la grâce. Neuchâtel: Delachaux et
Niestlé, 1962.
(See his Nachfolge)

Bonnard, Pierre. "El Sermón de monte." Cuadernos
teologicos 9-10 (1954) 40-54.

_____. "Le Sermon sur la montagne." Revue de thé-
ologie et de philosophie 3 (1953) 233-46.

_____. Le Sermon sur la montagne. Neuchâtel/Paris:
1956.

Bonsirven, Joseph. "'Nisi fornicationis causa.' Comment
résoudre cette 'Crux interpretum'?" Recherches de science religieuse 35 (1948) 442-64.

Bonus, Albert. "Righteousness and Almsgiving and St.
Matthew VI. 1." Expository Times 11 (1899-1900) 379-81.

_____. "St. Luke VI. 19." Expository Times 18 (1906-
07) 287-88.

Borg, M. "New Context for Romans 13." New Testament
Studies 19 (1973) 205-18.

Bornhäuser, Karl B. Die Bergpredigt. Versuch einer zeit-
genössischen Auslegung. Gütersloh: C. Bertelsman, 1923
(1927).
A scholarly commentary.

_____. Jesu Bergspredikan. Försök till tidhistorisk
tolkning. Övers. C. Sandegren. Stockholm: Svenska
missionsförbundet, 1930.
(See his Die Bergpredigt)

_____. The Sermon on the Mount, Interpreted in the Light
of Its Contemporaraneous World of Creeds, Customs and
Conditions. Trans. Rev. and Mrs. C. Sandegren. Madras:
Christian Literature Society for India, 1951.
(See his Die Bergpredigt)

Bornkamm, G. / Fascher, E. / Frör, K. "Bergpredigt,"
in Die Religion in Geschichte und Gegenwart I. 3. Aufl.
Tübingen: J. C. B. Mohr, 1957, 1047-53.

Bornkamm, Günther. "'Bittet, suchet, klopfet an.'" Evangelische Theologie 13 (1953-54) 1-5.

_____. "Die Gegenwartsbedeutung der Bergpredigt." Uni-
versitas 9 (1954) 1283-96.

_____. "Gerechtigkeit und Gesetz Christi" [Sermon text:
Mt. 6, 24-34], in Zuwendung und Gerechtigkeit. Heidel-
berger Predigten III. Hrsg. von Paul Philippi. Claus
Westermann zum 60. Geburtstag am 7 Oktober 1969.
Göttingen: Vandenhoeck & Ruprecht, 1969, 36-42.

_____. "The History of the Exposition of the Sermon on
the Mount," in Jesus of Nazareth. Trans. Irene and
Fraser McLuskey with James M. Robinson. New York:
Harper, 1960, 221-25.
(his "Die Gegenwartsbedeutung der Bergpredigt")

_____. "Zur Geschichte der Auslegung der Bergpredigt,"
in Jesus von Nazareth. 2. Aufl. Stuttgart: W. Kohlhammer Verlag, 1957, 201-4.
(his "Die Gegenwartsbedeutung der Bergpredigt")

Bossuet, Jacques B. Erklärung der Bergpredigt. Übers.

156   Bibliography

J. M. Jimensee. Bern: Jenni; Leipzig: Volkmar,
1824.

_____. The Sermon on the Mount. Trans. F. M. Capes.
London: Longman, Green, 1900.
(See his Le Sermon sur la montagne)

_____. Le Sermon sur la montagne. Paris: 1900.
Meditations for a forty-seven-day period.

Bourbeck, Christine. Was sagt uns die Bergpredigt heute?
Stuttgart: Quell-Verlag, 1948.
A sermon.

Bousset, D. "Bergpredigt," in Die Religion in Geschichte
und Gegenwart. Tübingen: J. C. B. Mohr, 1909, 1038-
42.

Bouwman, Gilbert. "Bergpredigt," in Bibel-Lexikon. 2.
Aufl. Einsiedeln: Zürich: Köln: 1968, 193-95.

Bowman, John W., and Trapp, Roland W. The Gospel from
the Mount. Philadelphia: Westminster Press, 1957.
Interpretation used in teaching and in lectures delivered
at the Southern Baptist Theological Seminary. Includes the
author's translation or paraphrase.

Brandt, Wilhelm. "Sinn und Bedeutung der Bergpredigt."
Vorträge der Erziehungs und Schulkonferenz, pp. 57ff.

_____. "Der Spruch vom lumen internum." Zeitschrift
für die neutestamentliche Wissenschaft 14 (1913) 97-116.

Braun, Heinrich S. Selig seid ihr. Radioansprachen zur
Bergpredigt. Innsbruck: Wien: München: Tyrolia, 1960.

Braun, Maria. Die Bergpredigt des Herrn. Bochum:
Schacht, 1928.

Brekke, Egil. Bergprekenen idag. Oslo: Gyldendal, 1935.

Bretscher, Paul M. "Brief Studies: The Light of the
World." Concordia Theological Monthly 30 (1959) 931-36.

_____. "Log in Your Own Eye (Matt. 7: 1-5)." Con-
cordia Theological Monthly 43 (1972) 645-86.

Brewster, Harold S. The Simple Gospel. New York: Macmillan, 1922.
A pronounced social gospel emphasis.

Brewster, James. Lectures upon Our Lord's Sermon on the Mount. Edinburgh: Oliphant and Balfour, 1811.

Brillenburg Wurth, Gerrit. De Bergrede en onze tijd. Kampen: J. H. Kok, 1933.
A useful study which deals with various interpretations of the Sermon on the Mount such as Catholic, Lutheran, humanistic, eschatological. In addition, Brillenburg discusses the various motifs in the Sermon on the Mount. Finally, he deals with practical and ethical issues.

Bring, J. C. Die Bergpredigt Jesu. In 42 Betrachtungen ausgelegt. Herborn: Buchhandlung des Nassaur Colportagevereins, 1903.

_____. Jesu bjergpraediken udlagt i 42 betragtninger. Overs. Karl Schreiner. Steen, 1894.

Brouwer, Anneus M. De Bergrede. Zeist: G. J. A. Ruys' Uitg.-Mattschappij, 1930.
The first part forms an introduction to the Sermon on the Mount and deals with Christological, historical, and literary questions. The second part is a commentary.

Browder, Arville H. "The Sermon on the Mount and Its Significance for Contemporary Life." STM thesis. Richmong, Va.: Union Theological Seminary, 1970.

Brown, Charles R. "The Religion of a Layman. A Study of the Sermon on the Mount." Biblical World 53 (1919) 586-93; 54 (1920) 50-57, 122-29, 268-75, 363-70.

_____. The Religion of a Layman. New York: Macmillan, 1920.
A practical, ethical approach to the Sermon on the Mount.

Browne, John R. The Great Sermon. Boston: Stratford, 1935.
Deals primarily with brief expositions of the Beatitudes. A short concluding chapter interprets the remainder of the Sermon on the Mount.

Bruce, A. B. "The Wise and the Foolish Hearer." Expositor 9 (1879) 90-105.

Brückner, Wilhelm. "Über die ursprüngliche Stellung von Luk. 6, 39. 40=Matth. 15, 14; 20, 24. Ein Beitrag zur Evangelienkritik." Theologische Studien und Kritiken 42 (1869) 616-57.

Brüggemann, Theo. Gebete zur Bergpredigt. Basel: F. Reinhardt, 1971; Lahr: Ernst Kaufmann, 1971.
     Prayer meditations.

Bruppacher, H. "Was sagte Jesus in Matthäus 5:48?" Zeitschrift für die neutestamentliche Wissenschaft 58 (1967) 145.

Bryant, H. E. "Matthew V. 38, 39." Expository Times 48 (1936-37) 236-37.

Büchler, Adolf. "St. Matthew VI. 1-6 and Other Allied Passages." Journal of Theological Studies 10 (1908-09) 266-70.

Burchridge, A. T. "Singleness of Vision (Matt. VI. 22, 23; Luke XI. 33-36)." Expositor 6th ser 2 (1900) 277-87.

Burns, Vincent G. The Master's Message for the New Day. New York: Association Press, 1926.
     Meditations.

Burtness, J. H. "Life Style and Law: Some Reflections on Mt. 5:17." Dialog 14 (Winter 1975) 13-20.

Burtt, E. P. "A Free Translation of the Sermon on the Mount." Biblical World 3 (1894) 336-44.

Butkevich, Timofeĭ I. Nagornaĭa propoved'. Kharkov': Tip. Gub. pravleniĭa, 1893.
     Textual and critical analysis. Polemic against Tolstoy's interpretation of the Sermon on the Mount.

_____. "Nagornaĭa propoved'. Vera i Razum, 1895.

Cadbury, Henry J. "The Single Eye." Harvard Theological Review 47 (1954) 69-74.

Caird, G. B. "Expounding the Parables; the Defendant (Matthew 5:25f; Luke 12:58f)." Expository Times 77 (1965) 36-39.

Calvin, Jean. Auslegung der Evangelien-Harmonie. Übers.
Hiltrud Stadland-Neumann und Gertrud Vogelsbusch. Aus-
legung der Heiligen Schrift. Bd. 12. In Zusammenarbeit
mit anderen. Hrsg. von Otto Weber. Neukirchen-Vluyn:
Neukirchener Verlag, 1966.
(See his Harmonia ex evangelistus tribus composita,
Matthaeo, Marco & Luca)

_____. Commentary on a Harmony of the Evangelists,
Matthew, Mark, and Luke. vol. 1. Trans. William Prin-
gle. Grand Rapids: Eerdmans, 1949, 257-371.
(See his Harmonia ex evangelistis tribus composita,
Matthaeo, Marco, & Luca)

_____. Harmonia ex evangelistis tribus composita,
Matthaeo, Marco, & Luca. Genevae: Eustathii Vignon,
1595.

_____. A Harmony of the Gospels, Matthew, Mark and
Luke. 3 vols. Edinburgh: St. Andrew Press, 1972.
Sermon on the Mount section is in vol. 1, 167-242.
(See his Harmonia ex evangelistis tribus composita,
Matthaeo, Marco & Luca)

_____. Jezus spreckt zalig. Calvin Opera XLVI, 771-886.
Vert. W. H. van der Vegt. Franeker: T. Wever, 1951.

Camargo, Satilas do Amaral. O carácter à luz do Sermao
da montanha. São Paulo: Livraria Independente Editora,
1952.
Meditations.

Campbell, Donald K. "Interpretation and Exposition of the
Sermon on the Mount." Th.D. thesis. Dallas Theological
Seminary, 1953.

Carpenter, Spencer C. The Sermon on the Mount. London:
S. P. C. K., 1940.

Carpenter, William B. The Great Charter of Christ; Being
Studies in the Sermon on the Mount. London: Isbister,
1895; New York: T. Whittaker, 1899.
Sermons.

Carpus. "The Sermon on the Mount." Expositor 1 (1875)
70-88, 128-42.

Carr, A. "Salt." Expository Times 26 (1914-15) 139-40.

Carré, Ambroise-Marie. Béatitudes pour aujourd'hui. Paris.
Cerf, 1963.
Sermons.

_____. Bergpredigt heute. Übers. Karl Hermann Berg-
ner. Rottenburg (Neckar): Bader'sche Verlag, 1964.
(See his Béatitudes pour aujourd'hui).

_____. Las Bienaventuranzas hoy. Trad. Salvador
Cabré. Barcelona: Estela, 1967.
(See his Béatitudes pour aujourd'hui)

_____. L'Homme des béatitudes. Paris. Cerf, 1962.

_____. Der Mensch der Bergpredigt. Übers. Karl Her-
mann Bergner. Stuttgart: Schwabenverlag, 1964.
(See his L'Homme des béatitudes)

Carré, Henry B. "Matthew 5:1 and Related Passages."
Journal of Biblical Literature 42 (1923) 39-48.

Castellini, G. "Struttura letteraria di Mt. 7, 6." Rivista
biblica 2 (1954) 310-17.

Chafer, Lewis S. "The Sermon on the Mount." Bibliotheca
Sacra 108 (1951) 389-413.

Chambers, Oswald. Men jag säger eder. Studier i Bergspredikan. Övers. Sven Stolpe. Uppsala: Lindblad, 1939.
(See his Studies in the Sermon on the Mount)

_____. Studies in the Sermon on the Mount. Cincinnati:
God's Revivalist Press, 1915; London: Simpkin Marshall,
1932 (1941); London: Marshall, Morgan & Scott, 1955.
Six brief studies.

_____. Vuorisaarnan sanoma. Suomentanut Kalle Kor-
honen. Lahti: 1948.
(See his Studies in the Sermon on the Mount)

Chappel, Clovis G. The Sermon on the Mount. Nashville:
Cokesbury, 1930.
Sermons.

Chavannes, C. G. "Matth. 7. 7-11." Theologisch tijdschrift
29 (1895) 72-76.

Christblumen, oder die Bergpredigt Christi und die letzten
  Reden Christi im Johannes, rhythmisch behandelt von
  Karl Buchner. Mit einer Vorrede von Ernst Zimmermann.
  Leipzig: L. Schumann, 1827.

Chrysostom, Joannes. The Preaching of Chrysostom; Homilies on the Sermon on the Mount. Edited by Jaroslav Pelikan. Philadelphia: Fortress Press, 1967.
    Sermons. One section of the Introduction by Jeroslav
  Pelikan deals with Chrysostom as an expositor of the Sermon on the Mount.

Clarke, W. K. Lowther. "The Excepting Clause in St.
  Matthew." Theology 15 (1927) 161-62.

_____. "Studies in Texts." Theology 5 (1922) 37-38
  [Mt. 5:22].

_____. "Studies in Texts." Theology 20 (1930) 43-44
  [Mt. 5:48].

Clavier, H. "Matthieu 5. 29 et la non-résistance." Revue
  d'histoire et de philosophie religieuses 37 (1957) 44-57.

Clemm, Heinrich W. Theologische Untersuchung der Frage:
  Ob die heilige Schrift A. T. dunkel und zweideutig ware,
  wenn die hebräischen Punkte kein göttliches Ansehen hät-
  ten? Nebst einer Erklärung des Spruchs Christi Matthäus
  5, 18. Tübingen: 1753.

Cohon, Beryl D. Jacob's Well; Some Jewish Sources and
  Parallels to the Sermon on the Mount. New York: Book-
  man Associates, 1956.
    Lists Jewish sources and parallels to the Sermon on the
  Mount, primarily from the Old Testament, but also from
  the Talmud, Midrash, liturgy, Philo, and the Apocrypha.

Cohu, John R. The Sermon on the Mount as Viewed from
  the Modern Standpoint: a Series of Addresses. London:
  Skeffington and Son, 1908; New York: Whittaker, 1908.
    Sermons.

Coiner, H. G. "Those Divorce and Remarriage Passages;
  Matt. 5:32, 19:9; I Cor. 7:10-16." Concordia Theological
  Monthly 39 (1968) 367-84.

Coleridge, Henry J. The Sermon on the Mount. 2 vols.

London: Burns and Oates, 1878.
Commentary.

Collett, Samuel. A Paraphrase of the Fifth, Sixth and
Seventh Chapters of Matthew, with Proper Soliloquies at
Every Period. 2d ed. London: J. Noon, 1737 (1746).

Collins, Edward M., Jr. "A Critical Edition of the Thirteen Sermons by John Wesley on the Sermon on the
Mount." Doctoral dissertation. Ohio Univ., 1965.
The thirteen sermons on the Sermon on the Mount are
examined to see to what extent Wesley's sermons might be
recreated in the manner in which they were spoken.

Collis, M. M. P. "An Analysis of the Sermon on the Mount
as Given in the First Gospel." Expositor 8th ser. 5
(1913) 146-60.

Colton, Clarence E. Sermon on the Mount; Thirty Messages
of Spiritual Power. Grand Rapids: Zondervan, 1960.
Sermons.

Colwell, E. C. "Has Raka a Parallel in the Papyri?"
Journal of Biblical Literature 53 (1934) 351-54.

Conner, J. "Matthew V. 18." Expository Times 38 (1926-
27), 469.

Connick, C. Milo. Build on the Rock: You and the Sermon
on the Mount. New York: Revell, 1960.
A popular treatment of the understanding and practical
application of the Sermon on the Mount.

_____. "Sermon on the Mount Put to Work." Together
(1957) 46-48.

Conrad. Die Bergpredigt; ihrer Behandlung und Auslegung
in der Schule. Brandenburg: J. J. Wiesike, 1860.
Address on teaching the Sermon on the Mount in
schools.

Cooley, William F. "What Has the Sermon on the Mount
to Do with the Gospel?" Christian Literature 10 (1893-
94) 1699-73a.

Corbach, Liselotte. Die Bergpredigt in der Schule. Göttingen: Vandenhoeck & Ruprecht, 1956 (1962).

Methods of teaching and teaching plans for the study
and teaching of the Sermon on the Mount in schools.

_____. Bjergpraédikenen. Fortolkningundervisning.
Overs. og bearb. Elisabeth Kieldrup Jørgensen og Theodor
Jørgensen. København: Rasmus Fischer, 1970.
(See her Die Bergpredigt in der Schule)

Corbin, M. "Nature et signification de la loi évangélique."
Recherches de science religieuse 57 (1969) 5-48.

Cordier, Leopold. Jesus und das Glück. Betrachtungen
über die Bergpredigt. Herborn: Oranien-Verlag, 1923.

Couroyer, B. "De la mesure dont vous mesurez il vous sera
mesure." Revue biblique 77 (1970) 366-70.

Couvée, D. J. "De Bergrede," in Vragen van dezen Tijd IV.
Culemborg: Uitgeversbedrijf "De Pauw," 1933.

_____. Met Jezus op den berg. Kampen: J. H. Kok,
1941.

Crouzel, Henri. "Le texte patristique de Matthieu V. 32 et
XIX. 9." New Testament Studies 19 (1972) 98-119.

Crowe, Charles M. Sermons from the Mount. Nashville:
Abingdon, 1954.
Sermons.

Cullmann, Oscar. "Das Gleichnis vom Salz. Zur frühesten
Kommentierung eines Herrenworts durch die Evangelisten,"
in Vorträge und Aufsätze 1925-1962. Tübingen: J. C. B.
Mohr; Zürich: Zwingli Verlag, 1966, 192-201.

_____. "Que signifie le sel dans la parabole de Jésus?
Les évangélistes premiers commentateurs du Logion."
Revue d'histoire et de philosophie religieuses 37 (1957)
36-43.

Currie, S. D. Matthew 5:39a--Resistance or Protest? Harvard Theological Review 57 (1964) 140-45.

Custer, Stewart. "The Sermon on the Mount." Biblical
Viewpoint 1 (1967) 85-91.

Daily, Starr. Magnificent Love; a Gospel of Divine Love

Based on the Sermon on the Mount. Evesham, Worcester-
shire, England: Arthur James Pub., 1962; Westwood,
N.J.: Revell, 1964.
   Meditations. For Daily the understanding of the Sermon on the Mount depends upon the reader's discovery and
application of one spiritual key--Love.

Dalisda, E. Die Bergpredigt. Beiträge zur Lehrerbildung
und Lehrerfortbilding. Heft 35. Gotha: E. F. Thiene-
mann, 1906.

D'Angelo, Fr. "A proposito del testa di Matteo V, 32 e
XIX, 9." Asprenas V (1958) 81-89.

Daniel, Constantin. "'Faux prophètes': surnom des Es-
séniens dans le Sermon sur la montagne." Revue de
Qumran 7 (1969) 45-79.

Dannenbaum, Hans. Bergpredigt Jesu, Gesetz und Evangelium der Jüngergemeinde. Gladbeck: Schriftenmissions-
Verlag, 1955.

Darrett, J. D. M. "The Light under a Bushel: The Hanuk-
kah Lamp?" Expository Times 78 (1966-67) 18.

Daube, David. "Matthew V. 38 f." Journal of Theological
Studies 45 (1944) 177-87.

Davidson, W. Hope. "Note on Matthew V. 39." Expository
Times 22 (1910-11) 231.

Davies, William D. Die Bergpredigt. Exegetische Unter-
suchung ihrer jüdischen und frühchristlichen Elemente.
Übers. Gertraud Reim/Günter Reim. München: Cladius
Verlag, 1970.
   (See his The Sermon on the Mount)

_____. Bergspredikan. Ett bidrag till fördjupad för-
ståelse. Övers. Stig Lindhagen. Stockholm: Verbum,
1971.
   (See his The Sermon on the Mount)

_____. "Matthew 5, 17-18," in Mélanges bibliques rédi-
gés en l'honneur de André Robert. Paris: Bloud et Gay,
1957, 428-56. Also: Christian Origins and Judaism.
London: Darton, Longman & Todd, 1962, 31-66.

_____. The Sermon on the Mount. New York, Cambridge University Press, 1966; Cambridge: University Press, 1966.

Lectures on the historical setting of the Sermon on the Mount. A briefer form of the main views developed in his The Setting of the Sermon on the Mount.

_____. The Setting of the Sermon on the Mount. New York: Cambridge University Press, 1962; Cambridge: University Press, 1964.

A substantial study dealing with the influences, within and without the Church, and the circumstances out of which the Sermon on the Mount emerged. Davies questions the extreme view of source-criticism that the Sermon on the Mount is a collection of diverse sayings arranged by an editor. Matthew and the other composers of the Gospels are not mere editors but are in a real sense "authors." Thus Matthew regarded the Sermon on the Mount as a unit. Davies suggests that the form of the Sermon on the Mount may have been fashioned under the impact of Jamnia and that it may be the Christian answer to Jamnia.

Davis, G. Herbert. "The Practice of the Sermon on the Mount." Expository Times 11 (1899-1900) 382.

Davis, W. Hersey. "Don't Hide Your Light?" Review and Expositor 33 (1936) 400-01.

Daxer, Georg. Die Bergpredigt und der Kreig. Leipzig: Krüger, 1916.

Deatrick, E. P. "Salt, Soil, Savior (Mt 5:13, Mk 9:50, and Lk 14:34-35)." Biblical Archaeologist 25 (1962) 41-48.

Dehn, Günther. "Die Bergpredigt als ethisches Problem." Die Zeichen der Zeit. Heft 6. Munchen: C. Kaiser Verlag, 1950.

Delaporte, L. "Matthieu VII, 4-27, d'après un papyrus de la Bibliothèque Nationale." Revue biblique 25 (1916) 560-64.

Delcor, M. "Les attachés littéraires, l'origine et la signification de l'expression biblique 'Prendre à témoin le ciel et la terre'." Vetus Testamentum 16 (1966) 8-25.

Delling, G. "Das Logion Mark X, 11 (und seine Abwundlun-
gen) im Neuen Testament." Novum Testamentum 1 (1956)
263-74.

Denison, Stephen. The White Wolfe. London: Printed by
George Miller, for Robert Milbovrne, 1627.
Sermon on Matt. 7:15.

Descamps, A. "Esaai d'interprétation de Mt. 5, 17-48.
'Formgeschichte' ou 'Redaktionsgeschichte'?" in Studia
Evangelica. Berlin: Akademie-Verlag, 1959, 156-73.

Deutscher Evangelischer Kirchentag, 14th, Stuttgart, 1969.
Arbeitsgruppe Gottesfrage. Gottesfrage heute. Vorträge
und Biblearbeit in der Arbeitsgruppe Gottesfrage des 14.
Deutschen Evangelischen Kirchentages Stuttgart 2. Aufl.
1969. Stuttgart: Kreuz-Verlag, 1969.
    Contains six Bible studies on the Sermon on the Mount
by six pastors and professors, given at the 14th Deutschen
Evangelischen Kirchentag Stuttgart 1969.

Dewailly, L. M. "Kristologi och Etik in Jesu Bergspredikan;
av E. Bijer." Revue biblique 68 (1961) 269-72. (review
article)

Dewitt, Samuel A. Sermon on the Mount. New York: Published by the author, 1940.

_____. The Sermon on the Mount. New York, Strathmore
Press, 1948.
    King James Version text set to rhyme and rhythm. In-
tended for voice, reed, and string. 500 copies printed.

Dibelius, Franz. "Zwei Worte Jesu." Zeitschrift für die
neutestamentliche Wissenschaft 11 (1910) 188-92.

Dibelius, Martin. "Die Bergpredigt," in Botschaft und
Geschichte I. Tübingen: J. C. B. Mohr, 1953, 80-174.
    (See his The Sermon on the Mount)

_____. The Sermon on the Mount. New York: Charles
Scribner's Sons, 1940.
    An eminent work by a pioneer of Form Criticism. The
Sermon on the Mount is a collection of radical, absolute
commands and sayings. They are signs of the Kingdom of
God which cannot be fully performed in this age. For
Dibelius the Sermon on the Mount is not an ideal but an

eschatological stimulus intended to make men well acquainted with the pure will of God. Moreover, this "stimulus" should challenge men to perform signs of our own
time as individuals, as communities, as churches, and if
possible as nations. While he rejects Schweitzer's interim
ethic, Dibelius does see eschatology as the pervading background of the Sermon on the Mount. This work gives one
a good insight into the methodology of Form Criticism as
it is applied to the Sermon on the Mount.

Diem, Harald. Luthers Lehre von den zwei Reichen, untersucht von seinem Verständnis der Bergpredigt aus. Ein
  Beitrag zum Problem: "Gesetz und Evangelium." München: C. Kaiser Verlag, 1938.
    An analysis of Luther's interpretation of the Sermon on
  the Mount with special emphasis on his teaching on conscience and on the "two kingdoms."

Diem, Hermann. "Predigt über Lukas 6, 20-31." Evangelische Theologie 14 (1954) 241-46.

Dimitroff, Stojam. Der Sinn der Forderungen Jesu in der
  Bergpredigt. Diss. Bern: 1938.
    A detailed study which gives special attention to the
  eschatological interpretation of the Sermon on the Mount.

Dmitrievskiĭ, F. Nagornaîa beseda Gospoda nashego Iisusa
  Khrista o blazhenstvakh, zapovedîâkh i o nravstvenno-
  sovershennoĭ zhizni chelovecheskoĭ. Sankt Peterburg:
  1893.

Dods, Marcus, and Denny, James, and Moffatt, James.
  The Literal Interpretation of the Sermon on the Mount.
  London: Hodder and Stoughton, 1904.
    Three brief essays which were originally published
  in the British Weekly as a result of the correspondence in
  its columns.

Doktor, T. "De Exegese van Mattheüs 5:17-48." Vox theologica 9 (1937-38) 175-80.

Dorr, Karl R. Bergpredigt in diese Zeit. Wien: Cura
  Verlag, 1966.
  Sermons.

Drumwright, Huber L., Jr. "A Homiletical Study of the
  Sermon on the Mount: the Ethical Motif in Matthew 5-7."
  Southwestern Journal of Theology 5 (1962) 65-76.

———. "Problem Passages in Luke; a Hermeneutical Approach." Southwestern Journal of Theology 10 (1967) 45-58.

Dupont, Jacques. "L'appel à imiter Dieu en Matthieu 5, 48 et Luc 6, 36." Rivista biblica 14 (1966) 137-58.

———. Les Béatitudes. 3 vols. Bruges: Abbaye de Saint-André, 1954 (1958); Paris: J. Gabalda et Cie, 1969.
An extensive and scholarly study of the literary problems of the Matthean and Lucan parallels of the Sermon on the Mount and the Beatitudes. The entire second volume is on the Beatitudes.

———. "'Soyez parfaits' (Mt. V, 48) 'Soyez miséricordieux' (Le. VI, 36)," in Sacra Pagina II. Paris: Gebalda; Gembloux: Duculot, 1959, 150-52.

Dupont-Sommer, A. "Note archéologique sur le proverbe évangélique: Mettre la lampe sous le boisseau," in Mélanges Syriens offerts à Monsieur René Dussaud II. Paris: Geuthner, 1939, 789-94.

Dyck, Anni. Höher als alle Vernunft. Basel: Agape-Verlag, 1965.
Thirty short stories from various centuries and countries on the themes of the Sermon on the Mount.

Dykes, James O. The Laws of the Kingdom. New York: Robert Carter and Brothers, 1873.
An exposition of Matthew 5:17-6:18 which treats the relation of the New Law to the old under the principle that Jesus came to fulfill and not destroy the Old Law.

———. The Manifesto of the King; an Exposition of the Sermon on the Mount. New York: Carter, 1881; London: James Nisbet, 1881 (1887) (1891).
This volume contains three books which were published previously under their respective titles in three separate volumes.
(See his The Beatitudes of the Kingdom)
(See his The Laws of the Kingdom)
(See his The Relations of the Kingdom to the World)

———. The Relations of the Kingdom to the World. New York. New York: Robert Carter and Brothers, 1874.
An interpretation of the Sermon on the Mount concern-

ing its teaching on the relations of the Kingdom to the
world, and its relevance to Christians wrestling with the
perennial problem of the demands of Christ and culture.
Deals with Matthew 6:19 to the end of the Sermon.

Easton, Burton S. "The Sermon on the Mount." Journal
of Biblical Literature 33 (1914) 228-43.

Eberhardt, F. W. "The Social Imperatives of the Kingdom
of God on Earth." Review and Expositor 37 (1940) 163-
72, 286-94, 397-407.

Eddleman, H. Leo. Teachings of Jesus in Matthew 5-7.
Nashville: Convention Press, 1955.
Intended for study and teaching.

Edlund, Conny. Das Auge der Einfalt. Eine Untersuchung
zu Matth. 6, 22-23 und Luk. 11, 34-35. Uppsala: Alm-
qvist & Wiksells Boktryckeri, 1952.
A doctoral dissertation which analyzes Jesus' saying
regarding the eye as the lamp of the body. Much of the
study is devoted to the roots of this concept in the Old
Testament and intertestamental periods.

Edwin, Einar. Jesu Bergpreken til mennsker i dag. Oslo:
H. Aschehoug, 1949.
Popular exposition of various themes related to the Sermon on the Mount. Based on addresses given in the Fa-
gerborg Church in the fall of 1948.

Eger, Karl. Die Botschaft Jesu von der Herrschaft Gottes.
Worte Jesu aus der Bergpredigt für die Gegenwart ausgelegt. Berlin: Furche Verlag, 1925.

Eichholz, Georg. "Die Aufgabe einer Auslegung der Bergpredigt," in Tradition und Interpretation. München: C.
Kaiser Verlag, 1965, 34-56.

_____. Auslegung der Bergpredigt. Neukirchen-Vluyn:
Neukirchener Verlag, 1965 (1970). Eichholz's primary intention is to present a theological profile of Matthew as it
is reflected in the Sermon on the Mount. The first Evangelist reveals his Christology--what Christ was for him.
A significant study which in its course of development enters into "dialogue" with 19th and 20th century New Testament scholarship.

Elliot, J. H. "Die Antithesen der Bergpredigt. Gesetz und Eschatologie." Lutherische Rundschau 18 (1968) 19-29.

_____. "Law and Eschatology; the Antitheses of the Sermon on the Mount." Lutheran World 15 (1968) 16-24.

Emmanuel a S. Marco, P. "Quaerite ergo primum regnum Dei et iustitiam eius (Mt. 6, 24-33)." Verbum Domini 10 (1930) 281-86.

Emmerich, K. "Prayer in the Inner Chamber," in "And Other Pastors of thy Flock"--A German Tribute to the Bishop of Chichester [The Right Rev. George K. A. Bell]. edited by Franz Hildebrandt. Printed for Subscribers at the University Press, Cambridge, 1942, 6-18.

Emmet, C. W. "The Teaching of Hermas and the First Gospel on Divorce." Expositor 8th ser. 1 (1911-A) 68-74.

Engel, Ingrid. Gottesverständnis und sozialpolitisches Handeln. Eine Untersuchung zu Friedrich Naumann. Göttingen: Vandenhoeck & Ruprecht, 1972.
    This is a revision of Die Bergpredigt in den sozialen Spannungen des 19. Jahrhunderts. Eine Untersuchung zu Friedrich Naumann. Diss. Marburg: 1970. Engel discusses Naumann's understanding of the Kingdom of God in relation to his social-political thought. He also deals with the change in Naumann's thought about the Kingdom of God and the Sermon on the Mount which resulted from his trip to Palestine.

Engelmann, Fridolin. Die Bergpredigt Jesu Christi. Waldbröl: Haupt, 1938.

Ensfelder, J. Th. "Etude exégétique sur Matthieu V, 21 & 22." Revue de théologie 2 (1851) 171-75.

Ervast, Pekka. The Sermon on the Mount; or, The Key to Christianity. London: Theosophical Publishing House, 1933.

L'esposition sur le sermon que nostre seigneur fit en la montaigne côtenant les huyt beatitudes. Paris: F. Regnault, 1510?

Evers, M., and Marx, Herman. Die Bergpredigt. Berlin: Reuther und Reichard, 1899 (5. Aufl. 1907).

Eyton, John. The Lord Jesus Christ's Sermon on the Mount;
with a Course of Questions and Answers, Explaining that
Valuable Portion of Scripture, and Intended Chiefly for the
Instruction of Young Persons. Wellington and Iron Bridge:
F. Houlston and Son, 1806 (1811) (1819).

_____. El Sermon de Jesu-Christo en el Monte, explicado
en preguntas y respuestas. Segunda edicion, corregida y
aumentada. Londres: J. Davis, 1828.

Falk, A. E. Grundlinjer till Jesu bergspredikan. Lysekil:
Tr. Lysekilsposten, 1927.

Feine, Paul. "Über das gegenseitige Verhältnis der Texte
der Bergpredigt bei Matthäus und Lukas," in Jahrbücher
für Protestantische Theologie, 1885, 1-35.

Fensham, F. C. "Legal Background of Mt VI:12." Novum
Testamentum 4 (1960) 1-2.

Ferrar, W. J. "A Note on St. Matthew VII. 9." Expository
Times 17 (1905-06) 478.

Feuillet, A. "Morale ancienne et morale chrétienne d'après
Mt. V:17-20; comparaison avec la doctrine de l'épître aux
Romains." New Testament Studies 17 (1971) 123-37.

Fiebig, Paul. Die Gleichnisse Jesu und die Bergpredigt in
Verbindung mit rabbinischen Parallelen erläutert für die
Schüller und Schülerinen höherer Leharanstalten. Tübin-
gen: J. C. B. Mohr, 1911 (1914).
   A brief study guide for students of Jesus' parables and
the Sermon on the Mount.

_____. Jesu Bergpredigt. Rabbinische Texte zum Ver-
ständnis der Bergpredigt ins deutsche Übersetzung, in ihren
ursprachen Dargeboten und mit Erläuterungen und Lesarten
versehen. Göttingen: Vandenhoeck & Ruprecht, 1924.
   A compilation of passages from rabbinical literature
which parallel or shed light on the Sermon on the Mount.
The texts are in German and Hebrew.

_____. "Der Sinn der Bergpredigt." Zeitschrift für sys-
tematische Theologie 7 (1929-30) 497-515.

_____. "Das Wort Jesu vom Auge." Theologische Studien
und Kritiken 89 (1916) 499-507.

Findlay, James A. The Realism of Jesus; a Paraphrase and
   Exposition of the Sermon on the Mount. London: Hodder
   and Stoughton, 1922; New York: George H. Doran Co.,
   1924.
      First section is author's paraphrase. Presents the
   Sermon on the Mount as a practical way of life possible
   in this world.

Fitzgerald, Ernest A. There's No Other Way. Nashville:
   Abingdon, 1970.
   Sermons.

Fletcher, Alfred E. The Sermon on the Mount and Practical
   Politics. London: Griffiths: 1911.
      A discussion of the relation and relevance of the Ser-
   mon on the Mount to social problems.

van der Flier, A. "Een fijn trekje in de kekening der
   Farizeën in de Bergrede (Mt. 6. 2, 5)." Nieuwe theologische studien 1 (1918) 111.

Flusser, David. "Die Tora in der Bergpredigt," in Juden
   und Christen lesen dieselbe Bibel. Hrsg. Heinz Kremers.
   Duisburg: Braun, 1973, 102-13.

Fonck, L. "Attendite a falsis prophetis (Mt. 7, 15-21)."
   Verbum Domini 2 (1922) 198-204.

_____. "Surdus et mutus sanatur (Mt. 7, 31-37)." Ver-
   bum Domini 4 (1924) 231-36.

Forbes, John. The Symmetrical Structure of Scripture; or,
   The Principles of Scripture Parallelism Exemplified, in an
   Analysis of the Decalogue, the Sermon on the Mount, and
   Other Passages of the Sacred Writings. Edinburgh: Hamilton, 1854.
      In six of twenty-six sections Forbes analyses the Ser-
   mon on the Mount according to the principles of "parallelism" which was discovered by Bishop Lowth. The author's intention is to attempt to rescue the study of parallelism from the disrepute in which it has fallen and to
   show its value for the investigation of the true meaning
   and connexion of Scripture. For this purpose the Sermon
   on the Mount is his major example.

Ford, J. M. "Reflections on W. D. Davies. 'The Setting
   of the Sermon on the Mount.'" Biblica 48 (1967) 623-28.

Foreman, Kenneth J. "A Possible Interpretation of Matthew 7." Interpretation 1 (1947) 66-67.

Fox, Emmet. Die Bergpredigt. Eine allgemeine Einführung in das wissenschaftliche Christentum. Übers. Eugene W. K. Schwartz und William M. Conn. Dt. Überarb.: Käthe Blenkner. 2. Aufl. Karlsruhe-Durlach: Dups, 1958. (See his The Sermon on the Mount)

_____. El Sermón del monte y la Oración Dominical. New York, Harpers, 1945. (See his The Sermon on the Mount)

_____. The Sermon on the Mount; a General Introduction to Scientific Christianity in the Form of a Spiritual Key to Matthew V, VI, and VII. New York: Church of the Healing Christ, 1934; New York: Harpers, 1938; New York: Grossett & Dunlap, 1944.
Sermon on the Mount offers principles and techniques, which if rightly applied, will lead to health, peace of mind, and spiritual development.

_____. Le Sermon sur la montagne: La clé du succès dans la vie. Trad. J. Denis. Paris: Astra, 1969. (See his The Sermon on the Mount)

_____. Le Sermon sur la montagne et l'Oraison Dominicale. New York: Harpers, 1943. (See his The Sermon on the Mount)

Frickart, A. "Die Composition der Bergpredigt." Theologische Zeitschrift der Schweiz 6 (1889) 193-210; 7 (1890) 43-52, 107-25.

Fridrichsen, Anton. "Bergspredikan i kristendomsundervisningen." Kyrka och skola 4 (1944) 1-13.

_____. "Fullkomlighetskravet i Jesu förkunnelse." Svensk teologisk kvartalskrift 9 (1933) 124-33.

Friedlander, Gerald. The Jewish Sources of the Sermon on the Mount. New York: Bloch Publishing Co., 1911; London: George Routledge and Sons, 1911; New York: Ktav Publishing House, 1969.
An analysis of the Sermon on the Mount in the light of contemporary Jewish thought. In a broader framework the book sets forth the relationship between Christianity

and Judaism. A polemical and apologetic work.

Frindte, Dietrich. "Die Auslegung der Bergpredigt als
Versuch eines rechten Schriftverständnisses." Evangelisches Erziehen 16 (1964) 225-31.

Fritzsche, Christoph F. Observationes ad Matth. V, 29.
30. 39. Halle: Schwetschke u. S., 1828.

Frost, Bede. Founded upon a Rock; an Introduction to the
Sermon on the Mount. New York: Macmillan, 1935.
Sermons and meditations.

Fuchs, Ernst. "Jesu Selbstzeugnis nach Matthäus 5." Zeitschrift für Theologie und Kirche 51 (1954) 14-34.
Also: Zur Frage nach dem historischen Jesus. Tübingen: J. C. B. Mohr, 1960 (1965), 100-25.

_____. "Die volkommene Gewissheit. Zur Auslegung von
Matthäus 5:48," in Neutestamentliche Studien für Rudolf
Bultmann zu seinem 70. Geburtstag am 20. August 1954.
Berlin: A. Töpelmann, 1957, 130-36.
Also: Zur Frage nach dem historischen Jesus. Tü-
bingen: J. C. B. Mohr, 1960 (1965) 126-35.

Fullerton, Kemper. "Raka." Expository Times 15 (1903-04)
429-31.

Gallo, St. "Structura sermonis montani." Verbum Domini
27 (1949) 257-69.

Genung, George F. The Magna Charta of the Kingdom of
God; Plain Studies in Our Lord's Sermon on the Mount.
Philadelphia: American Baptist Publishing Society, 1900.
Popular work on the relation of the Sermon on the
Mount to Christian ethics.

George, A. "La justice à faire dans le secret." Biblica
40 (1959) 590-98.

Gerecke, Karl. Wir Deutschen im Kampfe um die Ideale.
Gegen Prof. D. Baumgartens-Kiel "Bergpredigt und Krieg."
Baunschweig: F. Wagner, 1916.

Gerhardsson, Birger. "Geistiger Opferdienst nach Matth 6,
1-6," in Neues Testament und Geschichte. Historisches
Geschehen und Deutung in Neuen Testament. Oscar Cull-

mann zum 70. Geburtstag. Zürich: Theologischer Verlag; Tübingen: J. C. B. Mohr, 1972, 16-21.

Gesner, Herbert M. The Life Worth Living, or, The Religion of Christ; a Systematic and Popular Exposition of the Greatest Religious Document the World Has Ever Seen, Commonly Known as the Sermon on the Mount. Boston: Richard G. Badger, 1915.
Principles for Christian living derived from the Sermon on the Mount.

Giavini, G. "Abbiamo forse in Mt. 6, 19-7, 11 il primo commento al 'Pater Noster'?" Rivista biblica 13 (1965) 171-77.

Gideon, Virtus E. "Preaching Values in Matthew 5." Southwestern Journal of Theology 5 (1962) 77-88.

Gillie, R. C. "The Sermon on the Mount." Expository Times 40 (1928-29) 21-25.

Gilmour, S. MacLean. "Interpreting the Sermon on the Mount." Crozer Quarterly 24 (1947) 47-56.

van Gilse, J. "Exegetische Studiën." Theologisch tijdschrift 10 (1876) 537-48 [Mt. 6: 22, 23; Jn. 19: 11].

Ginoulhiac, Jacques-Marie-Achille. Le Sermon sur la montagne avec des réflexions dogmatiques et morales. Lyon: P. N. Josserand, 1872.

Girgensohn, Herbert. Die Bergpredigt. Eine Auslegung für die Gemeinde. Witten: Luther-Verlag, 1962.
An interpretation which views the Sermon on the Mount, not as a call to abstract ethical rules, but as the call of Jesus in a concrete community. The central theme of the Sermon on the Mount is love which grows and finds expression in a community. Girgensohn emphasizes the sociological dimension of the Sermon on the Mount.

Gladkov, B. I. Nagornaia propoved' i Tsarstvo Bozhie. Sankt Peterburg: 1907.

Glasson, T. Francis. "Carding and Spinning: Oxyrhynchus Papyrus No. 655." Journal of Theological Studies 13 (1962) 331-32.

_____. "Chiasmus in St. Matthew VII. 6." Expository
Times 68 (1956-57) 302.

Gloag, Paton J. "Our Lord's View of the Sixth Commandment." Expository Times 4 (1892-93) 492-96.

Göss, Georg F. D. Reden über die Bergpredigt nach neuen
Ansichten. Übersicht und exegetische Rechtfertigung.
Ulm: 1823.

Gössmann, Wilhelm, und Gössmann, Elizabeth. Die Bergpredigt. München: Hueber, 1965.

Gomes, M. M. "A Argumentação de Jesus no Sermão da
montanha." Revista eclesiástica brasileira 10 (1950) 333-
51.

González Ruiz, J. M. "El divorcio en Mt. 5, 32 y 19, 9,"
in Semana Biblica Española XII. Madrid: 1952, 513-28.

Goppelt, Leonhard. Die Bergpredigt und die Wirklichkeit
dieser Welt. Stuttgart: Calwer Verlag, 1968.
Brief study which views the Sermon on the Mount as a
call to follow Jesus in the real life of this time.

Gore, Charles. The Sermon on the Mount; a Practical Exposition. London: John Murray, 1896; New York: E. P.
Dutton, 1913.
Gore's intention is to assist ordinary people to medi-
tate on the Sermon on the Mount in the Revised Version,
and to apply its teaching to their own lives. It is designed
for practical reflection rather than intellectual study. This
work appeared in many later editions.

_____. The Social Doctrine of the Sermon on the Mount.
London: Percival, 1892; Oxford: Horace Hart, 1895;
Oxford: Christian Social Union, 1895.
A brief work which summons the church to exercise
her authority in matters of social morality. The Sermon
on the Mount supplies the fundamental law of the Lord's
Kingdom. This may be broadly expressed as the principle of the sonship and brotherhood of man as based on
the Fatherhood of God.

_____. "The Social Doctrine of the Sermon on the Mount."
Economic Review 2 (1892) 145-60.

Gossip, Arthur J. "The Sermon on the Mount." Expository
Times 39 (1927-28) 342-47.

Goumaz, L. "Le Sermon sur la montagne constitue-t-il tout
l'évangile?" Revue de théologie et de philosophie 36
(1903) 105-35.

Govett, Robert. The Sermon on the Mount Expounded. London: James Nisbet, 1861; London: Thynne, 1932 (1934).

Graaf, Johannes de II. In gesprek met de Bergrede. 's-
Gravenhage: Boekcentrum, 1957 (1961).

Gräsbeck, H. Bergspredikan och Jesu Versamhet. Helsing-
sons: 1949.

Grässmann, Frithjof. "Die Bergpredigt in der Bibelwoche,"
in Praxis Ecclesiae; Praktische Theologie als Hermeneutik,
Katechetik und Homiletik im Dienste der Kirche. Festschrift für Kurt Frör. In Verbindung mit Rudolf Bohren
und Manfred Seitz. Hrsg. von Dietrich Stollberg. München:
C. Kaiser Verlag, 1970, 373-90.

Graff, Johannes de. In gesprek met de Bergrede. 's-
Gravenhage: Boekancentrum, 1958 (1961).
    A brief analysis of the Sermon on the Mount in terms
of its character, validity or relevance, and ethics.

Grant, Frederick C. "The Sermon on the Mount." Anglican
Theological Review 24 (1942) 131-44.

Grawert, Friedrich. Die Bergpredigt nach Matthäus auf ihre
äussere und innere Einheit mit besonderer Berücksichtigung
des genuinen Verhaltnisses der Seligpreisungen zur ganzen
Rede neu untersucht und dargesteilt. Marburg: Elwert,
1900.
    A fairly brief study which concentrates on the setting
and design of the Sermon on the Mount.

Grayston, Kenneth. "Sermon on the Mount," in Interpreter's
Dictionary of the Bible. vol. 4. New York: Abingdon,
1962, 279-89.

Greenhough, John G., and others. The Sermon on the
Mount. 3 vols. New York: Methodist Book Concern,
1906.

Greenwood, D. "Moral Obligation in the Sermon on the
Mount." Theological Studies 31 (1970) 301-9.

Greeven, Heinrich. "Zu den Aussagen des Neues Testaments uber die Ehe." Zeitschrift für evangelische Ethik
1 (1957) 109-25.

Gregory, Sadie. The Sermon on the Mount; a Bible Study
Course for Seniors. The Canadian Council of Churches,
Dept. of Christian Education, 1947.
A study course for high school students.

Griffiths, J. Gwyn. "Wisdom about Tomorrow." Harvard
Theological Review 53 (1960) 219-21.

Groenewald, E. P. "Grond vir egskeiding volgens Matthëus."
Nederduitse gereformeerde teologiese tydskrif 1, no. 4
(1960) 5-12.

Grosse, Ernst T. C. De consilio quod Christus in oratione
montana secutus sit. Göttingen: Vandenhoeck und Ruprecht,
1818.

Grüllich, A. Zur unterrichtlichen Behandlung der Bergpredigt
des Herrn Jesu Christi in den Schulen, beim Konfirmande-
nunterrichte oder bei den religiösen Unterredungen mit der
erwachsenen Jugend. Meissen: H. W. Schlimpert, 1886
(1908).

Grundmann, Walter. "Die Bergpredigt nach der Lukasfas-
sung," in Studia Evangelica I. Berlin: Akademie-Verlag,
1959, 181-89.

_____. Die Frage der ältesten Gestalt und des ursprüng-
lichen Sinnes der Bergrede Jesu. Weimar: Verlag
Deutsche Christian, 1939.

Guelich, Robert A. "Mt. 5:22: Its Meaning and Integrity."
Zeitschrift für die neutestamentliche Wissenschaft 64
(1973) 39-52.

Günther, H. "Die Gerechtigkeit des Himmelreiches in der
Bergpredigt." Kerygma und Dogma 17 (1971) 113-26.

Guindon, Roger. "Le 'De Sermone Domini in Monte' de S.
Augustin dans l'oeuvre de S. Thomas d'Aquin." Revue
de l'Université d'Ottawa 28 (1958) 57-85.

Gutzwiller, Richard. Gedanken zur Bergpredigt. Zürich:
NZN Verlag, 1945 (5. Aufl. 1947).

Gyllenberg, Rafael. "Religion und Ethik in der Bergpredigt."
Zeitschrift für systematische Theologie 13 (1936) 682-705.

Haaren, Jan Jozef van. De troost der Bergrede. Hilver-
sum: Paul Brand, 1961 (1963).

Haas, Joseph. Die Seligen. Variationen über die Bergpredigt. Oratorium nach den Worten der Heiligen Schrift
und des Angelus Silesius. Op. 106. Mainz: Schott's
Sohne, 1956 (1959).

Häring, Bernhard. Liebe ist mehr als Gebot. Lebens-
erneuerung aus dem Geist der Bergpredigt. München:
E. Wewel, 1968.
    Meditations on a wide range of ethical questions. Här-
ing makes frequent reference to the Sermon on the Mount
as a pattern for the Christian life.

_____. La morale del Discorso della montagna. Alba:
Edizioni Paoline, 1967.
    An examination of the ethics of the Sermon on the Mount
with emphasis on the relationship to Catholic moral theology.

_____. "The Normative Value of the Sermon on the
Mount." Catholic Biblical Quarterly 29 (1967) 375-85.

Hahn, Philipp M. Die Erklärung der Bergpredigt Jesu
Christi. 2. Aufl. Basel: Reihm, 1885.

Hall, Alfred H. "The Gospel in the Sermon on the Mount."
Bibliotheca Sacra 48 (1891) 322-31.

Hamaide, Jacques. La discours sur la montagne: charte de
vie. Paris: Le Centurion, 1973.
    Deals primarily with the Beatitudes. In the first chap-
ter there is a brief history of interpretation of the Sermon on the Mount. This is followed by the relationship of
the Sermon on the Mount to the Law, eschatology, and
Christology, and a discussion of the Kingdom of God. Sermon on the Mount is the heart of Christianity and a charter of life.

Hamilton, E. L. Laws of the Kingdom; as Contained in the

Sermon on the Mount; a Series of Addresses. 3d ed.
London: Pickering & Inglis, 1957. (Originally published
as The Laws and Principles of the Kingdom of Heaven.
London: Marshall Brothers, 1927).
Sermons.

Hammelsbeck, Oskar. "Die Bergpredigt in Andacht und Unterricht." Evangelische Theologie 5 (1938) 212-21.

Hammerton-Kelly, R. G. "Attitudes to the Law in Matthew's
Gospel; a Discussion of Matthew 5:18." Biblical Research
17 (1972) 19-32.

Handtmann, Gottfried. Der Weg der Kirche. Gedanken zur
Kirchenfrage auf Grund der Bergpredigt. Stettin: Fischer
& Schmidt, 1929.

Hannula, J. R. Vuorisaarnan oppilaan näkökulmasta. Tam-
pere: 1955; Oulu: 1935 (1936).

Hansen, Olav. "Zum Verständnis der Bergpredigt. Eine
missionstheologische Studie zu Mt 5, 17-18," in Der Ruf
Jesu und die Antwort der Gemeinde. Exegetische Untersuchungen. Joachim Jeremias zum 70. Geburtstag gewidmet von seinem Schülern. Hrsg. von Eduard Lohse
gemeinsam mit Christoph Burchard und Berndt Schaller.
Göttingen: Vandenhoeck und Ruprecht, 1970, 94-111.

Harder, Günther. "Jesus und das Gesetz (Matthäus 5. 17-
20)," in Antijudaismus in Neuen Testament? München:
C. Kaiser Verlag, 1967, 105-18.

Ha-Reubeni, M. et Mme. Éphraïm. "Les lis des champs:
recherches sur les plantes de l'évangile." Revue biblique
54 (1947) 362-64.

Hargrove, Hubbard H. At the Master's Feet; a Series of
Expository Sermons from the Sermon on the Mount. Nash-
ville: Broadman Press, 1944; Grand Rapids: Baker Book
House, 1963.
Sermons.

Harms, Claus. Die Bergrede des Herrn. In 21 Predigten
vorgetragen. Kiel: Universitäts-Buchhandlung, 1841.
Sermons.

Harnisch, O. Die Bergpredigt des Herrn nach dem Evan-

gelium des Matthäus für Seminaristen und Lehrer erläutert.
Breslau: C. Dulfer's Verlag, 1901.

Harries, John. The Gospel of Righteousness; or, Short
Studies, Homiletical and Expository on the Sermon on the
Mount. London: Charles H. Kelly, 1893.
Sermons.

Harris, Edward N. "Is the Sermon on the Mount Homiletically
Defensible?" Bibliotheca Sacra 75 (1918) 331-83.

Hartog, Arnold H. de. De Bergrede. Overdenkingen en
overwegingen. Amsterdam: U. M. Holland, 1936.

Hasler, Viktor. "Das Herzstück der Bergpredigt. Zum
Verständnis der Antithesen in Matth 5, 21-48." Theologische Zeitschrift 15 (1959) 90-106.

Hatch, W. H. P. "A Note on Matthew 6:33." Harvard
Theological Review 38 (1945) 270-72.

Hatzfeld, Johannes. Ist die Bergpredigt für Feiglinge?
Paderborn: Bonifacius-Druckerei, 1937 (1940).

Haven, S. V. Kristi Bjergprædiken. Faaborg: Hagerup,
1880.

Hayes, Doremus A. The Heights of Christian Living; a
Study of the Sermon on the Mount. New York: Abingdon,
1929.
Rules for Christian living. Strong pacifist emphasis.

Hedley, P. L. "'The Mote and the Beam' and 'The Gates
of Hades.'" Expository Times 39 (1927-28) 427-28.

Heim, Karl. Die Bergpredigt Jesus für die heutige Zeit
ausgelegt. Tübingen: Furche-Verlag, 1946 (1948) (1949).
Six studies presented at the Evengelical Academy in Boll.

_____. Die Bergpredigt Jesus in ihrer praktischen Ge-
genwartsbedeutung. 3. Aufl. Hamburg: Furche-Verlag,
1959.
Brief studies on various themes in the Sermon on the
Mount such as: murder, divorce, prayer, retaliation.

Heinemann, J. "Nochmals Matth. 5, 42ff." Biblische
Zeitschrift 24 (1938-39) 136-38.

Heinen, Anton. Die Bergpredigt Jesu Christi. Gladbach:
Volksverein Verlag, 1921 (1926).

Heinrici, C. F. Georg. Die Bergpredigt (Matth. 5-7. Luk.
6, 20-49). Leipzig: Alexander Edelmann, 1899; Leipzig:
Dürr'sche Buchhandlung, 1900.
    Source and textual criticism.

_____. Die Bergpredigt (Matth. 5-7. Luk. 6, 20-49).
Begriffsgeschichtlich untersucht. Leipzig: Dürr'sche
Buchhandlung, 1905.
    An analysis of the various concepts and categories found
in the Sermon on the Mount.

Heinzelmann, Gerhard. "Das richtige Verständnis der Bergpredigt." Theologische Studien und Kritiken 108 (1937-
38).

Heitmüller, Friedrich. Das Evangelium der Bergpredigt.
Hamburg: Christliche Gemeinschaftsbuchhandlung, 1929.
    Popular treatment in homiletical style.

Hendriksen, William. The Sermon on the Mount. Grand
Rapids: Eerdmans, 1934.
    Outline and brief commentary of Sermon on the Mount
text. Includes questions for discussion and reading and
study helps.

Henke, Oskar. Die Bergrede Jesu. Gotha: F. A. Perthes,
1895.

Henry, Carl F. H. "The Biblical Particularization of the
Will of God: the Sermon on the Mount," in Christian
Personal Ethics. Grand Rapids: Eerdmans, 1957, 278-
326.
    A useful sketch and evaluation of seven appraisals of
the Sermon on the Mount. These are: (1) humanistic;
(2) liberal; (3) dispensational; (4) interim-ethic; (5) existential; (6) Anabaptist-Mennonite; (7) Reformed.

Henson, William E. The Inaugural Message of the King; a
Brief Exposition of the Sermon on the Mount. New York:
Vantage Press, 1954.

Hering, Jean. "Le Sermon sur la montagne dans la nouvelle
traduction anglaise de la Bible." Revue d'histoire et de
philosophie religeuses 42 (1962) 122-32.

Hermann, Rudolph. Die Bergpredigt und die Religiös-Sozialen.
Leipzig: A. Deichert, 1922.

Herr, Johannes. Erläuterungs-spiegel, oder, Eine gründliche
Erklärung von der Bergpredigt unsers Herrn Jesu Christi.
Lancaster, Pa.: Johann Bär und Söhne, 1854.
A spirited plea for self-examination, upright living, and
conversion, using the Sermon on the Mount as one's model.

_____. The Illustrating Mirror; or, A Fundamental Illus-
tration of Christ's Sermon on the Mount. Lancaster, Pa.:
Elias Barr, 1858.
(See his Erläuterungs-spiegel...)

Herwerden, Claudius Henricus van. Jezus Christus in de
Bergrede beschouwd als een voorbeeld voor den Kanzel-
rednaar. Groningen: 1829.

Hezel, Wilhelm F. Die Bergrede und das Gebet Jesu als
Probe einer neuen Übersetzung der ganzen Bibel. Dorpat:
1808.

Hildebrand, Christian. Die Bergpredigt. Ein Unterricht über
die wahre und falsche Frömmigkeit ... mit eine Predigt
Luthers über die Liebe. Essegg: Pfarrer Hildebrand,
1906.
Practical study.

Hill, Daniel H. A Consideration of the Sermon on the Mount.
Philadelphia: William S. and Alfred Martinen, 1858.
Fairly lengthy work with few subject or topical divisions.
Practical emphasis.

Hirsch, Emmanuel. "Die Bergpredigt." Deutsches Volkstum
20 (1938) 820-6.

Hjerl-Hansen, Borge. "Le rapprochement poison-serpent dans
la prédication de Jésus (Mt. VII, 10 et Luc XI, 11)."
Revue biblique 55 (1948) 195-98.

Hodtke, Otto. Die Bergpredigt und moderne Sittlichkeit.
Koslin: A. Hoffmann, 1907.

Hofer, Philipp. Die Methodik der Bergpredgt des Herrn.
Ein Beitrag zur Theorie der Katechese. Wien: H. Kirsch,
1903.

Hofmeyr, N. J. Met Jezus op den berg. Blikken in de
Bergrede. Utrecht: P. den Boer, 1908.

_____. Zu Jesu Füssen. Betrachtungen über die Berg-
predigt. Übers. G. Holten-Weber. Barmen: Buchhandlung des blauen Kreuzes, 1911.

Hogg, Charles F., and Watson, J. B. On the Sermon on
the Mount. 3d ed. London: Pickering and Inglis, 1947.
    Popular commentary. A concluding section lists
parallels between the teachings of the Sermon on the
Mount and the Epistles.

Hoh, I. "Christus humani civilisque cultus fautor." Verbum
Domini 2 (1922) 204-06.

Holl, Adolf. Augustins Bergpredigtexegese nach seinem
Frühwerk. De sermone domini in monte libri duo. Wien:
Herder, 1960.
    A discussion of Augustine's method and principles of
Biblical interpretation as exemplified in Book II of his
commentary on the Sermon on the Mount.

Holl, F. J. de. De autoriteit der Bergrede. Vlugschriften
van de Studieclub van moderne theologen. 7 Assen:
Van Gorcum & Comp's Boekh., 1928.

Hollensteiner, Karl. Glaube, Liebe, Hoffnung. Ein Buch
über die Bergpredigt. Berlin: Rehtwisch & Langewort,
1898.

Holm, Ivar. Handledning till bergspredikan och den kristna-
tros-och livsåskådningen. Stockholm: Magn. Bergvall,
1922.

Holtzclaw, Brooks. "A Note on Matthew 5, 21-48," in
Festschrift to Honor F. Wilbur Gingrich, Lexicographer,
Scholar, Teacher and Committed Christian Layman.
Leiden: Brill, 1972, 161-63.

Holzmeister, U. "'Nemo potest duobus dominis servire'
(Mt. 6, 24)." Verbum Domini 3 (1923) 304-06.

_____. "Die Streitfrage über die Ehescheidungstexte bei
Matthäus 5, 32 und 19, 9." Biblica 26 (1945) 133-46.

_____. "De veritate sermonum in Scriptura relatorum."
Verbum Domini 10 (1930) 135-41.

_____. "Vom Schlagen auf die rechte Wange (Mt. 5. 39)"
Zeitschrift für katholische Theologie 45 (1921) 334-36.

Honeyman, A. M. "Matthew V. 18 and the Validity of Law."
New Testament Studies 1 (1954-55) 141-42.

Horn, Friedmann, und Reissner, Erich L. G. Der innere
Sinn der Bergpredigt. Zürich: Swedenborg Verlag, 1963.
Brief expositions by various authors.

Horneck, Anthony. Several Sermons upon the Fifth of St.
Matthew. 3d ed. London: Printed for Batley, 1717.
Sermons.

Hove, J. ten. "Het zout der aarde." Theologisch tijdschrift 46 (1912) 252-54.

Hubenthal, Adolf. Die Bergpredigt als Botschaft an die evangelische Frau. Bielefeld: Bechauf, 1953.

Huber, Hugo H. Die Bergpredigt. Eine exegetische Studie.
Göttingen: Vandenhoeck & Rupprecht, 1932.
Scholarly work dealing with higher critical and textual
questions.

Hulbert, C. B. "The Theology of the Sermon on the Mount."
Homiletic Review 34 (1897) 163-66.

Hunt, Gladys M. The God Who Understands Me; 15 Studies
in the Sermon on the Mount for Neighborhood, Student,
and Church Groups. Wheaton, Ill.: Harold Shaw, 1971.

Hunter, Archibald M. Design for Life; an Exposition of the
Sermon on the Mount. London: SCM Press, 1953.
A brief, readable guide to critical and ethical issues.

_____. Ihr sollt vollkommen sein; die Bergpredigt als
Ethik der Gnade. Übers. Horst Weiss. Kassel: Oncken-
Verlag, 1968.
(See his Design for Life)

_____. "The Meaning of the Sermon on the Mount." Ex-
pository Times 63 (1951-52) 176-79.

_____. A Pattern for Life; an Exposition of the Sermon
on the Mount. Philadelphia: Westminster Press, 1953
(1965).
(See his Design for Life)

Hurley, M. "Christ and Divorce." Irish Theological Quarterly 35 (1968) 58-72.

Hutton, W. R. "Make a Tree Good?" Expository Times 75
(1963-64) 366-67.

Ibbeken, Hermann G. Die Bergpredigt Jesu. Wissenschaft-
lich-populär ausgelegt. Metz: G. Lang, 1888; Einbeck:
J. Ibbeken, 1888 (1890).
     A verse by verse commentary.

Ich aber sage euch. 6 Bibelarbeiten über die Bergpredigt
     beim 14. Deutschen Evangelischen Kirchentag, Stuttgart
     1969. Stuttgart: Berlin: Kreuz-Verlag, 1969.
     Six Bible studies on the Sermon on the Mount by six
pastors and professors, given at the 14th Deutschen Evangelischen Kirchentag Stuttgart 1969.

The Inaugural Address of the Kingdom of Heaven. Louisville,
     Ky.: John P. Morton, 1885.
     A translation of the Sermon on the Mount with a run-
ning comment and notes.

Innokentii, episkop. Nagornaia propoved' Khrista Spasitelia.
     Ekzegeticheskoe issledovanie. Astrakhan': 1915.

Ish Yehudi, pseud. Bo u-re'eh. 2d improved and enl. ed.
     by J. I. Landsman. London: Hebrew Christian Testimony
to Israel, 1913.
     Brief popular exposition.

Jaeger, Ch. "À propos de deux passages du Sermon sur la
montagne.--Matthieu 5, 21 et 33." Revue d'histoire et
de philosophie religieuses 18 (1938) 417-18.

James, Truman. "He." Fort Wayne, Ind.: Hoosier Press,
1927.
     Brief popular discussion, followed by a literary presen-
tation of the setting for the Sermon on the Mount. Includes selected parts of the Sermon.

Jameson, John G. The Gospel of the Kingdom in the Sermon
on the Mount (from Matt. V, 13 onwards). London: W.
Hodge, 1951.
     Meditations.

Jenkins, Isaac C. The Sermon on the Mount. Nashville:

Cokesbury Press, 1925.
Meditations.

Jentzen, F. G. De indole ac ratione orationis montanae.
Lübeck: von Rohden, 1819.

Jeremias, Joachim. Die Bergpredigt. Stuttgart: Calwer
Verlag, 1959 (1960) (7. Aufl. 1970).
A brief, readable interpretation which employs the
techniques of source and form analysis to probe the question of the aim of the Sermon on the Mount. Jeremias
understands its original function as a catechism for con-
verts to Christianity, and hence also its contemporary
relevance.

_____. Bjergpraedikenen--frihedens lov. Overs. Karen
Thormann. København: Det økumeniske Center, 1969.
(See his Die Bergpredigt)

_____. "Die Lampe unter dem Scheffel." Zeitschrift
für die neutestamentliche Wissenschaft 39 (1940) 237-40.
Also: Abba. Studien zur neutestamentlichen Theologie
und Zeitgeschichte. Göttingen: Vandenhoeck & Ruprecht,
1966, 99-102.

_____. "'Lass allda deine Gabe' (Mt. 5, 23f.)." Zeit-
schrift für die neutestamentliche Wissenschaft 36 (1937)
150-54.
Also: Abba. Studien zur neutestamentlichen Theologie
und Zeitgeschichte. Göttingen: Vandenhoeck & Ruprecht,
1966, 103-07.

_____. "Matthaus 7, 6a," in Abraham unser Vater.
Juden und Christen im Gespräch über die Bibel. Fest-
schrift für Otto Michel zum 60. Geburtstag. Hrsg. von
Otto Betz, Martin Hengel, Peter Schmidt. Leiden: E. J.
Brill, 1963, 271-75.
Also: Abba. Studien zur neutestamentlichen Theologie
und Zeitgeschichte. Göttingen: Vandenhoeck & Ruprecht,
166, 83-87.

_____. Palabras de Jesús. El sermón de la montaña.
El Padre Nuestro. Trad. José Maria Bernáldeg Montalvo.
Madrid: Fax, 1968.
(See his Die Bergpredigt)
Also includes translation of Das Vater-Unser im Lichte
der neuren Forschung. Stuttgart: Calwer Verlag, 1962.

_____. Paroles de Jésus. Le Sermon sur la montagne.
Le Notre-Père dans l'exégèse actuelle. Trad. Dom
Marie Mailhé. Paris: Cerf, 1963 (1967).
   (See his Die Bergpredigt)
   Also includes translation of Das Vater-Unser im Lichte
der nueren Forschung. Stuttgart: Calwer Verlag, 1962.

_____. The Sermon on the Mount. Trans. Norman Per-
ris. London: Anthone Press, 1961; Philadelphia: Fortress, 1963.
   (See his Die Bergpredigt)

Jesus and His Disciples (Filmstrip). Cinema Corp. of
   America, 1948.

Johnson, Franklin. "The Plan of the Sermon on the Mount."
   Homiletic Review 24 (1892) 360-65, 550-53.

Johnson, Sherman. "Sermon on the Mount," in Twentieth
   Century Encyclopedia of Religious Knowledge. vol. 2.
   Grand Rapids: Baker Book House, 1955, 1018-20.

Jones, E. Stanley. Bergspredikans Kristus. En praktisk
   livsfilosofi. Över. Th. Avidson. Stockholm: Nya bok-
   förlags, 1934.
   (See his The Christ of the Mount)

_____. The Christ of the Mount; a Working Philosophy
of Life. New York: Abingdon, 1931.
   This book came out of discussions about the Christian
   message held in Indian ashrams. The Sermon on the
   Mount is presented as a working philosophy of life and
   as the main moral content in the word "Christian."

_____. Christus op den berg. Vert. Johanna E. Kuiper.
Amsterdam: H. J. Paris, 1933.
   (See his The Christ of the Mount)

_____. Vuorisaarnan Kristus. Suomentanut Aune Krohn.
Porvoo: 1933.
   (See his The Christ of the Mount)

Jongsma, Lieuwe S. De Bergrede van onzen Heere Jezus
   Christus uitgelegd. Kampen: Uitgave van het Gere-
   formeerd Traktaatgenootschap "Filippus," 1916.
   Practical treatment.

Jordan, Clarence. Sermon on the Mount. Philadelphia:
Judson Press, 1952 (1970).
The late founder of Koinonia Farm interprets the Sermon on the Mount in the arresting, down-to-earth style
reminiscent of his "Cotton Patch" version of the New Testament Gospels and Epistles.

Jordan, Paula. Die Bergpredigt. Wandbilder zur Bibel. Nr.
5. Kassel: Stauda; Stuttgart: Verlag "Junge Gemeinde,"
1957.

Josaphat, Carlos P. de Oliveira. O Sermão da Montanha.
São Paulo: Livraria Duas Cidades, 1967.

Josefson, R. "Bergpredikans plats i den kristna etiken."
Ny kyrklig tidskrift 19 (1950) 43-55.

Joüon, Paul. "Matthieu V, 43." Recherches de science
religieuse 20 (1930) 545-46.

_____. "Notes philologiques sur les Évangiles.--Matthieu
5, 21." Recherches de science religieuse 17 (1927) 540.

Juárez Muñoz, J. Fernando. El Sermón de la Montaña.
Guatemala: Talleres Gutenberg, 1944.
Meditations.

Just, J. Die Bergpredigt als Beispiel des Lehrens Jesu.
Leipzig: H. Beyers und Sohn, 1917.

Kahlefeld, Heinrich. Der Jünger. Eine Auslegung der Rede
Lk 6, 20-49. 2. Aufl. Frankfort am Main: J. Knecht,
1962 (1965).
A critical interpretation of the Lucan Sermon on the
Mount.

_____. "Selig ihr Armen." Bibel und Leben 1 (1960)
55-61.

Kaiser, Paul. Die Bergpredigt des Herrn ausgelegt in
Predigten. Leipzig: A. Deichertsche Verlagsbuchhand-
lung (George Böhme), 1904 (1912).
Sermons.

_____. The Law in the Light of the Gospel. Burlington,
Iowa: German Literary Board, 1909.
Sermons.

Kallus, Reiner. Bergpredigt. Augsburg: Verlagsverein
Lebendiges Wort, 1970.

Karmeluk, J. Die proletarische Bergpredigt. Zürich:
Buchhandlung des schweizerischen Grütlivereins, 1904.

Katz, Peter. " Πῶς αὐξάνουσιν. Matt. VI. 28. " Journal of
Theological Studies 5 (1954) 207-09.

Keck, Leander E. "The Sermon on the Mount, " in Pittsburgh
Festival on the Gospels. vol. 2. Pittsburgh: Pittsburgh
Theological Seminary, 1970, 311-22.

Kepler, Thomas S. Jesus' Design for Living. New York:
Abingdon, 1955.
Devotional studies.

Kertelge, Karl. "Die Bergpredigt als Thema heutiger Ver-
kündigung, " in Das Evangelium auf dem Weg zum Menschen.
Hrsg. Otto Knoch, Felix Messerschmid, Alois Zenner.
Frankfurt am Main: J. Knecht, 1973, 25-34.

Kessel, Robert. Die Gleichnisse Jesu und die Bildreden
der Bergpredigt. Nach der Auffassung der neueren Zeit
für die Schulpraxis erklärt und gewürdigt. 2., vermehrte
und verbesserte Aufl. Hamburg: Beyer & Söhne, 1909.

Kierkegaard, Søren Aabye. Ce que nous apprennent les lis
des champs et les oiseaux du ciel. Paris: F. Alcan,
1935.
(See his Hvad vi leare af lilierne pas marken...)

_____. Christelige taler. Kjøbenhaven: C. A. Reitzel,
1848 (1862); Glydendal, 1939.
Part I is on "The anxieties of the heathen" and is a
discussion of anxiety under seven heads. Based on Matt.
6:24-34.

_____. Christian Discourses and the Lilies of the Field
and the Birds of the Air and Three Discourses at the
Communion on Fridays. Trans. Walter Lowrie. London:
Oxford University Press, 1939 (1952).
(See his Christelige taler and his Lilien paa Marken...)

_____. Christliche Reden. Übers. W. Kütemeyer und
Chr. Schrempf. Jena: E. Diederichs, 1929; Göttingen:
Vandehoeck & Ruprecht, 1955.
(See his Christelige taler)

_____. Consider the Lilies, Being the Second Part of "Edifying Discourses in a Different Vein." Trans. A. S. Aldworth and W. S. Ferrie. London: C. W. Daniel, 1940.
(See his Hvad vi leare af lilierne pas marken...)

_____. Discours chrétiens. Traduction et introduction de P. H. Tisseau. Neuchâtel: Delachaux et Niestlé, 1952 (1967).
(See his Christelige taler)

_____. Gli ucceli dell'aria e i gigli del campo. Roma: Edizioni della Bussola, 1945.
(See his Hvad vi leare af lilierne pas marken...)

_____. The Gospel of Suffering and The Lilies of the Field. Trans. David F. Swenson and Lillian Marvin Swenson. Minneapolis: Augsburg Pub. House, 1948.
(See his Lilien paa Marken...)

_____. Hvad vi leare af lilierne pas marken og af himmelens fugle. Kjøbenhavn: C. A. Reitzel, 1847.
Three discourses on Matt. 6:24-34.

_____. I gigli dei campi e gli uccelli del cielo. Milano: Fratelli Bocca, 1945.
(See his Hvad vi leare af lilierne pas marken...)

_____. Die Lilien auf dem Felde; drei Reden. Übers. und mit einem Nachwort versehen von Friedrich Hansen-Löve. Wien: Herder, n.d.
(See his Hvad vi leare af lilierne pas marken...)

_____. Die Lilien auf dem Felde und die Vögel unter dem Himmel. Zusammengestellt von A. Bärthold. 2. Aufl. Halle: Fricke, 1885.
(See his Lilien paa Marken...)

_____. Lilien paa Marken og Fugeln under Himlen. Kjøbenhavn: C. A. Reitzel, 1849 (1854) (1865); Glydendal, 1906 (1943); Samlerens forlag, 1943.
Three discourses on Matt. 6:24-34.

King, George B. "Consider the Lilies." Crozer Quarterly 10 (1933) 28-35.

_____. "A Further Note on the Mote and the Beam

(Matt. VII. 3-5; Luke VI. 41-42)." Harvard Theological
Review 26 (1933) 73-76.

_____. "The Mote and the Beam." Harvard Theological
Review 17 (1924) 393-404.

King, Guy H. New order; an Expositional Study of the Sermon on the Mount. London: Marshall, Morgan and Scott,
1943.
    Lectures delivered before parish Bible School. Prac-
tical and popular approach.

King, Henry C. The Way of Life, a Revised and Enlarged
Reprint of Those Portions of the Author's Ethics of Jesus,
Dealing with the Sermon on the Mount, with a Special Discussion of War and the Teaching of Jesus. New York:
Macmillan, 1918.
    Practical and popular interpretation. In two brief,
concluding chapters King discusses pacifism and nonresistance in relation to Jesus' teaching.

The Kingdom of Heaven (Motion picture) Harmon Foundation,
1930.

Kittel, G. "Die Bergpredigt und die Ethik des Judentums."
Zeitschrift für systematische Theologie 2 (1924-25) 555-94.

Klein, G. "Mt 6, 2." Zeitschrift für die neutestamentliche
Wissenschaft 6 (1905) 203-04.

Kling, Christoph F. Die Bergpredigt Christi nach Matthäus.
Für nachdenkende Christen erklärt. Marburg: Elwert,
1841.

Klöpper, Albert. "Zur Stellung Jesu gegenüber dem
mosaischen Gesetze (Matth. 5, 17-48)." Zeitschrift für
wissenschaftliche Theologie 39 (1896) 1-23.

Klostermann, Erich. "Zum Verständnis von Mt. 6, 2."
Zeitschrift für die neutestamentliche Wissenschaft 47
(1956) 280-81.

Knorzer, Wolfgang. Die Bergpredigt. Modell einer neuen
Welt. Stuttgart: Verlag katholisches Bibelwerk, 1968
(1970).
    A brief interpretation which treats both critical and
practical questions.

Kock, Gösta. Sammanfattning av bergspredikans religiösa och etiska grundtankar. Stockholm: G. Lindström, 1932.

Köhler, Konrad. "Zu Mt. 5, 22." Zeitschrift für die neutestamentliche Wissenschaft 19 (1919-20) 91-95.

König, Hans-Joachim. Ich aber sage Euch. Der Gemeinde zur Bibelwoche 1965/66. Zeichnungen von Gerd Wilk. Berlin-Friedenau: Christlicher Zeitschriftenverlag, 1965.

Kraeling, Carl H. "Seek and You Will Find," in Early Christian Origins. Studies in honor of Harold R. Willoughby, edited by Allen Wikgren. Chicago: Quadrangle Books, 1961, 24-34.

Krarup, Jens. Kristendom--for og impod. 6 bibeltimer over Jesu bjergprædiken. København: De Unges Forlag, 1968.
Six study lessons for young people. Includes discussion questions.

Krause, Christian. "The Sermon on the Mount in Ecumenical Thought Since World War II." Lutheran World 15 (1969) 52-59.

Kretzer, Max. Die Bergpredigt. 3. Aufl. Dresden: Leipzig: E. Pierson's Verlag, 1898; 7. Aufl. Leipzig: P. List, 1925.
Novel.

Kühn, H. "Das Problem der Bergpredigt." Neue kirkliche Zeitschrift 25 (1914) 227-50, 251-67.

Kürzinger, Josef. "Zur Komposition der Bergpredigt nach Matthäus." Biblica 40 (1959) 569-89.

Kuhn, Johannes, comp. Die bessere Gerechtigkeit. Die Bergpredigt zwischen Utopie und Realität. Stuttgart: Quell Verlag, 1969.
Essays, mostly by pastors.

Kutsch, E. "'Eure Rede aber sei ja ja, nein nein.'" Evangelische Theologie 20 (1960) 206-18.

Kylander, K. F. Förklaring till Jesu bergspredikan. För skolar och vid självstudier. Stockholm: Norstedt, 1902.

Lamote, J. Die Bergrede. Grond van elke kritiek, opgave
tot echtheid. Antwerp: Patmos, 1972.

Lamsa, George M. The Kingdom on Earth. Lee's Summit,
Mo.: Unity Books, 1966.
    An imaginative account which tries to reenact the orig-
inal setting of the Sermon on the Mount. Most of the
book deals with the Beatitudes and the Lord's Prayer.

Lancelot, John B. Guidance from the Mount. London:
Church Book, 1937.

Langley, James A. "Critique of Contemporary Interpretations of the Sermon on the Mount, with Special Reference
to Albert Schweitzer, Reinhold Niebuhr, and C. H. Dodd."
Th. D. thesis. Southwestern Baptist Theological Seminary,
1956.

Lanwer, Bernhard. Die Grundgedanken der Bergpredigt auf
dem Hintergrunde des Alten Testamentes und Spätjudentums.
Hiltrup: Herz-Jesu-Missionhaus, 1934.
    Examines the Sermon on the Mount against the back-
ground of the understanding of the Kingdom of God and the
Law in the Old Testament and late Judaism. The subject
of the Sermon on the Mount is the universality and law of
God's Kingdom. While Jesus was in the Jewish tradition,
his ethic is something new. It excels and transcends the
old righteousness in an unequalled loftiness.

_____. Jesu Stellung zum Gesetz. Mt 5, 17-48 auf dem
Hintergrunde des AT und Spätjudentums. Diss. Katholisch-
Theologischen Fakultät der Universität Münster i. W. Hiltrup: 1933.
    A study of the nature of law in the Old Testament and
in late Judaism and of Jesus' attitude toward it as expressed in the first part of the Sermon on the Mount.

Lapide, Cornelius A. Commentarii in quatuor Evangelia.
    A commentary on the four Gospels which was part of
Lapide's celebrated commentaries on all the Canonical
Books except Job and Psalms. Editions appeared in:
1638, 1639, 1641, 1660, 1695, 1712, 1732, 1734-35, 1737,
1747, 1767, 1896, 1935- .

Lapide, P. E. "Die Bergpredigt, Theorie und Praxis."
Zeitschrift für evangelische Ethik 17 (1973) 369-72.

Laurila, Kaarle S. Leo Tolstoi und Martin Luther als Ausleger der Bergpredigt. Helsinki: Suomalainen Tiedeakatemia, 1944.
An analytical and critical essay on Tolstoy's and Luther's interpretations of the Sermon on the Mount. This
is followed by a brief discussion of the views of Emil
Brunner and Carl Starge on the Sermon on the Mount.

Lebreton, Jules. "Le discours sur la montagne et les béatitudes." Revue pratique d'apologétique 28 (1919) 321-43.

_____. "Le Sermon sur la montagne," in Lumen Christi:
la doctrine spirituelle du Nouveau Testament. Paris:
Beauchesne, 1947, 141-57.

Leeming, Bernard and Dyson, R. A. "Except It Be for For-
nication?" Scripture 8 (1956) 75-82.

Lees, Harrington C. The King's Highway; a Series of Expository Studies in the Sermon on the Mount. London:
Marshall Bros., 1910.

Légasse, Simon. Les pauvres en esprit: Evangile et non
violence. Paris: Editions du Cerf, 1974.
A commentary on Matthew 5.

Lerle, E. "Realisiebare Forderungen der Bergpredigt?"
Kerygma und Dogma 1 (1970) 32-40.

Le Seur, Eduard. Die Bergpredigt und der Krieg: vier
Kreigspredigten. Berlin: M. Warneck, 1915.
Sermons.

Le Seur, Paul. Jesu Angriff auf die verdorbene Religion.
Eine kurze Einführung in die Bergpredigt. Berlin:
Hochweg-Verlag, 1936.

Ley, Wilhelm. Ich aber sage euch. Jesu Bergrede in zeit-
gemässen Gesprächen mit Jugendlichen. 12 Hefte. Wup-
pertal-Barmen: Umbruch-Verlag, 1935.

Liese, H. "De iustia evangelica (Mt. 5, 20-24)." Verbum
Domini 12 (1932) 161-67.

Lifschitz, Feitel. Zur Sozial-und Wirtschafts-Philosophie der
Bergpredigt. Bern: D. Schermann, 1931.

Ligon, Ernest M. The Psychology of Christian Personality.
New York: Macmillan, 1935 (1950) (1961).
    Considers the teachings of Jesus in the Sermon on the
Mount in light of the psychology of personality. Each
section of the Sermon is dealt with according to three
problems: (1) Description of the Christian personality;
(2) Teachings of Jesus examined psychologically; (3) How
can the Christian personality be developed? Ligon is convinced that the problems of human nature find their solution in the teachings of Jesus.

Lilje, Hanns. Anweisung zum Leben. Einführung in die
Bergpredigt. Hamburg: Furche-Verlag, 1958.
    Brief, popular treatment.

Lindberg, O. E. Bergspredikan och det verliga lifvet. La-
holm: Tr. Laholms typografiska anstalt, 1922.

Lindblom, Johan. Jesu bergspredikan. Stockholm: Sveriges
kristliga studentrörelse, 1927.

Linderholm, Emanuel. Jesu bergspredikan i kortfattad utläg-
gning för folkskolans undervisning och självstudium.
Stockholm: Norstedt, 1922.

Lindsay, Alexander D. The Moral Teaching of Jesus; an
Examination of the Sermon on the Mount. London: Hodder and Stoughton, 1937.
    Six addresses which examine the nature of Jesus' teach-
ing concerning perfection, desire, reverence, non-resistance, relations of men and women, divorce.

Linton, O. "Bergspredikan." Svenskt Bibliskt Uppslagverk
I, 222-33.

_____. "St. Matthew 5:43." Studia Theologica 18 (1964)
66-79.

Ljunghoff, Johannes. Bergspredikan. Lund: Gleerup, 1939
(1954).

Ljungman, Henrik. Das Gesetz erfüllen--Matth. 5.17ff. und
3.15 untersucht. Lund: Gleerup, 1954.
    A scholarly monograph on the meaning of Jesus' words
regarding the fulfilling of the law.

Lloyd-Jones, David M. Studies in the Sermon on the Mount.

2 vols. Grand Rapids: Eerdmans; London: Inter-Varsity
Fellowship, 1959-60.
Sermons.

Lohse, Eduard. "Ich aber sage euch," in Der Ruf Jesu und
die Antwort der Gemeinde. Exegetische Untersuchungen.
Joachim Jeremias zum 70. Geburtstag Gewidmet von
seinem Schülern. Göttingen: Vandenhoeck & Ruprecht,
1970, 189-230.

Loosley, Ernest G. The Challenge from the Mount. London:
Epworth Press, 1964.
For Loosley the key concept for interpreting the Sermon on the Mount is repentance. He assumes that what
Jesus was appealing for was a radical change of mind and
heart, and a new outlook on life, a new moral orientation, a revaluation of all values.

Lovestam, E. " Αποστάσιον --en gammalpalestinensisk
skilsmässoterm." Svensk exegetisk Arsbok 27 (1962) 132-
35.

Lovette, Roger. For the Dispossessed. Philadelphia: United
Church Press, 1973.
Sermons.

Loy, Matthias. The Sermon on the Mount. Columbus, Ohio:
Lutheran Book Concern, 1909.
A practical, topical study.

Luck, Ulrich. Die Vollkommenheitsforderung der Bergpredigt.
Ein aktuelles Kapitel der Theologie des Matthäus. München: C. Kaiser Verlag, 1968.
A brief study of the Sermon on the Mount and the theology of the Gospel of Matthew.

Lührmann, D. "Liebet eure Feinde; Lk 6:27-36; Mt 5:39-
48." Zeitschrift für Theologie und Kirche 69 (1972) 412-
38.

Lüthi, Walter, und Brunner, Robert. Der Heiland. Ein
Gang durch die Bergpredigt. Basel: F. Reinhardt, 1936
(7. Aufl. 1949?).
A series of studies presented to Bible classes in the
Oekolampad community center. Popular treatment.

_____ und _____. The Sermon on the Mount. Trans.

Kurt Schoenenberger. Edinburg: Oliver and Boyd, 1963;
Toronto: Clarke, Irwin, 1963.
(See his Der Heiland: Ein Gang durch die Bergpredigt)

Luther, Martin. Commentary on the Sermon on the Mount.
Trans. Charles A. Hay. Philadelphia: Lutheran Publish-
ing Society, 1892.
(See his Das fünffte, sechste und siebend Capital S.
Matthei...)

_____. D. Martin Luthers Auslegung der Bergpredigt
Matthäus 5-7. Hrsg. von Erwin Mühlhaupt. Mit einen
einführenden Aufsatz von Paul Althaus über Luther und die
Bergpredigt. Göttingen: Vandenhoeck & Ruprecht, 1961.
(See his Das fünffte, sechste und siebend Capital S.
Matthei...)

_____. Enarrationes doctissimae & lectu utilissimae
Doctoria Martini Lutheri ... in quintū, sextum, & septi-
mum capita Matthaei pro concionibus pronūciatae & excep-
tae. Per vincentium Obsopoeum in latinum sermonem
traductae. Haganoae: Ex officina Seceriana, 1533.
(See his Das fünffte, sechste und siebend Capital S.
Matthei...)

_____. Das fünffte, sechste und siebend Capital S.
Matthei, gepredigt und ausgelegt durch D. Mart. Luther.
Wittenberg: J. Klug, 1532 (1534); J. Weiss, 1539.
An extensive commentary on the Sermon on the Mount
based upon a series of sermons delivered at Wittenberg.
Luther makes frequent reference to the Old Testament
and relates it to the Sermon on the Mount. A funda-
mental theme running through the commentary is Luther's
defense of his doctrine of the two kingdoms against the
"Papists" and the Anabaptists.

_____. T. Martti Lutherukselta kirjoitettu Herramme
Jesuksen Kristuksen Wuorisaarnan, eli P. Mattheuksen
Ewangeliumin 5-7 nen lu'un selitys, jonka on Ruotsista
suomentanut Karl Isaac Nordlund. Helsingisä: 1845.
(See his Das fünffte, sechste und siebend Capital S.
Matthei...)

_____. Works. vol. 21. The Sermon on the Mount
and the Magnificat. Edited by Jeroslav Pelikan. St.
Louis: Concordia Publishing House, 1956.
(See his Das fünffte, sechste und siebend Capital S.
Matthei...)

Lutz, Nelly. Unvergleichliches Leben. Die Botschaft der
Bergpredigt. München: Evangelischer Verlag A. Lempp,
1939.

Lyttelton, E. Studies in the Sermon on the Mount. London:
Longmans, Green, 1905.
    The author divides the Sermon on the Mount into
twenty-two topics and presents a brief, popular treatment
of each.

_____. "The Teaching of Christ about Divorce." Journal
of Theological Studies 5 (1904) 621-28.

Ma, Kyŏng-il. Wanjŏn e ŭi tojong. Seoul: Taehan Kidok-
kyo Sŏhoe, 1970.

McAfee, Cleland B. Studies in the Sermon on the Mount.
New York: Revell, 1910.
Sermons.

McArthur, Harvey K. Understanding the Sermon on the
Mount. New York: Harpers, 1960.
    The primary purpose of this book is to deal with the
practical, historical, and theological problems raised by
the Sermon on the Mount. McArthur examines historically various views of interpreting the Sermon on the Mount
under the following headings: the Sermon and the Mosaic
tradition; the Sermon and the Pauline tradition; the Sermon and the Eschaton; the Sermon and ethics. This work
is a good source for a history of interpretation of the
Sermon on the Mount.

McGillivray, Donald. "Matthew VII. 6." Expository Times
27 (1915-16) 46.

Macgregor, W. M. "The Sermon on the Mount." Expository Times 39 (1927-28) 293-97.

Macintyre, William. Exposition of the Sermon on the Mount,
Matt. V-VII. Edinburgh: Theobald, 1854.

MacMunn, V. C. "Who Compiled the Sermon on the Mount?"
Expository Times 35 (1923-24) 221-25.

Macrakis, Apostolos. The Interpretation of the Gospel Law
and Commentary on the Epistle to the Hebrews. Trans.
D. Cummings. Chicago: Orthodox Christian Educational

Society, 1955.
First half of the book is a commentary on the Sermon
on the Mount.

Mahoney, A. "A New Look at the Divorce Clauses in Mt 5,
32 and 19, 9." Catholic Biblical Quarterly 30 (1968) 29-
38.

Maine, Louis Auguste de Bourbon. Méditations sur le
sermon de notre-Seigneur sur la montagne. Paris:
Palmé, 1884.
Meditations.

Manek, J. "On the Mount--on the Plain, Mt 5:1, Lk 6:17."
Novum Testamentum 9 (1967) 124-31.

Mánek, Jindřich. Dům na skále; Ježíšovo kázání na hoře.
Praha: Blahoslav, 1967.
First part deals with critical questions relating to the
Sermon on the Mount. There follows a verse by verse
commentary. Contains text according to the Nestle transla-
tion of 1960.

Margoliouth, D. S. "Studies in the Sermon on the Mount."
Expositor 7th ser. 9 (1910) 42-50, 143-52, 210-17.

Marquardt, G. "Die Bergpredigt des Mt.--Ev. Eine meister-
lich disponierte Komposition des Evangelistes." Bibel und
Kirche 13 (1958) 81-4.

Marriott, Horace. The Sermon on the Mount. London: Society for Promoting Christian Knowledge, 1925; New York:
Macmillan, 1925.
A sizeable work which seeks to combine the critical,
exegetical, and expository. A notable feature is Marriott's
attempt to reconstruct the Q text of the Sermon on the
Mount. A large part of the book deals with textual and
source analysis and with parallels and affinities to the Sermon on the Mount in pre-Christian Jewish literature.

Martin, G. Currie. "'Know No Despair!'" Expository
Times 8 (1896-97) 141.

Massaux, É. "Le texte du Sermon sur la montagne de Matthieu utilisé par saint Justin." Ephemerides theological
Lovanienses 28 (1952) 411-48.

Mattheus: De Bergrede. Naschrift van W. K. Grossouw.
's-Gravenhage: Daamen, 1968.

Mau, Johann A. Die Bergpredigt Christi nach St. Matthäus.
Homiletisch bearbeitet, und in 24 Predigten dargestellt.
Hamburg: Perthes, Besser, und Mauke, 1836.
Sermons.

May, Eric. "'... For Power Went Forth from Him...'
(Luke 6, 19)." Catholic Biblical Quarterly 14 (1952) 93-
103.

Mayhew, William H. "The Sermon on the Mount." New
Church Review 3 (1896) 192-203.

Mee, A. J. "'Ye are the salt of the earth.'" Expository
Times 46 (1933-34) 476-77.

Meier, Henry A. The Sermon on the Mount. Cleveland,
Ohio: Central Publishing House, 1924.
Meier views the Sermon on the Mount as belonging to
the Gospel of the Kingdom and as being the real Gospel.
A verse by verse commentary.

Meinertz, Max. "Zur Ethik der Bergpredigt," in Aus Ethik
und Leben. Festschrift für Joseph Mausback. Hrsg. von
Max Meinertz und Adolf Donders. Münster in Westfalen:
Aschendorffsche Verlagsbuchhandlung, 1931.

Meister, Leonhard. Betrachtungen über Jesu Bergpredigt.
1796.

Merentitis, Konstantin J. "Die Bergpredigt Jesu," in
Eucharistērion. Festschrift für Hamilcar S. Alivisatos.
Athens: 1958, 242-61.

Metzger, Bruce M. Index to Periodical Literature on Christ
and the Gospels. Compiled under the direction of Bruce M.
Metzger. New Testament Tools and Studies vol. VI. Leiden: E. J. Brill, 1966.
The section on the Sermon on the Mount (Matt. 5-7)
consists of pp. 216-34. Luke 6:17-49 is on p. 307.

Metzler, Burton. Light from a Hillside. Elgin, Ill.:
Brethren Press, 1968.
Popular work emphasizing the Sermon on the Mount as

a guide to right moral conduct. Includes suggestions for
discussion and study and a proposed study course organization.

Meyer, Frederick B. The Directory of the Devout Life;
Meditations on the Sermon on the Mount. New York:
Revell, 1904; The Sermon on the Mount; the Directory of
the Devout Life. Grand Rapids: Baker Book House,
1954 (1959).
Popular, practical treatment.

Mezger, Manfred. Zuruf an Hungrige. Predigten für jeder-
mann. Nr 8. Bad Connstatt: Müllerschön, 1969.

Michaelis, Wilhelm. "'Die Gerechtigkeit' in der Bergpredigt." Kirchenblatt für die reformierte Schweiz 89 No.
12 (June 15, 1933).

Miegge, Giovanni. Il Sermone sul monte. Torino: Claudi-
ana, 1970.
Extensive scholarly commentary.

Miguez Bonino, José. El mundo nuevo de Dios. Estudios
biblicos sobre el Sermón del monte. Buenos Aires: 1955.

Militz, Annie R. The Sermon on the Mount. rev. ed.
New York: Absolute Press, 1904; London: L. N. Fowler,
1916.
Brief verse by verse, popular commentary.

Miller, John W. The Christian Way; a Guide to the Christian
Life Based on the Sermon on the Mount. Scottdale, Pa.:
Herald Press, 1969.
This book grew out of Miller's experience of using the
Sermon on the Mount in instructional work with candidates
for church membership. It focuses, not so much on the
meaning of the text for its original audience, as on its
significance for our lives today. There are questions for
self-examination based on the Beatitudes and a "covenant
for Christian disciples."

Miller, Robert H. The Life Portrayed in the Sermon on the
Mount. Boston: W. A. Wilde, 1934.
Popular, didactic treatment.

Millington, C. "A Spoilt Masterpiece," in Studia Evangelica.
Berlin: Akademie-Verlag, 1959, 506-09.

Minear, Paul S. "Ask, seek, knock! (Matt. 7:7 and Luke 11:9)." Thesis Theological Cassettes 2 no. 4 (1971).

_____. "Yes or No; the Demand for Honesty in the Early Church." Novum Testamentum 13 (1971) 1-13.

Möller, Johann F. Commentatio in effatum Christi: Matth. 5, 13. Erfurt: Keyser, 1832.

Møller, P. Wernberg. "A Semitic Idiom in Matt. V. 22." New Testament Studies 3 (1956-57) 7-73.

Moffatt, James. "Exegetica. --Matthew V. 39." Expositor 8th ser. 7 (1914-A) 89.

_____. "Exegetica. --Matthieu V. 39." Expositor 8th ser. 8 (1914-B) 188-89.

_____. "Literary Illustrations of the Sermon on the Mount." Expository Times 15 (1903-04) 508-11.

_____. "Sermon on the Mount," in The Encyclopedia Biblica, vol IV. New York: Macmillan, 1903, cols. 4375-4391.

Mojzes, P. "Anger, Worship, and Unity (Mt 5:23-24)." Editorial. Journal of Ecumenical Studies 9 (1972) 576-78.

Moldenhawer, Johann H. D. Erklärung der Bergpredigt Jesu. 2 Thle. Hamburg: 1783.

Monier, Prosper. Le Sermon sur la montagne. Marseille: Publiroc; Paris: Desclée de Brouwer et Cie, 1938; Lyon: Besacier, 1951; Toulouse: Apostolat de la Prière, 1959. Meditations. Contains numerous quotations from a wide variety of sources.

_____. El Sermón de la montaña. Bilboa: Desclee de Brouwer; Madrid: Meri, 1959. (See his Le Sermon sur la montagne)

Monneron, Henri. Le Sermon sur la montagne. Lausanne: Bridel, 1889.

Montefiore, Claude G. Rabbinic Literature and Gospel Teachings. London: Macmillan, 1930. Pages 1-201 constitute a commentary on the Sermon on the Mount in light of the rabbinic texts. A conciliatory interpretation from the viewpoint of Liberal Judaism.

Montizambert, Eric St. Lucian Percy. The Flame of Life; an Interpretation of the Sermon on the Mount. Greenwich, Conn.: Seabury Press, 1955.
Practical interpretation designed to help persons develop a deeper understanding of the Christian faith.

Moore, Theophilus W. The Analysis and Exposition of Our Lord's Sermon on the Mount. Sanford, Fla.: Sanford Publishing Co., 1886.
Sermons.

Morant, Peter. Der Geist der Bergpredigt. Baden: Meierhof Druckerei, Martin Gyr, 1949.
Brief exposition.

Morgan, Edward J. No Thought for Tomorrow. Grand Rapids: Eerdmans, 1961.
Meditations. Sermons.

Morrison, J. H. "'Ye are the salt of the earth.'" Expository Times 46 (1934-35) 525.

Mosbech, H. "The Ethics of the Sermon on the Mount," in Spiritus et Veritas. Festschrift für K. Kundziņš. Duluth: 1953, 121-34.

Moule, C. F. D. "Matthew V. 21, 22." Expository Times 50 (1938-39) 189-90.

_____. "Uncomfortable Words. The angry word. Matthew 5:21f." Expository Times 81 (1969) 10-13.

Mounce, R. H. "Synoptic Self-portraits." Evangelical Quarterly 37 (1965) 212-17.

Müllendorff, Julius. Die Bergpredigt. 2. verb. Aufl. Sursum corda! 1. Innsbruck: F. Rauch, 1902.

Müller, David H. Die Bergpredigt im Lichte der Strophen-Theorie. Biblische Studien. V. Alfred Hölder, 1908.

Müller, Hermann. Zum Eidesverbot der Bergpredigt. Paderborn: Bonifacius-Druckerei, 1913.

Müller, Johannes. Die Bergpredigt, verdeutscht und verge-
genwärtigt. München: C. H. Beck, 1906 (1911) (1920,
6th ed.) (1923, 7th ed.) (1929, 8th ed.)
 A practical work relating the Sermon on the Mount to
 personal and social life.

_____. De Bergrede in onze taal en voor onzen tijd.
Vert. Bella Jansen. Zeist: J. Ploegsma, 1924.
(See his Die Bergpredigt)

_____. Bergspredikan tolkad för vår tid. Övers. Anna
Collan. Uppsala: Lindblad, 1922.
(See his Die Bergpredigt)

_____. Le Sermon sur la montagne transposé dans notre
langage et pour notre temps. Trad. S. Godet. Saint
Blaise: Foyer Solidariste, 1912.
(See his Die Bergpredigt)

Mueller, Ullrich F. "Zu Mt 5, 13." Biblische Zeitschrift
6 (1908) 363.

Mueller, William A. "Self-Defense and Retaliation in the
Sermon on the Mount." Review and Expositor 53 (1956)
46-54.

Müssle, Marainne. Die Humanität Jesu im Spiegel der Bergpredigt. München: J. Pfeiffer, 1971.
 A series of essays by twelve authors each of whom interprets a section of the Sermon on the Mount.

Murray, Mrs. W. John. The Sermon on the Mount. Jackson
Heights, N.Y.: The author, 1939.

Myers, William V. Design for Happiness. Nashville:
Broadman Press, 1961.
 A psychological interpretation of the Sermon on the
Mount which views it as a source of psychological prin-
ciples for personal adjustment.

_____. "Psychological Elements in the Sermon on the
Mount." D.R.E. thesis. Southwestern Baptist Theological
Seminary, 1945.

Nägelsbach, Friedrich. "Die Einheit der Bergpredigt."
Neue kirchliche Zeitschrift 39 (1928) 47-76.

_____. "Die hohen Forderungen der Bergpredigt (Mt. 5: 33-42)." Neue kirkliche Zeitschrift 30 (1919) 510-32.

_____. "Der Schlüssel zum Verständnis der Bergpredigt." Beiträge zur Förderung christlicher Theologie 20 (1916) 431-61; also Gütersloh: C. Bertelsmann, 1916.

Nagel, Walter. "Gerechtigkeit--oder Almosen?" Vigiliae Christianae 15 (1961) 141-45.

Nagornaiâ beseda Spasiteliâ s kommentariiâ mi iz tvorenii luchshikh tolkovnikov. Pekin: 1910.

Nauck, W. "Salt as a Metaphor in Instructions for Discipleship." Studia Theologica 6 (1952) 165-78.

Nestle, Eberhard. "Eine kleine Korrektur zur Vulgata von Luk. 6, 17." Zeitschrift für die neutestamentliche Wissenschaft 8 (1907) 240-41.

_____. "Luke VI. 19." Expository Times 17 (1905-06) 431.

_____. "Matt. V. 22." Expository Times 11 (1899-1900), 381-82.

_____. "Matt. VI. 3." Expository Times 13 (1901-02) 524-25.

_____. "Matth 6, 16." Zeitschrift für die neutestamentliche Wissenschaft 15 (1914) 94.

_____. "Matt. VI. 24=Luke XVI. 12." Expository Times 19 (1907-08) 284.

_____. "Matt. VII. 25, 27." Expository Times 19 (1907-08) 237-38.

_____. "The Salt of the Earth and the Light of the World." Expository Times 20 (1908-09) 565.

Nielsen, Svend A. Bjergpraedikenen. En gennemgang i 12 bibeltimer. Udg. af KFUM og KFUK's Halandsudvalg. Aalborg: 1953.

_____. Vuorisaarna. Raamatuntutkisteluopas. Pieksämäki: 1960.
    (See his Bjergpraedikenen)

Nötges, Jakob. Die Bergpredigt des Tabernakels. Warendorf i. Westfalen: J. Schnell, 1925.

Nötscher, F. "Das Reich (Gottes) und seine Gerechtigkeit." Biblica 31 (1950) 237-41. Also: Vom Alten zum Neuen Testament. Gesammelte Aufsätze. Bonn: P. Hanstein, 1962.

Nome, John. "Bergprekenens betydning i den cristne etikk." Tidesskrift for theologi og kirke 22 (1951) 49-68.

Norberg, Gunnar. Jesu Bergspredikan. Handledning vid undervisning i kristendomskunskap. Stockholm: Svenska bokförlaget (Norstedt), 1946.

Norton, Arthur M. "Motives to which Christ Appealed in the Sermon on the Mount." Th. M. thesis. Central Baptist Theological Seminary, 1959.

Norwood, F. W. "The Sermon on the Mount." Expository Times 39 (1927-28) 408-11.

Nygren, Anders. "Bergpredigt," in Evangelisches Kirchenlexikon. vol. I. Göttingen: Vandenhoeck & Ruprecht, 1956, 392-95.

Öhrn, Arnold T. Är Bergspredikan evangelium? Övers. Yngve Lindblom. Stockholm: B.-M:s bokförlag, 1939. (See his Er Bergprekenen evangelium?)

_____. Er Bergprekenen evangelium? Oslo: Norsk litteraturselskap, 1939.
  An evangelical interpretation which seeks to relate the themes of ethics and salvation (grace) in the Sermon on the Mount.

_____. The gospel and the Sermon on the Mount. New York: Revell, 1948. (See his Er Bergprekenen evangelium?)

Oertel, Heinrich G. De oratione Iesu montana ejusque consilio. Inaug. diss. Wittenberg: 1802.

Oesterley, W. O. E. "The Study of the Synoptic Gospels Exemplified by Matthew V. 21, 22." Expositor 6th ser. 12 (1905) 17-32.

Oestrup, J. "Zu Matth. VII, 6." Zeitschrift der deutschen

morgenländischen Gesellschaft 59 (1905) 155-58.

Offerhaus, H. R. "Rondom de verheerlijking op den Berg."
Theologisch tijdschrift 49 (1915) 317-24, 384-95.

Offermann, Henry. "Studies in the Gospel of Matthew."
Lutheran Church Review 45 (1926) 1-16, 109-16; 46 (1927)
129-44, 242-53, 348-60.

O'Hara, J. "Christian Fasting (Mt. 6, 16-18)." Scripture
19 (1967) 3-18.

Oliveira, Carlos J. O sermão da montanha. São Paulo:
Duas Cidades, 1967.
Critical and theological commentary.

Olivieri, Olivo. "Dico enim vobis, quia nisi abundaverit
iustia vestra plus quam scribarum et pharisaeorum non
intrabitis in regnum caelorum." Biblica 5 (1924) 201-05.

_____. "Nolite iurare omnio." Biblica 4 (1923) 385-90.

Omkaranda, Swami. Der universelle Geist der Bergpredigt.
Schopfheim: Schwab, 1968.

Oort, H. De Bergrede. Assen: L. Hansma, 1905.
A critical commentary.

O'Rourke, John J. "A Note on an Exception: Mt. 5:32 (19:
9) and 1 Cor. 7:12 Compared." Heythrop Journal 5 (1964)
299-302.

Orr, Peter. "The Will of My Father." Scripture 4 (1950)
146-48.

Palomero, G. "El sermón de la montaña." Cultura bíblica
3 (1946) 33-36.

Park, John E. The Wonder of His Gracious Words; an Ex-
position of the Sermon on the Mount. Boston: Pilgrim
Press, 1909.
Practical and homiletical in style.

Parker, Hankins F. Earth's Greatest Sermon; a Practical
Application of the Sermon on the Mount. New York:
American Press, 1966.

Patton, Carl S. "The Deviations of Matthew and Luke in the Sermon on the Mount." Biblical World 48 (1916) 288-90.

Pauw, D. de. De bergboodschap. Radiokwartiertjes. Mechelen: D. de Pauw, 1937.

Peacock, Heber F. "The Text of the Sermon on the Mount." Review and Expositor 53 (1956) 9-23.

Pennington, Chester A. The Word among Us. Philadelphia: United Church Press, 1973.
Reflections on parts of the Sermon on the Mount and on the Lord's Prayer in "quasi-poetic" form.

Pentecost, J. Dwight. Design for Living. Chicago: Moody Press, 1975.
Studies based on preparation for classroom and pulpit ministry.

_____. "The Purpose of the Sermon on the Mount." Bibliotheca Sacra 115 (1958) 128-35, 212-17, 313-19.

Percy, J. Duncan. "An Evil Eye." Expository Times 54 (1942-43) 26-27.

A Periodical and Monographic Index to the Literature on the Gospels and Acts Based on the Files of the Ecole Biblique in Jerusalem. Pittsburgh: Clifford E. Barbour Library, Pittsburgh Theological Seminary, 1971.
The section on the Sermon on the Mount (Matt. 5-7) consists of pp. 14-29. Luke 6:17-49 consists of pp. 166-67.

Perles, Felix. "Zur Erklärung von Mt 7, 6." Zeitschrift für die neutestamentliche Wissenschaft 25 (1926) 163-64.

Pernot, Hubert. "Une correction à Luc VI, 35." Comptes rendus. Académie des Inscriptions et Belles-Lettres (1929) 277-80.

Perry, Alfred M. "The Framework of the Sermon on the Mount." Journal of Biblical Literature 54 (1935) 103-15.

_____. "'Pearls before Swine.'" Expository Times 46 (1934-35) 381-82.

Pesch, W. "Zur Exegese von Mt. 6, 19-21 and Lk. 12, 33-34." Biblica 41 (1960) 356-78.

Peterborough, W. C. "The State and the Sermon on the
Mount." Fortnightly Review 53 (1890) 33-46.

Peters, John P. "On Matthew V. 21-22." Journal of
Biblical Literature 11 (1892) 131-32.

Peterson, Erik/Wünsch. "Bergpredigt," in Die Religion in
Geschichte und Gegenwart I. Tübingen: J. C. B. Mohr,
1927, 907-13.

Pfeifer, Hermann. Die Bergpredigt nach Matthäus. Leipzig:
Dürrsche Buchhandlung, 1913.

_____. Ethik in der Volksschule. Die Bergpredigt nach
Matthäus und dem 1. und 3. Hauptstück. 3. und 4. Aufl.
Leipzig: Dürrsche Buchhandlung, 1913.

Pfendsack, Werner. Ihr seid das Salz der Erde. Eine
Auslegung der Bergpredigt Jesu. Basel: F. Reinhardt,
1966.
    Sermons.

Pfister, Benjamin. Die Bergpredigt. Bern: Francke, 1929.
    Sermons.

Phillips, C. A. "Luke 6, 24:"ὍΟτι ἀπέχετε τὴν παράκλησιν
ὑμῶν." Bulletin of the Bezan Club 6 (1929) 27-29.

Phillips, John A. D. The Sermon on the Mount. Published
for the Catholic Biblical Association in Victoria. Melbourne: Central Catholic Lib., 1965.

Pick, B. Zweihundert und zwölf Dispositionen über die
Bergpredigt. Oswego, N.Y.: Lutherischen Kirchenfreunde,
1870.
    Sermon outlines.

Pink, Arthur W. An Exposition of the Sermon on the Mount.
Swengel, Pa.: Bible Truth Depot, 1950; Grand Rapids:
Baker Book House, 1953 (1959).
    Series of expository articles which appeared first in
the author's monthly magazine Studies in the Scriptures.

Pinson, Ernest R. "Some Revolutionary Teachings of Jesus
in the Sermon on the Mount." Th.D. thesis. New Or-
leans Baptist Theological Seminary, 1945.

Pitman, John R. A Practical Commentary on Our Blessed
Lord's Sermon on the Mount; Valedictory Address to His
Disciples; and Parables; Together with a Brief Paraphrase
and Corrections of the Authorized Version. London: J.
Darling, 1852.
First 200 pages are a verse by verse commentary on
the Sermon on the Mount. There follows a commentary
on John 14-17 and a section on the parables.

"The Place of the Sermon on the Mount in the Christian
System." Bibliotecha Sacra 54 (1897) 381-83.

Plotzke, Urban W. Bergpredigt; von der Freiheit des christlichen Lebens. Frankfort am Main: J. Knecht, 1960
(1963).
Sermons.

_____. Gebot und Leben. Geistliche Reden über die
Bergpredigt. Köln: Bachem, 1954.
Sermons.

Plummer, George W. The Applied Psychology of the Sermon on the Mount. New York: Seminary of Biblical Research, 1927.
Brief, practical treatment.

Poiger, Benedikt. Katholisches Gespräch über die Worte des
Herrn, Matth. VI, 19, 20. München: 1814.

Pokorný, Petr. Der Kern der Bergpredigt. Hamburg: Herbert Reich Evangelischer Verlag, 1969.
Using the methods of redaction and tradition criticism
Pokorný shows that the Sermon on the Mount gives us insights into how the early Christian community understood
and applied the message of Jesus. But it also affords answers to the problems for human existence involved in following Jesus today.

Ponce de la Fuente, Constantino. Confession of a Sinner,
the Sermon on the Mount, and Christian Doctrine. Nashville: Publishing House of the M. E. Church, South, n.d.

_____. "El Sermón que nuestro Señor Jesu Cristo hizo
en el monte." Traduzido en castellano por el doctór Constantino. Reformistas antiquos españoles. Madrid: 1863,
tomo XIX, 238-74.

Poortman, E. B. A. "De exegese van Matthëus 5:17-48."
Vox theologica 9 (1937-38) 181-87.

Pott, V. J. Commentatio de natura atque indole orationis
montanae. Braunschweig: Schulbuchhandlung, 1789.

Prabhavananda, Swami. Bergspredikan och Vedanta. Kristi
budskap i Ramakrishnas efterföljd. Övers. Gunnar Ander-
sson, Inga Heikel. Stockholm: Proprius, 1970.
(See his The Sermon on the Mount according to Vedanta)

_____. The Sermon on the Mount According to Vedanta.
Hollywood, Calif.: Vedanta Press, 1964; London: G.
Allen and Unwin, 1964; New York: New American Library, 1972.
Prabhavanada finds in the Sermon on the Mount an essential unity between the message of Jesus and that of
Hindu seers and sages. Vedanta with its emphasis on
God-realization is paralleled in the Sermon on the Mount
in Jesus' declaration that God can be seen and that divine
perfection can be achieved. In order that men might attain this supreme goal, Jesus taught the renunciation of
worldliness, the contemplation of God, and the purification
of the heart through the love of God. These are the Sermon on the Mount's underlying themes according to Prabhavanada. This is a lucid interpretation with frequent references to Sri Ramakrishna and other Hindu saints, and
it gives vivid insights into the Sermon on the Mount from
a non-Christian, Eastern tradition.

Presting, B. Die Bergpredigt das Gesetz des Reiches Gottes.
Gotha: G. Schloessmann, 1894 (1896).

Pritchett, Carl R. "Studies in the Sermon on the Mount."
Master's thesis. Richmond, Va.: Union Theological
Seminary, 1936.

Proost, Karel F. De Bergrede, hare herkomst en strekking.
Amsterdam: J. Brandt & Zoon, 1914.
A substantial study on source analysis and eschatology
and ethics, followed by a commentary.

Purdy, Alexander C. "Biblical Theology and the Sermon on
the Mount." Religion in Life 15 (1946) 498-508.

Pyle, J. G. "The Sermon on the Mount." Putnam's Magazine 7 (1909-10) 285-88.

Quimby, Chester W. Sermon on the Mount; Jesus' Description of the Christian Life; a Questionnaire. New York:
Methodist Book Concern, 1927.

Rabinowitz, Jacob J. "The Sermon on the Mount and the
School of Shammai." Harvard Theological Review 49
(1956) 79.

Rad, Gerhard von. "Die Stadt auf dem Berge." Evangelische
Theologie VIII (1948-9) 439-47. Reprinted in Gesammelte
Studien zum Alten Testament. München: C. Kaiser Ver-
lag, 1958, 214-24.

Ragaz, Leonhard. Die Bergpredigt Jesu. Bern: Herbert
Lang and Cie, 1945; Hamburg: Furche Verlag, 1971.
Ragaz interprets the Sermon on the Mount from the
viewpoint of a religious socialist. It shows a new way to
Christ and the Kingdom of God--a way which leads to the
revolution of Christendom and of the world.

_____. Il Sermone sul monte. Milano: Ed. di Com-
munità, 1963.
(See his Die Bergpredigt Jesu)

Raikes, Walter A. "Thou Fool." Expository Times 4 (1892-
93) 514-15.

Rand, James F. "Problems in a Literal Interpretation of the
Sermon on the Mount." Bibliotheca Sacra 112 (1955) 28-
38, 125-36.

Rassmussen, Im. Eilstrup. Bjergpraedikenens etiske Problem,
Besvarelse af en Prisopgave. København: P. Haase &
Søns, 1948.
Treats the personal and social ethical problems raised
by the Sermon on the Mount. Contains a historical survey
of these questions from Luther to Bultmann.

Rau, Johann W. Untersuchungen die wahre Ansicht der Bergpredigt betreffend. Erlangen: J. J. Palm, 1805.

Rausch, J. W. "The Principle of Nonresistance and Love of
Enemy in Mt 5:38-48." Catholic Biblical Quarterly 28
(1966) 31-41.

Reaves, Edw. S. "What Did Jesus Teach about Forgiving?"
Review and Expositor 18 (1921) 282-86.

Reid, James. "The Sermon on the Mount." Expository
Times 39 (1927-28) 486-90.

Reisterer, A. "Die Bergpredigt." Theologische Praktische
Quartalschrift (1897) 30-46, 583-88, 812-18.

Richards, H. J. "Christ on Divorce." Scripture 11 (1959)
22-32.

Ridderbos, Herman N. "De exegese van Mattheus 5:17-48."
Vox theologica 9 (1937-38) 162-69.

_____. De strekking der Bergrede naar Mattheus.
Kampen: J. H. Kok, 1936.
    Doctoral dissertation which deals with exegetical, criti-
cal, and practical problems. It contains many references
to, and analyses of, previous interpretations of the Sermon on the Mount.

Riegler, Johann G. Bergpredigt Jesus Christus, kritisch-
historisch-praktisch erklärt, zur Belehrung und Betrachtung dargestellt. Bamberg: J. G. W. Schmidt, 1844.
    An extensive commentary which emphasizes historical,
critical, and philological problems.

Riemann, Otto. Die Bergrede unseres Herrn Jesu Christi
Evangelium Matthäi Kap. 5-7, in 27 Predigten für die
Gemeinde der Gegenwart ausgelegt. Berlin: Schriften-
vertriebsanstalt, 1911.
    Sermons.

Riesenfeld, Harald. "Vom Schätzesammeln und Sorgen--ein
thema urchristlicher Paränese, zu Mt. VI 19-34," in
Neotestamentica et patristica. Eine Freundesgabe, Herrn
Professor Dr. Oscar Cullmann zu seinem 60. Geburtstag
überreicht. Leiden: Brill, 1962, 47-58.

Riethmüller, Otto. Die Stadt auf dem Berge. Einführung in
die Bergpredigt Matth. 5-7. Berlin: Burckhardthaus-
Verlag, 1936.

Riga, Peter J. Be Sons of Your Father. Staten Island,
N.Y.: Alba House, 1969.
    Readable interpretation of "that which constitutes the
central core of the life and moral activity of the follower
of Christ"--the Sermon on the Mount.

Rivas, Gabry. El Sermón de la Montaña. Managua, Nicaragua: Editorial La Nueva Prersa, 1945.
Primarily an exposition of the Beatitudes with a social action emphasis.

Robinson, Arthur W. Studies in the Teaching of the Sermon on the Mount. London: Student Christian Movement, 1922.
Brief, popular study which sets forth the main thoughts of Jesus' teaching in the Sermon on the Mount.

Rocca, Annette di. Selig seid ihr! Jesu Verheissungen bei der Bergpredigt in einer Betrachtung für die Munschen unserer Zeit. Gröbenzell bei München: Hacker, 1958.

Rodrigues, Hippolyte. Les origines du Sermon de la montagne. Paris: Michael Levy, 1868.
Contains parallels to the Sermon on the Mount from the Old Testament and rabbinical literature. The Sermon on the Mount text and the parallels appear on opposite pages.

Roehl, Gerhard. Bergpredigt und neue Erziehung. Erkentnisse eines Suchenden. Jena: Zwing, 1932.

Rogge, Christian. Federzeichnungen zur Bergpredigt. Berlin: Vaterländischer Verlag und Kunstanstalt, 1911.

Roland-Gosselin, M. D. "Le Sermon sur la montagne et la théologie thomiste." Revue des sciences philosophiques et théologiques 17 (1928) 201-34.

Rongen, Hieronymous. Das Lied vom neuen Menschen. Gedanken über die Bergpredigt. Einsiedeln: Benziger, 1934.

Rothuizen, Gerardus T. De hand aan de ploeg. Klein commentaar op de Bergrede. Aalten: De Graffschap, 1960.

Rüger, H. P. "Mit welchem Mass ihr messt, wird euch gemessen werden (Mt 7:2, Gen 38:25-26)." Zeitschrift für die neutestamentliche Wissenschaft 60 (1969) 174-82.

Runestam, Arvid. "Bergspredikans etiska problem." Svensk teologisk kvartalskrift 2 (1926) 107-24.

_____. "Das ethische Problem der Bergpredigt." Zeitschrift für systematische Theologie 4 (1926-27) 555-72.

Sachse, D. "Bergpredigt als Grundlage für die Unterweisung

im christlichen Wandel." Zeitschrift für den evangelischen christlichenen religions-Unterricht 8 (1897) 214-20.

Sandegren, C. "Be Ye Perfect!" Expository Times 61 (1949-50) 383.

_____. "A Mostly Misunderstood Section of the Sermon on the Mount." Evangelical Quarterly 23 (1951) 134-38.

Sanders, John Oswald. Real Discipleship; a Devotional Exposition of the Sermon on the Mount. Grand Rapids, Mich.: Zondervan Pub. House, 1972.
Popular devotional exposition.

van Santvoord, George. "The Teacher." Anglican Theological Review 30 (1948) 156-58.

Savage, Henry E. The Gospel of the Kingdom: or, The Sermon on the Mount Considered in the Light of Contemporary Jewish Thought and Ideals. London: Longmans, Green, 1910.
A detailed study comparing the teaching of the Sermon on the Mount with the contemporary religious attitude of the Jews. This approach hopefully helps one to more nearly arrive at the original force of its message.

Schabert, Arnold. Die Bergpredigt. Auslegung und Verkündigung. München: Claudius Verlag, 1966.
Commentary and sermons.

Schade, Gerhard. Was steht in der Bergpredigt? Leipzig: Schloessmann, 1936.

Schaefer, Carol J. "A Study in the Exegesis of Matthew 6: 22 through Analysis of Alpha pi lambda omicron upsilon sigma." Doctoral dissertation. Brown Univ., 1963.

Schearer, John B. The Sermon on the Mount. Richmond, Va.: Presbyterian Committee of Publication, 1906.

Schenz, Alphons. Die Bergpredigt in ihrer ursprünglichen Schönheit. Augsburg: Filser, 1929.
A literary and textual analysis which uses "Architektonik" methods.

Schepper, Pieter I. De Bellamy-gedachte en de Bergrede. Hoorn: Vermonde Zonen, 1937.

Discusses the relationship between the thought of Edward Bellamy and Matthew 5.

Scher, Andrew R. Master Speech: the Sermon on the Mount; a Nonsectarian Interpretation of Matthew 5-7; with Questions and Answers for Study. New York: Exposition Press, 1952 (1954).

Schieder, Julius. Die Bergpredigt. Fünf Vorträge. Nürnberg: Lätare-Verlag, 1948.
Many aspects of the Sermon on the Mount discussed in brief sections.

Schinle, Gertrudis. Salz der Erde. Meditationsgedanken zur Bergpredigt des Matthäusevangeliums. Leutesdorf am Rhein: Johannes-Verlag, 1968.
Meditations.

Schlatter, Adolph. Die Gabe des Christus. Eine Auslegung der Bergpredigt. Essen: Freizeiten-Verlag zu Delbert im Rheinland, 1928.
Brief popular treatment.

_____. "Zur Auslegung von Matth. 7, 21-23," in Greifswalder Studien. Theologische Abhundlungen Hermann Cremer zum 25 jährigen Professonenjubiläum dargebracht. Gütersloh: C. Bertelsmann, 1895, 83-105.

Schlingensiepen, Hermann. Die Auslegung der Bergpredigt bei Calvin. Berlin: 1927; Diss. Bonn: 1927.
Brief monograph on Calvin's interpretation of the Sermon on the Mount centering on the themes of Christ as an interpreter of the Law and on the concept of love.

Schmauch, Werner. "Reich Gottes und menschliche Existenz nach der Bergpredigt," in Theologische Existenz Heute. Neue Folge 64. München: Kaiser Verlag, 1958, 5-19.

Schmidt, Karl O. Die Religion der Bergpredigt als Grundlage neugeistigen Tatchristentums. Pfullingen: Baum, 1930.

_____. Die Religion der Bergpredigt als Grundlage rechten Lebens. Freiburg: Hermann Bauer, 1955 (1962).
Practical interpretation of the Sermon on the Mount and its relevance to life.

Schmitz, O. "Thurneysen's christologische Deutung der

Bergpredigt." Jahrbuch der Theologischen Schule Bethel,
1948, 17-36.

Schnackenburg, Rudolf. "Bergpredigt," in Lexikon für Theologie und Kirche II. 2. Aufl. Freiburg im Breisgau:
Herder, 1958, 223-27.

_____. "Die Bergpredigt Jesu und der heutige Mensch,"
in Christiliche Existenz nach dem Neuem Testament I.
München: Kösel-Verlag, 1967, 109-30.

_____. "Ihr seid das Salz der Erde, das Licht der Welt.
Zu Matthaus 5, 13-16," in Mélanges Eugène Tisserant vol.
I. Città del Vaticano: Biblioteca Apostolica Vaticana,
1964, 365-87.

Schnappinger, Bonifaz M. Commentatio biblica in sermonem
Christi in monte, Matth. cap. V. VI. VII. Heidelberg:
1794.

Schneider, Gerhard. Botschaft der Bergpredigt. Aschaffenburg: Paul Pattloch; Stein am Rhein: Christiana-Verlag,
1969.
Commentary preceded by brief criticism.

Schneider, Johannes, & Beyer, H. W. Jesu Bergspredikan.
Övers. Bo Reicke. Uppsala: Nytestamentliga seminariet,
1944.
(See his Der Sinn der Bergpredigt)

_____. Der Sinn der Bergpredigt. Berlin: Furche Ver-
lag, 1936.
Brief general study composed of five lectures.

Schneider, Paul. "Bergpredigt und Christenleben." Neue
kirkliche Zeitschrift 37 (1926) 591-610.

Schneller, Ludwig. Die Bergpredigt. Köln: Palästinahaus,
1923.

_____. Die Bergpredigt in zwanzig Predigten ausgelegt.
Leipzig: H. G. Wallmann, 1924.
Sermons.

Schrödter, Franz A. Christi Bergpredigt, frei übersetzt für
ungelehrte Bibelleser und Landschulen. Altona: Ham-
merich, 1796.

Schruers, Paul. "La paternité divine dans Mt. V, 45 et VI,
26-32." Ephemerides theologicae Lovanienses 36 (1960)
593-624.

Schubert, Kurt. "Bergpredigt und Texte von En Fešha."
Theologische Quartalschrift 135 (1955) 320-37.

_____. "The Sermon on the Mount and the Qumran
Texts," in The Scrolls and the New Testament, edited by
K. Stendahl. New York: Harpers, 1957, 118-28.

Schürmann, Heinz. "Die Warnung des Lukas vor der Fal-
schlehre in der 'Predigt am Berge' Lk. 6, 20-49."
Biblische Zeitschrift 10 (1966) 57-81.

_____. "Wer daher eines dieser geringsten Gebote
auflöst..." Biblische Zeitschrift 4 (1960) 238-50.
Also: Traditionsgeschichtliche. Untersuchung zu den
synoptischen Evangelien. Düsseldorf: Patmos-Verlag,
1968, 126-36.

Schullerus, Adolf. Die Bergpredigt. Für die Gemeinde
erläutert. Hermannstadt: W. Krafft, 1906.
Detailed commentary with practical emphasis.

_____. Die Bergrede in Predigt und Unterricht. Göttin-
gen: Vandenhoeck & Rupprecht, 1918.
A practical interpretation intended to aid the pastor
in his preaching and teaching ministries.

Schulte, Anton. Bergpredigt; up to Date. Duisburg-Ruhrort:
J. Brendow, 1967.
Section by section commentary by an evangelist, written
so that contemporary man might better come to know
Jesus and his help for daily life.

Schwalb, M. "Le discours sur la montagne et les textes qui
y sont rattachés." Revue de théologie 8 (1861) 257-91.

Schwartz, Anton von. Der Geist Christi. Betrachtungen
über die Bergpredigt. 2 Bd. Immensee/Schweiz: Verlag
des Missionshauses Bethlehem, 1921.

Schwarz, Günther. "Matthäus V:13a and 14a." New Testament Studies 17 (Oct. 1970) 80-6.

_____. "Matthäus VI:6-13/Lukas XI:2-4; Emendation

und Rückübersetzung." New Testament Studies 15 (1969) 233-47.

_____. "Matthäus 7:6a. Emendation und Rückübersetzung." Novum Testamentum 14 (1972) 18-25.

_____. "Matthäus 7:13a. Ein Alarmruf angesichts höchster Gefahr." Novum Testamentum 12 (1970) 229-32.

Schweizer, Eduard. "'Der Jude im Verborgenen..., dessen Lob nicht von Menschen, sondern von Gott kommt.' Zu Röm 2, 28f und Mt 6, 1-18," in Neues Testament und Kirche. Festschrift für Rudolf Schnackenberg. Hrsg. Joachim Gnilka. Freiburg (im Breisgau), Basel, Wien: Herder, 1974, 115-24.

_____. "Matth. 5, 17-20--Anmerkingen zum Gesetzesverständnis des Matthäus." Theologische Literaturzeitung 77 (1952) 479-84.

_____. "Noch einmal Mt 5, 17-20," in Das Wort und die Wörter. Festschrift Gerhard Friedrich. Stuttgart: W. Kohlhammer, 1973, 69-73.

Schwencke, Friedrich. "Das Auge ist des Liebes Licht." Zeitschrift für wissenschaftliche Theologie 55 (1914) 251-60.

Seale, M. S. "Ethics of Malāmatīya Sufism and the Sermon on the Mount." Muslim World 58 (1968) 12-23.

Sedir, Paul. Le Sermon sur la montagne. Solleville-lez-Rouen: Legrand, 1921; Paris: Âmities Spirituelles, 1951.

Seeberg, Reinhold. Zur Ethik der Bergpredigt. Leipzig: Deichert, 1934.
    Study of the ethics of the Sermon on the Mount.

Seitz, O. J. F. "Love Your Enemies; the Historical Setting of Matthew V:43f; Lukc VI:27f." New Testament Studies 16 (Oct. 1969) 39-54.

Semmelink, J. H. "Theologisch-exegetische opmerkingen." Nederlands theologisch tijdschrift 1 (1946-47) 340-46.

The Sermon on the Mount (Filmstrip). J. S. van den Nieuwendijk, Zeist, Netherlands.

The Sermon on the Mount. Historical introduction by Ernest
   F. Scott. Trans. by Edgar J. Goodspeed. Chicago:
   American Institute of Sacred Literature, 1926.
   Brief exposition by Scott followed by Goodspeed transla-
   tion.

Sermon on the Mount Now. (Motion picture) Kirby Brum-
   field. Released by Mass Media Associates, 1972.
   A collage of contemporary images, patterned with a
   reading of Matthew 5-7, communicates that Jesus' message is relevant for today.

The Sermon on the Mount; a Practical Exposition of St.
   Matthew V-VI. 8; Including the Beatitudes. 3 vols.
   Manchester: J. Robinson, 1903; Cincinnati: Jennings &
   Graham; New York: Eaton & Mains, n. d.
   A collection of sermons by many authors. The ar-
   rangement of the sermons is in sequence so that they
   form a homiletical commentary on the Sermon on the
   Mount.

Shafto, G. R. H. The School of Jesus; a Primer of Discipleship. London: Student Christian Movement, 1920.
   The second half of Shafto's work consists of brief comments on various topical divisions of the Sermon on the
   Mount. These are preceded by the author's paraphrase of
   the text. Includes discussion questions.

Shearer, John B. The Sermon on the Mount. Richmond,
   Va.: Presbyterian Committee of Publication, 1906.
   Topical arrangement with an evangelical emphasis.

Shears, Hubert. Christ or Betham? A Criticism of Dr.
   Gore's Work on the Sermon on the Mount. London:
   Williams & Norgate, 1927.
   Shears believes that Gore in his interpretation of the
   Sermon on the Mount has embraced Bentham's fallacy of
   applying the principles of physical science to social
   phenomena. Gore attempts the impossible task of recon-
   ciling two fundamentally different points of view. He ig-
   nores character and regards actions as mere physical
   facts. He brings the precepts of the Sermon on the Mount
   down to the mere sociological level by transforming them
   into proverbs.

Sheldon, Frank M. The Teaching on the Mount; a Study Outline. Boston: Pilgrim Press, 1926.

Shellabaer, William G. The Sermon on the Mount in Verse;
and also the Scriptural Portions on which the Verses are
Based. Illus. by Elsie Anna Wood. Cairo: Malay Nile
Mission Press, 1931.
In Arabic.

Shinn, Roger L. Sermon on the Mount. Philadelphia:
United Church Press, 1962.
Popular exposition. Includes questions for study and
discussion.

_____. The Sermon on the Mount; a Course for Older
Young People and Adults. Teacher's edition. Philadelphia: Christian Education Press, 1954.
A quarter's guide which includes a section for the
teacher and one for the students. The teacher's section
includes: suggestions for preparation, suggested class
procedure, activities. The student's section contains expositions, suggested Bible readings, and questions for
thought and discussion.

Sickenberger, Joseph. "Zwei neue Äusserungen zur Ehe-
bruchklausel bei Mt." Zeitschrift für die neutestamentliche Wissenschaft 42 (1949) 202-09.

Sidebottom, E. M. "'Reward' in Matthew V. 46, etc." Expository Times 67 (1955-56) 219-20.

Sinclair, W. M. "Lessons from the Sermon on the Mount."
Good Words (1894) 571-6.

Sivananda, Swami. Les Béatitudes. Le Sermon sur la
montagne, tel qu'il est enseigné dans l'Inde. Trogen:
1957.

Sjöberg, E. "Das licht in dir. Zur Deutung von Matth. 6,
22f Par." Studia theologica 5 (1951) 89-105.

Skalitsky, M. G. A. "A Critical Edition of Annianus' Latin
Version of John Chrysostom's Homilies (15-18) on Matthew
V." Doctoral dissertation. Fordham, 1969.

Skeat, T. C. "The Lilies of the Field." Zeitschrift für die
neutestamentliche Wissenschaft 37 (1938) 211-14.

Skibbe, Eugene M. "Pentateuchal Themes in the Sermon on
the Mount." Lutheran Quarterly 20 (1968) 44-51.

Skovgaard-Petersen, C. Jesu Bjergpraediken. En Discipels
Tanker om Mesterens Ord. København: Lohse, 1936.

Skvireckas, J. "Nesipriešinkite piktans ['Non resistere
malo' Mt. 5, 39]." Σωτήρ 5 (1928) 15-21.

Sladek, Paulus F. "'Liebet eure Feinde...' (Mt. 5, 44).
Ein moral-psychologischer Vertrag," in Kirche, Recht
und Land. Festschrift Adolf Kindermann. Königstein im
Taunus (Sudentendt. Priesterwerk e. V.); München (Acker-
mann-Gemeinde), 1969, 30-48.

Smailes, Frederick W. "Perfect" Man According to the Pattern Showed on the Mount; a Study in the Sermon on the
Mount. London: Skeffington and Son, 1925.

Smirnov, A. Nagornaiâ beseda Iisusa Khrista v besedakh.

Smith, C. Ryder. "The Evil Eye." Expository Times 54
(1942-43) 26.

Smith, David. "Raka!" Expository Times 15 (1903-04) 235-
37.

Smith, George B. The Christian Charter; a Study of the
Sermon on the Mount. London: Salvationist Publishing
and Supplies, 1972.
Meditations.

Smith, H. "Ante-Nicene Interpretations of the Sayings on
Divorce." Journal of Theological Studies 20 (1919) 356.

Smith, Morton. "Mt. 5. 43: 'Hate thine Enemy.'" Harvard
Theological Review 45 (1952) 71-73.

Smith, Richard M. "The Old and the New." The Quarterly
Review of the M. E. Church, South 16 (1894) 312-24.

Smith, Ronald Gregor. "Studies in Texts." Theology 45
(1942) 93-95 [Mt. 5:48].

Smith, W. Taylor. "Matthew V. 14." Expository Times 8
(1896-97) 138.

Smith, Walter C. The Sermon on the Mount. Edinburgh:
Edmonston and Douglas, 1867.
Sermons.

Söderblom, Nathan. Jesu Bergspredikan och vår tid. Stockholm: Ahlen and Sönners Förlag, 1933.
This study begins with Söderblom's interpretation of the Sermon on the Mount. There follows a discussion of the revolutionary, Roman Catholic, Luther's, and modern interpretations. He then discusses such issues as non-swearing, marriage, anxiety, and prayer as reflected in the Sermon on the Mount. A significant work which is also useful as a guide to Scandanavian interpretation of the Sermon on the Mount.

_____. "Le sens des commandements de Jésus dans le discours sur la montagne." Revue de théologie et de philosophie 30 (1897) 247-63.

Soiron, Thaddaeus. Die Bergpredigt Jesu. Formgeschichtliche, exegetische und theologische Erklärung. Freiburg im Breisgau: Herder, 1940 (1944).
A lengthy and substantial exegesis which gives special attention to form critical and theological questions.

Sommer, Carl Ernst. Die Bergpredigt. Unterweise mich, Herr, nach deinem Wort. Gruppenarbeit unter Jugendlichen über Bibel und Kirche. H. 5. Frankfurt am Main: Anker-Verlag, 1953.

Soucek, J. B. "Salz der Erde und Licht der Welt. Zur Exegese von Matth 5:13-16." Theologische Zeitschrift 19 (1963) 169-79.

Southouse, Albert J. The Men of the Beatitudes. Cincinnati: Jennings and Pye; London: Hodder and Stoughton, 1903. Meditations on the Sermon on the Mount.

Spear, Samuel T. "The Sermon of Christ on the Mount." Independent 42 (1890) 1479-80.

Speyr, Adrienne von. Bergpredigt. Betrachtungen über Matthaeus 5-7. Einsiedeln: Johannes Verlag, 1948. Meditations.

Sprenger, Paul. Die Bergpredigt. Witten: Bundes-Verlag, 1947.

Stadtland-Neumann, Hiltrud. Evangelische Radikalismen in der Sicht Calvins. Sein Verständnis der Bergpredigt und der Aussendungsrede (Matth. 10). Neukirchen-Vluyn: Neukirchener Verlag, 1966. Issued also as thesis, Göt-

tingen, with title "Reformatorischer Radikalismus," 1963.
An analysis of Calvin's interpretation of the Sermon on
the Mount.   This book gives a good picture of the theological differences between Calvin and the "Täufer" in
their respective understandings of the Sermon on the
Mount.

Stafford, Geoffrey W.   The Sermon on the Mount, the Charter of Christianity.   New York: Abingdon, 1927.
Sermons.

Stamm, Frederick K.   Seeing the Multitudes.   New York:
Harpers, 1943.
Sermons.

Stange, Carl. "Zur Ethik der Bergpredigt."   Zeitschrift
für systematische Theologie 2 (1924-25) 37-74.

Staudinger, Josef.   Die Bergpredigt.   Wien: Herder, 1957.
An extensive and wide-ranging study which treats such
questions as: Jesus and the Law, the true piety, the
meaning of the Beatitudes, the Lord's Prayer and the
synoptic question, the Sermon on the Mount and demythol-
ogization.

_____.   El Sermón de la montaña.   Trad. Jose Bellock
Zimmermann.   Barcelona: Herder, 1962.
(See his Die Bergpredigt)

Steinhausen, Wilhelm.   Die Bergpredigt.   Fünf Wandbilder
in der Aula des Kaiser Friedrich-Gymnasiums zur Frankfurt am Main.   München: G. D. W. Callwey, 1906.

Steinmann, Alphons.   Die Bergpredigt, exegetisch-homiletisch
erklärt.   Pederborn: F. Schöningh, 1926.

_____.   "Die Bergpredigt; kritische Bemerkungen zu
einer neuen Auslegung," in Braunsberger Vorlesungver-
zeichnis für Sommer 1925.   Braunsberg: 1925.

Steinmeyer, Franz L.   Die Rede des Herrn auf dem Berg.
Berlin: Verlag von Wiegandt und Griebin, 1885.
Scholarly study in which the concept of justice or
righteousness is a key category of interpretation.   Steinmeyer uses Greek terminology freely.

Stinette, Charles R.   "The Kingdom of God and the Sermon

on the Mount." STM thesis. Hartford Theological
Seminary, 1943.

Stockmeyer, Immanuel. Die Bergpredigt Jesu Christi aus-
gelegt in fünfunddreissig Predigten. Basel: Verlag von
R. Reich vormale C. Detloffs Buchhandlung, 1891.
Sermons.

Stoger, Alois. Ich aber sage euch. Die Bergpredigt leben-
dig gemacht. München: J. Pfeiffer, 1952.

Stoll, Raymond. "The Sermon on the Mount." American
Ecclesiastical Review 104 (1941) 193-209, 301-18, 395-411.

Stolz, Johann J. Geist der Sittenlehre Jesu, in Betrachtungen
über die ganze Bergpredigt. 3 Thle. Lemgo: Meyer,
1792-1793.

Stosch, G. Die Bergpredigt Jesu als Evangelium. Gütersloh:
C. Bertelsmann, 1918.

_____. Der pastoraltheologische Ertag der Bergpredigt.
Berlin: Wiegandt & Grieben, 1898.

Stout, James C. "Matthew 7:9-11--A Translation." Biblical
Review 3 (1918) 132-37.

Strack, Hermann L., und Billerbeck, Paul. Kommentar zum
Neuen Testament aus Talmud und Midrash. Erster Band.
"Das Evangelium nach Matthäus," 189-474. München:
Beck, 1922 (1965).

Stramare, Tarision. "Matteo divorzista?" Divinitas 15
(1971) 213-35.

Strang, Lewis C. The Master and the Modern Spirit. New
York: Roland Publishing Co., 1925.
A liberal, modernistic apologetic which views Jesus as
a rebel against dogmatism and conformity. The work is
not a commentary or interpretation but a series of speculations and opinions. The Sermon on the Mount is a sort of
backbone or connecting link on which these speculations and
opinions are hung.

Streeter, Burnett H. War, This War and the Sermon on the
Mount. London: Oxford University Press, 1915.

Stubbs, Charles W. Christ and Economics in the Light of
the Sermon on the Mount. London: Ibister, 1893.
Sermons. Pronounced social gospel accent.

The Student World, vol. XXX, no. 8, 1937.
Entire issue on the Sermon on the Mount.

Stüler, Christoph B. 37 Predigten über das 5., 6. und 7.
Kapitel Matthäus, gehalten in Berlin im Jahre 1828 und
1829. Halle: Mühlmann, 1843.
Sermons.

Sturz, H. A. "Sermon on the Mount and Its Application to
the Present Age." Grace Journal 4 (1963) 3-15.

Sutcliffe, Edmund F. "Not to Resist Evil." Scripture 5
(1952) 33-35.

_____. "Not to Swear at all." Scripture 5 (1952) 68-69.

_____. "One Jot or Tittle, Mt. 5. 18." Biblica 9 (1928)
458-60.

Sweet, Ralph T. Moments on the Mount. Austin, Texas:
R. B. Sweet Co., 1963.

Szczygiel, Paul. "Die Bergpredigt (Mt 5-7) nach ihrer
strophischen Struktur," in Pastor bonus 1921/22, 449-60,
508-17.

Székely, Edmond B. Sermon on the Mount. Tecate, Calif.:
Essene School of Life, 1948.

Tafi, A. "'Excepta fornicationis causa' (Mt. 5, 32)."
Verbum Domini 26 (1948) 18-26.

Tait, Andrew. The Charter of Christianity: an Examination
in the Light of Modern Criticism, of Our Blessed Lord's
Sermon on the Mount, and Its Ethical Precepts Compared
with the Best Moral Teaching of the Ancient World. London: Hodder & Stoughton, 1886.
An extensive, critical commentary which makes frequent
references to early Christian and classical literature.

Tannehill, R. C. "Focal Instance as a Form of New Testament Speech; a Study of Matthew 5:39b-42." Journal of
Religion 50 (1970) 372-85.

Tetzlaff, Emil. Bergpredigt und Eddalehre. Zur Veran-
schaulichung des hohen Gesittungsstandes unserer Vorfahren
zu einander in Beziehung gebracht. Zeitz: Sis-Verlag,
1921.

Thielicke, Helmut. Die Bergpredigt. 2. Aufl. Stuttgart:
Quell-Verlag, 1950.
Sermons.

_____. "Ich aber sage euch..." Auslegungen der Berg-
predigt in Stuttgarter Gottesdiensten. Stuttgart: Quell-
Verlag, 1946.
Sermons.

_____. Das Leben kann noch einmal beginnen. Ein Gang
durch die Bergpredigt. Stuttgart: Quell-Verlag, 1956
(1958) (1960) (1961) (1962) (1965).
Sermons.

_____. Het leven kan opnieuw beginnen. Vert. D. J.
Couvée. Wageningen: Zomer & Keuning, 1966.
(See his Das Leben kann noch einmal beginnen)

_____. Life Can Begin Again. Trans. John W. Dober-
stein. Philadelphia: Fortress Press, 1963.
(See his Das Leben kann noch einmal beginnen)

Thiersch, Heinrich W. Die Bergpredigt Christi und ihre
Bedeutung für die Gegenwart. Augsburg: 1878.

_____. Kristi Bjergpraediken og dens Betyding for Nutiden.
København: Schiødte, 1873.

Thimme, Hans. Die Bergpredigt: Hören und Tun. Berlin:
Christlicher Zeitschriftenverlag, 1965.
Eight studies prepared for the 28th Bible Week 1965/
1966.

Tholuck, August. Ausführliche Auslegung der Bergpredigt
Christi nach Matthäus. 3. Ausg. Hamburg: Friedrich
Perthes, 1845.
A verse by verse commentary preceded by an introduction which deals with critical problems. A classic
nineteenth-century work which has a predominant evangelical emphasis.

_____. Die Bergpredigt. Gotha: Friedrich Perthes,

1856. Die Bergrede Christi. 5. Aufl. 1872.
Extensive, critical commentary regarded for many years
as a classical work.

_____. Commentary on the Sermon on the Mount. Trans.
from the fourth and revised edition by R. Lundin Brown.
Philadelphia: Smith, English; New York: Shelden, 1855
(1860); Edinburgh: T. and T. Clark, 1860 (1869).
(See his Die Bergpredigt)

_____. Exposition, Doctrinal and Philological, of Christ's
Sermon on the Mount. Trans. Robert Menzies. Edinburgh: T. Clark, 1834-37.
(See his Philologisch-theologische Auslegung der Bergpredigt...)

_____. Philologisch-theologische Auslegung der Berg-
predigt Christi nach Matthäus, zugleich ein Beitrag zur Be-
gründung einer reinbiblischen Glaubens und Sittenlehre.
Hamburg: Friedrich Perthes, 1833.
An extensive, critical exposition which interprets the
Sermon on the Mount by the method of comparing it with
parallel passages. Tholuck also refers to many early and
contemporary sources and scholars.

Thomas Aquinas, Saint. Catena aurea.
A series of extracts from the Fathers and ecclesiastical
writers for the elucidation of the Four Gospels. Published in many editions and translations. It is among the
most widely diffused works of Aquinas.

Thome, Josef. Selig seid ihr! Gedanken zur Bergpredigt.
Regensburg: Pustet, 1937.

Thompson, Ernest T. The Sermon on the Mount and Its
Meaning for Today. Richmond, Va.: John Knox Press,
1946 (1953) (1961).
A readable and popular interpretation which holds that
the Sermon on the Mount is a practical way of life for individuals and society.

Thomson, D. G. S. De Bergrede. Uitleg en consequenties
van het Evangelie. Uitg. van de vereeniging Godsdienst
en rede. Rijswijk (Z. H.): V. A. Kramers, 1938.

Thornton, Henry. Family Commentary upon the Sermon on
the Mount. Edited by R. H. Inglis. London: J. Hatchard

and Son, 1835.
Verse by verse commentary in homiletical style. This
work is also contained in his Family Prayers: to which
Is Added, a Family Commentary upon the Sermon on the
Mount. Edited by the Rev. Manton Eastburn. New York:
Swords, Stanford, 1837; and in his Family Prayers and
Prayers on the Ten Commandments. Boston: Houghton,
Mifflin, 1887.

_____. Sermon on the Mount. London: J. Hatchard,
1853.

Thurn, Wilhelm E. Reine Übersetzung der Bergrede Jesu,
nach der praktischen Vernunft dargestellt und für Jeder-
mann lesbar gemacht. 2 Bde. Lemgo: Meyer, 1799.

Thurneysen, Eduard. Die Bergpredigt. München: C. Kaiser Verlag, 1936 (1963) (6. Aufl. 1965).
In keeping with his emphasis on the theology of the
Word of God, Thurneysen insists that the Sermon on the
Mount must be interpreted so that its Christological and
eschatological content is brought to light. A brief but
significant theological study.

_____. The Sermon on the Mount. Trans. William C.
Robinson. Richmond, Va.: John Knox Press, 1964.
(See his Die Bergpredigt)

_____. Le Sermon sur la montagne. Trad. Emile
Marion. Genève: Editions Labor et fides, 1958.
(See his Die Bergpredigt)

_____. Ein Stück Bergpredigt. Predigt uber Luk. 6,
27-38. Basel: Reinhardt, 1950.

Thy Kingdom Come--Beginning in Me; Studies in the Sermon
on the Mount. Circle program material. Atlanta: Committee on Woman's Work, Presbyterian Church in the U.S.,
n.d.
Study guide for women's circles.

Tiling, Magdalene von. Von der besseren Gerechtigkeit.
Erläuterungen zur Bergpredigt. Stuttgart: F. Steinkopf,
1929.

Tolson, G. T. "Universals and Particulars in the Sermon
on the Mount." Expository Times 57 (1945-46) 82.

Tolstoi, Lev Nikolaevich. My Religion. Trans. from the
French by Huntingdon Smith. New York: Thomas Y.
Crowell, 1885; London: Walter Scott, 1889.
(See his V chem moîa viêra?)

_____. V chem moîa viêra? Genêve: M. Elpidine,
1884 (1886) Izd. 2., dop. i ispr. 1888; Berlin: Izd. G.
Shteinitsa, 1902.
A confessional statement in which Tolstoy describes
the change in his life when he discovered that the doctrine of Jesus is simple, practical, and conducive to the
highest happiness. This "awakening" resulted from his
reading of the Sermon on the Mount. A sizeable portion
of this book is devoted to an exposition of the Sermon on
the Mount. He emphasizes particularly the concept of
nonresistance which entirely changed his understanding of
the doctrine of Jesus.

Touw, H. C. "De exegese van Matthëus 5:17-48." Vox
theologica 9 (1937-38), 169-74.

Traub, Friedrich. "Das Problem der Bergpredigt." Zeitschrift für Theologie und Kirche 17 (1936) 193-218.

Trench. Nagornaîa propoved' Gospoda nashego Iisusa
Khrista. Moskva: 1880.

Trench, Richard C. Die Erklärung der Bergpredigt aus den
Schriften des hl. Augustinus. Übers. Ed. Roller. Neu-
kirchen: Buchhandlung des Erziehungsvereins, 1904.
(See his Exposition of the Sermon on the Mount...)

_____. Exposition of the Sermon on the Mount, Drawn
from the Writings of St. Augustine. London: 1844; 2nd
ed. rev. and improved. London: J. W. Parker, 1851;
3rd ed. rev. London: Kegan Paul, 1886.
The book begins with a lengthy essay on "Augustine as
an Interpreter of Scripture." The remainder of the book
is an exposition of the Sermon on the Mount based on
Augustine's writings. These include not only his Exposition of the Sermon on the Mount, but also his Sermons,
his Letters, his Exposition of the Psalms and his controversial Tracts.

Troitskii, A. D. Khristova Nagornaîa propoved'.

Troitskii, F. Nagornaîa beseda Iisusa Khrista. Kazan':
1889.

Turlington, H. E. "Jesus and the Law." Review and Expositor 53 (1956) 34-45.

Tyndale, William. An Expoficion vpon the V. VI. VII.
Chapters of Mathew, which Thre Chapters Are ye Keye &
the Dore of the fcripture, and the Reftoring Agayne of
Christes Lawe Corrupte by the Papists. Compyled by
Wyllyam Tindal. Newly set forth and corrected accord-
inge to his first copye. London: by Wyllyam Hill, ca.
1550.

_____. An Exposicion vppon the V. VI. VII. Chaptres of
Mathew, which Thre Chaptres Are the Keye and the Dore
of the Scripture. Antwerp: Joannes Grapheus, 1533?

Ulbrich, Martin. Die Bergpredigt unseres Heilands. Kurz
ausgelegt als Handreichung für Diakonen und Diakonissen.
Gütersloh: C. Bertelsmann, 1906.

Ulrich, Johann J. De hoogste wysheit op de hoogtens
roepende. Of, De guldene, zoe genaamde Bergpredikatie,
van den grooten leeraar Jesus Christus: begreepen in het
V. VI. en VII. capittel des Evangelium van Mattheus; in
verscheide predikation verklaart en op de conscientie
toegepast. Gravenhage: Isaac van der Kloot, 1735-39.
    Sermons which comprise an extensive homiletical com-
mentary.

van Unnik, W. C. "Die Motivierung der Fiendesliebe in
Lukas VI, 32-35." Novum Testamentum 8 (1966) 284-300.

Vaccari, A. "La clausola del divorzio in Mt. 5, 32; 19, 9."
Rivista biblica 3 (1955) 97-119.

_____. "De matrimonio et divortio apud Matthaeum."
Biblica 36 (1955) 149-51.

Vaganay, L. "L'absence du Sermon sur la montagne chez
Marc." Revue biblique 58 (1951) 5-46.

_____. "Existe-t-il chez Marc quelques traces du Ser-
mon sur la montagne?" New Testament Studies 1 (1955)
192-200.

Vaĭt, É. G. Razmyshleniĭa o Nagornoĭ propovedi Iisusa
Khrista. Petrograd: 1915.

Valdes, Juan de. Juan de Valdes Commentary upon Our
Lord's Sermon on the Mount. Reprinted from the com-
mentary itself, published 1882. Trans. and edited by
John T. Betts. London: Trübner, 1882.
Verse by verse commentary in homiletical style.

Varillon, F. "Le Sermon sur la montagne." Masses
Ouvrières 4 (1948) 33, 34, 36, 38, 39.

Vaughan, Charles J. Characteristics of Christ's Teaching,
Drawn from the Sermon on the Mount. London: Strahan,
1866 (1874); London: S. P. C. K., 1894; New York:
Wilbur B. Ketcham, 19--?
Popular exposition. Homiletical style.

Vawter, Bruce. "The Divorce Clauses in Mt. 5, 32 and
19, 9." Catholic Biblical Quarterly 16 (1954) 155-67.

Vecchi, Jos. "In locum quendam Salviani observationes."
Vigiliae Christianae 4 (1950) 190-92.

Ventro, F. Il sermone sulla montagne e le parabole com-
mentate per le scuole medie. Catania: 1926.

Verkuyl, Johannes. Chotbah dibukit. Djakarta: Badan
Penerbit Kristen, 1968.

Vietor, Hans. Auf Felsengrund. 22 Predigten über die
Bergpredigt. Witten/Ruhr: Luther-Verlag, 1954.
Sermons.

Vigeveno, H. S. Climbing up the Mountain, Children.
Glendale, Calif.: G/L Regal Books, 1968.
Popular treatment intended to show that the Sermon on
the Mount is meaningful, relevant, and helpful.

Vinogradov, N. Nagornaĩa propoved' Spasiteliâ. Uchene o
blazhenstvakh. Moskva: 1892 (1894).

Viotti, Johannes. "Sasom en som har makt (Matt. 7:29," in
Ordet och tron. Festkrift för E. Billing. Uppsala: Diakonistyrelsen, 1931, 173-92.

Vitalis, Justus. Die Bergpredigt. Flugschriften des neuen
Frankfurter Verlages. VIII. Frankfurt am Main: Neuer
Frankfurter Verlag, 1902.

Vogels, Heinrich J. "Synoptische Studien zur Bergpredigt,"
in Bonner Zeitschrift für Theologie und Seelsorge I (1924)
123-36.

Votaw, Clyde W. "Jesus' Ideal of Life." Biblical World 35
(1910) 46-56.

_____. "Sermon on the Mount," in Hastings, James, ed.
A Dictionary of the Bible. extra vol. New York: Charles
Scribner's Sons, 1904, 1-44.
An extensive, scholarly article dealing with the origin
and transmission, interpretation, and the relation of the
Sermon to the teaching of Jesus as a whole.

Vuorisaarna. (Matteuksen evankeliumin V. VI ja VII luku.)
Jeesuksen hyvä sanoma totuuden etsijöille. Kreikankieles-
tä suomentanut ja selittänyt Pekka Ervast. Helsinki:
Ruusu-Risti, 1925 (1943) (1952).

Wahlström, Gunnar. Bergspredikans Kristus och korset.
Stockholm: De ungas förlag, 1934.

Walker, Dean A. "Idealism and Opportunism in Jesus'
Teaching: A Study of Matt. 5:17-20." Biblical World
17 (1901) 433-38.

Ward, James E. The Master on the Mount. New York:
Longmans, Green, 1943.
Sermons.

Warner, N. "Mattheus 5:17." Gereformeerd theologisch
tijdschrift 48 (1948) 33-50.

Warner, Richard C. The Sermon on the Mount; in Five Discourses, Preached in Chelwood Church. London: Longman, 1840.
Sermons.

Wayland, Daniel S. Sermons, Preached in the Parish Church
of Bassingham, near Newark-on-Trent. 2 vols. London:
J. Hatchard, 1021-32.
Volume 2 contains sermons on the Sermon on the Mount.

Waylen, Hector. Mountain Pathways; a Study in the Ethics
of the Sermon on the Mount. London: Sherratt and Hughes,
1909; 2nd ed. London: Kegan Paul, Trübner, 1912.
The Sermon on the Mount forms a new Code of Ethics.

Raises various ethical issues such as nonresistance, marriage, swearing oaths. Contains author's translation of the Sermon on the Mount with extensive notes.

Weatherlake, Robert C. On the Mount; Studies in Matthew 5-7. Melbourne: Joint Board of Christian Education of Australia and New Zealand, 1973.

Weber, Hans E. Die Bergpredigt. Bibelstunden über Beruf und Berufung. Gütersloh: C. Bertelsmann, 1939.

Webster, Charles A. "The Mote and the Beam (Luke VI. 41, 42 = Matt. VII. 3-5)." Expository Times 39 (1927-28) 91-92.

Weener, J. "Mt. 5. 33-37." Nieuwe theologische studien 4 (1921) 74-79.

Wehmeyer, Ludwig. Das Marcus-Evangelium und die Bergpredigt aus Matthäus (Kap. 5-7), für Schule und Haus zum leichteren Verständnis bearbeitet. Kassel: E. Hühn, 1898.

Wehnert, Bruno. Jesu Bergpredigt psychologisch und philosophisch erklärt für Lehrer und Schüler. Tübingen: J. C. B. Mohr, 1914.
A discussion of numerous topics found in the Sermon on the Mount as well as a wider treatment of such questions as Jesus and Paul, Jesus and Nietzsche, etc.

Weinel, Heinrich. Die Bergpredigt. Leipzig: B. G. Teubner, 1920.
The major part of this work is a comparative study of the Sermon on the Mount with parallels in other religious literature. A useful feature of the book is a setting of the Matthean and Lucan texts of the Sermon on the Mount in parallel columns.

Weir, T. H. "Matthew V. 20." Expository Times 23 (1911-12) 430-31.

Weise, Manfred. "Mt. 5, 21f.--ein Zeugnis sakraler Rechtsprechung in der Urgemeinde." Zeitschrift für die neutestamentliche Wissenschaft 49 (1958) 116-23.

Weismann, J. "Zur Erklärung einer Stelle in der Bergpredigt." Zeitschrift für die neutestamentliche Wissenschaft 14 (1913) 175-76.

Weiss, Bernhard. "Die Besetzauslegung Christi in der Bergpredigt." Theologische Studien und Kritiken 31 (1858) 50-
94.

Weiss, Hugo. Die Bergpredigt Christi in ihrem organischen
Zusammenhang erklärt. Freiburg: Herder, 1892.

Wendling, E. "Zu Matthäus 5, 18.19." Zeitschrift für die
neutestamentliche Wissenschaft 5 (1904) 253-56.

Werkenthin, Annabel R. Twenty Studies of Christian Action
and Jesus' Ten Ways of Happiness from Sermon on the
Mount. Lawrence, Kan.: Miller Print Shop, 1938.
    Study guide with positive and negative admonitions for
    Christian living.

Wernberg-Møller, P. "A Semitic Idiom in Matt V:22." New
Testament Studies 3 (1956) 71-73.

Wesley, John. "Upon Our Lord's Sermon on the Mount,"
in Works. 3rd ed. vol. V. London: John Mason,
1829, 247-433.
    Thirteen discourses on the Sermon on the Mount, ex-
    cluding Matt. 5:21-48.

_____. "Upon Our Lord's Sermon on the Mount," in
Works. vol. I. New York: B. Waugh and T. Mason,
1833, 177-306.
    (See London edition)

Wessenberg, Ignaz H. K. Die Bergpredigt unsers Herrn
und Erlösers. Constance: Wallis, 1820 (1825).

West, Edward N. God's Image in Us; a Meditation on
Christ's Teachings in His Sermon on the Mount. Cleveland, Ohio: World Publishing Co., 1960.
    Meditations.

Westman, Sigurd. Jesu Bergspredikan. Göteborg: Pehrs-
sons förlag, 1925.
    Relatively brief exposition intended for study and medi-
    tation.

Westrup, Folke. Lärjungens väg, med Bergspredikan i
blickpunkten. Stockholm: Diakonistyrelsens bokförlag, 1957.
    Meditations.

Wetter, Gillis P:son. "Den litterära karaktären av Jesu "Bergpredikans" första del, " in Till Ärkebiskop Söderbloms sextioårsdag 1926. Stockholm: Diakonstyrelsen, 1926, 449-67.

White, Ellen G. Gedanken vom Berg der Seligpreisungen. Hamburg: Internationale Traktatgesellschaft, 1913; 16. Aufl. Hamburg: Vollmer & Bentlin, 1946. (See her Thoughts from the Mount of Blessing)

_____. Leuchtende Spuren. Zürich: Advent-Verlag, 1967. Contains two previously published works: Der Weg zu Christo and Gedanken vom Berg der Seligpreisungen. (See her Thoughts from the Mount of Blessing)

_____. Love Unlimited: Combining Steps to Christ, and Thoughts from the Mount of Blessing. Mountain View, Calif.: Pacific Press, 1958. (See 1896 edition of Thoughts from the Mount of Blessing)

_____. Thoughts from the Mount of Blessing. Battle Creek, Mich.: International Tract Society, 1896; Mountain View, Calif.: Pacific Press, 1900 (1928) (1948) (1956). Meditations. This work has been printed in many languages.

_____. Vuorisaarna. Suomentanut Kaisu Salmela. Hameenlinna: 1958. (See her Thoughts from the Mount of Blessing)

White, Thomas. Πανθεολογία, or the Summe of Practical Divinity Practiz'd in the Wilderness, and Delivered by Our Saviour in his Sermon on the Mount. Being Observations upon the Fourth, Fifth, Sixth, and Seventh Chapters of St. Matthew. To which is Prefixed a Prolegomena or Preface by Way of a Dialogue, Wherein the Perfection and Perspicuity of the Scripture Is Vindicated from the Calumnies of Anabaptists and Papists. London: A. M. for Jos. Cranford, 1654.

Whitefoord, B. "The Christian 'Nil Desperandum': A Study of St. Luke VI. 35." Expositor 6th ser. 5 (1902) 218-24.

Whyte, Alexander. "Christ the Interpreter of Nature (Mt. VI. 24-34)." Expositor 3rd ser. 2 (1885) 224-32.

Wichmann, Heinrich. Gedankengang der Bergpredigt nach Matthäus. Wernigerode: Angerstein, 1882.
Text of a lecture given in a Gymnasium course.

Wiessen, Pastor. "Zu Matth. 5, 17. 20." Zeitschrift für die neutestamentliche Wissenschaft 3 (1902) 336-52.

Wilder, Amos N. "The Sermon on the Mount." Bulletin of the General Theological Library 37 (Oct. 1944).

_____. "Sermon on the Mount," in Interpreter's Bible, vol 7. New York: Abingdon, 1951, 155-64.

Willard, Conrad R. "The Sermon on the Mount in the Writings of the Ante-Nicene Fathers from New Testament Times to Origen." Th. D. thesis. Central Baptist Theological Seminary, 1956.

Williams, Hermon P. "The Project of Jesus, or, The Sociological Significance of the Sermon on the Mount." Th. D. thesis. Madison, N.J.: Drew University, 1929.
A study of the Sermon on the Mount which shows the "sociological wisdom of Jesus." Along with his other designations, Jesus should be seen as the "great Engineer now functioning in social development."

Willis, Donald G. The Sermon on the Mount. New York: Carlton Press, 1972.
Devotional meditations.

Wilson, Frank T. Unconditional Spiritual Surrender; Studies from the Sermon on the Mount. Philadelphia: United Presbyterian Church, 1946.

Wilson, Harold C. "The Salt of the Earth." Expository Times 35 (1923-24) 136-37.

Wilson, James P. "In Matthew VII. 25 is προσέπεσαν a Primitive Error Displacing προσέκοψαν?" Expository Times 57 (1945-46) 138.

Windisch, Hans. The Meaning of the Sermon on the Mount. Trans. S. MacLean Gilmour. Philadelphia: Westminster Press, 1951.
(See his Der Sinn der Bergpredigt)

_____. Der Sinn der Bergpredigt. Leipzig: J. C. Hin-

richs, 1929 (1937).
Windisch holds that historical and theological exegesis
should be strictly differentiated. His intention is to examine selected problems of the Sermon on the Mount and
to show what historical and critical exegesis, distinguished
from modern philosophical and theological exegesis, has
taught us to see. The essence of his view is that the Sermon is essentially a collection of commandments and that
these are practicable in the sense that Jesus expected them
to be obeyed as a condition of salvation. The depth and
scope of this work are most impressive, and it is one of
the finest studies on the Sermon on the Mount.

Winkelhofer, Sebastian. Reden über die Bergpredigt unsers
Herrn Jesus Christi. München: J. Lentner, 1812.
   Sermons.

Wissmann, Erwin. Die Bergpredigt und die Gleichnisse
Jesu im Unterricht. Berlin: Topelmann, 1939.
   Intended for study and teaching. An appendix gives
brief interpretations of the parables.

Wöllner, E. Präparationsskizzen. Die Bergpredigt, Jako-
busbrief und Galaterbrief. Für den Schulgebrauch und zur
Vorbereitung auf die 2. Lehrerprufüng und das Mittle-
schulexamem. Ausgearbeitet nach den 5 Formalstufen.
Langensalza: H. Beyer & Söhne, 1907.

Woellner, Frederic P. The Highlands of the Mind; a Psychological Analysis of the Sermon on the Mount. Pasadena,
Calif.: Sunday Morning Press, 1930.
   A psychological defense of the Sermon on the Mount
which seeks to probe the type of mind revealed in it and
the type of mind of those who follow it.

Wolf, Rudolf. Die Bergpredigt, in Schulandachten dargeboten.
Halle: E. Strien, 1899.

Wood, James D. The Sermon on the Mount and Its Application. London: Geoffrey Bles, 1963.
   A readable introduction to the Sermon on the Mount
which treats such questions as: The Sermon on the Mount
and the Dead Sea Scrolls, the ethics in the Sermon on the
Mount, the Kingdom and eschatology, marriage and divorce, nonresistance.

Wood, W. S. "The Salt of the Earth." Journal of Theological Studies 25 (1924) 167-72.

Woods, F. H. "The Moral Teaching of the Sermon on the
Mount." Expository Times 4 (1892-93) 254-59.

Worden, Ronald D. "A Philological Analysis of Luke 6:20b-
49 and Parallels." Ph.D. thesis. Princeton Theological
Seminary, 1973.
    Luke's Sermon on the Plain is compared with corres-
ponding parts of Matthew in order to explain differences
in the wording of comparable clauses. Two hundred ten
differences in the wording are identified and evaluated as
to probable origin. The separate results are combined in
a reconstructed text of the Q Sermon. The dissertation
surveys the history of theories about Q or Synoptic sources
like Q from the eighteenth century to contemporary studies
in the redaction criticism of Q.

Worsley, Thomas. The Province of the Intellect in Religion
Deduced from Our Lord's Sermon on the Mount, and Considered with Reference to Prevalent Errors. 6 vols.
London: John W. Parker, 1845-50.
    A wide-ranging apologetic and interpretation of the Ser-
mon on the Mount which includes volumes on the Patri-
archs as setting forth the things of the Sermon on the
Mount and on the Apostles as the completion of the Patri-
archs.

Wrege, Hans-Theo. Die Überlieferungsgeschichte der Bergpredigt. Tübingen: J. C. B. Mohr, 1968.
    A substantial, scholarly analysis using literary and
form critical methods.

            . Untersuchungen zur Überlieferungsgeschichte des
Spruchgutes der Bergpredigt. Diss. Gottingen, 1963.

Wright, Thomas H. The Sermon on the Mount for Today.
Edinburgh: T. & T. Clark, 1927; New York: Charles
Scribner's Sons, 1927.
    Wright seeks to arrive at the meaning of Jesus in the
Sermon on the Mount and to show its validity for contemporary issues. The Sermon on the Mount represents
the highest moral and spiritual discernment achieved by
any human, but is also the Word of God. Homiletical
style.

Wright, William B. Master and Man; or, The Sermon on
the Mount Practiced on the Plain. Boston: Houghton,
Mifflin, 1894.

Largely a discussion of five of the Beatitudes. Each
Beatitude is followed by a biography of a person exempli-
fying it.

Wünsch, Georg. Die Bergpredigt bei Luther. Tübingen:
J. C. B. Mohr, 1920.
A study of Luther's interpretation of the Sermon on the
Mount with special reference to social ethics.

_____. "Bergpredigt und Kultur der Gegenwart."
Christliche Welt 35 (1921) 586-89.

Yates, J. E. "Studies in Texts." Theology 44 (1942) 48-
51 [Mt. 5:44].

Zambelli, Ernesto. Meditazioni sul Vangelo. Il Vangelo
dell'infanzia e il Discorso della montagna. Brescia: La
Scuola, 1970.
The second half of this work consists of meditations on
the Sermon on the Mount--the first half of meditations on
the Nativity.

Zerwick, M. "De matrimonio et divortio in Evangelio."
Verbum Domini 38 (1960) 193-212.

Žilka, František. Ježišova kázáni na hoře. Praha: Kalich,
1931.
Practical exposition of the Sermon on the Mount. Includes author's translation of the text.

Zoller, I. "Il discorse sulla montagna e la letteratura
biblico-rabbinica." Richerche religiose (1931) 497-517.

Zorell, Franciscus. "Ἀρκετός, Mt. 6, 34: 'Sufficit diei
malitia sua.'" Biblica 1 (1920) 95-96.

Zuber, Albert. Bergpredigt (Gesänge). Zürich: Orell
Füssli Verlag, 1940.

BEATITUDES CRITICISM,
INTERPRETATION, SERMONS, MEDITATIONS, ETC.

Ackermann, August. Werde selig! Gedanken zu den acht
Seligkeiten. Einsiedeln: Benziger, 1952; Gersau
(Schweiz): R. Müller, 1961.

Adeney, Walter F. "The Beatitudes." Expositor 5th ser. 2
(1895) 365-76.

Ainsworth, Percy C. The Blessed Life; Short Addresses on
the Beatitudes. London: Epworth Press, 1923.
    Previously published under the title: The Heart of
Happiness; the Blessed Life as Revealed in the Beatitudes.
(See his The Heart of Happiness)

_____. The Heart of Happiness; the Blessed Life as Re-
vealed in the Beatitudes. New York: Revell, 1910.
Sermons.

Alexander, William. The Eight Beatitudes. London: W.
Jackson, 1821.

Allen, Charles L. The Beatitudes. Westwood, N.J.: Revell, 1967.
Meditations. Contains drawings by Ismar David.

Allen, R. Earl. Divine Dividends; an Inspirational Reading
of the Sermon on the Mount. Nashville: T. Nelson, 1974.
Sermons on the Beatitudes.

Anderson, Robert. Discourses on the Beatitudes. London:
J. Hatchard and Son, 1837.
Sermons.

Arnold, Frank S. The Octave of Blessing; a Present-day
Application of the Beatitudes. Chicago: Theodore Reese,
1895.
Sermons.

Asensio Nieto, Félix. Le Beatitudini. Roma: Libreria
Editrice dell'Università Gregoriana, 1970.
(See his Las Bienaventuranzas)

_____. Las Bienaventuranzas; avances de luz en el An-
tiguo Testamento y luz llena en el Nuevo. Bilboa: Editorial el Mensajero del Corazón de Jesús, 1958.
A method of exegesis whereby the author relates the
Beatitudes to the Old Testament and attempts to find their
roots there.

Ashrea, 1665, by E. M. Facsimile reprint of the 1st ed.
London: W. P., 1665. Varously attributed to Edward
Manning and Edward Mico. Menston, Yorkshire, England:
Scolar Press, 1970.
The Beatitudes are symbolized by a grove in which are
eight trees. Each tree is emblematic of one of the Beati-
tudes. The author describes the characteristics of these
respective trees and relates them to the Christian life.
A meditation on each of the Beatitudes follows the em-
blematic tree which symbolizes it.

Bailey, T. Arthur. Messages of the Beatitudes. London:
R. Scott, 1914.

Baker, Eric W. The Neglected Factor; the Ethical Element
in the Gospel. New York: Abingdon, 1963.
Popular exposition of the Beatitudes. Delivered as the
Fred J. Cato Lecture at the General Conference of the
Methodist Church of Australasia.

Baker, Gordon P. "Constant Meek." Interpretation 7 (1953)
34-41.

_____. In the School of Christ; the Meaning of the Beati-
tudes for Today. Nashville: Tidings, 1962.
Sermons.

Bannach, Horst. Das erträumte und das wirkliche Glück.
Eine Auslegung die Seligpreisungen. Hamburg: Furche-
Verlag, 1957.

Barclay, William. The Beatitudes and the Lord's Prayer for
Everyman. New York: Harper and Row, 1968 (1975).
(See his The Plain Man Looks at the Beatitudes. This
work is combined with The Plain Man Looks at the Lord's
Prayer.)

_____. Freut euch frohlocket. Eine Anleitung zum Ver-
ständnis der Seligpreisungen. Übers. Annemarie Oesterle.
Kassel: Oncken-Verlag, 1968.
(See his The Plain Man Looks at the Beatitudes)

_____. The Plain Man Looks at the Beatitudes. London:
Collins, 1963.
The substance of lectures given over the years to the
author's students in Trinity College, Glasgow. A good
synthesis of scholarship and readability.

Barrett, George W. Christ's Keys to Happiness. New
York: World Publishing Co., 1970.
Meditations. Relates the Beatitudes to the seven say-
ings of Jesus on the cross.

Bartina, Sebastián. "Los macarismos del Nuevo Testamento; estudio de la forma." Estudios eclesiásticos 34
(1960) 57-88.
Also: Semana Biblica Espanhola XIX (1958) 319-49.

Bassi, D. "Le Beatitudini nella struttura de De Sermone
Dei in Monte e nelle altre opere di S. Agostino." Miscel-
lanea Agostiniana 2 (1931) 915-31.

Batdorf, Irvin W. Interpreting the Beatitudes. Philadelphia:
Westminster Press, 1966.
A critical exegesis which seeks to bridge the gulf between the scholar and the layman. Views the Beatitudes
in light of contemporary source materials. A good, readable work which uses the Beatitudes to introduce a wide
range of historical and critical problems and interpretations.

The Beatitudes for today: with selected scriptures. Compiled and illustrated by Royal V. Carley. Norwalk, Conn.:
C. R Gibson Co., 1975.
Each Beatitude is followed with selected scriptural passages. Illustrated with photographs in black and white and
color.

Beaucamp, E. "La salutation inaugural du livre des
Psaumes." Eglise et Théologie 1 (1970) 135-46.

Behringer, William. Mary and the Beatitudes. Staten Island,
N.Y.: Alba House, 1964.
Mary has not added any new doctrine or development to

the Beatitudes. But she is an example of a person who has given a total and complete adherence to the life expressed in the Beatitudes. She shows what a complete living of the Beatitudes means--and in the context of an ordinary human life.

Benedict, Wayland R. New Studies in the Beatitudes and the Lord's Prayer. Cincinnati: Earhart and Richardson, 1894.
    Lectures delivered at the University of Cincinnati. Practical treatment.

Bereczky, Albert. Der Becher fliesst über. Eine Auslegung der Seligpreisungen für unsere Zeit. Übers. Liselotte M. Somoskeőy und Hans Bürki-Fillenz. Wuppertal: R. Brockhaus, 1956; Berlin: Evangelische Verlagsanstalt, 1958.
    (See his Boldogok)

_____. Boldogok. Jézus nyolc Boldogmondása. 2. kiad. Budapest: Magyarorsz. Ref. Egyház Egyet. Konventje, 1949.
    Sermons.

Berger, Klaus. "Die sogenannte Sätze heiligen Rechts im N. T." Theologische Zeitschrift 28 (1972) 305-30.

Bernasconi, E. Las Bienaventuranzas. Trad. Alejo Oria León. Zalla: Edic. Paulinas, 1960.

Bertrangs, Albert. Les Béatitudes. Trad. du néerlandais. Bruxelles: La Pensée catholoqie; Paris: Office général du livre, 1962.

Bessières, Albert. Les Béatitudes et la civilisation. Paris: Éditions Spes, 1943.
    The way of the Beatitudes is presented as an antidote to the maladies that afflict our civilization. The Beatitudes express the primacy of the Spirit and of love.

Besson, Nicolas François Louis. Les Béatitudes de la vie chrétienne; ou, La dévotion envers le Sacré Coeur. Paris: Bray et Retaux, 1879.
    Devotional studies on the Sacred Heart including a section on the Beatitudes.

Best, E. "Matthew V. 3." New Testament Studies 7 (1960-61) 255-58.

Black, Matthew. "The Beatitudes." Expository Times 64
(1952-53) 125-26.

Bläser, Pedro. "Las Bienaventuranzas (Mt. 5, 3-10; Lc.
6, 20-26)." Revista biblica 18 (1956) 20-24, 91-97.

Blauvelt, Mary T. Ultimate Ideals. Boston: Sherman,
French, 1917.
Popular exposition of the Beatitudes.

Blunt, Hugh F. The New Song; Thoughts on the Beatitudes.
Ozone Park, N.Y.: Catholic Literary Guild, 1941; St.
Nazians, Wis.: Society of the Divine Savior (Salvatorian
Seminary) Publishing Dept., 1945.
Practical and popular interpretation.

Boehmer, J. "Die erste Seligpreisung." Journal of Biblical
Literature 45 (1926) 298-304.

Bohren, Rudolf. Seligpreisungen der Bibel--heute. Zürich:
Stuttgart: Zwingli Verlag, 1963; Neukirchen-Vluyn: Neu-
kirchener Verlag des Erziehungsvereins, 1969.
Sermons.

Bolo, Henry. Béatitudes. Les coeurs détachés. Les doux et
humbles. Paris: R. Haton, 1899.
Practical interpretation.

_____. The Beatitudes: the Poor in Spirit, the Meek and
Humble. Trans. Madame Cecelia. London: Kegan Paul,
1906.
(See his Béatitudes. Les coeurs détachés. Les doux
et humbles)

Boreham, Frank W. The Heavenly Octave; a Study of the
Beatitudes. London: Epworth Press, 1935 (1936); New
York: Abingdon, 1936; Grand Rapids: Baker Book House,
1968.
Sermons.

Bourbeck, Christine. Das Alter im Lichte der Seligpreisungen. Gladbeck: Schriftenmissions-Verlag, 1963.

Bourne, Arthur. "The Guide of the Beatitudes." Wesleyan
Methodist Magazine 120 (1897) 213-16.

Bowman, John Wick. "An Exposition of the Beatitudes."
Journal of Biblical Literature 15 (1947) 162-70.

_____. "Travelling the Christian Way--the Beatitudes."
Review and Expositor 54 (1957) 377-92.

Braumann, G. "Zum traditionsgeschichtlichen Problem der
Seligpreisungen Mt. 5, 3-12." Novum Testamentum 4
(1960) 253-60.

Bretscher, Paul G. The World Upside Down or Right Side
Up? St. Louis: Concordia, 1964.
    Bretscher begins with the conviction that man's vision
and values are inverted and that Jesus Christ has come
to convert them right side up. Applying this typology to
the Beatitudes, he finds in them the most dramatic dichotomy between the life that is right side up and that which
is upside down.

Brett, Jesse. The Blessed Life; Devotional Studies of the
Beatitudes. London: Longmans, Green, 1903.

Brown, Milton P. "Matthew as εἰρηνοποιός (Matt. 5:9),"
in Studies in the History and Text of the New Testament
in Honor of Kenneth Willis Clark. Salt Lake City: University of Utah Press, 1967, 39-50.

Brown, R. E. "The Beatitudes According to Luke," in New
Testament Essays. Milwaukee: Bruce, 1965, 265-71.

Buchholz, Friedrich. "Predigt über Matthäus 5. 1-12."
Evangelische Theologie 14 (1954) 97-104.

Buitendijk, S. H. De Zaligsprekingen des Heeren. Does-
borgh: Van Schenk Brill, 1866.
    Sermons.

Bunch, Taylor G. The Beatitudes. Washington, D.C.: Review and Herald, 1938.
    Brief interpretation in homiletical form.

_____. The Road to Happiness. Washington, D.C.: Re-
view and Herald, 1960.
    Sermons.

Burns, Sister Fernando. "Use of Beatitudes in the Guidance
Program in High School." Masters' thesis. Catholic
University of America, 1944.

Burr, John. The Crown of Character; a Study of the Beatitudes of Our Lord. London: J. Clarke, 1932.

Burroughs, Jeremiah. The Saints Happinesse. London:
Printed by M. S. for Nathaniel Brook, and for Thomas
Parkhurst, 1660; Edinburgh: James Nichol; London:
James Nisbet; Dublin: G. Herbert, 1867.
Sermons.

Buttrick, George A. The Beatitudes; a Contemporary Meditation. Nashville: Abingdon, 1968.
Meditations. Illustrations by Diana Blank.

Buzy, D. "Béatitudes, " in Dictionnaire de Spiritualité I.
Paris: G. Beauchesne et ses Fils, 1937, col. 1298-1310.

Canclini, Santiago. Más allá de la violencia: las bienaven-
turanzas de Jesús y el christianismo auténtico. Buenos
Aires: Junta Bautista de Publicaciones, 1974.
Brief, popular expositions.

Capecelatro, Alfonso. Le virtú christiane. 2. ed. Roma:
Desclée, 1913.
The first part of the book discusses faith, hope, love,
and the cardinal virtues. This is followed by Jesus' view
of virtue as expressed in the Beatitudes.

Carré, Ambrosius-M. Quand arrive le bonheur: les béatitudes. Paris: Editions du Cerf, 1974.
Concentrates on such crucial questions as suffering,
peace, violence, in light of the Beatitudes. The Beatitudes are the way of blessedness or happiness for man.

Casabona, J. "Encore Mathieu V, 3." Bulletin de l'Association Guillaume Budé. 1960, 106-12.

Cazelles, H. "Béatitude. I--L'Idée de béatitude dans la
Sainte Écriture, " in Catholicisme I. Paris: Letouzey et
Ané, 1948, col. 1342-46.

Chapin, Edwin H. Discourses on the Beatitudes. Boston:
Universalist Publishing House, 1853; Abel Thomkins, 1855
(1860).
Sermons.

Charles, R. H. "The Beatitudes." Expository Times 28
(1916-17) 536-41.

Chevignard, B. M. "Bienheureux vous qui êtes pauvres."
Lumière et Vie 7 no. 39 (1958) 53-60.

Chevré, Henry. Les Béatitudes, mon curé parle. Paris: Beauchesne et ses Fils, 1942.
Meditations.

Chevrot, Georges. Les Béatitudes. Bruges: Desclée de Brouwer, 1952.

_____. Las Bienaventuranzas. 2. ed. Trad. Luis Horno Livria. Madrid: Rialp, 1959 (1962) (1966) (1970). (See his Les Béatitudes)

_____. The Eight Beatitudes. Trans. J. A. McArdle. Dublin: Scepter, 1959.
(See his Les Béatitudes)

Chew, B. "Happiness of Heaven." Christianity Today 7 (Jan. 18, 1963) 12-14.
Sermon.

Chrysostom, John. Les Béatitudes. Montreal: Fides, 1944. In Les grands auteurs spirituels vol. 1, no. 2, 1944-46.
Homilies.

CISCA. "The Eight Beatitudes, the Truly Christian Way of Life." Journal of Religious Instruction 11 (1940) 146-70, 242-63, 328-49; (1941) 417-34.

Clarke, W. K. Lowther. "Studies in Texts." Theology 47 (1944) 131-33 [Mt. 5:5].

Clowes, John. Sermons on the Beatitudes, and on Several Other Important Subjects of Christian Life and Doctrine. Leamington: Rose and Lapworth, 1825.
Sermons.

Coleridge, Henry J. The Preaching of the Beatitudes. London: Burns and Oates, 1881 (1892).
A commentary intended to assist meditation. Emphasizes the theological and practical meaning of Jesus' teaching.

Colunga, A. "Bienaventurados los mansos porque ellos poseeran la tierra." Salmanticensis 9 (1962) 589-97.

Corley, D. H. "The Modius." American Journal of Semitic Languages and Literature 39 (1922-23) 71.

Cotter, W. E. P. "The Meek." Expository Times 33
(1921-22) 280.

Crock, Clement H. The Eight Beatitudes. New York:
Joseph F. Wagner, 1953.
    Popular study. Chapters on each of the eight Be-
atitudes are preceded by discussions on the moral and
physical setting of the Beatitudes and of beatitudes in
general.

Crum, George C. The Mount of Blessing; or, Lectures
on the Beatitudes. New York: Methodist Book Concern, 1848; Cincinnati: L. Swormstedt & Poe, 1854
(1859).

DeCarlo, Cornelio. Se vuoi vivere felice. Isola del Gran
Sasso: Eco, 1968.
    Meditations.

Delastre, Jehanne Marie. Béatitudes pour un petit enfant.
Marcy-l'Etoile: A. Rivoire, 1948.

Delebecque, Édouard. "À propos de Matthieu, V. 3." Bulletin de l'Association Guillaume Budé. 1959, 326-31.

Delimat, Casimir A. Ascent; Spiritual Progress According
to the Beatitudes. New York: St. Paul Publications,
1960.
    A practical interpretation which views the Beatitudes
as general principles of morality and a compendium of
religious perfection.

D'Elpidio, Raimondo. Le Beatitudini oggi. Napoli: Edizioni Domenicane Italiane, 1969.
    A study dealing with critical, theological, and practical
issues. Can be used for spiritual exercises, retreats,
conferences, and study and teaching.

Devine, Minos. The Religion of the Beatitudes. London:
Macmillan, 1918.
    Addresses given during Lent. Author endeavors to re-
enforce the teaching of the Beatitudes by illustrations
from history, biography, and literature. Contains brief
appendix on Tolstoy and the Sermon on the Mount; Luke's
version of the Beatitudes; other points of view on the Beatitudes; a Quaker's view of war in the light of the Sermon on the Mount.

Dillenberger, Josef. Der neue Mench. Seligpreisungen und Tugendleben. Einsiedeln: Benziger, 1949.
This work begins with a discussion of St. Thomas' interpretation of the cardinal virtues. There follows a study of the Beatitudes which compares them with the cardinal virtues as a standard for the virtuous life.

Dobrosmyslov, D. "Evangel'skie zapovedi o blazhenstvakh kak uchenie o vysshikh stepeniakh khristianskoi nravstvennosti sravnitel'no s vetkhozavetnym zakonom." Vera i Razum 11, 1889.

Dodd, C. H. "The Beatitudes " in Mélanges bibliques en l'honneur de André Robert. Paris: Bloud et Gay, 1957, 404-10.
Also: "The Beatitudes: a Form Critical Study," in More New Testament Studies. Manchester: Manchester University Press, 1968, 1-10.

Doll, Ludwig C. K. Der sichere Weg zur Seligkeit, dargelegt in acht Predigten über die Seligpreisungen unseres Herrn und Heilandes, Matth. 5, 3-12. Neukirchen bei Moers: Missions-Buchhandlung Stursberg & Cie, 1885. Sermons.

Dumont, C. J. "Les Béatitudes et l'esprit d'unité." Vie spirituelle 88 (1952) 5-19.

Dupont, Jacques. Les Béatitudes. 2 vols. Bruges: Abbaye de Saint-Andre, 1954 (1958); Paris: J. Gabalda et Cie, 1969.
An extensive and scholarly study of the literary problems of the Matthean and Lucan parallels of the Sermon on the Mount and the Beatitudes. The entire second volume is on the Beatitudes.

_____. "Béatitudes égyptiennes." Biblica 47 (1966) 185-222.

_____. "L'interpretation des Béatitudes." Foi et Vie 65 (1966) 17-39.

_____. "Les pauvres en esprit," in A la recontre de Dieu: Mémorial Albert Gelin. Le Puy: Editions Xavier Mappus, 1961, 265-72.

_____. "Les πτωχοί τῷ πνεύματι de Matthieu 5, 3 et les רוח ענוי de Qumrân," in Neutestamentliche Auf-

sätze. Festschrift für Josef Schmid zum 70. Geburtstag.
Hrsg. J. Blinzler, O. Kuss, F. Mussner. Regensburg:
Verlag Friedrich Pustet, 1963, 53-64.

Dykes, James O. The Beatitudes of the Kingdom. London:
James Nisbet, 1872; New York: Robert Carter, 1873.
Popular exposition.

Eifert, William H. The Lamb and the Blessed; a Series of
Sermons for Lent and Easter. St. Louis: Concordia
Publishing House, 1964.
Sermons.

Ejarque, R. "Beati pauperes spiritu." Verbum Domini 8
(1928) 126-33, 234-37, 334-41.

Elliott, Norman K. Great Is Your Reward; Living the Beatitudes. Westwood, N.J.: Revell, 1966.
Presentation of the Beatitudes as guidelines, methods,
means, and insights by which one may attain fulfillment,
happiness, and wholeness. Homiletical style.

Emtrage, Harold G. Addresses on the Beatitudes. London:
Skeffington and Son, 1929.

Estang, Luc. Les Béatitudes. Paris: Gallimard, 1945.

Evans, Colleen T. A New Joy. Old Tappan, N.J.: Revell:
1973.
Describes the relevance of the Beatitudes for the religious life of modern woman.

Eyton, Robert. The Beatitudes. 2d ed. London: Kegan
Paul, Trench, Trübner, 1896.
Sermons.

Fachinetti, Vittorino. Le beatitudini. 2 ed. Milano: S.
Lega eucaristica, 1933.

Faivre, Nazaire. Les Béatitudes. Apostolat de la presse,
n. d.

Farano, Vincenzo M. Le Beatitudini. Roma: Centro Vo-
lontari della Sofferenza, 1969?
Spiritual exercises.

Farrer, John. Sermons on the Mission and Character of
Christ and on the Beatitudes. Oxford: University Press,

1804.
Book of sermons, the last half of which is on the Beatitudes.

Fischer, Gustaf A. Predigten über die acht Seligkeiten.
München: J. Lindauer, 1834.
Sermons.

Fisher, Robert H. The Beatitudes. New York: Charles
Scribner's Sons, 1912.
A popular study designed to aid ministers, laymen,
and Sunday School teachers.

————. The Beatitudes. Edinburgh: T. and T. Clark,
1937.
Sermons.

Fitch, William F. "Beatitudes." Eternity 11 (Aug. 1960)
9-11; (Sept. 1960) 15-17; (Oct. 1960) 11-13f.; (Dec. 1960)
25-28f.; 12 (Feb. 1961) 21-23; (April 1961) 15-17f.; (June
1961) 12-14f.; (Aug. 1961) 12-14f.; (Oct. 1961) 20-22f.;
(Nov. 1961) 11-13f.

————. The Beatitudes of Jesus. Grand Rapids: Eerdmans, 1961.
Popular interpretation with frequent use of poetry. Illustrations by Armand Merizon.

Fix, Kar. Die sieben Seligpreisungen in der Offenbarung
Jesu Christi. Neue Schriften der Volksmission. Nr. 76.
Schorndorf/Württemberg Aarburg: Harfe-Verlag, 1957.

Flusser, D. "Blessed Are the Poor in Spirit." Israel Ex-
ploration Journal 10 (1960) 1-13.

Fonck, L. "'Beati...!' (Mt. 5, 1-12)." Verbum Domini 2
(1922) 321-27.

Foston, Hubert. The Beatitudes (Matt. V:3-9) and the Contrasts (Luke VI:20-26): a Study in Methodic Interpretation.
London: James Clarke, 1911.
An exposition which stresses the symmetry of the Beatitudes which is manifested by a balanced reference to
the inner and the outer life in each of the Beatitudes.
They express life's inward condition and its outward social conduct.

Franck, César. Les Béatitudes. Oslo: A. W. Brøggers

boktr., 1932.

Frankemölle, H. "Die Markarismen (Mt. 5:1-12; Lk. 6:20-
23). Motive und umfang der redaktionellen Komposition."
Biblische Zeitschrift 15 (1971) 52-75.

Franzmann, M. H. "Beggars before God. The First Beatitude." Concordia Theological Monthly 18 (1947) 889-99.

Friedrich, Hans. Nur selig! Betrachtungen über die sieben
Seligpreisungen des Herrn. Gross-Salze: E. Strien, 1912.

Fritzsche, Klara. Die Seligpreisungen Jesu: Vortragsdich-
tungen. Berlin-Friedrichshagen: Jugendbund-Buchhandlung,
1922.

Garbett, James. The Beatitudes on the Mount, in Seventeen
Sermons. London: Hatchard, 1854.
       Sermons.

Gardeil, A. "Béatitudes évangéliques." Dictionnaire de
théologie catholique 12 (1923) 515-17.

Gauthier, François Louis. Réflexions chrétiennes sur les
huit Béatitudes; ou Les huit moyens enseignés par Jesus-
Christ, pour parvenir au véritable bonheur. Paris: B.
Morin, 1783.
       A lengthy exposition which employs frequent Scriptural
references as well as references to the Church Fathers.

George, Augustin. "La 'Forme' des Béatitudes jusqu'à
Jésus," in Mélanges bibliques rédigés en l'honneur de
André Robert. Paris: Bloud et Gay, 1957, 398-403.

_____. "Hereux les coeurs purs! Ils verront Dieu!
(Matth. 5.8)." Bible et Vie chrétienne 13 (1956) 74-79.

Gilbert, Jesse S. Blessed Are They; or, Thoughts on the
Beatitudes. Paterson, N.J.: Carleton M. Herrick, 1890.
       Sermons.

Graham, William F. Het Geheim van het Geluk. Vert.
T. B. van Houten. Zwolle: La Rivière & Voorhoeve,
1956.
       (See his The Secret of Happiness)

_____. Das Geheimnis des Glücks. Hinweise zu einem

glücklichen Leben nach den Seligpreisungen der Bergpredigt. Übers. Ulrich Wever. Wuppertal: Brockhaus,
1956 (1960).
(See his The Secret of Happiness)

_____. Le Secret du bonheur. Trad. Madeleine Blan-
denier. Vevey: Ed. des Groupes Missionaires, 1956.
(See his The Secret of Happiness)

_____. The Secret of Happiness. Garden City, N.Y.:
Doubleday, 1955 (1968).
    The well-known evangelist gives a practical interpreta-
tion of the Beatitudes as a formula for personal happiness.

_____. El secreto de la felicidad. Trad. Ramón Taibo
Sienes. Barcelona: Alturas, 1968 (1969) (1970).
(See his The Secret of Happiness)

Gregory of Nyssa, St. The Lord's Prayer and the Beatitudes.
Trans. and annotated by Hilda C. Graef. Westminster,
Md.: Newman Press, 1954; London: Longmans, Green,
1954.
Sermons.

Griffith, Arthur L. Pathways to Happiness; a Devotional
Study of the Beatitudes. New York: Abingdon, 1964.
    Brief popular exposition of each of the eight Beatitudes.
Each exposition is concluded with a prayer.

Grounds, V. C. "Mountain Manifesto." Bibliotheca Sacra
128 (1971) 135-41.

Guder, Eileen L. Living in Both Worlds. Grand Rapids:
Zondervan, 1968.
    Emphasizes the practical guidelines for Christian con-
duct found in the Beatitudes.

Gyldenvand, Lily M. Invitation to Joy. Minneapolis: Augsburg, 1969.
Meditations.

Haering, Theodor von. Die Seligpreisungen Jesu, Matth. 5,
1-12. Hamburg: E. Salzer, 1918.
Sermons.

Hahn, Traugott. Die Seligpreisungen. Kurze Bibelstunden
über Matth. 5, 1-12. Gütersloh: C. Bertelsmann, 1924.

Hall, Charles A.   The Blessed Way.   London: New-Church
Press, 1929.

Haller, Eduard.   Heil und Friede unter dem Kreuz.   Eine
Anleitung wie wir in den Seligpreisungen Jesu leben sollen.
Neuendettelsau: Freimund-Verlag, 1959.

Hambleton, John.   Sermons on the Beatitudes.   London: J.
Hatchard and Son, 1831.
Sermons.

Hamby, Warren C.   Eight Keys to Happiness; a New Look at
the Beatitudes.   Westwood, N. J. :   Revell, 1969.
Sermons.

Hastings, Robert J.   Take Heaven Now!   Nashville: Broadman
Press, 1968.
Sermons.

Hatzfeld, Johannes.   Die acht Seligpreisungen in unserer Zeit.
Paderborn: Bonifacius-Druckerei, 1948.

Hayes, Doremus A.   The Heights of Christian Blessedness; a
Study of the Beatitudes.   New York: Abingdon, 1928.
    A lengthy study with a strong pacifist emphasis.   About
a third of the book is devoted to the seventh Beatitude.

Heard, Gerald.   Die Bergpredigt.   Die Exerzitienschule der
Seligpreisungen.   Zürich: Origo Verlag, 1959.
    (See his The Code of Christ)

_____.   The Code of Christ; an Interpretation of the Beati-
tudes.   New York: Harper, 1941.
    A series of addresses which forms a sequel to the
author's book on the Lord's Prayer.   The Beatitudes are
the consequences of prayer.   They show the divine policy,
the line of action, possible to those who have become pro-
ficient in the life of prayer.   Heard interprets the Beatitudes by the categories of purgation, proficiency, perfection.

Heim, Karl.   Der Himmel auf Erden.   Predigt über die Selig-
preisungen Jesu.   2. Aufl.   Stuttgart: Quell-Verlag der
Evangelischen Gesellschaft, 1947.
Sermons.

Heitmüller, Friedrich.   Die Glückseligkeit der Jünger Christi.
Hamburg: Christliche Gemeinschaftsbuchhandlung, 1929.

Herder, Johann G.   "Uber die Seligpreisungen Jesu. Matth.
5, 1-12," in Sämmtliche Werke.   Zur Religion und Theologie.   Neunter Theil.   Stuttgart und Tübingen: J. G.
Cotta, 1828, 189-201.

Hirzel, Rudolf.   Und er sprach: "Selig sind...!"   St. Gallen:
Verlag der Evangelischen Gesellschaft, 1945.
Nine sermons.

Hobbs, Herschel H.   Showers of Blessings.   Grand Rapids:
Baker Book House, 1973.
First third of the book consists of meditations on the
Beatitudes.   The remainder consists of meditations on
various aspects of the Christian life.

Hutchison, Harry.   The Beatitudes and Modern Life.   New
York: Morehouse-Barlow, 1960.
Practical treatment which views the Beatitudes as the
essence of personal Christianity and as the dynamic expression in personal living.   Includes an appendix with
questions for private meditation or group discussion.

Hyslop, James.   The Blessing that Maketh Rich; Meditations
on the Beatitudes.   New York: Loizeaux Brothers, 1951.
Meditations.

Insolera, Vincenzo.   Le Beatitudini evangeliche.   Stile della
vita christiana.   Roma: Stella Matutina, 1971.
Meditations.

Instruction chrétienne sur les huit Béatitudes par demandes
& résponses.   Tirée des SS. Pères de l'Eglise, & en
particulier de S. Augustin.   Avec des prières & aspirations
sur chaque instruction.   Paris: Witte, F. Crevier, 1732.
Explication of the Beatitudes and their relationship to
the blessed life in question and answer form.

Jameson, John G.   The Way of Happiness; or, The Prelude
to the Good News; a Study of the Beatitudes.   London:
W. Hodge, 1946.
A popular exposition of each of the eight Beatitudes.
As the title suggests, the Beatitudes are the way to hap-
piness.

Johnston, Howard A.   The Beatitudes of Christ; a Study of
the Way of the Blessed Life.   Chicago: Winona Publish-

ing Co., 1905.
  Sermons.

Jones, Arthur. "'Blessed are the pure in (of) heart, for
  they shall see God' (Matt. V. 8)." Expository Times 31
  (1919-20) 522-43.

Jones, John D. The Way into the Kingdom; or, Thoughts on
  the Beatitudes. London: Religious Tract Society, 1900;
  Allenson, 1934.

Jordan, John. Sermons on the Beatitudes. Ripon: 1830.
  Sermons.

Kaiser, Paul. Blessed Are Ye: a Series of Sermons on the
  Beatitudes. Burlington, Iowa: German Literary Board,
  1906.
  Sermons.

Karch, Georg. Über die Makarismen. Aschaffenburg:
  Wailandt's Wittib, n. d.
  Scholarly monograph on the Beatitudes.

Kealy, Gerard A. "The Reaction of Junior Boys in High
  School to the Beatitudes." Masters' thesis. Catholic
  University of America, 1952.

King, Henry C. "The Fundamental Conditions of Happiness
  as Revealed in Jesus' Beatitudes." Biblical World 24
  (1904) 180-87.

Kleine, Richard. Die acht Seligpreisungen der Bergpredigt.
  Die Richtlinien des Reiches Gottes als Predigtreihe.
  Paderborn: Schöningh, 1935.

Klöpper, A. "Über den Sinn und die ursprungliche Form der
  ersten Seligpreisung der Bergpredigt bei Matthäus." Zeitschrift für wissenschaftliche Theologie 37 (1894) 175-91.

Koch, Robert. "'Beati mundo corde' (Mt. 5. 8)." Verbum
  Domini 20 (1040) 9-18.

Kühn, W. E. Die Seligpreisungen. Andachten. Gütersloh:
  Gütersloher Verlagshaus, 1961.

Kühnel, Josef. Die acht Seligkeiten. Meitingen bei Augsburg: Kyrios-Verlag, 1951.

Kuperschmid, Alfred. Ihnen gehört das Himmelreich. Eine Handreichung für die Stille. Bern: Berchtold Haller Verlag, 1961.
Meditations on the Beatitudes.

Landriot, Jean François Anne Thomas. Les Béatitudes évangéliques. 2 vols. Paris: Palmé, 1866-67.
Conferences for women.

Lang, Hugo. Die acht Seligkeiten. Rundfunkpredigten. München: Glocken, 1946 (1947).
Sermons.

Lang, Marshall B. "The Beatitudes in the Twenty-third Psalm." Expository Times 10 (1898-99) 46-47.

Lasance, Francis X. The Beatitudes. New York: Benzinger, 1940.
Contains selections of devotional literature arranged under each of the Beatitudes. Concluding section gives brief exemplifications of the eight Beatitudes in the lives of saints.

Lathbury, Clarence. The Code of Joy. Germantown, Pa.: Swedenborg Publishing Assoc., 1902.
Practical treatment of the Beatitudes as the requisites of perfect manhood.

Laubscher, Friedrich. Die Regierungserklärung Jesu. Die acht Seligpreisungen als das Programm des Christenlebens. Stuttgart: Verlag Junge Gemeinde, 1965.
Devotional exercises intended for students.

Lavallée, Fleury. Béatitudes. 2-e éd. Paris: Vitte, 1927.
Meditations.

Lawson, William. Good Christian Men Rejoice; the Meaning and Attainment of Happiness. New York: Sheed and Ward, 1955.
Practical study which sees the Beatitudes as the fulfillment of the self in God. They are blessings which mean our present happiness.

Légasse, Simon. "Les pauvres en esprit et les 'volontaires' de Qumran." New Testament Studies 8 (1962) 336-45.

Lemonnyer, A. "Le Messianisme des 'Béatitudes.'" Revue des sciences philosophiques et théologiques 11 (1922) 373-89.

Livingston, William J. B. "A Critical and Homiletical Treatment of the Beatitudes." Masters' thesis. Richmond, Va.: Union Theological Seminary, 1945.

Lopez Melus, Francisco Maria. Perspectivas de las Bienaventuranzas. 2. ed. Madrid: Casa de la Biblia, 1967.

Lowrie, Sarah D. Meditations on the Beatitudes. n. p., n. d. Meditations.

Lüthi, Walter. Les Béatitudes. Trad. Roland Revet. Neuchâtel: Delachaux et Niestlé, 1963.
(See his Die Seligpreisungen)

_____. Die Seligpreisungen. Ausgelegt für die Gemeinde. Basel: Friedrich Reinhardt, 1961.
Addresses given before various audiences.

_____. De Zaligsprekingen. Voor de gemeente verklaard. Vert. T. Van der Veen. Franeker: T. Wever, 1963.
(See his Die Seligpreisungen)

Luttichau, S. Graf von. Frohbotschaft. Die Auslegung von Matthäus 5, 1-12. 2. Aufl. Berlin: F. Zillessen, 1920. Sermons.

McCann, Samuel N. The Beatitudes. Elgin, Ill.: Brethren Publishing House, 1913. Meditations.

Macchioro, Vittorio. "The Meaning of the First Beatitude." Journal of Religion 12 (1932) 40-49.

McCown, C. C. "The Beatitudes in the Light of Ancient Ideals." Journal of Biblical Literature 46 (1927) 50-61.

MacDonald, William C. "The Singer of the Beatitudes." Theology Today 5 (1948) 13-14.

Mackay, Macintosh. A Practical Exposition of the First Ten Verses of the Fifth Chapter of the Gospel by Matthew. In Forty-one Sermons, Preached in the Parish Church of Dunoon, 1840-42. 2 vols. Edinburgh: W. Whyte, 1844-45. Sermons.

McKelvey, Gertrude D. Stories to Live by. Philadelphia:
John C. Winston Co., 1943 (1948).
Juvenile work. Illustrations by Pelagie Doane.

Mackintosh, Robert. "The Beatitudes." Expository Times
26 (1914-15) 415-18; 32 (1920-21) 519-20.

McLaren, Alexander. The Beatitudes and Other Sermons.
London: Alexander and Shepheard, 1896.
Sermons.

_____. A Garland of Gladness; Devotional Studies
in the Beatitudes. Grand Rapids: Eerdmans,
1945.
Sermons.

McMillan, Robert M. Happiness Is God's Gift. Nashville:
Broadman Press, 1970.
Practical interpretation with illustrations.

Martin, Hugh. The Beatitudes. London: S. C. M. Press,
1952; New York: Harper, 1953.
Brief study with questions for discussion.

Martinez, Louis-Marie. Les Béatitudes. Inclus. dans:
Le Saint-Espirit, tome 4. Trad. Arsène Croteau. Paris:
Téqui, 1962.

Masterman, John H. B. Aspects of Christian Character; a
Study of the Beatitudes. London: Longmans, Green, 1921.
Practical study designed for Lenten devotional reading.

Mather, Increase. Sermons Wherein Those Eight Characters
of the Blessed Commonly Called the Beatitudes Are Opened
and Applied in Fifteen Discourses. Boston: N. E.
Printed by B. Green, for Daniel Henchman, 1718.
Sermons.

Matthew 5:5 [Motion picture] Franciscan Communications
Center, 1973.

Matthews, Charles H. S. The Way to Happiness; Thoughts
on the Beatitudes. London: S. C. M. Press, 1934.

Maturin, Basil W. Laws of the Spiritual Life. New York:
Longmans, Green, 1908 (1916); Baltimore: Carroll Press,
1951.
Practical interpretation which presents the Beatitudes

as principles or laws of the spiritual life.

Maydieu, Augustin J. Les Béatitudes. Lyon: Éditions de
l'Abeille, 1943.
Sermons.

Mayer, Joseph E. Die acht Seligpreisungen Jesu. Wien:
Herder, 1948.
Homiletical expositions.

Meek, Frederick M. The Life to Live. New York: Oxford
University Press, 1955.
Sermons preached during Lent.

_____. Strong in the Strength which God Supplies (The
Mourners). A sermon preached in the Old South Church
in Boston, March 14, 1954.

Merchant, Jane. Blessed Are You. New York: Abingdon,
1961.
Series of devotional readings arranged under each of
the Beatitudes. Each devotional includes a Scripture
verse, a poem, and a prayer.

Meuss, Eduardus. Μακαρισμῶν. Jesu Christi usu ecclesiae publico receptorum historia. Vratislaviae: C.
Dülferum, 1865.
Academic address on the Beatitudes given at the in-
auguration of Professor P. O. Muneris.

Meyer, Frederick B. Blessed Are Ye; Talks on the Beati-
tudes. New York: Thomas Whittaker, 1898; Grand Rapids:
Baker Book House, 1955 (1971).
Sermons.

Michaelis, Christine. "Die P-Alliteration der Subjektsworte
der ersten 4 Seligpreisungen in Mt. V, 3-6 und ihre Bedeutung für den Aufbau der Seligpreisungen bei Mt., Lk.,
und in Q." Novum Testamentum 10 (1968) 148-61.

Michelet, Marcel. Les Béatitudes. St.-Maurice: Saint-
Augustin, 1939; N'empêchez pas la musique. 2. éd. St.-
Maurice: Saint-Augustin, 1974.
Popular exposition.

Miller, Andrew. Meditations on the Beatitudes and Christian
Devotedness. London: 1878.

Miller, James R. The Master's Blesseds; a Devotional
    Study of the Beatitudes. New York: Revell, 1898.
    Meditations.

Moberly, George. Sermons on the Beatitudes, with Others
    Mostly Preached before the University of Oxford. Oxford:
    J. Parker, 1860 (1870).
    Sermons.

Modersohn, Ernst. Selig, Selig. Betrachtungen über die
    Seligpreisungen der Bergpredigt. Neumünster: G. Ihloff,
    1923.

Morin, G. "Sermon inédit de S. Augustin sur les huit Bé-
    atitudes." Revue Bénédictine 34 (1922) 1-13.

Mortimer, Alfred G. The Laws of Happiness; or, The Be-
    atitudes as Teaching Our Duty to God, Self, and Neighbor.
    New York: E. and J. B. Young, 1888.
    Sermons.

Moulton, James H. "Synoptic Studies; I. The Beatitudes."
    Expositor 7th ser. 2 (1906) 97-110.

Müssle, Marianne. Der politische Jesus. Seine Bergpredigt.
    München: J. Pfeiffer, 1969.
    Essays on the Beatitudes by various authors.

Murphy, Charles. Blessed Are You; Beatitudes for Modern
    Man. New York: Herder and Herder, 1971.
    Popular approach which views the Beatitudes as the way
    of joy which is the way of the Christian life. Homiletical
    in style.

Murray, Jon E. "'The Beatitudes.'" Interpretation 1 (1947)
    374-76.

Nicolmann, Margarete. Die Seligpreisungen des Herrn in
    Mutterleben. Berlin: Sonnenweg-Verlag, 1938.

Nielsen, R. Die Seligpreisungen unsers Herrn in seiner
    Bergpredigt, in neun Predigten vorgetragen. Lübeck:
    1838.

Eeen nieuw volk. Tien meditaties over de Zaligsprekingen,
    uitgesproken in de "Avondstilten" in de Oude Kerk te Am-
    sterdam, door K. H. Miskotte, R. Dijkstra, G. A. den

Hertog, J. K. Lofvers, S. F. H. J. Berkelbach van der
Sprenkel, H. Voorham, A. H. Edelkoort. Amsterdam:
W. ten Have, 1941.

Norris, John. Practical Discourses upon the Beatitudes of
Our Lord and Saviour Jesus Christ. 2 vols. London:
Printed for S. Manship, 1699-1707.
Volume 1 contains sermons on the Beatitudes.

Nygaard, Norman E. The Heart of the Gospel; Studies in
the Beatitudes. N.Y.: Hobson, 1945.

Overduin, Jacobus. Gods grote verrassing. De Zaligsprekingen. Kampen: J. H. Kok, 1961 (1969).
Practical interpretation.

Pass, Herman L. The Divine Commonwealth; a Study in the
Beatitudes. London: A. R. Mowbray, 1936.
The first part of the book contains a discussion of
Jesus' teaching on the nature and scope of the Kingdom of
God. There follows an exposition of the Beatitudes as
summarizing in themselves the character and outlook of the
ideal citizen of the Kingdom. In three appendices the author discusses Augustine on the Beatitudes and the number,
order, and text of the Beatitudes. In the other the Beatitudes are given in seven English versions from Cover-
dale to Moffatt.

Paul, W. F. "Interprétation pratique des huit Béatitudes
tirées de l'Evangile selon Saint Matthieu, V, 3-10," in
Festschrift zu der zweiten Säcularfeier des Friedrichs-
Wederschen Gymnasiums zu Berlin veröffentlicht von dem
Lehrer-Kollegium des Friedrichs-Wederschen Gymnasiums.
Berlin: Weidmannsche Buchhandlung, 1881, 73-84. Also
published separately in 1887.
Brief exposition.

Peabody, Francis G. "The Peace-Makers." Harvard Theological Review 12 (1919) 51-66.

Pegarski, Bernard. The Olive Branch: the Ideal Home. The
Beatitudes. The Lord's Prayer. Montreal: Fides, 1943.
A book of meditations in three parts: the ideal home;
the Beatitudes; the Lord's prayer.

Peltier, Jean. Béatitudes. Saint-Calais (Sarthe): Lefeuvre,
1948.

Pendleton, William F. The Ten Blessings; a Series of
  Twelve Sermons. Bryn Athyn, Pa.: Academy Book
  Room, 1922.
    Sermons.

Pendleton, Winston K. Pursuit of Happiness; a Study of the
  Beatitudes. St. Louis: Bethany Press, 1963.
    A confessional statement by a newspaper man about how
  the Beatitudes have enriched his life.

Perrin, Joseph Marie. Die acht Seligkeiten als Botschaft
  der Freude. Übers. Joséphine Enekel. 2. Aufl. Basel:
  Freiburg: Wien: Herder, 1960.
    (See his L'Évangile de la joie)

_____. Het evangelie van de vreugde. Vert. H. J. G.
  Severens. Deurne (N. Br.): Sint Willibordus-Uitgeverij,
  1963.
    (See his L'Évangile de la joie)

_____. L'Évangile de la joie. Paris: Aubier, 1954.
    An interpretation of the Beatitudes in which joy is the
  central motif. The discussion of the Beatitudes is preceded and followed by sections on "Christian joy" and
  "Holiness through joy." Perrin holds that the Beatitudes
  impart no ordinary joy, but our Lord's joy itself.

_____. Gospel of Joy. Trans. P. D. Gilbert. West-
  minster, Md.: Newman Press, 1957.
    (See his L'Évangile de la joie)

Peters, Hermann. Die Seligpreisungen der Bergpredigt.
  Elberfeld: Evangelische Gesellschaft für Deutschland, 1932.

Peterson, Lancie E. The Beatitudes: a Latter-Day Saint
  Interpretation. Salt Lake City: Deseret Book Co., 1964.
    This book grew out of seminary and institute lectures
  given by the author. Contains frequent references to
  Mormon sources.

Pfister, Benjamin. Die Seligpreisungen. Bern: A. Francke,
  1926.
    Ten sermons.

Pichery, E. "Les Béatitudes." Vie spirituelle 11 (1924)
  105-34.

Pieper, Pastor in Sieburg. Die Seligpreisungen der Bibel
und die "Seligkeit," mit besonderer Berücksichtigung von
Matth. 5, 3ff. Elberfeld: R. L. Friderichs, 1876.
    Brief monograph on the Biblical meaning of blessedness
and the Beatitudes.

Pirot, Louis. "Béatitudes évangéliques," in Dictionnaire de
la Bible. Suppl. L Paris: Letouzey et Ané, 1928, col.
927-39.

Plotzke, Urban W. Gebot und Leben. Köln: J. P. Bachem
Verlag, 1954.
    Sermons.

_____. God's Own Magna Charta. Trans. J. Holland
Smith. Westminster, Md.: Newman Press, 1963.
    (See his Gebot und Leben)

Portaluppi, Angelo. Commento alle Beatitudini. Roma:
Sales, 1942.

Prince, Thomas. Ten Lectures on the Beatitudes. London:
Rivington, 1818.

Procknow, Herbert V. Meditations on the Beatitudes. Boston: W. A. Wilde, 1952; Inspirational Thoughts on the
Beatitudes. Grand Rapids: Baker Book House, 1970.
    Meditations.

Przybylaki, Lothar. Seligpreisungen als Feuer Gottes in
der Welt. Dortmund: C. Neumetzler, 1928.

Ragsdale, Ray W. Foundation for Reconciliation; the Beatitudes. Nashville: Tidings, 1960.
    Brief expositions with questions for discussion.

Rambach, Johann J. Betrachtungen über die acht Seligkeiten.
Jena: 1723.

Ranson, Guy H. "Persecuted for Righteousness' Sake."
Review and Expositor 53 (1956) 55-60.

Read, David H. C. The Pattern of Christ. New York:
Charles Scribner's Sons, 1967.
    Sermons.

Redhead, John A. Finding Meaning in the Beatitudes. Nashville: Abingdon, 1968.
Sermons.

Reid, James. The Key to the Kingdom; Studies in the Beatitudes. New York: George H. Doran Co., 1926.
Popular interpretation in homiletical style.

Reynolds, Myra. "Illustrations of the Beatitudes from English
Literature." Biblical World 11 (1898) 51-52.

Rezevskis (Resewski), Janis. "Die Makarismen bei Matthäus
und Lukas, ihr Verhältnis zueinander und ihr historischer
Hintergrund, " in Studia Theologica I. Riga: 1935, 157-
69.

Rice, Hillery C. God's Happy People. Anderson, Ind.:
Warner Press, 1965.
Sermons.

Richards, William C. The Mountain Anthem; the Beatitudes
in Rhythmic Echoes. Boston: Lothrop, Lee & Shephard,
1884.

Ridgeway, Charles J. The Mountain of Blessedness; a Course
of Addresses on the Beatitudes. London: Skeffington and
Son, 1888.
Sermons.

Rieger, Conrad. Richtiger und leichter Weg zum Himmel
durch acht Stufen der Seligkeit. Stuttgart: 1744.

Rife, J. Merle. "Matthew's Beatitudes and the Septuagint, "
in Studies in the History and Text of the New Testament
in Honor of Kenneth Willis Clark. Salt Lake City: University of Utah Press, 1967, 107-12.

Rijckenborgh, J. van. Het mysterie der Zaligsprekingen.
Met acht tekeningen van Henk Leene en muziek van Jos
Damme. Haarlem: Hora est, 1946.

_____. Das Mysterium der Seligpreisungen. Braun-
schweig: Ernst Gottschalk, 1960.

Rittelmeyer, Friedrich. Die deutsche Not im Licht Jesu.

Acht Kanzelreden über die Seligpreisung. München: C.
Kaiser Verlag, 1919.
Sermons.

Roberts, Robert E.   The Happy Heart; a Study in the Beatitudes.   London: Epworth Press, 1936.
Sermons.

Rohrdants, Theodor.   Das Eingangstor ins Himmelreich.
Schwerin: F. Bahn, 1925.
Sermons.

Romanes, Ethel.   Thoughts on the Beatitudes.   Milwaukee:
Morehouse, 1917.

Rongione, Louis A.   Conferences on the Beatitudes.   Philadelphia: Peter Reilly Co., 1959.
Conferences given on two occasions to Catholic Sisters.

Russell, Elbert.   The Beatitudes; a Series of Studies.   Garden City, N.Y.:   Doubleday, Doran, 1929.
Talks given at Lake Junaluska, N.C. which emphasize
the practical bearing of the Beatitudes on some contemporary problems and of the meaning of their blessedness.

Russell, William H.   "The Eight Beatitudes in the School
Program."   The Catholic Educational Review 26 (1928)
193-202.

St. George, Arthur.   The Blessings of Christian Philosophy;
Being a Treatise on the Beatitudes.   In a Familiar Dialogue between Doctor and Parishioner.   London: Printed
for W. Innye R. Manby, 1738.
Intended to acquaint the reader with the necessary
graces of the Christian life and a plea against "conceited
infidels and profane libertines." In a dialogue form between pastor and parishioner.

Saldarini, Giovanni.   Le Beatitudini evangeliche.   Milano:
O. R., 1969 (1971).
Meditations.

Sangran, Joaquín.   Las Bienaventuranzas.   Sevilla: Gráf.
Salesiana, 1969.

Schaumann, Leopold.   Die Seligpreisungen der Bergpredigt.
Königsburg: Verlag unter dem Kreuz, 1934.

Schenkel, Ernst. Die Seligpreisungen Jesu. Kirchenlengern/ Westfalen: Warte-Verlag, 1961.

Schick, Erich. Die Seligpreisungen. Jesu Seligkeitsworte als Geisteshilfe für den Weg des Jüngers. Hamburg: Furche-Verlag, 1954. Meditations.

Schmitthenner, Adolf. Die Seligpreisungen unseres Herrn. Praktisch ausgelegt und aus seinem Nachlasse. Hrsg. von Heinrich Bassermann. Tübingen: J. C. B. Mohr, 1908.

Schmitz, Emil. Les Béatitudes de l'Évangile et les promesses de la démocratie sociale. Trad. Abbé L. Collin. Paris: P. Lethielleux, 1902.
An exposition of the Beatitudes which relates them to social and political questions.

Schumm, Robert. Gifts of Grace; 13 Beatitudes. Danville, Ill.: Interstate Printers and Publishers, 1969.
Brief practical studies which seek to relate the Beatitudes to contemporary disciples.

Schweitzer, E. "Formgeschichtliches zu den Seligpreisungen Jesu." New Testament Studies 19 (1973) 121-26.

Seaver, George. The Beatitudes. London: S. P. C. K., 1948. Meditations.

Seligpreisungen heute. Band I. Foto-Text-Plakate. Eine Serie/9 Plakate. Gladbeck: Schriftenmissions-Verlag.

Die Seligpreisungen in Bildern unserer Zeit. Foto: Horst Baumann u. a. Gelnhausen: Burckhardthaus-Verlag, 1963.

Serafim, Archimandrite. Nashata nadezhda. Sofia: Sinodalno IZD-VO, 1957. Meditations.

Serval, Claude. Les Béatitudes. Editions du Scorpion, 1961.

Sheen, Fulton J. The Cross and the Beatitudes. New York: P. J. Kennedy and Sons, 1937.

Sermons which correlate the Beatitudes and the Seven
Last Words.

_____. Kreuz und Bergpredigt. Übers. Irene Steidle.
Aschaffenburg: Pattloch, 1956.
(See his The Cross and the Beatitudes)

Sibinga, J. Smit. "'Zalig de armen van geest.'" Vox
theologica 29 (1958) 5-15.

Simmons, Arthur. The Measure of a Christian; a Study of
the Beatitudes. London: Epworth Press, 1936.
Popular treatment which views the Beatitudes as giving
the answer to the question: What does it mean to be a
Christian?

Sloan, Mersene E. The Immortals, Who They Are; the Beatitudes in Daylight. St. Paul, Minn.: The Way Press,
1932.
Popular expositions.

Sloman, A. "'Blessed Are the Poor in Spirit,' Matt. V. 3;
cf. Luke VI. 20." Journal of Theological Studies 18
(1916-17) 34-35.

Smith, Charles Z. The Divine Constitution. Los Angeles,
Calif.: De Vorss, 1952.
Brief interpretation of each Beatitude arranged in ques-
tion and answer form.

Sockman, Ralph W. The Higher Happiness. New York:
Abingdon-Cokesbury, 1950.
A practical interpretation which draws on a wide range
of illustrations and quotations.

Stafford, Russell H. Paradoxes of the Kingdom; and Interpretation of the Beatitudes. Boston: Fort Hill Press,
1929.
Sermons.

Stamm, Frederick K. Seeing the Multitudes. New York:
Harper, 1943.
Sermons.

Steck, O. H. Israel und das gewaltsame Geschick der
Propheten. Untersuchungen zur Überlieferung des deu-
teronmistischen Geschichtsbildes im Alten Testament,

Spätjudentum und Urchristentum. Neukirchen-Vluyn: Neukirchener Verlag, 1967.

Stewart, Agnes M. Stories of the Beatitudes. New York:
D. & J. Sadler, n.d.

Stewart, Irma. The Beatitudes. New York: Privately
printed, 1948.
Meditations.

Stories on the Beatitudes. The Third.... n.p., n.d.

Stramare, P. T. "Le Beatitudini e la critica letteraria."
Rivista biblica 13 (1965) 31-39.

Strecker, G. "Die Makarismen der Bergpredigt." New
Testament Studies 17 (1971) 255-75.

Swayne, William S. The Beatitudes. Milwaukee: Morehouse, 1913.

Talks with a Child on the Beatitudes. Philadelphia: J. B.
Lippincott, 1868.
Exposition for children in story form.

Tapp, Roland W. New Light on the Beatitudes. Philadelphia:
Westminster Press, 1966.
Brief exposition in tract form. Contains King James
Version text and Tapp's paraphrase.

Tasker, John G. "Beatitude," in Hastings, James, ed. A
Dictionary of Christ and the Gospels. vol. 1. New York:
Charles Scribner's Sons, 1906, 176-80.

Tebbe, Walter. "Die zweite Seligpreisung (Matth. 5, 4)."
Evangelische Theologie 12 (1952-53) 121-28.

Tholuck, Friedrich A. "Uebereinstimmung unter den Ausle-
gern des n. Test., nebst einer Beurteilung der Auslegungen von Mt. 5, 3-5." Theologische Studien und Kritiken
5 (1832) 325-54.

Thurneysen, Eduard. Die Seligpreisungen. Predigt über
Matth. 5, 1-10. Basel: Reinhardt, 1943.
Sermons.

272 Bibliography

Tolzien, Gerhard. Die Seligpreisungen im Kriege. Kriegs-
Betstunden. Schwerin in Mecklenburg: F. Bahn, 1917.

Torrance, Thomas. The Beatitudes and the Decalogue. London: Skeffington and Son, 1921.

Tremel, Y. B. "Béatitudes et morale évangélique." Lumière et Vie 21 (1955) 83-102.

Tummer, Matthias. Predigtgedanken über die acht Seligkeiten. Angermund: Verlag Der Pflug, 1947.

Tuttle, R. G. "What Is Your Pleasure?" Christianity Today
2 (Aug. 18, 1958) 5-6.

Uhlig, Ewald. Die Seligpreisungen. Leipzig: Arwed
Strauch, 1916.
Sermons.

Van Roey, Joseph Ernest. Les Béatitudes évangéliques.
Liége: La Pensée catholique; Paris: Casterman, 1939.

Vann, Gerald. The Divine Pity; a Study in the Social Implications of the Beatitudes. New York: Sheed and Ward,
1946; Garden City, N.Y.: Doubleday, 1961; London:
Fontana, 1956 (8th impression, 1971).
A practical interpretation of the first seven Beatitudes.
In each of the seven chapters given to the Beatitudes there
is a discussion of one of the seven sacraments.

_____. Das göttliche Erbarmen. Eine Studie über die
Auswirkungen der Seligpreisungen im Gemeinschaftsleben.
Übers. Franz Ludwig Greb. Bonn: Verlag des Borro-
mäus-Vereins, 1950.
(See his The Divine Pity)

Vattioni, F. "Le beatitudini nella S. Scritura." Studi Sociali
2. Roma: 1962, 469-91.

Vernotte, P. et Delebecque, E. "À propos d'une interprétation de Mattieu, V, 3." Bulletin de l'Association
Guillaume Budé. 1960, 100-05.

Vila, David. Bienaventuranzas. Tarrasa, España: Editorial
Clie, 1967.
Sermons.

Vogel, Heinrich. Selig sind. Kurze Auslegung der Seligpreisungen. Berlin: Haus und Schule, 1948.
Brief interpretations of each of the Beatitudes.

_____. Selig sind. Die Seligpreisungen Matthäus 5, 1-12
ausgelegt in acht Predigten. Bad Salzuflen: MBK-Verlag,
1948.
Sermons.

Vowinckel, Emanuel. Die Seligpreisungen der Reichsgenossen.
Bethel bei Bielefeld: Verlagshaus der Anstalt Bethel, 1913.

Waitz, Hans. "Eine Parallele zu den Seligpreisungen aus
einem ausserkanonischen Evangelium." Zeitschrift für die
neutestamentliche Wissenschaft 4 (1903) 335-40.

Walker, Harold B. Ladder of Light; the Meaning of the Beatitudes. New York: Revell, 1951.
Practical approach which seeks to relate the Beatitudes
to the problems of ordinary living.

Walter, N. "Die Bearbeitung der Seligpreisungen durch
Matthäus," in Studia Evangelica IV. Berlin: Akademie
Verlag, 1968, 246-58.

Ward, John W. G. The Beauty of the Beatitudes. New York:
Revell, 1931.
Sermons.

Washburn, Edward A. The Beatitudes and Other Sermons.
New York: Dutton, 1884.
First 100 pages are sermons on the Beatitudes.

Watcyn-Williams, Morgan. The Beatitudes in the Modern
World. London: Student Christian Movement Press, 1935;
New York: Round Table Press, n.d.
Sermons preceded by two brief studies on the Kingdom
of God.

Watson, Alexander. Sermons on the Beatitudes. London:
Masters, 1850.
Sermons.

Watson, Thomas. The Beatitudes: an Exposition of Matthew
5:1-12. New ed., revised in layout. London: Banner of
Truth Trust, 1971.

A lengthy exposition with an evangelical emphasis.
Originally published, London, 1660.

Weir, T. H. "Matthew V. 3." Expository Times 24 (1912-
13) 44.

Wenzel, Theodor. Stille und unruhige Gedanken über die
Seligpreisungen. Berlin: Christlicher Zeitschriftenverlag,
1951.

Werder, Eberhard von. Die Wegweiser Gottes! Betrachtungen
über die Seligpreisungen. Dresden: Leipzig: Ungelenk in
Kommission, 1937.

Who Are the Blessed? or, Meditations on the Beatitudes.
Philadelphia: Lindsay and Blackiston, 1856.
Sermons by Gottlob F. Krotel.

Widmayer, Eliot. "The Attitude of Third Year High School
Boys toward the Beatitudes." Masters' thesis. Catholic
University of America, 1953.

Windisch, Hans. "Friedensbringer--Gottessöhne. Eine re-
ligionsgeschichtliche Interpretation der 7. Seligpreisung."
Zeitschrift für die neutestamentliche Wissenschaft 24
(1925) 240-60.

Wirt, Sherwood E. The Cross on the Mountain. New York:
Crowell, 1959; Magnificent Promise: a Fresh View of the
Beatitudes from the Cross. Chicago: Moody Press,
1964; London: Marshall, Morgan & Scott, 1965.
Popular treatment which seeks to interpret the Beatitudes, not so much as descriptions of the "ideal" life as
of the "crucified" life.

Wu, John C. H. The Interior Carmel: the Threefold Way
of Love. New York: Sheed and Ward, 1953.
A work on the spiritual life which interprets the Beatitudes as the "eight degrees of love." The author relates the "eight degrees of love" to the three stages of
the spiritual life set forth by St. John of the Cross.
These are: the purgative way, the illuminative way, the
unitive way.

_____. Inwendige Karmel. Wegen van de liefde. Hil-
versum: Paul Brand, 1963.
(See his The Interior Carmel)

De Zaligsprekingen en eenige andere dichterlijke ontboezemin-
gen. Door een vriend van bedrukten. Uitgegeven ten
behoeve van eene weduwe met 6 jeugdige kinderen. Dor-
drecht: H. J. Koebrugge, 1878.

Zarin, S. M. Zapoviêdl blazhenstva. Petrograd: Sinodal'-
naîâ tipografiîâ, 1915.
Scholarly analysis of the Beatitudes.

Zodiates, Spyros. The Pursuit of Happiness; an Exposition
of the Beatitudes of Christ in Matthew 5:1-11 and Luke
6:20-26, Based upon the Original Greek Text. Grand
Rapids: Eerdmans, 1966.
The author emphasizes the basic difference between
"blessed" and "happy." "Blessed" refers to the one
whose sufficiency is within him, while "happy" refers to
the one whose sufficiency comes from outside sources.
This is a lengthy book of meditations with an evangelical
emphasis.

APPENDIX

"Sermon on the Mount" in Various Languages

Africaans Bergrede

Albanian Predikim' i Malit

Arabic Mawᶜazat al-Jabal

Armenian Leran Kᶜaroz

Basque Juanac predicatcen
du mendi gainbatean

Batak Djamita na di dolok

Bengali Parbbate datta
Yíśura upadeśa

Bulgarian Propoved v planin-
ata

Burmese Thạhkin hkạrittaw
danmạ deithạnạ

Catalan Sermó en la montanya

Chinese Tun Shan pao hsün

Czech Kázání na hoře

Danish Bjerprædiken

Dutch Bergrede

English Sermon on the Mount

Estonian Mäejutlus

Finnish Vuorisaarna

French Sermon sur la
montagne

Gaelic Searmoin Chrìosd
air a' bheinn

German Bergpredigt

Greek Hē epi tou orous homilia

Gujarati Pahad parnu Bashan

Hebrew Derashat ha-har

Hindi Parvatapara kā pravacana

Hungarian Hegyi beszéd

Icelandic Fjallræðan

Indonesian Chotbah Tuhan Yésus
dibukit

Irish Seanmóir Chríost san
tslíabh

Italian Discorso della montagna

Japanese Sanjō no suikun

Javanese Piwulangé Gusti ana
ing gunung

Korean Sansang e kyohun

Lappish Jesus oapat vare alde

Latin Sermo in monte

Latvian Kalnasprediķis

Lithuanian Pamokslas nuo kalno

Malayalam Kristuvinṭe malayil
vecculḷa prasaṅgaṃ

Marathi Ḍoṅgarāvaracā upadesá

Norwegian Bergprekenen

Panjabi Pahāṙī vā'z

Persian Moueza Faraz-e Kūh

Polish Kazanie na górze

Portuguese   Sermão da Montanha
Romanian   Predica de pe munte
Romansh   Predgia sül munt
Russian   Nagornaiîa propoved'
Serbo-Croatian   Govor na gori
Sinhalese   Kanda u̇da deśanava
Slovak   Kázeň na vrchu
Slovenian   Govor na gori
Spanish   Sermón de la Montaña
Swahili   Matangazo ya mlimani
Swedish   Bergspredikan
Tae'   Pangadaranna Puang
    Jesu dao tanete
Tamil   Kiṟistu malaiyiṉmēl
    upatēcittal
Turkish   Hazreti Isa'nin dağ
    va'zi
Ukranian   Nahorna proporid'
Urdu   Pahā̇ri vā'z
Vietnamese   Bài giảng trên
    núi
Welsh   Y bregeth ar y mynydd
Wendic   Prědowanje na horje

BIBLICAL REFERENCES INDEX

279

GENERAL INDEX

Aanby, Sigurd S. 143
Abel, F. M. 143
Abernathy, A. R. 143
Achelis, Ernest C. 143
Ackermann, August 242
Adams, Frank D. 143
Adeney, Walter F. 143, 242
Ahlberg, Adolf 143
Ahlberg, P. V. 143
Aicher, Georg 144
Ainsworth, Percy C. 242
Alexander, William 242
Alexandrian school 10
Allegorical interpretation
    9-10, 12, 16
Allen, Charles L. 144, 242
Allen, Erastus D. 144
Allen, Isaac N. 144
Allen, J. P. 144
Allen, R. Earl 242
Allgeier, A. 144
Allstrom, Elizabeth C. 144
Almsgiving 154
Anabaptists 2, 4, 20, 21,
    24-26, 27-28, 29-34, 35,
    36, 76, 78, 102, 107, 124,
    182, 198, 224-25, 237
Anderson, Robert 242
Andrén, Victor 144
Andrews, Charles F. 144
Annianus 222
Ante-Nicene Fathers 2, 3,
    5-9, 29, 36, 46, 61, 223,
    238
Antiochene school 9-10
Antonius Pius 7
Apocrypha 120, 161
Aquinas, Thomas 17-18,
    178, 215, 229
Archer, E. Wallace 144
Arendzen, J. P. 144
Arenson, Adolf 145

Arndt, Friedrich 145
Arnold, Eberhard 145
Arnold, Frank S. 242
Asensio Nieto, Félix 243
Asmussen, Hans 145
Atkins, Gains G. 145
Augsburger, Myron S. 145
Augustin, George 145
Augustine, Saint 2, 3, 9, 12-
    16, 19, 61, 145-47, 178,
    231, 244, 263, 264
Azibert, L'abbé 147

Bachmann, Johannes P. 31-32,
    147
Bacon, Benjamin W. 147
Bad Boll 152
Bäumlein, W. 147
Bahnsen, Wilhelm 147
Bailey, T. Arthur 243
Baillie, Donald M. 148
Bainton, Roland H. 31
Baker, Abijah R. 148
Baker, Eric W. 243
Baker, Gorden P. 243
Balmforth, Ramsden 148
Baltensweiler, Heinrich 148
Bannach, Horst 243
Baptists, German 37
Barclay, Robert 35, 36
Barclay, William 148, 243-44
Barnette, Henlee 148
Barnhouse, Donald Grey 63-64,
    65
Barrett, George W. 244
Barth, Fritz 148
Barth, Karl 44, 77, 83
Bartina, Sebastián 244
Barton, George A. 148
Bartsch, Hans W. 148
Bassermann, Heinrich 148

282